Northwest Vista College
Learning Resource Center
3535 North Ellison Drive
San Antonio, Texas 78251

In Search of Sunjata

D1559817

In Search of Sunjata
The Mande Oral Epic as History, Literature and Performance

EDITED BY

Ralph A. Austen

Indiana University Press
Bloomington and Indiana

Table of Contents

IV. Literature

V. Performance

*Contains items cited in more than one chapter. Items unique to a single chapter
are cited at the end of the respective chapter.

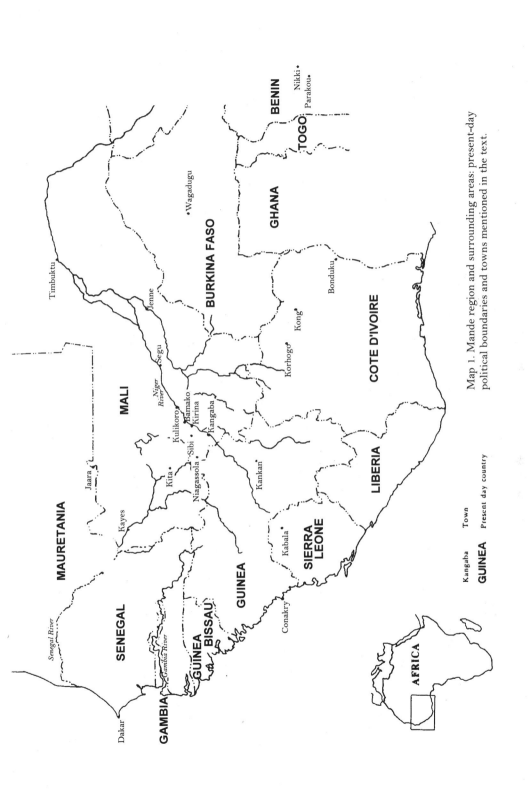

Map 1. Mande region and surrounding areas: present-day political boundaries and towns mentioned in the text.

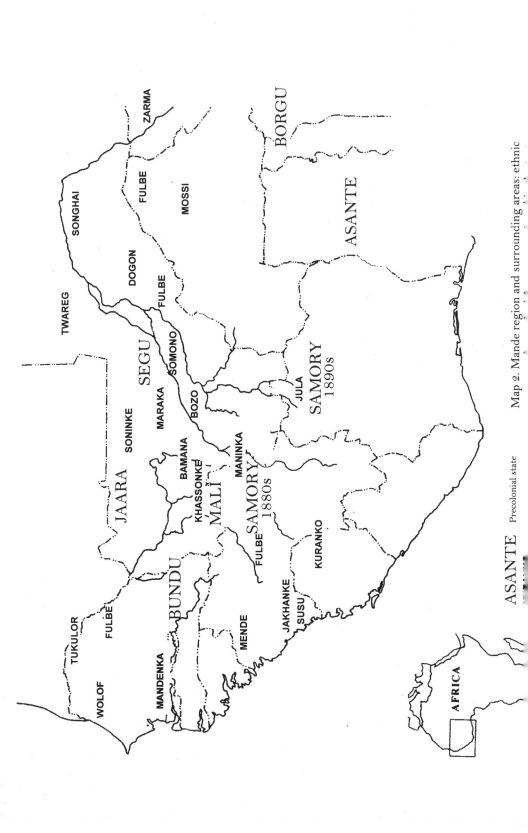

Map 2. Mande region and surrounding areas: ethnic

ASANTE Precolonial state

In Search of Sunjata

Editor's Introduction

Ralph A. Austen

In a much-publicized response to demands for multicultural revision of college humanities programs, the Nobel prize novelist Saul Bellow rhetorically demanded that he be introduced to "the Tolstoy of the Zulus? The Proust of the Papuans?" (Atlas 1988: 31). If students of Africa ever took up Bellow's challenge, the most obvious candidate for such monumental status would have to be the *Sunjata* epic, a narrative that celebrates the founder of the thirteenth century Mali empire in the western Sudan. This is a work that has already found a wide readership not only among Africanists, but also in the syllabi of universities as well as secondary and middle school general literature courses.

Most specialists on African history or oral literature would, however, reject the very terms in which Bellow poses his question. Not only do we instinctively resist the very concept of literature as a six-foot shelf of decontextualized "Great Books," but we are particularly uncomfortable with identifying any one written version of *Sunjata* as its canonical version and even more so with designating a particular performer or, still worse, any transcriber/interpreter of performances, as "the Milton of the Mande."

The essays in the present volume are thus at once a testament to the universal appeal of African cultural production and a set of inquiries into the very particular conditions under which such works come into existence and reach their audiences within Africa. The context here is not even "Africa" but rather a specific region of the continent, the Manden and surrounding areas of West Africa, whose internal contours and external boundaries will be more fully identified below.

The single written version of *Sunjata* that has already achieved something like canonical status, in classrooms as well as the footnotes of colleagues less deeply involved than the present authors in either oral literature or Mande studies, is that of D. T. Niane (1960, 1965).[1] But, as noted explicitly and implic-

---

[1] In a more formal gesture of canonization, the editors of the *Norton Anthology of World Masterpieces* (Mack 1995:2334-88) have also designated *Sunjata* to represent premodern Africa, but chosen a written version (Johnson 1986) which is closer to oral performance than Niane, although less easily accessible to readers, see also Austen, infra.

itly in almost every chapter of this volume, most serious research into the *Sunjata* epic has occurred subsequent to the 1960 publication of Niane's text, which thus loses much of its claim to represent the "authentic" voice of Mande "tradition." Our collective search for Sunjata does not, however, reject Niane but rather treats his work as one of many possibilities for studying the epic and giving it new forms of contemporary life.

The effort is truly collective, initiated through a modest but intense international conference in which most of these essays were discussed and whose proceedings have been examined by even those authors who did not attend.[2] As co-convener (along with David William Cohen and Ivor Wilks) of the conference, I will not use this introduction to assume, even in summary form, the voices of my fellow authors. We have not come to any general consensus about the *Sunjata* epic—indeed, as will be seen in cross references within the essays, some of us remain in disagreement over major issues.[3] However we have all read and listened to one another so that the volume can at least claim to represent a common discourse within which some new understanding of *Sunjata* has been achieved and the groundwork laid for what we hope will be continuing research and analysis.

The purpose of this introduction, then, is to identify the general terms under which the essays were conceived and organized and also to provide a more concrete guide to the physical and cultural geography of the Mande world, which is our common reference point.

The Terms of Inquiry

The bases of our search for *Sunjata* are set out in the subtitle of the volume "as history, literature, and performance." These terms do not imply that there are very clear disciplinary boundaries between the various sections of the book, and they also omit the perspective of anthropology, which informs all of us to greater or lesser degrees. However, by explicating what is meant by the categories that have been used, I can provide anyone who has browsed this far with at least some idea of what the body of the book contains (those totally unfamiliar with the terrain may want to skip to the last section of the introduction and the subsequent chapter by John W. Johnson).

---

[2] See "*Sunjata* Epic Conference," November 13–15, 1992, Institute for the Advanced Study and Research in the African Humanities, Northwestern University, transcript at NorthwesternUniversity Library. The only contributors to the present volume who did not participate in the conference are Jan Jansen and Robert Newton.

[3] Some of the unresolved questions include interpretations of specific narrative passages, the relationships between praise poetry and the epic, the specificity of genre terminology in Mande oral performance, the historical relationship between the epic and the septennial Kambalon ceremony at Kangaba in Mali, and the role of Arabic literacy in both the history and performance of the epic.

Although many of the contributors (including the editor) are officially designated as historians, none of us treat the textual content of the *Sunjata* epic as a reliable independent source for reconstructing what actually happened in the past.[4] In the time of Niane's pioneering work, scholars had more faith in the positive value of even such a stylized version of "oral tradition" as *Sunjata,* but in the intervening decades we have all become much more cautious.[5] Nonetheless, for the Mande peoples whose various versions of the epic have been recorded over the last century, the story of *Sunjata* is "history," and one task of this entire volume is to explore the forms of historical consciousness articulated in such beliefs. This last consideration, as demonstrated in the essay here by David Conrad, does not preclude the possibility of eventually returning to a more "positivist" historical approach of our own.[6]

For the moment, the history that the present authors themselves actually pursue is less that of the thirteenth-century events that the epic depicts than that of the text itself as an historical artifact. Ivor Wilks in particular tries to ascertain how much of the epic as we now know it actually can be traced back to the time of the undeniably historical figure, Sunjata, or his immediate successors. Seydou Camara and Ralph Austen concern themselves with the process by which, in a period probably not going back more than two or three hundred years from the present, the epic took and retained its "classical" form. The three essays in the second section of the book by Stephen Belcher, Mamadou Diawara, and Paulo de Moraes Farias trace the *Sunjata* epic and its performance tradition into lands beyond the core Manden, where it has been incorporated into other kinds of history and historical consciousness.

The treatment of the epic as literature comes closest to the experience almost all non-African audience—and a significant portion of African ones as well—will have of *Sunjata.* However, such an effort must remain sensitive to

---

[4] For a serious and well-informed effort to do this, but one which was not generally accepted at the 1992 Northwestern Conference (the author was present) see Tamari 1997: esp. 266–86.

[5] To trace this change, compare the defining methodological treatise of Africanist historiography in its most optimistic stage (Vansina 1960) with the revised views of the same author (Vansina 1985).

[6] In various conference presentations and comments over a number of years, Conrad (a very strong critic of Niane's work) has argued for the historicity of at least some elements within the *Sunjata* epic while being drawn, as evidenced by his contribution here, into at least preliminary focus on its more literary elements. The leading skeptic in this historiographic discussion has been John W. Johnson, whose prominent position in the present volume indicates something about the immediate state of the debate but not necessarily its ultimate outcome. For evidence of the very unsettled historiography of the Mali empire, see the exchange between Jan Jansen and Stephen Bühnen in *History in Africa* 23 (1996), pp. 87–128.

the context of this work in a specifically Mande oral tradition. Karim Traoré and David Conrad both venture to treat oral performances of *Sunjata* as texts, the first examining their relationship to hunting narratives (as well as the performances of hunting bards) and the second considering the representation of women within the epic itself. Stephen Bulman and James McGuire concern themselves with the transformation of the oral narrative into written text. Bulman surveys the various transcriptions or adaptations of the specific story of Sunjata, while McGuire examines a novel about a contemporary Mande hero produced by one of the leading Malian figures in Bulman's roster of transcribers.

Among current scholars of African culture and/or "oral literature" (for which the preferred term is now often "verbal art" or "orature"), the least controversial way to approach a work like *Sunjata* is to treat it as performance. That can be the case if researchers focus on performance as an aesthetic and social event; but in a collaborative book like the present, an attempt has been made to link the act of performing with literature and history—or at least the claims made in such realms by various interpreters of the epic, both expatriate and African. Thus the essay by Charles Bird is probably the *most* controversial contribution in the volume, because of both the doubt he casts upon various meanings attributed to the text of the epic and songs associated with its performance and the historical interpretation with which he concludes his own analysis. Jan Jansen's ethnography of the performers who produce the "official" version of the epic at a septennial ritual in southern Mali will also raise some hackles as it attacks assumptions made by many previous observers, including at least one fellow author in this book. Finally Robert Newton explores the medium by which most modern Mande audiences are exposed to the epic—neither live performance nor literary rendition but rather commercial electronic recording.

The Mande Setting

It is hoped that each of the chapters in this book can be appreciated on its own by a reader with some general interest in African studies or oral literature. The essay by John W. Johnson, which precedes the sections divided into "History," "Literature," and "Performance," offers a broad account of the content and social-cultural context of the *Sunjata* epic and should provide some orientation for the arguments that follow. However, the fullest understanding of the complete set of essays does require some acquaintance with specific features of the Mande landscape that cannot be reintroduced by each author. Thus the most general of these points (along with an accompanying map) are laid out here.[7]

---

[7] Some of the following material was extracted from preliminary versions of essays by other contributors, particularly David Conrad, John Johnson, Paulo de Moraes Farias, and Karim Traoré. For linguistic issues I have also consulted Dalby 1970 and Greenberg 1970 but am especially indebted to private correspondence from Valentin Vydrine (see also Vydrine 1995/96).

What follows makes no claim to be a definitive account of the very complex physical and cultural geography of the Mande world. Its main purpose is to establish a set of common terms that do not conflict with general scholarly usage and are limited to the areas covered in the essays. The orthography here (with the single exception of Moraes Farias's chapter) conforms to English usage and (in most cases) that of the postcolonial states of the region. However, since most of this area once formed part of French West Africa, there is also an established practice of French orthography for important local terms; this must be noted, because readers may encounter it in other texts and maps as well as some of the proper names and bibliographic citations used here. Thus a sound closest to the English *j* is often written as *di, dj,* or *dy* (Sundiata, Sundjata, or Sundyata vs. Sunjata), and *ou* can stand for either the consonant *w* or the vowel *u* (Ouagadougou vs. Wagadugu). In addition to orthography, the very terms used by the French for local ethnic groups, such as "Malinké" or "Bambara," are derived from Fulbe (Fulani) and/or Arabic rather than the languages of the peoples referred to. These labels will not be used here, but it should be noted (just as with the more obscure "griot" to be discussed below) that Mande peoples do themselves employ them when speaking in English or French, and they will also appear in the titles of cited works.

The terms used to distinguish between different portions of the Mande world (including "Mande" itself) are still in dispute among historians and linguists so that almost any system of usage, particularly one that is easily comprehensible to nonspecialists, must appear arbitrary. What unites all of these regions and communities is a set of closely related languages and a common set of cultural references that constitute the subject of this book. For present purposes, the various divisions of this world will be defined only in terms of location and language. "Mande" will be used here to indicate the entire population and area under discussion. "Manding" will refer to the mutually intelligible languages of the region linked to the medieval Mali empire and the *Sunjata* epic.

The local term for the probable center of historical Mali is transcribed here as "Manden." The Manden is located in the savanna and light forest lands of southern Mali and northeastern (Upper) Guinea, extending outward from either side of that stretch of the Niger River that flows northeast from around Kouroussa to somewhere near Bamako, the capital of modern Mali. The language (or dialect if one wants to emphasize the mutual intelligibility of all Manding speech systems) is Maninka (Malinké).

The secondary Manding zone (secondary, of course, only from the perspective of the *Sunjata* epic) is located in the drier savanna of central Mali along the Niger from Bamako to approximately Macina. The main language here is Bamana (Bambara), which has become, since the time of French colonialism or perhaps that of the eighteenth- and nineteenth-century Segu empire (which produced its own epic tradition), the most widely spoken form of Manding.

Beyond the Maninka-Bamana zones, the distribution and classification of Mande/Manding communities becomes very complicated and cannot be dealt with fully here. The trade in gold and other commodities from the medieval period onward dispersed major groups of Manding speakers from their homelands toward the eastern and southeastern savanna and forest lands of West Africa. In Burkina Faso and Cote d'Ivoire such communities have retained their Manding language, whose most widely used dialects are called Jula, which is also the Manding term for itinerant merchants. A consciousness of this commercial diaspora is strongly expressed in many versions of the *Sunjata* epic, but none of the papers in this collection examine the presence (or absence?) of the *Sunjata* narrative tradition among the Jula-speakers themselves.[8]

Several of these essays do discuss the *Sunjata* narratives among Mande-speakers in northwest Mali and eastern Senegal, such as the Khassonke and Mandinka. The Mandinka (as well as the Mande-speaking Mende of Sierra Leone) trace themselves to military conquerors from the Manden, although it is not clear how this expansion is linked to the history of the Mali empire. The Kuranko of the Sierra Leone highlands, an isolated and distant group of Mande-speakers, possess a particularly rich and well-studied narrative folklore that echoes many themes of the *Sunjata* epic (Jackson 1979).

The authors here also give considerable attention to the literature and performance practices of Mande-speaking Soninke peoples who are based in the Sahelian zone of northwestern Mali and neighboring regions in Senegal and Mauritania. The Soninke founded the Ghana or Wagadu empire, the medieval predecessor of Mali, and are associated in many accounts with Sumaworo,[9] the ruler of the intermediate Sosso empire that was overthrown by Sunjata.[10]

Specific Mande terms other than ethnolinguistic labels that occur throughout this book are defined in the chapters where they occur. However the concept of "casted" bards is so essential to every aspect of the *Sunjata* epic that its nomenclature (but not the nuances of *nyamakala* status)[11] needs to be dis-

---

[8] The first film of the *Sunjata* epic was produced in 1994 (too late to be discussed in this volume) in Burkina Faso and its language is Jula (Dani Kouyaté, "Keïta: The Heritage of a Griot").

[9] The rendition of the name of this critical figure in the *Sunjata* epic varies considerably among bards in different Mandekan subregions and is not even consistent within them, because many performers move from their home regions or use forms learned elsewhere. In the more southern Maninka areas the pronunciation most often heard is something like "Sumaworo" (Niane writes this as "Sumaoro"). For Bamana bards, but also those of the critical Maninka-speaking center of Kita, the usual transcription is "Sumanguru." However, John William Johnson, in his very widely cited recording of the Kita performer Fa-Digi Sisoko, writes "Sumamuru" (Johnson 1986). Given these circumstances, no single form of the name has been imposed on the contributors to the present volume.

[10] This view has recently been challenged in an important article that places Sumaworo among another group of Mande speakers, the Susu/Jallonke of South-Central Guinea (Bühnen 1994).

[11] See Johnson below, as well as Conrad and Frank 1995.

cussed here. The term "bard" is a reasonable translation of the function of these performers, also sometimes described in English as "praise-singers" although such identification gives little sense of the complex role that they occupy in Mande belief, ritual, and social relations. They are thus most properly designated by the Manding word *"jeli"* or *"jali"* (plural *jeliw/jaliw* or *jelilu/jalilu*) and, in several chapters here, the Soninke *"gesere."* However, in modern times the term "griot," whose etymology (whether Mande, Portuguese, or Arabic) is not precisely known, has come into wide local usage; it is thus freely deployed here as a synonym for more unambiguously indigenous terms.

Just as the Mande jeliw/griots are the ultimate source of our knowledge of the *Sunjata* epic, so the individual authors in this volume are the basis of its analytic power, and this introduction should now make way for their voices. However it is first necessary to acknowledge some otherwise invisible accompanists. These include: the staff of the Northwestern University Program of African Studies who organized our initial conference; MANSA (the Mande Studies Association) whose 1993 and 1995 conferences extended in critical ways the work of the original *Sunjata* epic Conference; Stephen Belcher, who (apart from contributing his own essay) edited the proceedings of the *Sunjata* conference and also translated three essays by other authors from French into English; my research assistants, Heather Barrow, Sara Pugach, J. Shields Sundberg, and Daniel Tarvella; and the Forschungsschwerpunkt Moderner Orient in Berlin, which supported a significant part of my editorial efforts.

Bibliography

Atlas, James. 1988. "Chicago's Grumpy Guru: Best-Selling Professor Allen Bloom." *New York Times Magazine*, Jan. 3, 23–25, 28.

Bühnen, Stephen. 1996. "Brothers, Chiefdoms and Empires: On Jan Jansen's 'The Representation of Status in Mande: Did the Mali Empire Still Exist in the Nineteenth Century?'" *History in Africa* 22: 111–20.

Dalby, David, ed. 1970. *Language and History in Africa*. London: Cass.

Jansen, Jan. 1996. "Polities and Political Discourse: Was Mande Already a Segmentary Society in the Middle Ages?" *History in Africa* 22: 121–28.

Kouyaté, Dani. "Keita: The Heritage of a Griot." Film, 1994.

Mack, Maynard (ed.). 1995. *The Norton Anthology of Modern Masterpieces: Expanded Edition*. New York: Norton.

Tamari, Tal. 1997. *Les castes de l'Afrique occidentale: artisans et musiciens endogames*. Nanterre: Société d'Ethnologie.

1. The Dichotomy of Power and Authority in Mande Society and in the Epic of *Sunjata*

John William Johnson

The epic *Sunjata* remains popular today over a large area roughly covering the same territory that was located in the medieval empire of Mali, plus an extension into surrounding and sometimes quite distant areas inhabited by minority Mande peoples.[1] This performance tradition is carried on in bardic families, whose endogamous "caste" status protects their monopoly over the recitation of *Sunjata* and other epics and oral literary forms as well as over certain well-defined social and socioeconomic roles. In this chapter I will attempt to analyze the dynamic opposition and sometimes cooperation between the traditional authority structures most often exhibited in Mali as a gerontocracy and the real power structure in Mande societies and how these concepts are reflected and propagated in the epic *Sunjata*.

To my knowledge, the dichotomy between power and authority in Mande society was first recognized by Nicholas Hopkins (Hopkins 1971 and 1972).[2] The tension between power exercised by the social group as a whole and that sought after by the individual in society is reflected in many places in the epic of *Sunjata*. Moreover, if one is to consider this epic a socially relevant and active piece of oral literature, then such a tension would seem to be suggested in

---

[1] In the different versions of this epic the hero's name has varied between Sunjata, Sonjata, Sunjara, and Sonjara. Mande folk etymologies assign varying meanings to both *Sun/Son* ("thief," or a contraction of the hero's mother's name, Sugulun/Sogolon) and *Jata/Jara* (both terms usually translated as "lion," but sometimes presented as surnames whose meaning has been lost).

[2] Both of these thorough studies of Mande society, as well as my own field notes, are employed throughout this essay as models for the analysis of the authority and power structures. Fieldwork was conducted in the Republic of Mali from November 1973 to February 1975.

the daily lives of real people in the Mande world. Firsthand fieldwork, and not just textual perusal, is necessary to determine the latter, and indeed it appears to be the case if we explore the social context of this remarkable heroic epic. Authority structures, of course, differ among all the ethnic groups in the Mande nation, but there does appear to be an underlying infrastructure marking significant similarities in most areas where the Mande peoples live and represent a majority of the local population. I shall, however, be cautious and confine my statements to the Maninka, Mandenka, and Bamana groups with whom I lived and conducted my own research in the Republic of Mali.

A number of social scientists since at least the time of Max Weber have explored the analytical distinction between authority structures and individual leadership, and this chapter is not the place to review their work. For my own analysis I shall employ the definitions presented by Robert Bierstedt (1954). Bierstedt marks a difference between authority—which he sees as the claimed possession of any organization—and leadership—which he sees as individual influence on the organization's members—in the exercise of power.

As we shall later see, in Mande cosmology, power is not perceived as a process, but rather as an entity to be stockpiled until enough is gained to enable the possessor to exercise social and political control over others. The stockpiling process is accomplished religiously, among other ways, through occult practices, such as conjuring and the preparation and wearing of amulets and talismans. Both authority figures and individuals outside the authority structure compete for control by practicing methods of gaining this occult power (*nyama*). Let me begin the analysis by looking more deeply into this cosmology, which serves as a constant backdrop to the struggle for social and political control.

In the worldview of Mande communities, humanity is divided into three categories. Social divisions are quite complex, but a great deal of social behavior is influenced by this three-patterned philosophy, and if we are to understand the relationship between power and authority, we must begin here with what Hopkins symbolizes as a vertical authority structure because of its tendency toward gerontocracy.

At the bottom of this structure one finds the population in this region who are remembered today as being the descendants of slaves or captives (*jon*) taken in times of war. Although there is, of course, no slavery practiced in Mali today, the genealogy of some families in certain areas is remembered as originating in slavery. Together with the descendants of people believed to have been adopted as orphans, these members of a lineage are not considered core members and may not hold office in the authority structure.

The second division of humanity, according to Mande belief, is made up of the casted members of society (*nyamakala*).[3] Four groups of families fill

---

[3] For a thorough study of the endogamous lineages in Mali, see N'Diayé (1970); also Conrad and Frank 1995.

this division: the bards (*jeli*), the blacksmiths (*numun*), the cordwainers or leather-workers (*garange*), and the Islamic praise-poets (*fune*). These families enjoy a monopoly over one or more specialized professions, and the bards especially play an important role of verbal and social mediation between other groups in Mande society. The nyamakala also do not hold office in the authority structure.

The majority of the population make up the third division of humanity, the freeborn (*horon*), which is further subdivided into commoner and royalty (*masalen*), the latter being made up of clans that, in many instances, trace their lineages back to Sunjata's era when their ancestors are believed to have been the rulers of the various sections of Old Mali in the thirteenth century. In other cases, the royal families establish their claims to the authority structure through ancestors believed to have played an important role at some crucial time during the history of the area where they live. The "core" segment of the royal family that Hopkins explored in Kita is believed to be made up of a sublineage descended from ancestors whose founding and delivery of the region from external threat ensures them an important place in the mythical charter of the town. I call this system "government by parable," as contrasted to Western constitutional and statutory legal structures. It is with the core lineage of royalty that we finally arrive at the pinnacle of the traditional authority structure of Mande society. And it is at this juncture that one generally finds the elderly in charge, some men waiting until they are very old indeed before they gain a prominent position in the ruling structure of a village. Their age often inhibits their ability to wield actual power, which makes it easy for others to manipulate them.

Mande authority structure revolves around the principle of *fa-siya* ("father-lineage-ness"), which generally means that everyone older than any given member of society is due respect and deference, while one accepts respect and deference from younger members of society. Built into the very naming of this system is its patrilineal bias, and it places into office the male considered to be the oldest son of the oldest son going back, as stated above, into the legendary past of the core lineage of the ruling lineage of the village. It is interesting to note that, because of the strict patrilineal derivation in the genealogy of this core lineage, the person who inherits the authority may not be the oldest member of the family. The most immediate representative of this principle is the *lu-tigi* ("household head" or "compound chief"), whose duties extend into the economic as well as the social affairs of those committed to his charge, mostly family members living in his compound, but also sometimes more distant relatives who may be temporarily residing there. I should point out that at this grassroots level of the authority system, every compound is based on family structure and has a lu-tigi, whether or not he is involved in the larger political structure beyond the door of his compound.

Authority at the village level is shared by two office holders, one with political credentials and one with a ritual commission still operating in most areas today. Both of these men are the elders at the sublineage tier of the two dominant families, and their offices are held by the authority of the legendary charter of the founding of the village. The first patrilineal family believed to have settled in the area is usually granted the ritual chieftaincy. Again, the eldest member of the core lineage of the family becomes the ritual chief (*dugu-kolo-tigi*, "earth-surface-master"), whose functions are mostly ritualistic. It is said that this man is the spiritual mediator between the local earth spirits and the village farmers, and it is his duty to maintain a balanced relationship between them by means of such occult activities as might be needed in any given situation. I was told in Mali that the ritual chief also has some authority in land tenure. The force of authority behind this office is based upon the belief that an ancestor of the ritual chief was the first immigrant to the area and had to come to terms with the local spirits of the land. Thus he maintains a special relationship with these spirits and is most qualified to mediate with them for the rest of the immigrants and inhabitants of the area.

The village political chief (*dugu-tigi*, "earth/village master") is usually associated with a power struggle in a legend composing a part of the mythical charter of the village. Sometimes the sublineage whose elder holds this office is thought to be the conqueror of the area or the sublineage whose ancestors prevented an external conquest at some time in the past, thus gaining the right to rule over the area. The other sublineages of a village are ranked according to the legendary account of their temporal arrival in the village. Note here that both these tenets of belief apply to the freeborn (horon) only. The casted families (nyamakala) and those believed to be descendants of former slaves (*jonlu*) and orphans (*falatolu*) are excluded in this ranking by the horon, although groups outside the horon may well have their own rankings.

Beyond the sublineage level of authority in the village lies the district (*kafo* or *jamana*), made up of several villages (often eight or more) and presided over by the titular head of a lineage. According to the principle of fa-siya, the district chief (*jamana-tigi*) is the senior man in the royal lineage (masalen) of the district, and rules by virtue of his place in the gerontocracy. It is difficult to determine what the duties of the jamana-tigi are in the modern state structure of Mali, but it is unlikely that this position ever represented anything like supreme authority. Modern beliefs hold that effective political unity in Old Mali ended at this district level, although, no doubt, the social and ethnic unity, then as now, extended to the clan and beyond to other related ethnic groups. The fact that no office of clan chief exists today reflects the fluidity of the concept of clan, which may be defined vaguely as everyone with the same surname. What is relevant here is the fact that, as Hopkins reports, "relations between the clans are molded after the relations between their ancestors in the time of Soundiata" (1971:101). I would add only that these relations are always subject to reinterpretation during each generation, in any given local situation, and in the various territories of the Mande peoples. In short, time and space must be taken into account when considering Hopkins's analysis and, as expected, one finds this reality mirrored in the many variants of the epic today; each version tells a slightly different story. Bards also state that Sunjata was able to unite the districts into a larger political unit and to attain the Mandenka title of *mansa*. Although the exact political duties of the mansa were different from those of monarchs in Europe, we might employ the term "emperor" as a rough translation of this Mande word. Many scholars now think that a mansa was something like a "chairman of the board" over the Mande gerontocracy, with most political decisions remaining at the local village level, a point to which I shall return later.

Still a part of the authority structure but not based upon the fa-siya system are a number of other units that cut across lineage segments and are thus termed "horizontal structures" by Hopkins. Perhaps the most important cross-lineage associations are the age-sets of youth and young men (*den-misen-ton, kamalen-ton*). These units are made up of the youth of the village, roughly of the same age within about a five-to-seven-year spread. Men join at their circumcision and remain in the *ton* until about the age of thirty-five. Women join at their excision and remain until their marriage or the birth of their first child, although their role is complicated by the fact that they are considered strangers (*dunan*, see below) in their husband's compound. Age-sets serve two main functions at the village level. They provide for much of the entertainment in the area, and they participate in collective, often charitable work. They do, however, sometimes make their political and social views known in the veiled speech of their theatrical and puppet performances, and are thus able to wield varying degrees of power, or at least pressure, at the village level.

Volunteer associations of a secular nature are smaller than the age-sets and often attract members from more than one village. These groups involve both men and women together and also concern themselves with charitable work and entertainment. They are often composed of members of different age-sets. Religious associations also exist and may be composed of age-set members and other variations of groups. The *komo* society, for instance, is a power association, concerned with the proper use of occult knowledge and is headed by a blacksmith. Again, these groups sometimes wield power but, especially with regard to the komo, are perhaps accused of attempting to influence local affairs more often than they actually do so.

While the fa-siya offices represent the warp in the fabric of Mande authority structures, and these other cross-lineage associations represent its weft, several other groups represent well-integrated, brocaded functions outside the freeborn authority structures altogether. I have already mentioned the casted families and the descendants of orphans and slaves. Other groups include strangers to the area, Muslim holy men, and hunters.

The stranger (dunan) is welcome in village life for several reasons. Potentially he or she may contribute to the prosperity of the region. He or she may serve as a client to his or her host (*ja-tigi*, "wraith-protector") and thus possibly increase the host's power in village politics. It was in this slot, for instance, that I found myself in my relationship with the authorities in the Institut des Sciences Humaines, to whom foreign scholars were "assigned" in the years when I did research in Mali.

The role of the Muslim holy man (*mori*) is more difficult to assess. As prayer leader and Quranic school master, the mori may be considered to fulfill pedagogical function. Together with the casted families and the hunters, the holy men are also involved in occult medicine, and this role is often used to influence the power structure of the area. Although deriving their authority primarily from ties to Islam, the mori, like most Mande groups, also utilize occult medicine when necessary. They often combine the two concepts of power when using the words of the Quran to perform divinations or to create amulets and potions.

While the stranger and the holy man, as well as the casted families, work in well-integrated ways with the lineages, the hunters' societies are isolated outside. Although they serve a definite function within Mande society, there are several characteristics about hunters' societies (*donson-ton*) that set them apart from society and cause them to be greatly feared. First, they go against the grain of society in that they represent a truly egalitarian strain of Mande social behavior, recruiting members from any and all strata, regardless of the original social status of the initiate. In short, lineage and "caste" authority is rejected outright, and this rejection is even institutionalized in the oath of allegiance the initiate takes when he joins a hunters' society.

Second, hunters spend a great deal of their time in the wilderness, considered the most dangerous place on earth in Mande cosmology, not only because of the threat of wild beasts found there, but also because of the uncontrollable spirits who inhabit this occult domain. Hunters' societies educate their initiates in the knowledge of control over the wilderness, which involves extensive training in occult medicine. But this esoteric knowledge is not shared with outsiders, and secret knowledge becomes an important factor in the relationship of hunters to non-initiates. Many believe that hunters are the people in Mande society most capable of rebalancing chaos at the cosmological level through their superior knowledge of the occult. The fear many have for them is based upon the belief that they are equally capable of upsetting that balance. I was once on a train in Mali that was stopped at a station when a hunter got on board. Those around the hunter began to smile and even laugh with extreme nervousness, thus indicating that his presence had introduced some potential danger into the space we were now sharing.

The institutionalized traditional authority structure in Mande society offers any of its members a ready conduit to real power and control over other people's lives. I do not think it was pure chance, for instance, that the first president of the modern independent state of Mali was a Keita. Likewise, it is interesting that the second president of the modern state was from the second family of power in Mali, the Taraweres.[4] One of the best-known episodes of the *Sunjata* epic describes how the hero was insulted by Jolof-fin Mansa, the ruler of the Gambia, when the Manden Mansa attempted to trade for horses in that land.[5] Enraged by the insult, Sunjata planned to do battle with the Gambian upstart but was confused when all his generals arrived to beg for generalship of the army except for Tura-Magan Tarawere. Seeking him out, Sunjata found him lying at the bottom of a grave, dug out but not filled in. When he asks what the Tarawere is doing in his grave before he is dead, Tura-Magan replies that if he is not to be given the generalship to avenge the insult from the Gambian upstart, he might as well be dead. This event resulted in Tura-Magan attaining the important praise-name Susare-jon, "Slave-of-the-Tomb."

Sunjata then gives Tura-Magan the generalship and the Tarawere ancestor conquers the Gambia, beheading its ruler, revenging the insult, and unquestionably becoming an important and powerful hero in his own right. Upon setting out on the road to return to the Manden, Tura-Magan observes a strange scene whereby a great eagle swoops down from the clouds and kills a mighty hawk flying at a lower level. The Tarawere warrior interprets this vision as a portent of his own imminent death, with himself in the role of the hawk and Sunjata in the role of the eagle. Sure enough, a small band of assassins arrives unexpectedly from the Mande and kills Tura-Magan, now a hero of such prowess as to threaten the power of his master. In my view, this is an important tale, as it establishes the Tarawere clan in Mali as a "legitimate" challenger to the authority of the Keitas. On the day that Musa Tarawere overthrew Mali's first postcolonial president, Modibo Keita, in a military coup, I was told that the Tarawere *faasa* (praise-poem), which alludes to this legend, was broadcast over the radio, thus legitimizing Musa's claim to authority.

Because of the restrictions of age, sex, and lineage affiliation in the Mande system of fa-siya, large numbers of ambitious people are excluded from the ranks of the authority structure. Methods of gaining real power other than through the traditional authority structure have therefore evolved over the years. In fact, a man of power (*faama*, or *mogo-tigi*) may rise to his position by completely circumventing the authority structure altogether. Circumventing the authority structure calls for dangerous and antisocial behavior characteristic of the Mande concept of the culture hero, of which Sunjata has become the prime model. Understanding heroic behavior is necessary to comprehend the relationship between power and authority and will take us to the Mande nuclear

---

[4] The name "Tarawere" is known outside of Mali by its francophone version, "Traoré." "Traoré" is also used for "Tarawere" in other chapters of this book even when making Malian references.

[5] The detailed version of this story cited here is one I collected myself.

family structure.[6]

In many ways, the nuclear family is the foundation of larger units of Mande social, religious, and political views of the world. Themes of sanctioned behavior in the family compound find their way into the society at large, and this behavior in the polygamous family is reflected by kinship terms. Rivalry (*fadenya*, "father-child-ness") is expected between half siblings (*fa-denlu*, "father's children"). Conversely, affection (*ba-denya*, "mother-child-ness") is expected between full siblings (*ba-denlu*). Thus Sunjata struggles with his half brother Mansa Dankaran Tuman, but is aided by his full siblings, Sugulun Kutuma and Manden Bukari.

By the linguistic process of metaphoric extension, these terms are encountered again in Mande worldview concerned with the cosmos. Now denoting the forces of social destruction (fa-denya) and social cohesion (ba-denya), a cosmos is perceived as polarized by a constant battle between change and stability, first one gaining the upper hand and then losing it to the other. In order to gain a reputation (*togo*) for himself, the hero must operate along the fa-denya axis. Violating social norms, especially those controlled by the traditional authority structure, provides a means for the individual to become a faama or mogo-tigi, a powerful person. Cosmologically, the act of violating norms is seen to release into the atmosphere vast amounts of occult power lying dormant toward the ba-denya axis. If the hero is strong enough, he will gain control over the released power and thus increase his stockpile of power and become that much stronger. If he is not strong enough—if his store of already accumulated occult power is not sufficiently great—he may be destroyed by the power he has released.

It is important for a Mande hero to perceive at what speed one must proceed in gaining and stockpiling occult power, for speed in these acts is related to Mande worldview concerning the concept of destiny. Destiny is seen as preordained but not as inevitable predestination. It is left up to individuals to discover their destinies and to progress toward their fulfillment carefully and at just the right speed. In this delicate balance, if they go too fast, they will not have stockpiled enough occult power to control the forces associated with power. In society, they may be stopped in their ambitious behavior by more powerful rivals. If they go too slow, they risk missing the flow that controls their eventual destiny. In society, his/her rival may gain the advantage through superior timing. Cosmologically, the hero must gain control of the occult power he releases through already having stockpiled enough power to resist the new influx of dangerous force. Again in social terms, the ambitious person must not make a

---

[6] For a discussion of the use of family terminology in Mande cosmology, see Bird (1976: 96–97), Bird and Kendall (1980: 14–17), Griaule (1973: 12), Hopkins (1971: 100), Jackson (1979: 100–101), and McNaughton (1988: 7–21). This discussion is also based on my own extensive field notes and observations.

career move before he/she is in a position to "get away with" the move.

The acquisition of real power is based on two things. Success in influencing public opinion is a necessity, for failure to accomplish this goal can cut short any ambition to power. The acquisition of wealth and clients (allies) is also a necessity, and this process involves both lineage and non-lineage associations, which leads to the growth of the mogo-tigi's retinue. A large retinue, in turn, leads to further growth in influencing public opinion (Hopkins 1972: 29). Moreover, the ability to cause others to believe that one has a great stockpile of occult power is a key element in the acquisition of power.

Wealth is obtained in numerous ways in one's normal life in the Mande world, with the most prestigious and respected methods being agriculture and commerce, both along the ba-denya axis. These are too slow for the hero; Sunjata's eulogy from the epic indicates the antisocial means employed by such a man to gain power:[7]

Minw be sene ke,	Those who would farm,
I ka sene ke!	Let them farm!
Minw be jago ke,	Those who would trade,
I ka jago ke!	Let them trade!
Minw be kele ke,	Those who would do
I ka jago ke!	battle,
Jata ye kele ke de!	Let them battle!
	It was battling that Sunjata
	did!

To influence public opinion and to attract a large retinue, one may begin at home by maintaining good relations with one's own patrilineage and matrilineage, as well as with one's spouse's two lineages. The maximum number of wives (four are allowed in Islam) increases the size of one's family and thus client lineage ties. Taking into account both paternal and maternal sides—and normative social rules exist for one's relationship to each—a man with four wives has ten extended families at his disposal, but it must be pointed out that extended families are complex social units. To employ them as clients in the search for power requires a great deal of skill in social interactions (or in cosmological terms, skill in the accumulation of occult power).

Together with familial and spousal clients, the hero seeks to stockpile other clients amongst horizontal structures, such as age-sets, esoteric cults like the komo, and voluntary associations. A large group of clients living in one's compound or supported by the mogo-tigi through generosity increases power.

---

[7] The variant of the eulogy employed here is the most complex one I collected in Mali. It was recited by the (then) national poet laureate Ban Sumana Sisòkò, a bard from the region around Segu in Bamana country.

Here, the stranger, the holy man, the hunter, and the casted families all come into play. The occult powers possessed by some of these groups helps the hero to establish a reputation of invulnerability.

All these processes and more are alluded to in the epic of *Sunjata*. Several episodes before the hero's birth are saturated with this topic. A major episode takes the narrative from Mecca, through the mythical founding of Mali, down to the time of Sunjata's father. This episode begins with the person called Jon Bilal (the Bilāl bin Rabah of Muslim history, a black slave, purchased by the Prophet and thought to be the second convert to Islam) and his relationship to the Prophet Muhammad.[8] Bilal's three sons are sent west to establish the country of the Manden, and there follows a struggle between the eldest of the three, whose traditional right it is under the principle of fa-siya to become the first ruler, and the youngest, whose heroic destiny it is to assume the title of mansa. A genealogical recitation follows this episode (just like the "begats" passages in the Bible), which advances the plot down to Sunjata's father Narè Magan, the Handsome. One of the main functions of this episode is to establish Sunjata's inheritance of *barakah*, the Muslim concept of grace laced with power, which becomes a syncretized Mande concept of Islamic occult power (in short, the Muslim equivalent of the local idea of occult power or nyama).

Another episode takes the plot from the ancient West African land of Du (or Do) down to Sunjata's mother, whose praise-name, according to one translation, is "Sugulun-of-the-Warts." Narè Magan, the handsomest man in the realm, is Sunjata's father, while Sugulun-of-the-Warts, the ugliest woman around, is his mother. In Du, the forces of chaos along the fa-denya axis have gained the upper hand in the form of the local ruler's disgruntled aunt, who transforms herself into a dangerous magic buffalo and is ravaging the countryside. The buffalo, by the way, is considered the most dangerous animal in the contemporary Malian bush. The king, in turn, calls for hunters, who, as I mentioned above, have an especially lethal monopoly of certain varieties of secret occult power, to restore the balance of ba-denya to the country. A pair of Tarawere hunters (recall the importance of this surname) arrive from the neighboring country of the Manden to defeat the aunt, and they are successful through the careful use of their occult knowledge. The reward for their success is Sugulun, the grandniece of the conquered buffalo woman. The hunters transport Sugulun to the king of the Manden and thereby provide the link-up between the Muslim barakah and the local nyama through the birth of our hero, Sunjata. Thus, through male and female lines, from Muslim and local sources, Sunjata is destined to inherit a vast stockpile of occult power from which to begin building

---

[8] Bilāl bin Rabah: for an outline of what Muslims believe about Bilāl bin Rabah see the *Encyclopedia of Islam* (1960: 1215). It is interesting to note that the American Black Muslim movement employed the name of this culture hero in the title of its newspaper, *The Bilalian News*.

his own personal supply of this critical resource.

Nowhere is the relationship between power and authority exhibited more clearly in the epic than in the conflict between Sunjata and his half brother Mansa Dankaran Tuman, with the co-wife rivalry between their mothers as a backdrop struggle. In the first part of this episode, the births of Sunjata and Dankaran Tuman occur at nearly the same moment, which gives rise to a struggle for succession. Variants sometimes declare Sunjata to be the first born, and sometimes Dankaran Tuman, son of Saman Berete, the senior wife, with additional complications provided by the order in which the messengers of their respective mothers are able to announce each of their births. The extended struggle that ensues is said by some bards to be the very origin of co-wife rivalry. In all versions, Dankaran Tuman somehow succeeds to the throne when old king Narè Magan dies, thus excluding Sunjata from an initial position of authority. For good measure, Saman Berete consults various practitioners of the occult and successfully conjures against Sunjata, leaving him paralyzed in the legs throughout his youth. Eventually a turning point must occur, of course, which will take the hero to the power he is destined to possess.

The bards who sing this narrative do not state explicitly that Sunjata is seeking power outside the traditional authority structure, but his goal is made clear in the episodes after he regains strength in his legs and is able to stand up. Sunjata is taken through a series of transformations, which become the classic Mande model for seeking power outside the fa-siya authority structure. At first, Sunjata is impotent, the limping hero symbolically castrated in the sense of that term used in Hays's work *The Limping Hero* (1971). To make up for lost time in the process of seeking power, Sunjata becomes associated with those skilled, secretive, and dangerous practitioners of the occult, the hunters' societies, the epitome of antisocial behavior. He also begins at once to seek ties with clients and other political and social groups, especially from the casted families, the most important of whom to him are the bard and the blacksmith. The bard will stamp his name in history, and the blacksmith will manufacture weapons for his army. Both bard and blacksmith will lend their knowledge of occult power to his store. A series of panegyric lines from a variant of the epic recited by Fa-Digi Sisòkò will illustrate Sunjata's search for clients among these groups (Johnson 1986: 132):

Hee Ala!	Ah God!
Son-Jara k'waa Manden.	Let Sunjata go to the Manden.
Sini-mogo l'a di.	He is the man for the morrow.
Sini-kene-mogo l'a di.	He is the man for the day to follow.
A jelilu marala,	He is to rule o'er the bards,
Ka numu mara,	He is to rule o'er the smiths,
Ka tun-tan-mogo ni saba.	And the three and thirty
A y'o mogo bee marala!	warrior clans.

He will rule o'er all these people!

The first transformation sees Sunjata overcome his symbolic castration through the acquisition of enough occult power to neutralize the senior co-wife's hex. Great iron bars, sevenfold forged, are not strong enough to hold him up. But the thin branch of the sacred custard apple tree, given to him by his mother and said to be imbued with great occult power, accomplishes what physical force fails to do.

Sunjata is thus transformed from a crippled youth to a strong young man. His act of joining the hunters' society moves him from the cosmological safety of his mother's compound on the ba-denya axis into the dangers of the wilderness on the fa-denya axis. His chief occupation, which he tries to disguise through unquestioned loyalty to his brother's royal position in the traditional authority structure, is the serious pursuit of occult knowledge. But the senior co-wife is not fooled like her incompetent son Mansa Dankaran Tuman; nor is the audience of the epic, for they are warned by the bard who laces his lines with a Mande proverb in several places.

Subaa ni mansaya!   Sorcerer and sovereignty!

Sunjata and his family are therefore exiled after the king's mother intimidates her son into casting his brother out, and what follows in succeeding episodes is a further series of transformations in which the hero's stockpile of occult power and his knowledge of it continue to increase. During his exile, Sunjata travels through several lands and is assisted by their monarchs in the acquisition of power; some of these hosts later serve as clients in supplying Sunjata's army with warriors or provisions.

The methods used in the acquisition of occult power sometimes lead to the violation of taboos, thus upsetting existing authority structures. In Fa-Digi Sisòkò's account, for example, one king offers Sunjata the sacrifice of the unborn child of a Muslim holy man, who is abroad on the Islamic pilgrimage (hajj). This act results in the release of a very potent form of nyama, which greatly strengthens the hero; but the hapless king, being no match for so much occult power in one place, is destroyed by it.

After Sunjata reaches the ultimate destination of his exile, the city of Mèma (identified in some versions as the capital of Wagadugu, or ancient Ghana), his half brother is defeated and deposed by a foreign, pagan king, Sumamuru Kantè. Now local public opinion changes and emissaries from the Manden are sent to plead with Sunjata to return and deliver the people from the new sorcerer king. When he returns, he is a very different man from when he left, but he still cannot match Sumamuru's store of occult power. Another plan must be put into action.

If the culture hero cannot gain more occult power than his enemy, then he must reduce his enemy's supply. Sunjata's sister, who has taken over the occult duties of the female line at the death of Sunjata's mother during his exile, is sent to seduce Sumamuru. This she does, thus learning the secret of his power. Countermeasures are taken that considerably reduce Sumamuru's occult store, resulting in his ultimate defeat.

Once the last adversary in the surrounding lands is subdued, the final transformation of Sunjata takes place. He takes off the traditional mud-dyed cloth of the hunter (*bogolan-fini*), a material symbol along the fa-denya axis of the heroic search for power outside the authority structure, and dons the embroidered robes of the town (*duloki-ba*), a material symbol along the ba-denya axis. In short, Sunjata becomes the new leader in the fa-siya authority structure, having arrived at his destiny by circumventing that very structure altogether. He then establishes a new order and is granted his own surname, Keita, symbolizing his having overcome his Konatè father's reputation,[9] an act required of every hero in the Mande worldview.

Bird and Kendall (1980:21) comment that, whereas written literature becomes frozen in time and space, reflecting the past historical period of its origin, "oral literature is constantly reshaped to its contemporary period—at least in its interpretation." Such is the case with the epic *Sunjata* and the other epics and praise-poems of the Mande culture. Whatever the original function, in the Mande world of today these poems reflect contemporary concerns and influence modern audiences. The bard, not being part of the authority structure, is licensed to comment on it and to act as a mediator between past and present. He is, at the same time, the conservative and the radical. He acts as "oral historian" and "keeper of the traditional worldview," a sort of oral archive. But he may also attempt to stir lazy youths into action, because action along the fa-denya axis, however dangerous to the individual and to the stability of society, is an important part of the tradition the bard is protecting and preserving. At the center of that fa-denya and ba-denya action is the struggle between the authority structure of the group status quo and the search for power by the individual seeking to make a name for himself both in the oral annals of the bard, and in the modern world of realpolitik.

Power and authority in any society are of ultimate importance to its people. Civil rights, police power, the army, economic wealth and its control, violation of the law and social norms, ambitious colleagues who use their fellow workers to their own advantage, and so on and so forth, are but a few life-and-death issues involved with power and authority. Every society has its own ways with dealing with these issues, of sanctioning power, punishing its misuse, symbolizing it in literature, and debating its outer limits. Mande culture is no

---

[9] Note that the word *jamu* in Maninka translates as both "surname" and "reputation." In the version recorded by D. T. Niane (1960/65) Sunjata again changes clothing at this point, now wearing Muslim robes to represent a more universal rulership which transcends (but by no means subdues) all axes of Manden power.

exception, and the epic *Sunjata*, though dealing with many other complex issues as well, is a major vehicle by which these questions are constantly debated and updated.

Bibliography

Bierstedt, Robert. 1954. "The Problem of Authority." *Freedom and Control in Modern Society*, Monroe Berger, Theodore Abel, and Charles H. Page, eds., 67–81. New York: D. Van Nostrand.

Cissé, Youssouf Tata and Wâ Kamissoko. 1988. *Soundjata, la gloire du Mali (La grande geste du Mali—Tome 2)*. Paris: Édition Karthala et Arsan.

Encyclopedia of Islam. 1960. New edition, Leiden: E.J. Brill.

Griaule, Marcel. 1973. "The Mothers Brother in Western Sudan." *French Perspectives in African Studies*, ed. P. Alexandre, 11–25. London: Oxford University Press.

Hays, Peter L. 1971. *The Limping Hero: Grotesque in Literature*. New York: New York University Press.

Hopkins, Nicholas S. 1971. "Manding Social Organization." In Carleton T. Hodge, ed., *Papers on the Manding*, 99–128. The Hague: Mouton for the Research Center for the Language Sciences at Indiana Unversity.

—. 1972. *Popular Government in an African Town: Kita, Mali*. Chicago: Chicago University Press.

Johnson, John William. 1980. "Yes Virginia, There Is an Epic in Africa." *Research in African Languages* 11, 4: 308–26.

McNaughton, Patrick. 1988. *The Mande Blacksmiths: Knowledge, Power and Art in West Africa*. Bloomington: Indiana University Press.

N'Diayé, Bokor. 1970. *Les Castes au Mali*. Bamako: Editions Populaires.

2. The History of the *Sunjata* Epic: A Review of the Evidence

Ivor Wilks

Introduction

A number of scholars have made major use of the *Sunjata* epic for purposes of historical reconstruction. Levtzion's account of medieval Mali, for example, depends heavily upon it; indeed, he describes this narrative as "a pivot in the historical traditions of the Malinke" (Levtzion 1973: 58). Others have regarded any such exercise as misguided. Innes, for example, takes a highly sceptical position: "Even if historians can establish that Sunjata did exist," he writes (1974: 26):

> I should regard with extreme suspicion any aspect of his life reported in the oral tradition. Indeed, I would need convincing that his career as it is recounted by the griots bears any relationship to the career of the historical Sunjata.

The student of the medieval period is thus faced with a dilemma. On the one hand there is no doubt that the griot custodians of the epic do regard it as preserving a knowledge of events which "really happened"; specifically, events to do with the emergence of imperial Mali. On the other hand, the very existence of Sunjata lacks external validation, insofar as we have no documented reference to him for something of the order of a century and more after his presumed *floruit*. This chapter, then, will be concerned not so much with the epic as history, but rather with the history of the epic: with matters of its development and transmission.

I suspect that many historians making use of the epic have worked with the premise that there is a positive correlation between the antiquity of the griot narratives and the veracity of their contents; that, in other words, the further back the origin of the texts can be pushed, the greater is the likelihood of their incorporating historical "fact." I doubt whether this is a safe assumption, for reflection will show that it discounts the whole genre of fiction. Folklorists have often subscribed to a contrary thesis, that, in the words of Innes, "there is reason to suspect the historicity of any purportedly historical account when similar accounts are found elsewhere in literature, either oral or written" (Innes 1974: 26). This discounts what is patently obvious, that veridical accounts of heroic figures, their wars and the like, will necessarily show similarities; human (or inhuman) behavior is remarkably consistent, regardless of place and time.

In this chapter I suggest that some items within the epic *Sunjata* may indeed date back to his era. Others are probably even older. I place much reliance on one methodological principle: *pluritas non est ponenda sine necessitate*, "multiplicity should not be postulated unnecessarily." William of Occam aside, I subscribe to the rational assumptions with which I grew up; most signally, perhaps, that a hypothesis which explains more is to be preferred to one explaining less. I make reference, for suggestive rather than truly comparative purposes, to the Celtic bardic tradition of the medieval period. I select it for the good reason that I have some knowledge of it, and in earlier papers have used the practices of the Mande griots to cast light upon those of their vanished Welsh and Irish counterparts.[1]

The epic *Sunjata* consists basically of three cycles of stories, the first to do with his birth and childhood, the second with his exile, and the third with his return to Manden and victory over the Sosso. Inserted into these is a fourth cycle of stories that concern the griot Bala Fasseke Kuyate and his relations with Sunjata's archenemy, Sumanguru. I draw upon various published recensions of the epic, some full linear texts, some no more than prose summaries. Belcher (1985: 227–58) listed sixteen versions, and more recently Bulman (1990: 19–94) has brought the count to thirty-five. My debt to those upon whose texts I have drawn will be obvious. Particular reference should also be made to the work of Charles Bird, which has so greatly stimulated recent interest in the field.

---

[1] "Arthur of Britain, Sunjata of Mali," University of Northern Iowa, 11th Annual Carl L. Becker Memorial Lecture, 1984; "In Defense of Orality: Mande Griots and Welsh Bards," Centre for Advanced Welsh and Celtic Studies, University of Wales, Aberystwyth, 1989. Without having access to these unpublished papers, in 1992 Michelle Gooze pursued many of the same themes in a Northwestern University honors thesis and I am in debt to her for obliging me to clarify my own thinking on many points.

Songs and Settings

Innes describes three styles of vocalization at the disposal of (in this case, Gambian) griots, namely, the speech, recitation, and song modes. Here I am particularly concerned with the third. Innes notes that the songs usually have to do with "outstanding incidents," and are often quite short. Each has a particular musical accompaniment, and the lines are clearly defined by the tune (Innes 1974: 15–20). Johnson notes that "bard and instrument seem to blend together," so that there is little aesthetic tension between the poetic line and the musical accompaniment. "Songs appear," he remarks, "at the major points in the narrative and seem to function like arias in grand operas, commemorating the major incidents in the plot" (Johnson 1986: 32–33, and compare Moser 1974: 35–36).

Moser has discussed at length the features of Maninka prosody, inter alia treating the complex patterns of alliteration, assonance, and the repetition of phrases and lines for euphonic as well as emphatic effect (1974: 43–116). He notes that the songs are distinguished from the narrative by their more melodic lines. Some impression of the scansion systems may be gained (even without the musical accompaniment) from a piece that Johnson describes as a eulogy to Sunjata (Johnson 1986: 18–19, and compare Diabaté 1970b: 37–39). I offer a sparser translation than Johnson's:

Minw bè sènè kè,	Those who farm,
I ka sènè kè.	Let them farm.
Minw bè jago kè,	Those who trade,
I ka jago kè.	Let them trade.
Minw bè kèlè kè,	Those who fight,
I ka kèlè kè.	Let them fight.
Jata ye kèlè kè.	Jata fought.

The melodic effect aside, the songs have less tangible but nonetheless important characteristics. Harris, who worked with the griot Pa Sanasi Kuyateh, of Sukurala in northern Sierra Leone, contrasts the *bologbili* with the *tulon bololu*. The first she describes as "the 'heavy' patterns or older songs," which carry "praises with greater historical and cultural resonance than other kinds of praise-words," and the latter as "the 'lighter' patterns that give advice and comment on social behavior for the most part." The former "carry a greater weight of obligation and responsibilty on the part of the praise-singer." Within the bologbili repertoire, moreover, are the *kele bololu*. These, Harris remarks:

are particularly heavy or powerful because they have death "behind" them. They accompanied warriors into battle and they have the weight of centuries of allusions to great heroes, warriors and their achievements and attributes within or "inside" them.

Harris was required to offer a goat or sheep for sacrifice before Pa Kuyateh was prepared to discuss aspects of the bologbili repertoire; otherwise, the griot said, the power inherent in it might spoil or destroy everything in her house (Harris 1989: passim). The words of Niane come to mind. "To acquire my knowledge," he reports Mamadu Kuyate of Djeliba Koro as saying:

> I have travelled throughout Mali. . . . Everywhere I was able to see and understand that which my masters were teaching me, between their hands I made an oath to teach that which is to be taught and to keep secret that which is secret. (Niane 1960: 153–54, but see Bulman 1990: 50-51)

Innes remarks that the words in each line of song are fixed or almost so; that is, there is little variation of text in different presentations (Innes 1974: 16). There is need for caution. It is salutary to keep in mind that items can be, and presumably always have been, added to the performance. Such improvisations may draw inspiration from existing sources, for example, hunters' songs, local "clan" traditions, or Muslim writings. Belcher tentatively identified over fifty songs and remarked that some address "the moment (and the patron) of the performance" (Belcher 1985: 227–33, 271, 296–320). An instructive example is that of Ibrahima Kanté's performance of the epic *Sunjata* at the request of Comrade N'Famara Keita, Minister of Energy in the People's Revolutionary Republic of Guinée, several times in the course of which Kanté introduced into the recital not only the minister, but President Ahmed Sekou Touré himself (Kanté, n.d.).

Of concern here, however, are not such improvisations, interesting as they are, but rather those songs that are relatively fixed in form and that are repeated by griots in widely dispersed localities, whose performances otherwise show such considerable differences that we may feel confident that the lines of transmission of the epic converge only in a distant past. How distant is a major concern of this paper. Of such songs, Belcher remarks:

> they are a "memorized" (i.e. fixed, stable) core that may serve to focus the narration around them. We could see a given

performance of *Sunjata*, then, as a series of linked episodes, at the core of each of which is the performance of a song, rather than as a succession of individual lines of poetry interrupted by songs. (Belcher 1985: 326)

Belcher has systematically compared versions of the popular song, "The Bow," which the griots use at different points in their performance of the epic (1985: 283–94). It is built around the refrain "bara kala ta le" (he took up the bow). Different epithets for Sunjata are, however, introduced into the song seemingly at the discretion of the singer. Thus, for example, Kele Monson Jabate of Kita could sing:

> O bara kala ta le,
> Simbon o bara kala ta le.
> Sugutigi, Simbon le, bara kala ta le.
> Jeli-ni-numulu-mara-baga bara kala ta le. . . .

and also,

> A, a, bara kala ta le,
> Simbon o bara kala ta le.
> Konte-muso de mago-nya-mogo bara kala ta le.
> Jeli-ni-numulu-mara-ba' bara kala ta le. . . .

The third lines translate, respectively, as "The master hunter, the Simbon, took up his bow," and "The protector of the Konte woman took up his bow" (Moser 1974: 268, 270). Johnson has a version of the song recorded from Fadigi Sisoko, also from Kita (Johnson 1978, II: 181–84):

> Bara kala ta le!
> Wula-tigi Sinbon ne!
> Bara kala ta le!
> Bara kala ta le!
> Jelilu ni numulu mara-mogo
> Bara kala ta!
> Bara kala ta le!

Johnson's translation is as follows:

> Took up the bow! / Simbon, Master-of-the-Bush! / Took up the bow! / Took up the bow! / Ruler of bards and smiths /

Took up the bow! / Took up the bow!

Belcher acknowledges that there is sometimes difficulty in deciding whether to treat certain texts as extreme variants of the same song, or as two songs showing parallel features. He notes, however, that usually—as with the versions of "The Bow" above—the matter is not in doubt:

> so that one may say the material belongs to the *Sunjata* tradition rather than to the individual griot's interpretation. The song occurs at similar moments in the story, and depends upon a standard refrain, but there is variation among the epithets used. (Belcher 1985: 293)

The burden of Belcher's study appears to validate Bird's view, expressed much earlier, that Manden heroic and epic works consist of "a series of songs tied together by narrative links." These songs, he argued, "seem to mark the major events of each story" (Bird 1972: 289).

The problem of the relationship between song and narrative is one that has long motivated students of Celtic bardic literature. Ifor Williams addressed the issue almost half a century ago, with reference to the ancient Welsh sagas. "In the early stages of the tradition," he suggested:

> the story teller knew the story by heart, at any rate the main lines of it. There was no need for him to be able to repeat it word for word, provided that he followed the original faithfully enough to bring in the stanzas, the *englynion*, at the right moment. These, however, had to be committed carefully to memory; metre, alliteration, rhymes, identical initial phrases, all these helped him to store them in his mind exactly as he first heard them. (Williams 1944: 23)

One example of a Welsh *englyn* may suffice to suggest the prosodic resemblances to the Manden songs:

Stafell Gynddylan ys tywyll heno,
Heb dan, heb wely.
Wylaf wers, tawaf wedy.

Cynddylan's hall is dark tonight, / Without fire, without bed. / I shall weep a while, then be silent.

Knowledge of the Celtic tradition has developed greatly since Williams wrote. His view expressed above has, however, stood the test of time. Bromwich, for example, has recently reiterated it:

> In the early literature of Wales and Ireland, in which both prose and poetry have been preserved by oral means over long periods, metrical conventions have ensured that verse has been retained in a more stable form than prose, since it is better able to guard its original structure in spite of partial modernization and corruption through failure of memory or at the hands of successive copyists. Prose, on the other hand, being unfettered by metrical constraints, can transmit the substance of oral stories without recognizing any obligation to transmit them in the exact words in which they were received; prose is continually renewed and revitalized as the language itself develops. (Bromwich 1991: 213)

The metrical patterns of the Mande songs, one assumes, similarly facilitated their accurate oral transmission from generation to generation of griots. The student of the Mande materials is, however, in one respect at a disadvantage vis-à-vis his Celtic counterpart. The problem is that our knowledge of the historical development of the Mande language and its dialects remains inadequate. Innes (1974: 12) has commented on the occurrence in Gambian texts of phrases that can no longer be understood. "As they are not part of everyday speech," he comments, "they set the griots' narrations apart and removed from the everyday world."

In 1969 Banna Kanute sang a song purportedly composed, on the orders of Sumanguru,[2] in praise of the smiths. It commences:

Sege ning Sirimang,
Tunkang ning mara mu. . . .

The griot knew that its meaning would be obscure to his audience. "As the Mandinka say," he assured them, "the eastern people understand the language of the griots./ All this is meaningful." He proceeded to attempt an exegesis of the song: "He (the original singer) said: 'Sege and Sirimang' / That is Sunjata and Susu Sumanguru Baamagana. . . ." and so forth (Innes 1974: 230–33).

The problem, however, may not lie in the difference between

---

[2] Banna Kanute says on the orders of Sunjata, but he was strangely confused on this matter (see Innes 1974: 29–30, 137; Okpewho 1979: 149, 267 n. 9).

western and eastern dialects of Mandekan. In 1925 Frobenius published
a version of the same song from eastern Mande:

> Sege ne sirima,
> Tunga in maramu. . . .

He was, however, unable to obtain any explanation of the meaning of
the lines (Frobenius 1921: VI, 35). It was not, in other words, simply a
matter of dialect as Banna Kanute thought. Frobenius was probably
correct in referring to "archaistisches," that is, in thinking that the song
preserves features of an older lexicon.

The mnemonic function of the Manden songs has been noted
by, inter alia, Belcher (1985: 88–89). The medieval Welsh bard had
recourse to a further mnemonic device not, I think we may be sure, used
by any Manden counterpart of the time: literacy. If the bard distrusted
his memory of the englynion, Williams continues:

> he could write them down on vellum, and by doing so would
> make it certain that these verse elements of the saga would be
> preserved intact for centuries, and that in their earliest and
> most primitive form. Later copyists might bungle their job,
> mis-copying through carelessness, or might deliberately and of
> choice change the orthography and subsitute more modern
> words and forms for those that had become obsolete or
> obscure in the course of time. Metre and alliteration would be
> a valuable check on this modernising process. You can
> modernise a prose story to your heart's content, but alliterative
> verse is not so easy to handle without spoiling the poetic form.
> Poetic form preserved the old grammatical form, the old
> phrase or word. (Williams 1944: 23)

There is a somewhat paradoxical result of the recourse that the
Welsh bards had to the written word. As the oral culture of the Welsh
died out in the sixteenth and seventeenth centuries (Jones 1992: xxix–
xxxvii), so the old sagas were for the most part lost. Only the songs
were preserved, and scholars have now to devote much time to guessing
at the narratives in which they were once embedded. The student of the
griots is in a somewhat more fortunate position, in having access to
living practitioners of an ancient tradition.

First-Singers

The griots who perform the *Sunjata* epic not infrequently refer
to the matter of transmission. "I obtained my knowledge from my father

Jeli Kedian," said Mamadu Kuyate, "who also obtained it from his
father" (Niane 1960: 12). Bamba Suso sang (Innes 1974: 40–41):

> This tune that I am now playing,
> I learned it from my father,
> And he learned it from my grandfather.
> Our grandfather's name—Koriyang Musa. . . .

I know of no such recital extending into the fourth generation,
and it does not seem that the griots thought it necessary to maintain long
chains of transmission comparable to the *isnads* for learning—
essentially chains of teachers—preserved by the Muslim scholars of
Mande (Wilks 1968: passim). The griots do, however, frequently refer
to those I shall call "first-singers."[3] They attribute songs embedded in
the narrative to particular individuals, and moreover to particular
individuals singing on particular occasions. Originality is not the issue
per se. The singers may draw upon earlier materials, most notably
perhaps on the songs of the Mande hunters, some of which are
presumably very ancient indeed (Bird 1972: 292; Bulmman 1990: 171–
88).

First-singers are "first" in a very specific sense. They are
represented as having sung of Sunjata during his lifetime: sung of his
childhood, of his struggles against the Sosso, and of the birth of
imperial Mali. The first-singers, morever, appear to be thought of as the
founders of the griot tradition: not that of the *donso-jeliw*, the hunters'
griots, but that of the casted jeliw, who came to constitute something
like an intellectual class within Manden society. At this stage I should
not and do not make any assumptions about the historicity of the first-
singers. However, surprisingly little attention has been paid to them in
the literature of the epic, and they merit more detailed consideration.

The first-singers are few in number. Three stand out in the
texts I have used, all being described (in some sense or other) as apical

---

[3] I have here adopted and adapted the Welsh concept of the *cynfeirdd*, the "first
bards" of the sixth to eleventh centuries. Of the considerable literature on the
bardic tradition I note—a relevant sample only—Ford 1975/76; Matonis 1978;
Haycock 1981; Caerwyn Williams 1984; Sims-Williams 1984.

in the development of the griot tradition:

> 1. Jankuma Duga (Jakuma Duga, Gnankouman Doua, Nyamkuma Dookha, Jankuma Doka, etc., and by translation, Doka the Cat) is referred to as *Kuyatelu mama,* "Kuyate ancestor" (Johnson 1979: II, 190–91; Johnson 1986: 148; 150; Moser 1974: 280).
>
> 2. Kalanjan Sangoyi is referred to as *Jabatelu mama,* "Jabate ancestor" (Moser 1974: 320–21; Diabaté 1975: 84–86; Johnson 1986: 121).
>
> 3. Tumu Manian (Tuntun Manian, Tumu Maniya, Tumuma Ninyan, etc.) is *Kuyatelu bemba,* "Kuyate ancestress" (Camara Laye 1984: 85–87, 91–92; Moser 1974: 266; Johnson 1986: 129, 145, 168).

Jankuma Duga is by far the best-known of the three first-singers. Indeed, most griots not only refer to his songs, but incorporate stories about him into their performances of the epic. There is, however, one conflict in their narratives that has to be addressed. Its resolution is not essential to the argument of this paper, but is relevant to the ease of presentation. In Niane's recension of griot tradition (1960: 40–41), Mamadu Kuyate presents Jankuma Duga as the griot of Sunjata's father. Nare Maghan gives his son a griot, saying:

> In Manden each prince has a griot; the father of Doua [that is, Duga] was my father's griot; Doua is my griot; the son of Doua, Balla Fasseke, is to be your griot.

Camara Laye's free translation of griot Babu Condé of Fadama has a passage to the same effect: that Gnankuman Dua, son of Dua, was the griot of Sunjata's father, and that Bala Fassali Kuyate, son of Gnankuman Dua, became Sunjata's griot (Camara Laye 1984: 72).

This treatment of Bala Fasseke Kuyate (Balan Fasege Kuyate, Bala Faaseega Kuyate, Balla Fassali Kuyate, Balla Faseke Kwate, etc.) as son of Jankuma Duga seems to be idiosyncratic.[4] Most texts, we shall see, firmly identify the two. They introduce Jankuma Duga into the narrative only after Sunjata is in exile in Mema. He was, they say, sent

---

[4] In this context it will be noted that Yves Person (1973: 205 n. 2, 207) implies that Niane collected much of his information not from Mamadu Kuyate but, like Camara Laye, from Babu Condé. Wa Kamissoko (1975: 192–93) refers to "Balla Faseke Kwate," but it is his translator who glosses this "son of Dyakouma-Doka."

on a mission to Sumanguru of the Sosso by Dankaran Tuman, brother
of Sunjata and ruler of the Manden in succession to Nare Maghan.

The story of Jankuma Duga's mission is found in many
recensions of the *Sunjata* epic. Belcher (1985: 244, 253, 256) and
Bulman (1990: 107–108) have most usefully listed its appearances. The
details of the story vary considerably between one performance and
another (Bulman 1990: 331–37). Essentially, Dankaran Tuman feared
the exiled Sunjata, who he knew was committed to his overthrow. He
sent his sister (or daughter) with Jankuma Duga to Sosso, to ask
Sumanguru to eliminate his rival. It is not my purpose here to attempt
any systematic collation of the texts, but I quote selectively from
several of them to give something of their flavor. The griot Magan
Sisoko—and I follow Johnson's translation (1979: II 145)—
commences the story thus:

> King Dankaran Tuman,
> He came and got his flesh-and-blood sister,
> And gave her to the Kuyate patriarch, Doka, the Cat,
> To take her to Susu Mountain Sumamuru [Sumanguru],
> That he might slay Magan Sun-Jata in Mema,
> Said he was afraid of him,
> And not to let him see the Manden again.

Moser (1974: 279) gives us Kele Monson Jabate's version of the same
event:

> Dangarantuman took his oldest daughter and sent her to
> Susukulu [*kulu*, "mountain"] Sumanguru.
> He called the ancestor of the Kuyates, Jakuma Doka.
> "Take this [sic] to Sumanguru.
> Tell him to raise an army.
> Tell him to go kill Magan Sunjata
> at the home of the ancestor of the Tunkaras, at Mema.
> Say he should not see the Manden again."

Finally, the version of Demba Kanute of Gambia, in the translation of
Innes (1974: 279):

> The men of Manding sent Nyankuma Dookha,
> Ordering him to go to Sumanguru
> And to ask him to help them with spear and bow,
> To announce that Sunjata's brothers had had news of him,
> And that he was in the land of Mansa Farang Tunkara.

They must go and kill him. . . .

Sumanguru was absent when Jankuma Duga arrived in Sosso.
The griot found Sumanguru's *balafon* in the palace, and played it.
Sumanguru returned, and was much angered. Jankuma Duga
immediately composed a song in his honor. Sumanguru, in turn much
enthralled, insisted that he should remain in Sosso as his griot.

The drama of the occasion is well captured in the performance
of Fadigi Sisoko (Johnson 1986: 150):

> He [Sumanguru] said, "Ah! What is your name?"
> "My name is Doka [Duga], the Cat."
> "Will you not remain with me?"
> "Not I! Two kings I cannot praise.
> I am Son-Jara's bard.
> From the Manden I have come,
> And to the Manden I must return."
> He laid hold of the Kuyate patriarch,
> And severed both Achilles tendons,
> And by the Susu [Sosso] balaphone set him.
> "Now what is your name?"
> "Doka, the Cat, is still my name."
> "Doka, the Cat will no longer do."
> He drew water and poured it over his head,
> And shaved it clean,
> And gave him the name Bala Faseke Kuyate.

Dembo Kanute's account has many of the same elements
(Innes 1974: 281). Sumanguru asked:

> What is your name?
> The griot replied, "My name is Nyankuma Dookha."
> Sumanguru said, "I am going to take your name from you;
> And apart from those with special knowledge,
> No one will know your name any more.
> I shall name you after my xylophone.
> What I am going to do to you,
> That is what I shall make your second name.
> The third will be your surname
> Your first name is Balo;
> I will cut your Achilles tendons;
> Your surname is Kuyate."

They call him Bala Faasege Kuyate.[5]

After the defeat of the Sosso, Sunjata conducted a search for Jankuma Duga. I choose Kele Monson Jabate's account of the matter (Moser 1974: 313–14):

> He came to get the ancestor of the Kuyates from the dead.
> He who does not know how to serve two kings.
> Someone said, "If somebody told a great lie now,
> you would see the ancestor of the Kuyates."
> One of the young men said, "On our way to join Magan Sunjata in Mema,
> all the Mema sheep had four horns."
> He rose to say, "You are lying.
> Who has ever seen sheep with four horns?"
> They grabbed the Kuyate ancestor and set him down.
> When he was ordered to rise, he could not rise.
> Sumanguru had cut his Achilles tendons and put tobacco in there,
> saying that there is nothing as sweet as a bard. . . .
> When Magan Sunjata shouted at the Kuyate ancestor to get up, he could not get up.

A son of Sumanguru, captured in the fighting, was made to help the griot. Fadigi Sisoko's version is as follows (Johnson 1986: 177–78):

---

[5] Diabaté (1975: 60) glosses this, saying that etymologically Bala Faseke Kuyate is made up of Bala (balafon) Fasere (witness) Kuyante (there is a secret between us). In other words, you've seen my balafon and played it; there is a secret between you and me.

"Had Sumanguru no child?" they queried.
"Here is his first born son," the reply.
"What is his name?"
"His name is Mansa Saman."
They summoned Mansa Saman
And brought forth Doka the Cat,
And placed him on Mansa Saman's shoulders,
Laying the balaphone on his head, serew!

The Songs of Jankuma Duga
I shall assume at this point that attributions of songs to
Jankuma Duga, to the Kuyate ancestor (or patriarch), and to Bala
Fasseke Kuyate are to one and the same person. In reviewing these
attributions, it should be reiterated that the first-singers, in the sense I
am using the term, may nonetheless draw themes and lines from older
repertoires, and particularly those of the hunters. "The Bow," parts of
which have been reproduced above, may well be a case in point.
According to Niane's prose text, "The Bow" was composed by
Bala Fasseke—identified as Sunjata's griot—to commemorate the
occasion upon which his master first (and belatedly) gained the use of
his legs and soon thereafter became a skilled hunter (Niane 1960: 40–
41, 47, 105, and compare Belcher 1985: 385–87). Fadigi Sisoko
introduces the song in much the same context, but without attribution.
Later, he has Tumu Manian, "the Kuyate matriarch," sing it at both the
beginning and end of Sunjata's exile to Mema (Johnson 1986: 141–42;
145–46; 168). Kele Monson has Tumu Manian sing it on four
occasions, all to do with the exile (Moser 1974: 266–70, 302–303), and
Magan Sisoko does likewise (Johnson 1979: I, 108, 112, 118). The
latter griot, however, takes up the song in another context, that of the
celebration of Sunjata's victory over Sumanguru. This time the singer is
"the Kuyate patriarch" (Johnson 1979: II, 191). Konaré Ba associates
"The Bow" with Sunjata's assumption of highest office: Bala Fasseke
sang it, "dedicated to Sunjata in honour of his taking power." It is
unfortunately unclear whose performance she is following (Konare Ba
1983: 83, and compare Niane 1960: 146).
Massa Diabaté, nephew of the griot Kele Monson, gives a
lengthy version of "The Bow," which he entitles "Sun Jata Fasa." A
fasa, essentially, commemorates an ancestor. Diabaté addresses the
matter of its first-singer. The traditionalists, he writes, generally
attribute the "refrain" of the song (presumably "bara kala ta le. . .") to
Tumu Manian, and the "couplets" to Bala Fasseke Kuyate—who
"improvised them after the victory of Sunjata over Sumanguru"

(Diabaté 1970a: 29n., and compare Diabaté 1975: 49n.). We have no need to pursue this matter here. "The Bow" appears to be associated with both Jankuma Duga (Bala Fasseke) and Tumu Manian, two of the first-singers.

A song having the accompaniment "Janjon" appears in most griot performances of the epic *Sunjata* at much the same point in the narrative (Belcher 1985: 311–12).[6] It is in praise of Sumanguru of the Sosso. The griot Magan Sisoko describes its first-singer variously, as "Kuyatelu mama" (the Kuyate ancestor), "Doka the Cat," and "Balan Fasege Kuyate" (Johnson 1979: I, 129, and II, 146–48, 150–51, 243n.). Kele Monson attributes it to Kuyatelu mama, Jankuma Doka. I follow his text as presented and translated by Moser (1974: 280–81; cf. Diabaté 1975: 58–59).

> Ye, ye, ye, aimari wo.
> Playing does not end the serious.
> Susu Sumanguru, I have found you gone.
> Sumanguru wears pants of human skin.
> Sumanguru wears a shirt of human skin.
> Sumanguru wears a hat of human skin.
> Sumanguru wears a shirt of human skin.
> Greetings to Sumanguru.
>
> Native king; first king.
> Playing does not end the serious.
> Susu Sumanguru, I have been here in your absence.
> Ye, ye, ye, aimari wo.
> Laughter does not end the serious.

Fadigi Sisoko gave a very closely related version of the song, attributing it to Jankuma Duga (Johnson 1986: 149, 150). There is some

---

[6] Other songs appear to use the same accompaniment (see Diabaté 1970a: 43–52; Bird 1971: 22).

change in the order of the lines, and clearly some difference in Moser's
and Johnson's understanding of the Maninka.

> Salute Sumamuru!
> Sumamuru came amongst us,
> With pants of human skin.
> Sumamuru came amongst us
> His coat of human skin.
> Sumamuru came amongst us
> With helm of human skin.
> The first and ancient king,
> The king of yesteryear.
> So, respite does not end resolve!
> Sumamuru, I found you gone.
> Oh! Glorious Janjon.

We have, in "Janjon" and in several other texts such as Duwa
mentioned below, perhaps items from an epic of Sumanguru which
became incorporated into *Sunjata*. The matter is highly conjectural, but
clearly the dramatic impact of collapsing the former into the latter is
greatly to enhance Sunjata's reputation by demonstrating just how
ferocious and fearsome an enemy he was able to overcome.

Belcher records numerous texts in which the song "Nyama,
Nyama, Nyama" appears (1985: 299–300). It was, according to Niane's
Mamadu Kuyate, composed by Bala Fasseke after Sunjata's celebrated
victory over Sumanguru (Niane 1960: 138). Babu Condé, if we follow
Camara Laye's text, maintained that it was created by Bala Fasseke
when Sunjata first walked, but that it was sung again, perhaps in
expanded form, in the aftermath of the victory (Camara Laye 1984:
135, 213). I follow the version sung by Banna Kanute in 1969, and the
translation made by Innes (1974: 230–31, but see also 204–205 and
206–207):

> Nyaama nyaama nyaama,
> Feng ne be dung na nyaama koro,
> Nyaama te dung na feng koro;
> Nyaama nyaama nyaama,
> Feng ne be bori la Sunjata ma,
> Sunjata te bori la feng ma.
> Saafuna taa wulu,
> Wulu meng mang a tu saafuna ye,
> Wo te a tu kulu ye.
> Sunjata ding kasi kang, Sumangguru,

Saa ka fisi malu ti, Sumangguru.

Thatching grass, thatching grass, thatching grass, / Other things go underneath thatching grass, / Thatching grass does not go underneath anything; / Thatching grass, thatching grass, thatching grass, / Others run away from Sunjata, / Sunjata does not run away from anyone. / A soap-taking dog, / A dog that does not leave soap alone, / Will not leave a bone alone. / Sunjata ding kasi kang, Sumanguru, / Death is better than disgrace, Sumanguru.[7]

Reference has already been made to "Sege ning Siriman," composed in praise of the smiths (and see Belcher 1985: 315–16). Despite its archaic linguistic features, Banna Kanute made use of it six times in the course of his performance. Five of these associate it with Bala Fasseke Kuyate, and one reference is particularly specific. Sumanguru told his griot, "I want you to sing the praises of the smiths so that I can hear" (Innes 1974: 157, 159, 185, 193, 205, 231). Banna Kanute also performs a song, the refrain of which is:

Kele le ka Manding tee,
Kele le ka Manding loo.

Demba Kanute rendered it

---

[7] In this context, Innes's translation of *nyama* seems preferable to that offered by, for example, Moser (1974: 257) and Camara Laye (1984: 135, 213): "filth." I am, however, familiar with the usage in which "nyama-nyama" is equivalent to the English "lowest of the low." The word is not so much ambiguous as encompassing: the sacred and the profane, as it were (see also Bird, infra).

Kele le ye Manding tee,
Kele le ye Manding loo. . . .

It is war that devastated Manden. / It is war that rebuilt
Manden.

Demba asked his audience,

Where did that song originate?
It originated with a griot.
Who was that griot?
He was called Nyankuma Dookha. . . .

Banna Kanute sang a closely related song, but to a different
accompaniment. He attributed it, again, to Bala Fasseke:

Janjung baa, kele le ka Janjung baa janjang,
Kele ka Jangung baa fanang loo.

Great Janjung, it is war that shattered Janjung, / War rebuilt
great Janjung. (Innes 1974: 232–33; 276–79)

Considerations of space dictate that we do no more than draw
attention to other songs having the same attribution. The following list
makes no claim to be exhaustive:

1. The griot Babu Condé, to follow Camara Laye's recension,
attributes to Jankuma Duga a song beginning "Trublu Kabala
Simbon." Camara Laye described it as an "incantation
composed of untranslatable nominalizations" (Camara Laye
1984: 95–96, 114).
2. Babu Condé attributes to Jankuma Duga a long speech
commencing "Minka an na din Mansa bara bi" delivered for
the young Sunjata (Camara Laye 1984: 121–22). The last six
lines appear to be song rather than narrative.
3. Babu Condé attributes the song "Sosso kémo dén Sumaoro"
(I Salute Thee Sumanguru the Ancient of Sosso) to Bala
Fasseke (Camara Laye 1984: 175–76). It is related to the song
in praise of Sumanguru, with the accompaniment Janjon,
discussed above.
4. Banna Kanute sang to the tune "Sunjata mang bori long":

Ee, Sunjata naata, Sumangguru,
Aa, Sunjata naata, Sumangguru. . . .

Ah, Sunjata has come, Sumanguru, / Ah, Sunjata has come, Sumanguru.

He attributes the song to Bala Fasseke (Innes 1974: 228–29).

5. Banna Kanute sang the song "Kankinya" to the melody of the same name. It has to do with the struggle against Sumanguru, and seems to be considered part of Bala Fasseke's repertoire (Innes 1974: 232–33).

6. A particularly popular song with the Gambian griots is one having the refrain "*nyankumolu khaba la*" (cats on the shoulder) (Belcher 1985: 309). Banna Kanute has Bala Fasseke singing it to Sunjata every morning (Innes 1974: 232–35).

7. Pa Kuyate of Sierra Leone sang the very well-known "Duwa." "The 'Duwa' pattern," he told Harris, "is particularly heavy; *Duwa ka gbili de!*" (Harris 1989: 2–4). Niane refers to it as the "Song of the Vultures" and, presumably following Mamadu Kuyate, has Bala Fasseke sing it first for Sumanguru and later for Sunjata on the eve of the battle of Krina (Niane 1960: 76, 118).

8. Niane (1960: 48) has the griot Mamadu Kuyate praising Sunjata in a song of which the first four lines are: "Space, space, space! / The lion has walked; / Antelopes, hide yourselves, / Avoid his path." It is attributed to Bala Fasseke.

9. Wa Kamissoko (1975: 194–95, 204–205) has Bala Fasseke sing in praise of Sunjata, "*Kani sinbo, kaninyokon sinbo* (Simbon the loved, Simbon the kind)."

10. Wa Kamissoko (1975: 364–65) has Bala Fasseke sing Boloba, which he describes as "the premier song of Manden." It is presumably the song recorded by Sidibé (1959: 51n.):

Sin ba kedi Jata,
Bolo ba kedi Jata,
Nye ba ti Jata.

Big leg-breaking Jata, / Big arm-breaking Jata, / Big eye-poking out Jata.

Magan Sisoko associates this song with the youth of Sunjata (Johnson 1979: I, 99–100, and see Belcher 1985: 310).

I am not arguing that these attributions are necessarily correct, but only that the griots do have a firm sense that songs were first sung by specific individuals to commemorate specific events. Jankuma Duga is unquestionably the most favored of those I have called the first-singers. At this stage I still refrain from making inferences to do with his historicity or otherwise. I do wish to argue, however, that we can be reasonably confident that the songs, the "heavy" songs, are older than the narratives in which they are embedded; older, that is, in at least the sense that their sheer metrical complexity (as with the Welsh poems), and their musical accompaniments, now lost in the Welsh tradition (Conran 1993), made them the most stable component within the developing epic.

The significance and sense of some of the griot songs may have become obscure over the course of time, particularly as words have either disappeared from everyday language or undergone changes in meaning. Some songs may well have been lost. But others are pivotal; the narrative is built around them. "Bara kala ta le" and "Boloba," for example, provide a firm structure for the story of Sunjata's triumph over physical handicap. The song in praise of Sumanguru, sung to the Janjon melody, and "Sege ning Siriman," in praise of his smiths, similarly structure the story of Dankaran Tuman's ill-judged embassy to Sosso. The popularity of some of these songs may lead griots to use them time and time again, in secondary contexts, but their content usually leaves little doubt as to where they essentially belong. It may be that close analysis and comparison of various versions of the epic will make it possible to reconstruct, conjecturally, something of the stemma of the epic, though I doubt whether anything like an ur-text will ever be within our reach. However that may be, here I turn rather to matters of external validation.

The Griots: Fourteenth-Century Witnesses

Ibn Fadl Allah al-`Umari of Damascus (1301–1349) spent much of his life in Cairo as a not altogether successful administrator. His *Masalik al-absar fi mamalik al-amsar* contains a lengthy account of Mali written, it seems, in the late 1330s. It includes a description of the court of Mansa Sulayman. Al-Umari thought his informant particularly reliable; he was Shaykh Abu Sa`id `Uthman al-Dukkali, who had spent thirty-five years in Mali.

The Malian ruler, we learn, sat in state on a large platform known as *banbi* (that is, Mande *bembe*). About thirty slaves stood behind him, one carrying his parasol. Two functionaries stood in front of him. The one was his *sayyaf*, "executioner" or perhaps "swordbearer" (Arabic). The other was his *shair*, "poet" (Arabic), who was also the *safir*, "intermediary" (Arabic), between him and the people (Levtzion and Hopkins 1981: 265). In this latter person it is difficult not to see the head griot of the time, the *mansa jeli,* who exercised functions as praise-singer to the king together with ones of a wider but related nature: roughly, attending to the loyalty of the the king's subjects. Fortunately, a much more detailed account of the court, written a decade and a half later, puts this matter beyond serious doubt.

Ibn Battuta (1304–1368) spent seven months in the Malian capital, from July 28, 1352, to February 27, 1353. On his return to Morocco he recounted his experiences to one of the literati attached to the court of Sultan Abu `Inan. This was Ibn Juzayy, who completed his transcription— subject to some final stylistic refinement—just two years after Ibn Battuta's return. Ibn Juzayy prided himself upon having faithfully conveyed the sense, and often the very words, of his informant. Nonetheless, there are passages that suggest that Ibn Juzayy drew some material from al-`Umari. Such contamination, if it is indeed present, does not detract from the evidential value of the text for present purposes.

Mansa Sulayman still presided over Mali in 1352-53. On Ibn Battuta's arrival in the capital he was met by various Muslim dignitaries and by "the interpreter (*turjuman*) Dugha, one of the respected and important Sudanese, who sent me a bullock. . . ." Weeks later Ibn Battuta, feeling that he was being ignored by the king, consulted the interpreter. "Speak with him," he was told, "and I will express what you want to say in the proper fashion" (Levtzion and Hopkins 1981: 288–89). The name "Dugha" is obviously the Maninka "Duga" (Doka, etc.). It certainly belonged, then, as present-day griots would have it, to the onomasticon of imperial Mali.

Ibn Battuta gave a description of the pavilion in which Mansa Sulayman conducted business. "Dugha the interpreter," he said:

> stands at the gate of the council-place wearing fine garments of silk brocade and other materials, and on his head a turban with fringes that they have a novel way of winding. Round his waist he has a sword with a golden sheath and on his feet boots and spurs. No one but him wears boots on that day. In his hand he has two short lances, one of gold and the other of silver, with iron tips. (Levtzion and Hopkins 1981: 290)

Up to this point we have a description of a senior functionary serving the ruler in the familiar enough role of dragoman. Ibn Battuta, however, also noted that every Friday, in the afternoon, and on the great

festival days, Duga assumed a different role. The king took his seat on
the bembe, surrounded by various dignitaries. Then, Ibn Battuta noted:

> Dugha the interpreter comes with his four wives and his slave
> girls. There are about a hundred of these, with fine clothes and
> on their heads bands of gold and silver adorned with gold and
> silver balls. A seat is set up for Dugha and he sits on it and
> plays the instrument that is made of reed with little gourds
> under it, and sings poetry in which he praises the sultan and
> commemorates his expeditions and exploits and the women
> and slave girls sing with him and perform with bows.
> (Levtzion and Hopkins 1981: 292–93)

Duga, playing a xylophone, singing poems in praise of the
king, accompanied by female singers: Ibn Battuta's testimony
demonstrates, surely beyond reasonable doubt, that Kele Monson and
Fadigi Sisoko and their fellow griots authentically represent, in their
contemporary performances, practices that were observable in Mali at
least by the mid-fourteenth century. But Ibn Battuta has more to tell us.

Duga had drummers with him, and "young followers who play
and turn somersaults in the air. . . ." The reader is referred to Camara's
photographs of griot (somersaulting) dancers and drummers (Camara
1976: plates 13–20). More to the point, Ibn Battuta spoke of other poets
who appeared after Duga had finished his recital. "They are called
jula," he said, "of which the singular is *jalf*." Mande "jeli" (griot) is
readily recognizable. Jula is presumably a metathesis for *jalu*, that is,
the plural jeliw.[8] Ibn Battuta described their strange attire; apparently
they wore bird-like masks and gowns of feathers. I shall refrain from
comment on this in the present context.[9] "They stand," reported Ibn
Battuta:

> in front of the sultan in this comical shape and recite their
> poems. I was told that their poetry was a kind of exhortation in
> which they say to the sultan: "This banbi on which you are
> sitting was sat upon by such-and-such a king and of his good

---

[8] Jalu is a by-name for the Jabate. It is just possible that Ibn Battuta heard
Jabate griots referred to this way, and assumed that it was the plural of jeli. I
think this unlikely.

[9] As a matter of sheer coincidence, however, it has been noted (Caerwyn
Williams 1971: 121) that the highly trained bard (*fili*) of medieval Ireland was
entitled to wear a distinctive dress of feathers!

deeds were so-and-so; and such-and-such a king and of his
good deeds were so-and-so; so you do good deeds that will be
remembered after you." (Levtzion and Hopkins 1981: 293)

The visitor to Mali made a further telling comment: "I was informed,"
he said, "that this act was already old before Islam, and they had
continued with it."

Ibn Battuta considered Mansa Sulaymân to be parsimonious.
He heard tell of Sulaymân's predecessor once removed, Mansa Musa.
He was less interested in Musa's well-known pilgrimage to Mecca in
1324, rather in his generosity. He cited several examples of it. One
recipient was Mudrik b. Faqqus. "Reliable people," said Ibn Battuta,
"informed me that he gave to Mudrik b. Faqqus 3,000 *mithqals* in a
single day." He added a rider to this: "his [Musa's] grandfather Sariq
Jata embraced Islam at the hands of the grandfather of this Mudrik"
(Levtzion and Hopkins 1981: 295). However we treat the problematical
"Sariq," we have here what can only be the first documentary reference
to Sunjata, who did indeed stand in the relationship of grandfather to
Mansa Musa; that is, he was Musa's "senior grandfather," senior
paternal brother of his real (or biological) grandfather, Abu Bakr
(Levtzion 1973: 71). No other plausible identification of Sariq Jata can
be offered without multiplying persons unnecessarily.

Ibn Battuta, then, should be read as authenticating the
existence of Sunjata, and as placing him in the second antecedent
generation to Mansa Musa, whose reign may be dated, with some
confidence, to 1312–37 (Levtzion 1973: 66). We know, moreover, that
some account of Sunjata's war against the Sosso was already current in
the late fourteenth century. It came to the attention of Abu Zayd` Abd
al-Rahman Ibn Khaldûn (1332–1406) in Cairo, and was recorded in his
Kitab al-'Ibar. Whoever the informant was, he knew Sunjata as Mari
Jata. This name is still known to present-day griots. It occurs many
times in Niane's recension of griot traditions (Niane 1960: especially
35–36). Niane also has Mamadu Kuyate sing "The Song to
Abundance": "He is come / And happiness is come. / Sunjata is here /
And happiness is here" (Niane 1960: 144). Sidibé (1959: 42) gives a
Malinke text:

> Na da dinye di ia?
> Soundiata na da digne di ia.
> Na da dinye di ia?
> Mari Diata na da dinye di ia.

Who has come to make the world happy? / Sunjata has come

to make the world happy. / Who has come to make the world
happy? / Mari Jata has come to make the world happy.

The relevant passage in Ibn Khaldûn reads:

> Then the authority of the rulers of Ghana dwindled away and
> they were overcome by the Susu, a neighbouring people of the
> Sudan, who subjugated and absorbed them. Later the people of
> Mali outnumbered the peoples of the Sudan in their
> neighbourhood and dominated the whole region. They
> vanquished the Susu and acquired all their possessions, both
> their ancient kingdom and that of Ghana as far as the Ocean on
> the west. They were Muslims. It is said that the first of them to
> embrace Islam was the king named Barmandana (thus
> vocalized by Shaykh Uthman), who made the Pilgrimage and
> was followed in this practice by the kings after him. Their
> greatest king, he who overcame the Susu, conquered their
> country, and seized the power from their hands, was named
> Mari Jata. *Mari*, in their language, means "ruler of the royal
> blood," and *jata* means "lion." (Levtzion and Hopkins 1981:
> 333)

The textual history of Ibn Khaldûn's writings is highly
complex. The reference to Shaykh `Uthman in the passage beginning
"They were Muslims . . ." and ending ". . . kings after him," has been
taken to indicate that the source of information on the Sosso and Mali
war was the traveler whom Ibn Khaldûn met in Egypt in 1393/94 and
described as "*faqih* of the people of Ghâna and one of their chief men."
However, the passage reads very much like an interpolation; Ibn
Khaldûn wished to make it clear, before proceeding with the story, that
the people of Mali—but not, by implication, those of Sosso—were
Muslim. Caution is therefore necessary. We cannot be sure of the
source of Ibn Khaldun's information about the war. Nonetheless, Ibn
Khaldun provides us with the earliest literary recension—albeit a very
brief one—of the story *Sunjata* as it had developed by the late
fourteenth century.

It is at this point that old William of Occam comes into his
own. Are we to argue the possibility that the songs about former rulers
sung by the griots in the mid-fourteenth century have all been lost, and
that when contemporary griots tell about Sunjata they sing songs that
have been composed—reinvented—at some more recent date? This
would seem singularly perverse. Or may we think that the songs that
contemporary griots attribute to the first-singers of the time of

Sunjata—Harris's "heavy" bologbili—are indeed the very songs sung by the griots in Mansa Sulayman's court?   All we know of the intense training of the griot, and of the mnemonic function of the elaborate metrical structure of the songs, incline me to accept the second thesis as the more economical, the more satisfactory in explanatory value, and hence the more acceptable. I note that Tamari (1991: 236) has recently made a similar point. I do not wish, of course, to suggest that the saga has not been expanded and developed as it has been retold and reperformed over the last half millennium. Indeed, we may guess that in the late fourteenth century the future epic consisted of little more than a series of metrical compositions—praise-songs—linked by a narrative that in time would be expanded and developed by individual griots expressing their own artistic capabilities within the framework of local and regional constraints.

When the original draft of this chapter was presented to the *Sunjata* Epic Conference on November 14, 1992, I had not seen Bulman's impressive but unpublished study of the subject. It is gratifying to note that his views on the history of the epic are by no means incompatible with those expressed here (Bulman 1990: 452–54).

Conjectures

First-singer Jankuma Duga became, by report, Bala Fasseke Kuyate in circumstances already described. He is also "the Kuyate ancestor," that is, the ancestor of the Kuyate who are the griots of the Keita kings of Manden. The relationship between the Kuyate and the Keita is represented as a contractual one. Kele Monson makes a brief addition to the story of the reunion of Sunjata and Jankuma Duga (Moser 1974: 314). Jankuma Duga was starving, so Sunjata:

> cut the flesh of his own chest and gave it to the Kuyate ancestor.
> The first thing he ate.
> It is that which is between the Kuyates and the royal family.

The Gambian griot Bamba Suso has a much longer version of the story; it has a different setting—the return from exile—and the flesh is taken from Sunjata's leg (Innes 1974: 59–61). Thus, Bamba Suso concludes:

> There is a special relationship
> Between the members of the Keita family and the members of the Kuyate family.
> Even today, if a member of the Kuyate family deceives a

member of the Keita family,
Things will go badly for him.
If a member of the Keita family deceives a member of the
Kuyate family,
Things will go badly for him.[10]

There is a rider, as it were, to this story. Bala Fasseke Kuyate
is said to have had three sons. Dembo Kanute (Innes 1974: 281), Fadigi
Sisoko (Johnson 1986: 151), and Babu Condé (Camara Laye 1984: 72,
207) all agree on their names. Babu Condé offers the most detailed
account. After the death of Bala Fasseke:

> his three sons shared the role of griot: Missa Kuyaté, the eldest
> son, inherited his father's balafon and guitar, and so became an
> instrumentalist griot. Missa Maghan Kuyaté, the second son
> and an old pupil of the Koranic School, kept the tarikh and
> became a traditionalist. Batru Mori, the third son, inherited the
> drum, and became, like his eldest brother, an instrumentalist
> griot. (Camara Laye 1984: 207)

One suspects that either Babu Condé (or more likely Camara
Laye) erred in linking Missa Maghan rather than Batru Mori with the
"Koranic School." "Mori" means "the Muslim," and the implication
may or may not be that the youngest son Batru Mori became a *fina*, that
is, one of the Muslim praise-singers who are regarded by the griots
proper as practitioners of an inferior trade. However this may be, it is
clear that the eldest son is seen as the true heir of Bala Fassake—and
his balafon.
        Genealogies are, of course, notoriously subject to
manipulation (see, e.g., Johnson 1986: 4). But not all genealogies can
be manipulated all the time, otherwise the exercise becomes a self-
defeating one! The burden of proof is, I think, on the skeptic who
wishes to doubt that the mid-fourteenth-century Duga, poet and
xylophonist to Mansa Sulayman and the earliest griot for whom we
have external validation, was not in a line that extended back to
Jankuma Duga. Indeed, since Mansa Sulayman almost certainly
belonged to the second generation descendent from Sunjata (Levtzion
1973: 71), it is not unreasonable to speculate that the mid-fourteenth-

---

[10] At some time along the line of transmission, this story was given an Islamic
cast. The Kuyate adopted a Muslim ancestor, Suraqa b. Malik b. Ju'shum, and,
in some accounts, had the Prophet Muhammad supplying his flesh to
"Surakate" (Conrad 1985: 39–49).

century griot was a grandson, or possibly great-grandson, of the first-singer of the same name. I have explored but rejected the possibility of arguing, with any degree of plausibility, that Ibn Battuta's Duga and the Jankuma Duga of the griots are one and the same person.

Reference to the fina, the Muslims who sang not only the praises of the Prophet but also of the heroes of Manden, requires us to address, albeit briefly, the matter of Islam. One may discern in the comments of Ibn Battuta something of the conflict between the griots on the one hand, conservative intellectuals concerned with the maintenance of the fabric of the Malian state as such, and on the other hand the Muslim scholars, radical intellectuals concerned with recreating that state in accordance with an Islamic vision of what constitutes a Rightful Caliphate. The bards of medieval Wales faced a comparable challenge from those who embraced a Christian vision of a Kingdom of God. In both cases the older values of society, expressed through the praise of famous heroes of the past, were confronted and progressively overlaid by newer values based less on history than on revelation.

The epic *Sunjata* was not immune to this process, and what may be referred to as its "Islamization" has been treated by Conrad (1985: 33–49). The songs, however, appear by and large to have been unaffected. Charles Bird recalled only one instance of a song displaying an Islamic feature, specifically, the appearance within it of the first part of the *shahada* (personal communication, November 1992). We may guess that the strong alliterative features of the Arabic "la ilaha illa Allah" (there is no god besides Allah) greatly facilitated its incorporation. Nevertheless, if Ibn Battuta's reference to Sunjata (Sariq Jata) becoming a Muslim has substance, then the appearance of the fina and the Islamization of the epic may well be early.

Paul Maas acutely remarked (1958: 17) that "an over-conscientious weighing of probabilities is liable eventually to stifle the germ of progress." The skeptic's suspicion of orally transmitted materials often seems to rest on no more than an intuition: that human memory is notoriously fallible and accurate transmission over considerable periods of time is, therefore, improbable. Africanists—some Africanists—have been taken as a model by Celtic—some Celtic—scholars. "Many people," Sims-Williams (1983: 24) argues:

> think that if you have only got tradition to go on you had better make the most of it. . . . but modern anthropologists and African historians would not agree. And although some writers like to suppose that Celtic oral tradition is peculiarly reliable,

this is not an opinion shared by experienced Celtic historians.[11]

Sims-Williams wrote before several painstaking and methodologically sophisticated studies by Koch appeared. A mass of Welsh genealogical material was committed to writing probably in the later tenth century. One of the pedigrees runs back through twelve generations to "Caratauc map [son of] Cinbelin map Teuhant." It has long been recognized that this is the independently attested sequence "Caratacus son of Cunobelinus son of Tasciovanus" (Bartrum 1966: 11, 127). The sound changes are regular. The grandfather is known from his coinage alone; he died ca. a.d. 5. His son and grandson are also known from the Roman historians: Cunobelinus died ca. a.d. 41, and Caratacus was taken to Rome as a prisoner in a.d. 51. Koch comments that this evidence "puts it beyond all doubt that Welsh tradition has remembered something of the pre-Roman Iron Age independently of Latin history" (Koch 1987a: 17, and see also 1987b: 264–72).

Koch treats what he aptly calls "a Welsh window on the Iron Age" in another context. A number of Welsh bardic stories were compiled, probably in the mid- to late eleventh century, into the famous Four Branches of the Mabinogion. The Third Branch contains the story of a certain Manawydan. Koch argues persuasively that it has to do with events in the late Celtic Iron Age, specifically the struggles of the Catuvellauni and Trinovantes for hegemony in Kent as known independently from Caesar's Gallic Wars and other contemporary Roman sources (Koch 1987a: 17–52). The issue here is not so much that of historicity as of transmission. All I wish to argue is that, within an institutionalized framework of instruction and training, oral texts may be passed on from generation to generation of bards—or griots—over very considerable periods of time. And the griots—like the bards—did indeed undergo an intensive training that has been described, inter alia, by Bird (1971: 18–20), Camara (1976: 124–29), and Johnson (1986: 24–25).

I note Austen's concern with locating—or rather, failing to locate—references to the *Sunjata* epic in the accounts of travelers in the half millennium between Ibn Battuta's visit to Mali (or as I argue, Ibn Khaldun's brief recension of the story) and the turn of the nineteenth century (Austen, infra). He is correct. There is, however, certainly evidence for the existence of the griot class. We may cite, for example, Mungo Park from the late eighteenth century. The love of music of the

---

[11] Elsewhere, however, Sims-Williams (1984: 173) advocates "comparative studies taking encomium from outside Celtic and Indo-European traditions, say from Africa, as a *tertium comparationis.*"

"Mandingoes," he wrote, is naturally connected with a taste for poetry, and he refers to the "singing men, called *Jilli* (i.e., jeli) *kea*" (Park 1799: 278–79).

In the introductory section to this paper I declined to assume a correlation between the antiquity of a tradition and the probability of its veracity. There is such a thing as a genre of fiction. But in the mid-fourteenth century, griots were referring the ruler of Mali to the deeds of his ancestors. It seems extremely implausible that they were indulging themselves in a fictional exercise; to the point, inventing a founder for imperial Mali and conjuring up his heroic conduct in an imagined war against the Sosso. It would be (William of Occam once again) an impoverished culture that, in such circumstances, had to invent a past for itself, and a desperate ruler—though one of an unquestionably powerful empire—who was prepared to be flattered by such inventions.

In this era of postmodernism, when a quest for "meaning" seems to have displaced that for "truth," and when the past is seen as something "constructed" or "invented," it is salutary to bear in mind that there are many, and among them the griots, who take a much gentler view of things, considering it important to preserve a knowledge of the past not only for what it may teach us, but because it is simply not good to forget those who made it.

I am reminded, in conclusion, of Niane's comment on the declining status of the Mande griots in the twentieth century, overtaken by the rapid changes in society:

> Today, when one speaks of griots, one thinks of that "caste of professional musicians" making a living on the backs of others; when one says "griots" one thinks of those numerous guitarists who populate our towns and try to sell their "music" in the recording studios of Dakar or Abidjan.
>
> If, today, the griot is reduced to capitalizing on his musical craft, or even to working with his hands in order to live, it has not always been that way in ancient Africa. Formerly griots were the Counsellors of Kings, they kept the constitutions of kingdoms by memory alone; each princely family had its griot in charge of preserving tradition. (Niane 1960: 7)

Niane romanticizes the traditional role of the griot in society, for it was only those demonstrating superior powers of memory and eloquence who became "Counsellors of Kings." Their less well-endowed peers (or younger relatives; see Jansen, infra) doubtless had

always to take to the roads, moving from place to place in search of a
livelihood. Mungo Park knew this. One or more of the "singing men,"
he wrote:

> may be found in every town. They sing extempore songs, in
> honour of their chief men, or any other persons who are
> willing to give "solid pudding for empty praise." But a nobler
> part of their office is to recite the historical events of their
> country: hence, in war, they accompany the soldiers to the
> field; in order, by reciting the great actions of their ancestors,
> to awaken in them a spirit of glorious emulation. (Park 1799:
> 278–79)

As a final conclusion I cannot refrain from citing Owen
Gruffydd, one of the last of the old Welsh bards. He bemoaned—in the
late seventeenth or early eighteenth century—the condition to which he
had been reduced as a result of the decline of patronage that had
followed the annexation of Wales by England and the subsequent
anglicization of the old Welsh gentry. I end by quoting two verses from
the memorable translation by Anthony Conran (in Jones 1977: 110–11):

> It pays
> Ill to have office nowadays,
> Unthieving givers are gone, and my ways
>   Are heavy and cold and long;
> And as I go, not a house I've seen
> Ready for praise, as it once had been—
> Serious song has gone from the scene,
>   There wants to hear me not one of the throng!
> Pure Welsh they do not willingly use:
> Twice better than the cywydd's muse
>   Is the pampered note of the English tongue.

> Betrayed
> To wander the world in search of aid,
> I have to keep my poet's trade
>   Hidden in my despair.
> Alas for the broken strength of the earth,
> True profit for the Muse of worth!
> To follow her now means fear and dearth,
>   Every hour a life of care.
> To tedious dust I'll soon belong:
> Farewell, dear Welsh and kindly song—

I may not take you with me there!

Bibliography

Bartrum, P. C. 1966. *Early Welsh Genealogical Tracts*. Cardiff: University of Wales Press.

Bromwich, Rachel. 1991. "The Tristan of the Welsh," in Bromwich, Jarman and Roberts, eds., *The Arthur of the Welsh*. Cardiff: University of Wales Press.

Caerwyn Williams, J. E. 1971. "The Court Poet in Medieval Ireland." *Proceedings of the British Academy*, LVII.

—. 1984. "Gildas, Maelgwn and the Bards." In R. R. Davies, R. A. Griffiths, I. G. Jones and K. O. Morgan, eds., *Welsh Society and Nationhood*. Cardiff: University of Wales Press.

Camara Laye. 1984. *The Guardian of the Word*. New York: Aventura.

Conran, Anthony. 1993. "Tribal Poetry and the Gogynfeirdd." *Planet. The Welsh Internationalist* 99, June/July.

Ford, Patrick. 1975/76. "The Poet as Cyfarwydd in Early Welsh Tradition." *Studia Celtica* X/XI.

Harris, L. A. 1989. "In the Hands of Others: A Yeliba in Maninka Society." Paper presented at the 32nd Annual Meeting of the African Studies Association.

Haycock, Marged. 1981. "Early Welsh Poetry," in P. Ryan, ed., *Memory and Poetic Structure*. London: Middlesex Polytechnic.

Jones, Gwyn. 1977. *The Oxford Book of Welsh Verse in English*. Oxford: Oxford University Press.

Jones, J. Gwynfor. 1992. *Concepts of Order and Gentility in Wales, 1540–1640*. Llandysul.

Koch, J. T. 1987a. "A Welsh Window on the Iron Age: Manawydan, Mandubracios." *Cambridge Medieval Celtic Studies* 14.

—. 1987b. "The Laureate Hero in the War-Chariot: Some Recollections of the Iron Age in the Gododdin." *Études celtiques* 24.

Maas, Paul. 1958. *Textual Criticism*. Oxford: Clarendon Press.

Matonis, A. T. E. 1978. "Traditions of Panegyric in Welsh Poetry: the Heroic and the Chivalric." *Speculum* LIII.

Sims-Williams, P. 1983. "Gildas and the Anglo-Saxons." *Cambridge Medieval Celtic Studies* 6.

—. 1984. "Gildas and Vernacular Poetry," in M. Lapidge and D. Dumville, eds., *Gildas: New Approaches, Studies in Celtic History V*. Boydell Press.

Wilks, Ivor. 1984. "Arthur of Britain, Sunjata of Mali." University of Northern Iowa, Eleventh Annual Carl L. Becker Memorial Lecture.

—. 1989. "In Defense of Orality: Mande Griots and Welsh Bards." Centre for Advanced Welsh and Celtic Studies, Universityof Wales, Aberstwyth.

Williams, Ifor. 1944. *Lectures on Early Welsh Poetry*. Dublin: Institute for Advanced Studies.

3. The Epic of *Sunjata*: Structure, Preservation, and Transmission

Seydou Camara

The study of Mande historical traditions raises many interesting questions concerning the relationship between orality and literacy. These traditions, mainly centered on the *Sunjata* corpus, appear to be a structured body of teaching, carefully maintained in certain specialized centers among which Kela, a small village some six kilometers southwest of Kangaba (cf. Jansen, infra), occupies a distinguished place.

A certain number of factors combine to make this region a world in which history and the transmission of history are endowed with great importance. Among others, these factors include:

—the maintenance of ancient relics or major cult-sites (tombs, for example), which allows the periodic or occasional evocation of the past
—the existence of teaching centers (*kumayoro*) and other cultural nodes; historical chronicles (*tarikhs* [Arabic]) and narratives; special keepers of the traditions, living around centers of power. These *nyamakala* (cf. Johnson, infra) are men of knowledge; together with the ruling men (men of power) they create a link of praxis and logos.

Nowadays, nyamakala are found scattered all over West Africa; hardly a single Mande village lacks them, and almost every chief of any importance maintains his own. Everywhere, these men, and particularly the jaliw, were and still are associated with the preservation and the transmission of historical traditions. However, their omnipresence in the lands of the Manden should not lead us to say that all the sites partially or completely occupied by them should be considered centers for the teaching of history.

In our opinion, the specialized teaching centers are not so numerous as some researchers would have us believe. By "school of history" we understand a center in which the process of acquiring knowledge of history is formalized: "students" are entrusted to a master who teaches them historical lore. Very few places meet that definition. In Kirina, Kita, Nyagasola, and Dugunikòrò one finds no such teaching. No outside jali come there to learn history. Nevertheless, one does find cults of regalia associated with the main characters of the Mande epic at certain of these places, thus lending support to their traditions and bolstering their claims to be considered major cultural centers. At any rate, "wherever nyamakala are found, each will speak a little" (*nyamakala be yoro o yoro, bee be doonin fo*), which means that each nyamakala is thought to teach history in some measure.

The traditions preserved in Kela are of the highest importance. For D. T. Niane (1974: 61) the Jabaté of that site are seen by most Malinke as possessors of the secrets of the Mande; they are feared by other griots. Y. Person (1963: 464) remarks that it is hardly surprising when one finds that the body of traditions about *Sunjata* presents very little difference among versions "since the common source is the famous school of Kela where this corpus was no doubt created."

The Epic *Sunjata*: An Infinity of Variants

The corpus bearing on the figure of Sunjata is more or less well known by most of the nyamakala in the Manden, and particularly in the areas inhabited by the Masaren-Keita. There are several variants that may intersect, which may differ on certain points, and that complete each other. We have collected, transcribed, and translated some twenty texts, not counting snatches of tale found here and there. These different "versions" resemble each other in their plots. However, one does note some divergences connected to the names of certain characters, to the sites involved, and in the causes of events.

As one of projects on behalf of the Niger Bend Project of the SCOA (Société Commerciale de l'Ouest Africaine) Foundation for the Promotion of Scientific Research in Africa in 1979, a team of scholars (including myself) was commissioned to record the Kela "version" of *Sunjata*. This rendition of the epic is performed publicly every seven years, on the occasion of the ritual reroofing of the Kamabolon of Kangaba, as well as at the funerals of high dignitaries. The Kela "version" enjoys an entirely unique prestige and, in the opinion of numerous researchers, it is the official version, from which all performances of *Sunjata* have been created.

The Story in Kela
Formal Structure

This narrative is a work of art based on a historical foundation. It includes several episodes that connect to each other in the following order:

— the creation of the universe and the origins of mankind
— the capture of Khaibar (by the forces of the Prophet Muhammad)
— the start of *mansaya* (kingship) in the Manden

— the epic of Sunjata, in the narrow sense (childhood, exile, return, reign)

— the clan praises and the genealogies of the principal clans of the Manden

— the list of the thirty families of the Manden

— the settlement and rule of the Kandasi branch of the Keitas in the Niger valley

A written document is involved, popularly known as a *tariku* (from *tarikh* [Arabic], "chronicle"), which the Mande distinguish from the *tare* (tale or fable) and other literary genres. One thinks of it then first of all as a text relating actual events. No doubt it does include a dose of the marvelous, but this appears particularly in the first large portion of the text, dealing with the most remote periods of history. That is where one finds mythological borrowings, where the real becomes intertwined with tale motifs and with current literary themes. Might this not be a device that allows for the filling in of forgotten material? Here one encounters difficulties in sorting out the events, in distinguishing characters, and in identifying places.

The aspects of the life of Sunjata that do not appear in this text are those dealing with the hero's initiation, his marital life, a comprehensive list of the territories conquered by his generals, and his demise. These are subjects on which the tradition in general has little to say. This silence can be explained not only by a sense of delicacy toward the hero, but also by the conscious desire to obscure certain elements that the hero's descendants might find discreditable. It is therefore difficult to obtain information on those questions, although they deserve elucidation.

Circumstances of the Recording

This "version" of the epic *Sunjata* was recorded on January 24, 1979, in Kela by a group composed of Madina Ly-Tall, Buna Bukari Juwara, and myself. The task became possible only after lengthy negotiations with the "royal" Keita family in Kangaba and with the Jabaté griots of Kela.

Once authorization had been obtained, the recording took place from 9:15 a.m. to 5 p.m. at the home of Manselu Jabaté, chief of the jali, and in the presence of N'Faly Berete, sent by the Keita of Kangaba to serve as a witness and also as a control. All the other Jabatés were also present, as well as a sizeable crowd attracted by the event. Jali Kanku Madi, then seventy years old, was the narrator. The musical accompaniment was provided by Jetenin Mori Jabaté, using a European guitar.

Lansine Jabaté, nephew of the performer (and presently the "master of the word"), served as respondent; throughout the performance, the singer called on him. After each break (change in cassette, meal-times, etc.) the story was picked up where it had left off.

The text, which exists in written form in Kela (and perhaps also in Kangaba) was given to us only in oral form. It was transcribed again by linguists, and then translated and annotated through our efforts, and published by the Association SCOA pour la recherche scientifique en Afrique Noire (Ly-Tall et al. 1987).

The Performance of the Narrator

A recitation session to which people may be invited is a major event, lasting several hours. The only elements are the musical instrument and the human voice. For the occasion, the narrator wears special clothing; he narrates his text in a declamatory tone. Basically, he does not recreate it; he only recites something that is fixed in writing, and which is the object of rigorous control. There is no dialogue with the audience, which remains silent and uninvolved with the story. However, the style employed is intended to induce in the audience a feeling of exaltation, a surge of admiration, of anger, of pity. But here we might distinguish situations of two types, or two sorts of *mansajigin* (epic performances): the ordinary sessions for teaching or rehearsal in Kela and the official sessions for the transmission of knowledge that take place in Kangaba.

In Kela the narrator may wear anything he chooses, for he is at home and he transmits his story to his brothers and his sons. The audience does not get involved through emotional reactions or signs of approbation. Still, each time a clan is involved, one of its representatives may interrupt the narration to offer a present and to request a blessing. In doing so, the emissary will apologize ahead of time and announce that he has a message to deliver.

In Kangaba things are much more formal. The *kumatigi* (master of the word) wears a special ritual costume with symbolic elements (a robe that is proof against sorcery) and on his head a *banbada* (the "crocodile-mouth" cap)(Ly-Tall et al. 1987).

The narrator of the text may play an instrument when he wishes, or if there is no other musician. But most of the time he will have an accompanist present, for it is difficult to play and to sing at the same time. The narrator remains seated, immobile, impassive, and does not engage in pantomime.

There are no interruptions of the story from the audience. During the offering of presents, the narration continues. Within the Kamabolon, drinking water or chewing tobacco is permitted, but to smoke or relieve oneself, one must leave the hut. Musical intervals allow the kumatigi to catch his breath, and at times people leave the hut and parade around the Kamabolon.

While the *bala* (xylophone) is the specialty of the Kuyate clan, the *n'koni* (four-stringed guitar) is the favorite instrument of the Jabatés of Kela, who are now likely to use the Spanish guitar in its place.

The narrator employs a solemn and marked style, exaggerating the traits of certain characters, sometimes personifying nature and inanimate objects. Of course, what he provides is a public version of the story, not the same as the secret version reserved for internal use both to preserve some historical truth and to maintain social cohesion.

Origin and Development of the Narrative

The origin of *Sunjata* is probably to be found in praise-names, in religious, ritual, or ceremonial songs, songs of a primitive nature. . . The work comes from a combination of all these elements. One of the songs incorporated into the epic, "Nyama! Nyama! Nyama!" appears to have been borrowed from the Komo, an initiatory society (cf. Bird, infra).

No doubt well before Sunjata came to power, itinerant performers crossed the land, reciting traditional songs and praising the heroes of the first warrior clans of the period. Only later, after the long development that led to the founding of the empire, did the nyamakala become more significant and enrich their repertoire with the deeds of Sunjata and his companions. At that point, they drew upon diverse sources (hunting, folklore, Islam) for a variety of themes which were then composed into a harmonious and cohesive whole, one which is continuously recreated.

As each clan had its praise-song, its heroes, and its epic, the process of harmonization must have begun as early as the court of Magan Sunjata. Since military victories were sung immediately after the battles, one may suppose that the narratives included many heroes and historical events. But over time some were forgotten and through a process of selection and arrangement, others were eliminated. This is how the epic *Sunjata* overtook the others and became widely diffused.

Thus, as the text was transported by the nyamakala, it changed according to individual interests; new variants appeared, especially after the fall of the empire and the increase in rivalry between different branches of the Keita dynasty.

The Kandasi branch of the Keita established a historical school in Kaaba (Kangaba) in close connection with the reroofing ceremony of the Kamabolon, during which the corpus of *Sunjata* traditions is subject to solemn recitation. According to D. T. Niane (1970: 60) this corpus, an indication of the years of crisis, was the first effort to provide the Malinke aristocracy with an image of itself and its world, intended to calm it. The teaching of history was first entrusted to the Kuyate and then to the Jabaté, who moved to Kela, where the Jawara act as guardians of the epic of Tira Magan Traore.

Function

History retains the life of great men only, and although it is based on historical recollection, this story serves to explain and especially to justify the ascent of Sunjata, by revealing his warrior's destiny as well as the way in which Maninka society works. It induces people to recognize their own identities, and leads them to act accordingly. One may find all the cultural and ideological data of the Mande within the epic; it can be considered truly an encyclopedia of Mande culture in the form of a metaphor of the initiatory path and of political legitimation. Hence its primarily political and ideological function, and its sociological underpinning.

A declamation of the text of the epic *Sunjata* is a powerful tool for mobilizing and exalting society; it confirms inherited bonds and renews the sense of identity by reactualizing it. Sunjata is a thirteenth-century hero who gives hope to the Mande people.

It is from the knot of forces concentrated in him that each individual may draw his own power.

At the Crossroads of the Oral and the Written

People talk readily of the importance of writing in the West, and some are very close to seeing there a proof of superiority over African civilizations. Thus we are wont to distinguish between societies with oral traditions and those with written traditions.

The first group, which includes the Mande as well as most African societies, is believed to have bound up their inner being, their memory, their sanctioned behaviors and their history with oral forms of communication. The second group enjoys much greater esteem, and until quite recently were the only ones believed to have a history, as the absence of writing was considered a handicap in the accumulation of knowledge.

In a purely oral universe, meaning one lacking any contact with writing, every reproduction of an utterance can be considered as a fresh creation (Goody 1979: 13). Consciously or not, each narrator is an author; he only repeats the narrative, he reorganizes it according to the circumstances, the interests, the tastes of the moment, and he will adapt it to different and even possibly contradictory purposes. The narrator may engage in a certain transformative work by recasting his stock of memorized elements, but it is possible that no process of permanent innovation is perceptible. And so, as Jean Derive also writes (1983: 14), as soon as it is spoken then oral text no longer exists except in memory, and to be maintained in existence it requires successive repetitions. The difficulty with reformulation in oral literature, according to Derive, stems from the fact that the material reference object, on the basis of which a second text would be formulated, cannot be caught: it has no isolated, concrete, material existence, and in fact it exists only in the memory of the speaker based on a sum of material objects perceived in succession. Given such a mode of presentation of knowledge, one cannot speak of fixed versions.

But the historical tradition of Kela does not function only within a system of orality; it also relies upon a graphic system, a model of concrete reference whose material existence is inscribed over time. Here we are dealing with a specific mode of communication that has been supported by a written document at least since the nineteenth century, but chooses to operate only through orality.

But why choose such a manner of presenting knowledge? The explanation is to be found in the importance accorded to writing in so-called cultures of orality, and particularly to the importance granted to the Arabic alphabet brought by Islam. Generally speaking, here as elsewhere, writing enjoys greater prestige than does ordinary spoken language. Hence the dictum of Horace: "*verba volant, scripta manent*" ("words may fly, but writing remains"), so dear to Europeans, and their disdain for oral tradition in matters of history. What is written is thought of as true. We have the examples of the Quran and of history books. Written transmission refers to the unchanging transmission of a content. Only information deemed important is treated in this way. Used for specialized and highly respected ends, writing appears as something magical that allows men a means to mark, to memorize, and to record.

Analysis of the style of Jali Kanku Madi of Kela shows that it is relatively stable, although it is not transmitted word for word. One finds all the characteristics of oral style (digressions, inappropriate repetitions, onomatopoeia, etc.). Some elements are apparently fixed, learned by heart: formulas for introduction, resumption, and closure; genealogical lists; songs; and the musical praises of the main heroes.

Thus, despite the oral transmission, the narrative from Kela rests upon a written base held in secret by the small circle of Jabaté griots. In response to the political upheavals of the nineteenth century a man named Bala Jabaté, also known as Siramori Balaba, the "griot" of Mansa Manbi Keita decided to write it down to preserve it as a part of the common heritage. He dictated it to a literate *sherif* (descendent of Muhammad) of the village who transcribed it in Maninka, the local language, using ajami Arabic script. This manuscript, which is purely a redaction of oral tradition, contributes in great measure to the prestige of the jali of Kela. It was later retranscribed by Bintu Faama, son of Balaba; we find him later in the service of a colonial district administrator, whom he accompanied as far as France.

The two manuscripts still exist, preciously preserved by the head of the Jabaté. Jali Mamadu Kone of Kangaba claimed, as of December 1979, that only the Jabaté of Kela could provide a true and faithful account of the history of the Manden, which they possessed as a book. This claim means that he bases the legitimacy of these professionals of memory on writing, which thus takes on considerable importance.

The preservation of such documents does entail some problems, particularly in Africa, where they are generally kept in a leather case. As paper is a fragile material, it deteriorates quickly and one must continually renew it. As soon as it begins to crumble, a document is handed over for recopying. This is how some mistakes slip into the contents.

Undoubtedly, even Nansa Baba Jabaté, who is a great Muslim scholar and the secretary (*sebelikela*) to the master of the word (*kumatigi*), serves as copyist! Indeed, to ensure the continuity of their system of training, the Jabaté of

Kela have always taken care to be educated in the Quranic schools kept by the Hayidara, said to be descendants of Ali and Fatima (daughter of the Prophet Muhammad), which have existed in the area for a long time. And so the life of Nansa Bala shows that this great marabout, paradoxically feared for his magical powers, studied the Koran for eleven years with Manbi Hayidara in Kela before making a Grand Tour throughout this region of West Africa to perfect his knowledge and to gain blessings from the great scholars. Successively, he traveled to Segu, Sinsani, Ké Masina, Jafarabé, Ja, Mopti, Jenné, Samatigila (Odjenné in Côte d'Ivoire), and Karifamoriya (Kankan, in Guinea). Apparently, he taught himself to play the n'koni and later initiated fourteen people in this instrument. But his apprenticeship in the art of speaking was particularly the work of one of his paternal uncles.

No doubt, this written tradition is the result of influence from Timbuktu and Jenne, as well as from the Futa Jallon, where a certain number of chiefs of Kangaba are said to have studied.

The speech performed by the artist, then, rests upon a written document, a tangible reference model that is reproduced at intervals and on special occasions. Its reformulation bears the stamp of the narrator, but the basic model is a fixed work, so long as no rewriting, agreed upon in theory by the group, has changed it. The people of Kela, confronted by the mystery of writing, have preserved the living and solemn character of orality in the teaching of history. The two modes of expression, oral and written, are bound up together; one cannot have the one without the other.

Conclusion

This study, based on the example of Kela, allows an appreciation of different aspects of the institutional preservation and transmission of history as they function in a society where writing, although long since known in the region, has become an important but secret means of communication. Mande culture is rich and highly varied. It includes a wide range of literary genres with full repertoires. Along with ordinary speech, there is forbidden speech involving society, which should not be questioned. People do believe that their history is secret and requires silence; in fact, this silence has had serious consequences for the place of Africa in the world.

The Keita, the imperial clan of Mali, were actors in one history, and they felt the need to preserve the traces of their past and their origins by developing the center of Kela, which in our day is considered the most prestigious school of the Manden. This center is staffed by jali bearing the patronymic of Jabaté, who live together with the Jawara (other gifted griots who serve the Traore). The classes include the young Jabaté of the village as well as many other outside jali who have come for training.

The collective past was drawn up the by Keita into a tradition that is thought to explain the foundation of the Mali empire. It has thus become a source of legitimation, rich in images, symbols, and models for action. To avoid being erased and forgotten, to mark their leadership in history, the old Keita chiefs and their retainers demonstrate and confirm the established hierarchies of the society through dramatic presentations staged at regular intervals or at special events (the reroofing of the Kamabolon, at funerals, at exhibitions of relics).

Considered an initial charter, and so treated by the discourse of power, the narrative held by the Jabaté of Kela constitutes a model for the Mande. It is a literary construction based on a historical core, speaking of local history infused by the universal themes of the classic hero.

Kela is a unique center in that, unlike others, it uses both methods of communication or transmission of knowledge at once: writing and speech. Most of the time, historians have asserted an imbalance of trustworthiness between these two means or forms of communication. In the case of writing, they say, documents are considered relatively stable; but with speech, given movement through time and space and the transmission from one generation to another, memories are erased, deeds are altered, and stories are changed. The Jabaté do not use one form or the other but both, retaining the written record for their internal and secret use and using it as a base for oral traditions that are for external and popular use. In fact, in both cases the storing of information and its transmission are never neutral; they are intended either to legitimate or to preserve values, truth, or a given social order. The stories play an ideological role by camouflaging a justification for social inequalities under cultural arguments.

Bibliography

Coulibaly, D. J. 1983. *Les récits de chasse considérés comme un genre narratif,*
    un répertoire: celui de Bala Jinba Jakité. Paris: Mémoire de DEA,
    EHESS.

Derive, Jean. 1986. "Le fonctionnement sociologique de la littérature orale
    l'exemple des Dioula de Kong (Côte d'Ivoire)." Thèse pour le doctorat
    ès - Lettres et sciences humaines, Paris III, Sorbonne Nouvelle.

Diawara, Mamadou. 1985. "La dimension sociale et politique des traditions
    orales du royaume de Jaara (Mali) du XVè siècle au milieu du XIXè
    siècle." Thèse pour le Doctorat de 3è cycle, Paris, EHESS.

Goody, J. 1979. *La raison graphique.* Paris: Editions de Minuit.

Meillassoux, Claude, and A. Sylla. 1978. *L'interprétation légendaire de l'histoire*
    de Jonkoloni (Mali). In *Anthropologie et Histoire.*

Sow, S. Y. 1985. "Etude comparée de trois versions de l'épopée de Sunjata."
    Mémoire de fin d'études, DER Lettres, Bamako: Ecole Normale
    Supérieure.

Traore, M. F. 1979. *Tiramakan Traoré.* Mémoire de fin d'études, DER Histoire,
    Géographie, Bamako: Ecole Normale Supérieure.

4. The Historical Transformation of Genres: *Sunjata* as Panegyric, Folktale, Epic, and Novel

Ralph A. Austen

This chapter will attempt what may initially appear to be two contradictory tasks: first, to "deconstruct" the *Sunjata* epic by revealing the contextual sources and motivations for its various components; and second, to defend its status as a "great book" whose power and broad appeal derives from an original distance between text and context. What I will argue is that even those oral versions of *Sunjata* recorded with the greatest degree of scholarly fastidiousness are themselves the product of historical development involving, among other things, encounters with written texts. From this perspective, the more directly literary versions of the epic created by Niane and others need not be rejected as "unauthentic," although I will try to demonstrate why some modern renditions of the epic seem to work better for their intended audiences than others. My hope is to use historical analysis to steer a path between Saul Bellow's call for a canonical African text (see "Introduction," infra) and a performance-based countercanon of oral literature.

The starting point for such an undertaking remains the oral *Sunjata* epic, but I will move both backward and forward in time from the first records of such a work: backward to reconstruct as far as possible the emergence of the epic from earlier Mande genres of oral poetry and narrative; forward to the written transcription of epic performances and their eventual transformation into the modern genre of the novel.

For the Mande themselves, *Sunjata* appears to occupy an ambiguous position between fixed written document— its putative Saul Bellow version— and pure performance process. The work belongs to a recognized genre, and even subgenre: *maana* as opposed to *faasa* (panegyric) or *tare* (folktale), but also *tariku* (historical epic), distinguishing the story of the great medieval ruler from the openly mythical and less textually stable hunting epics (Camara 1990:

43–47; Traoré, infra).[1]

For analytic purposes, the *Sunjata* epic could perhaps be most accurately described in current anthropological terminology as a "literary practice," i.e., an institutionalized performance whose content may vary considerably but centers around a coherent sequence of narrated episodes as well as certain concepts of heroic behavior.[2] However, just as we generally accept the formal oxymoron, "oral literature," I hope I will be excused if I occasionally refer to the standard content of *Sunjata* performances as "the text." This term is particularly justified in the case of the oral epic because, as will be argued below, this genre developed both at considerable remove from the historical context to which it explicitly refers and in active dialogue with written literature.

Before the Epic: Panegyric and Folktale

Historical studies of the epic in general have been properly criticized for their use of bad evolutionary models (Johnson 1982). However, in the case of *Sunjata* we have sufficient evidence, from the time of the thirteenth-century events it describes through the first records of its performance, to construct a plausible account of when and how it emerged. The evidence is strong enough so that, in contrast to most proponents of African "tradition," the leading Mande students of the *Sunjata* epic have concluded that its classic form did develop historically around the Mininjan region in the eighteenth century. Before discussing this critical moment, however, it is necessary to consider how the career of Sunjata was most probably represented in his own time and what other genres of oral literature entered into the formulation of the narrative core of the epic.

The much-disputed assertion by Ruth Finnegan (1970: 108–10) of the rarity of African epics rests upon a valid observation: that most oral heroic poetry on the continent takes the form of relatively brief and highly allusive panegyric rather than the extended narrative of the epic. The evidence of imperial Mali court poetry that we have from Ibn Battuta's visit about a century after Sunjata's death indicates that what he witnessed was panegyric rather than epic: the griots did not perform over long periods of time; their utterances appear to have maintained a single musical-poetic mode; and they referred to many ancestors of the ruler rather than elaborating on the career of a single individual.[3] Similarly, the very sparse evidence we have about the verbal content of griot performances from later European travelers in the Mande world again suggests panegyric rather than epic as the genre of heroic recitation.

---

[1] On the Arabic etymology of the terms for "epic," see below.

[2] For the episodes see Belcher 1985, Bulman 1990; on Sunjata and Mande concepts of the heroic career, Bird and Kendall 1980; Johnson, McGuire, infra.

[3] Hopkins and Levtzion, p. 293; for more extensive discussion of this material see Wilks, infra.

Panegyric should not, of course, be categorized as a primitive form of epic; it has its own rich aesthetic and social dynamic and remains alive and well in many parts of contemporary Africa, including the Manden. But it is precisely from studies of these contexts (Cope 1968; Opland 1983; Barber 1991; Vail and White 1991) that we know something of how panegyric works and why it does not easily translate (both literally and figuratively) into written literature. Panegyric generally does have an explicit narrative dimension, since it is, among other things a form of genealogy; however, the details of events are usually evoked only through allusion. The audience (such as that at the medieval Mali court) must therefore have detailed knowledge concerning the events alluded to. This information is derived from some type of informal narrative (oral history as opposed to oral literature) which is usually communicated in private rather than public settings.[4] The performed praise language may even be deliberately cryptic both to display the poetic skill of the performer and to convey in a subtle way sometimes discomforting messages to an incumbent ruler.

To those not intimate enough with the context, panegyric verses are thus opaque. If we assume, with Wilks, that some of the poetic fixed text of the contemporary *Sunjata* epic is retained from the time of the thirteenth- to fourteenth-century Mali empire, it is not clear that much of its original meaning is remembered anymore. Moreover, it is important to keep in mind how great a part of this court literature has been totally forgotten: the surviving panegyric refers only to Sunjata, some of his ancestors, and a few individuals around him (some, like Fakoli, partially mythic) whereas the praise-names along with the entire history of the rest of the Mali dynasty is lost to the modern jeliw (see table 4.1 below). A development like this is hardly surprising since the retention of such a body of literature and its accompanying informal knowledge is possible only if the context within which it developed has survived as well. Faasa, as genre, still thrives in the Manden but with the possible exception of the panegyric verse cited by Wilks, the specific body of medieval Mali court literature faded away with the decline of the empire to be replaced, shortly after the Keita dynasty lost its last vestiges of imperial power, with the less contextualized and less poetically dense genre of the epic.

While panegyric provides the richest poetics of the epic as well as its most intimate connection to historical memory, the immediate appeal of Sunjata's story rests upon its incorporation of narrative motifs identical to those found in more general Mande tales, particularly stories about hunters and the origins of griot-patron relationships.

In contrast to panegyric, there is no documentary evidence for the earliest appearance of such literary genres. However, we can safely assume that they

---

[4] For good examples of the link between narrative and panegyric see Webb and Wright 1976 (on Zulu materials) and Barber 1991: 28f. (on Yoruba *oriki* and *itan*). I would place in the category of such informal narrative/oral history the only other medieval source for *Sunjata*, Ibn Khaldun's report discussed in Wilks (infra) and Austen and Jansen (1996).

are quite old since they speak to institutions, beliefs, and practices that seem deeply rooted in Mande life and culture. The hunting narratives and their central concern with issues of power and gender are especially evident as the inspiration for some of the most compelling episodes in the *Sunjata* epic.[5] These include: the hunt for the buffalo wraith of Sunjata's mother, Sogolon; the transformation of the crippled child/animal Sunjata into an instant adult hunter; the encounters with witchcraft; the initiatory trials of Sunjata's exile; and the uncovering of the totemic secret of the rival emperor, Sumanguru, by a seductive female. The tales of griot-patron relations (Zemp 1966) are evoked throughout the epic, but particularly in the dramatic encounter between Sumanguru and Balla Fassake, the ur-ancestor of the royal Kuyaté griots.

This patently ahistorical material occupies a space within the epic that one might expect to contain fuller accounts of the rulers who preceded and particularly succeeded Sunjata.[6] Yet the *Sunjata* epic is distinguished from the epics of hunters (also called maana) precisely by the designation of tariku (from Arabic *tarikh*, "history"). This claim to historicity should not be dismissed on the grounds of its empirical indefensibility. It is part of the ethos that maintains the stability of the *Sunjata* narrative as well as its capacity to integrate the already complex issues of the hunting and griot narratives into a more comprehensive— and no less complex— account of the past and present Mande world.

The Emergence of the Epic: The Eighteenth-Century Mininjan and Beyond

The extended historical development of any oral literature is, by definition, difficult to document. What we have to work with are indirect references, analogies across time, space, and culture, and some degree of conjecture from the very absence of data. In the case of the *Sunjata* epic, we are confronted with a very striking combination of intensive sound and silence that points strongly toward a specific time, place, and set of circumstances for its composition.

Let us begin with the silences. The earliest references to any kind of oral *Sunjata* performances in the Manden occur, to the best of my knowledge, from the first stages in the French colonial occupation of the western Sudan at the end of the nineteenth century.[7] While the same limitations hold for the study of most African oral literature, in the case of the *Sunjata* epic we might expect to find some information in the many Arabic and European accounts for the Manden dating from the middle ages through the nineteenth century. However, ex-

---

[5] For fuller discussion of the meaning of hunting tales see Traoré (infra) and Bulman (1989; 1990: ch. 3).

[6] As is the case with the less widely performed epics of the much more recent Segu empire (Conrad 1990).

[7] Austen 1990: 37f. and Bulman, infra; on medieval Arab references to *Sunjata* (as Mari Jata) see Wilks, infra.

cept for Ibn Khaldun (and perhaps Ibn Battuta) none of the Arab documents, including the two great Timbuktu tarikhs (chronicles which do draw on local oral tradition) make any reference to *Sunjata*. Likewise most European travelers in the region describe frequent encounters with the jeliw who are the current guardians of the *Sunjata* narrative, but none mentions Sunjata or his epic, nor are jeliw even their sources for historical information.[8] This omission stands in stark contrast to the prominence of the *Sunjata* epic in the repertoire of contemporary jeliw.

Such negative evidence does not suggest that the *Sunjata* epic came into existence during the late nineteenth century. However, as with other African narratives discovered at this time (Hunwick 1994) we should not exclude the possibility of relatively recent composition inspired not by the colonial circumstances of transcription, but rather by earlier historical developments within Africa.

The positive indication of the Mininjan as the source for the epic comes from the two closely linked circumstances: first, the celebration every seven years at Kaaba/Kangaba, the site of the local kafu (chiefdom), of the major Kamabolon ritual that includes a performance of *Sunjata*; and second, the recognition of the jeliw responsible for this performance, the Jabaté of nearby Kela, as the masters from whom all jeliw of the region must learn the "correct" version of the epic (Johnson 1986: 25).

This evidence is sufficient to convince some of the leading expatriate and Mande researchers on the *Sunjata* epic to conclude that it originated at the time the Mininjan Kafu was founded and the Kamabolon ritual first established during the eighteenth century (Person 1962: 464; Niane 1974: 59–60; Camara, infra). This identification is perhaps too neat.[9] The oral traditions of the Mininjan indicate that the Kamabolon had some predecessors in (now relatively inactive) ritual centers of neighboring chiefdoms. The Jabaté also acknowledge some link between their knowledge of *Sunjata* and the Kuyaté, a jeli lineage more generally associated with the Keita (Camara 1990: 123, 304–11); it is even possible that other Kela groups such as the Haidara or Jawara, may have functioned as griots for the Kangaba rulers as recently as the early twentieth century.[10]

---

[8] The best list of these references to griots is Conrad 1990: 4; I have independently examined a very wide but undoubtedly not exhaustive set of the relevant travel accounts.

[9] Camara is also more cautious in his dissertation than his present paper about postulating "une ligne de demarcation rigoureuse entre une localité et une centre d'enseignement historique" (1990: 89); Jansen (1996b) is also skeptical about the pre-1900 history of the Kangaba Kamabolon ceremony.

[10] Vidal (1924) never specifies the Kela griots who are the source for his "legende officielle" but in an accompanying article (1923) names as informants for general historical information on the Mali empire the Haidara *fune* (Islamic bards; the Haidara in Kela are today considered to be *mori,* i.e., non-*nyamakala* marabouts); at Kangaba in April 1996

Despite the murkiness of our information and the absence of travelers' accounts on precolonial Kangaba to corroborate local oral traditions,[11] we can proceed with a tentative assumption that the epic, in its contemporary standardized form, arose somewhere in this subregion between the eighteenth and nineteenth centuries and has continued to be associated with small-scale Keita successor chiefdoms like the Mininjan Kandasi.

What remains of interest in analyzing the genesis of the epic, therefore, is its relationship to the historical events that link it with the time of Sunjata himself, the role of Islamic literacy in movement from earlier oral genres to the epic, and the circumstances surrounding the diffusion of *Sunjata* beyond its site (or sites) of origin.

Table 4.1 illustrates both the chronology of the Keita dynasty founded by Sunjata and the various genres of historical record by which it has been remembered. The chronology locates the Mininjan Kandasi of Kaaba/Kangaba (and by analogy, the other surviving Keita chiefdoms) at not only a great distance from Sunjata but also at several removes from Nyaani Musa Mamadu, the last Keita ruler with any real claim to an imperial status. The breaking up of the Keita lineage into these segmented lineages and sublineages thus marks the definitive end of an empire that had lost its hegemonic role in the region several centuries earlier.

The *Sunjata* epic, for all its claims to tariku, not only fails to provide us with much information about the empire in its heyday, but also omits most of the more proximate history of the Keita dynasty and Kandasi lineage, a history that is quite well known through other oral genres to the performers and at least their local audience. With the epic, unlike the case of panegyric, we are not dealing with poetic allusion to a body of knowledge that is being evoked indirectly, but instead an apparently deliberate suppression or exclusion of this knowledge from the entire discourse of literary performance.

In this process, Sunjata becomes both an ahistorical and a superhistorical figure. He is ahistorical for the reasons already noted in discussing what specific narrative information is omitted and included in his story. He is historical since he remains a verifiable human agent from the past and also because the narrative leaps across mundane history to a mythologized dynastic founder as response to the historical experience of alienation from the sources of material power.

Although the most powerful mythic content of the *Sunjata* narrative evokes the issues of masculine power and authority derived from the indigenous

---

informants of the Figira Keita dynasty, who asked not to be named, insisted that the Jawara had been the bards of the Kamabolon up until the mid-twentieth century.

[11] Jan Jansen (1996b) questions the historicity of all Mande genealogies but even he acknowledges that Kangaba was an important center for the eighteenth- and nineteenth-century version/remnant of the Mali empire.

Table 4.1
Keita Dynastic History and Its Major Sources

Regime	Era	Source
Sunjata (founding of Mali Empire vs. Sosso [Soninke] ruler Sumanguru)	1200s oral epic	b. Khaldun,[12]
Hegemony of Mali	ca. 1230– ca. 1400	b. Khaldun, b. Battuta, al-Umari
Hegemony of Songhai	ca. 1400– tarikhs[13]	Timbuktuca. 1591
Nyaani Musa Mamadu (last unitary Mansa/ Emperor)	late 1500s	Tarikhs, oral tradition[14]
3 successor lineages (Namagansi, Kurusi, Kandasi)	ca. 1600– present	Tarikhs, oral tradition, European texts
Tenenba-Koman, junior descendant, founds Mininjan subdivision of Knadasi	ca. 1700	oral tradition, epilogue to Kela version of epic[15]
Mansa Sèma s/o Tenenba-Koman settles at Kaaba/ Kangaba, builds Kamabolon	mid-1700s	oral tradition
Mininjan dominated by Segu (Bambara), Tukulor (jihadist) Samory (Juula) empires	late 1700s– 1887 (French conquest)	oral tradition, Segu, Tukulor and history, European texts

---

[12] On this source, see Austen and Jansen 1996.

[13] On the use of the epic and Arabic sources for Malian imperial history, see Ly-Tall 1977.

[14] For details of traditions and supporting sources for the rest of this table, see Person 1981 and Camara 1990: 100–169, 248–67.

[15] Ly-Tall et al. 1987: 71–74; the recitation of even this small, and very stylized, piece of recent oral tradition required prompting by the researchers; as Jansen (1996b) notes, it is only recited in such detail because of the special position that younger brothers hold in political genealogies.

subculture of hunting, the impulse to formulate the epic appears to be connected with the constitution of the Kamabolon ceremonies and their complex relationship to Islam. All observers of the Kamabolon ritual have noted its Islamic elements:[16] the base-seven calculation of its periodicity; the role of the Bereté clerical lineage in the actual ceremonies; the various evocations of the nineteenth-century jihadist al-Haj Umar Tal; and even the association of "Kaaba" with the site of the same name that is the center of Muslim pilgrimage to Mecca.[17]

It is significant that Islamic influence is most pronounced in the portions of the ritual linked to the reciting of the epic as opposed to the act of placing a new roof on the Kamabolon shrine. The latter is the final, and from a Mande perspective, most spiritually intense moment of the entire procedure. In this sense the ritual is a kind of model for the epic: a phenomenon centered around very profound local beliefs, practices, and memory but given its unique monumental form by confrontation with the universalist cosmology and grand narrative of Islam.

The Kangaba version of *Sunjata*, includes, like most such performances, a prefatory narrative tying its hero to the Prophet Muhammad through his alleged Meccan ancestor, the black servitor Bilal. However the main figure of the epic, Sunjata himself, rarely takes on a specifically Muslim identity (he is never given an Arabic-based first name), and his defeat of Sumanguru depends entirely upon the control of occult local knowledge in classical Mande terms (Bird and Kendall 1980). But Sunjata's claim to transcendent imperial status is tied to the very existence of the narrative as well as its use of varied (in different versions) references not only to Meccan ancestry but also to residence in the more Islamicized Mema (the imputed home of the Bereté clerics), the donning of Muslim robes at critical moments, and comparison with the generic Mediterranean world-conqueror, Dhu al-Qarnain.

Such a connection is reinforced by local claims that the oral composition is more like an Islamic text than either its core narrative content or performance might suggest. The Arabic-derived generic terms for the epic imply this quite literally. Tariku, as already noted, is both misleading and revealing about the relationship between the *Sunjata* story and known Arabic historical chronicles (tarikh) of the western Sudan. Maana has equally rich implications; it is a term probably derived from formal Islamic learning (with which the Jabaté jeliw

---

[16] My information on the Kamabolon ritual is drawn from descriptions of varying emphasis and from different years (Dieterlen 1955; Meillassoux 1968; Camara 1990: 334–49; de Ganay 1995). Unfortunately when Jan Jansen and I traveled to Kangaba for the scheduled 1996 reroofing ceremony, we discovered that it had been postponed (Jansen 1998).

[17] One local tradition reverses the history of the original Meccan Kaaba by claiming that the Mande version had first been a Muslim shrine now converted to "pagan" purposes (Niane 1959: 37).

are well acquainted) referring to the "significance," i.e., accepted understanding, of a primary text. In this case the equivalent of difficult passages from the Quran or Hadith collections might be the panegyric verses and songs that have survived from the distant past and now derive their meaning from the maana narrative.[18]

Finally, some people in Kangaba claim that the "true" version of the epic is preserved in a secret written Arabic text connected with the shrine (Camara 1990: 31–34). The jeliw are literate and might possibly have such a manuscript; however, the fact that it has never been seen, that the Jabaté themselves do not acknowledge its existence, and that their performances of *Sunjata* do vary somewhat in content suggests that the claim may be mythic.[19] Even if this is the case, like all serious myths, it embodies an important truth: that the establishment of a long, coherent, and relatively stable oral narrative of *Sunjata* could occur only in dialogue with written Islamic narratives.[20]

The Kamabolon ritual provides the *Sunjata* epic with a local context that is not immediately disturbed by either the lacunae in its account of history or the "mixing" of Islamic and local constructions. History is, after all, a subjective concept in any society, and Islam had been part of the Mande cultural landscape for centuries by the time the epic came into existence.[21] However, for the epic to become a work of "literature" with a capacity to communicate to a broader Mande audience, to say nothing of a universal one, it was necessary for even this contextual boundary to be breached.

In its Kamabolon version, the epic is neither aimed at such a general audience nor capable of reaching it. The intention is reflected in the aura of secrecy with which jeliw still surround the knowledge they claim to possess. It is quite possible that in the first century or so after its initial composition the entire formal narrative of *Sunjata* was considered a secret and not revealed on any public occasion other than the Kamabolon. This mystique may account for the

---

[18] The term "maana" is also used more generally by jeliw to describe narrative explanations of cryptic poetic texts.

[19] Another explanation, consistent with Camara's account of how the manuscript is used, may be that it contains little legible information but serves as a name list and/or mnemonic talisman for the jeliw; Wilks, at the 1992 Northwestern conference, described a manuscript of this kind shown to him by Karamoko Yusuf, b. Ibrahim Kamagatay of Bonduku in Ghana (see Wilks, FN/71, June 17, 1966, Africana Library, Northwestern University).

[20] A more radical possibility, which can be pursued only by closer examination of what Arabic texts were known in the Manden during the eighteenth and nineteenth centuries, is that the historical content of the *Sunjata* epic derives from Ibn Khaldun's writings rather than local oral tradition (Austen and Jansen 1996: 23–24).

[21] For a fuller discussion of the relationship between contemporary griots and the idioms and issues of Islam see Moraes Farias 1992.

absence of *Sunjata* accounts from the griot performances to which precolonial European travelers were privy during the eighteenth and nineteenth centuries.[22]

Obviously such total secrecy no longer prevails and, quite recently, two complete recordings were made of the "official" Kela *Sunjata* performance although not during the Kamabolon ritual (Ly-Tall et al. 1987; Jansen et al. 1995). However, this version is very difficult to follow in written form because many of the critical episodes are dealt with via allusion rather than explicit narrative. The knowledge assumed here on the part of the audience is not informally transmitted historical information, as in panegyric, but rather familiarity with previous performances. In any event, the effect is to produce a similar, or perhaps even more impenetrable, opacity for most hearers/readers since the Kaaba performance has now taken on some of the qualities of a liturgy.

The Kela Jabaté may thus remain the source for a stable version of the epic but its literary development— and very likely part of its creation— comes from the diffusion of this work into the repertoire of jeliw addressing much wider, truly "public" audiences.[23] Existing evidence gives no indication of how this process occurred or even whether the Kela version developed in dialogue with jeliw from the Kamabolon shrines that apparently existed in other Keita chiefdoms before the late nineteenth century.

One factor that probably played some role in diffusing the status and epic *Sunjata* was French colonial rule. Current historical and anthropological analyses of "the invention of tradition" argue that much of what has been presented as "indigenous" forms of cultural identity and production actually derives from the colonial experience (Hobsbawm and Ranger 1983; Amselle 1990). In the case of the *Sunjata* epic, the role of French colonialism remains unclear although it is an issue that might more easily be illuminated through further research than many of the other questions concerning the genesis of the work now familiar to us.

It is true that the French, despite their reputation for "assimilation," invested considerable intellectual energy in searching for the "true" local political systems that could be used to replace the recently defeated empires of Samory and the Tukulor. With this practice in mind, Kathryn Green (1990) suggests a major colonial influence in the regional influence of Kaaba and Sunjata, if not the epic. Green argues that: a) the French initially promoted the idea of

---

[22] Jansen (1995: 85–86) also notes that none of these travelers ever reached Kangaba, which (assuming that the Kamabolon ceremony was already established there by this time) may explain their failure to even mention Sunjata before the very late nineteenth century; for a situation in Kangaba as late as 1954 where griots refused to perform *Sunjata* in the presence of Europeans and provided their African assistants with only a truncated version of the narrative, see de Ganay 1995: 149, 169–71.

[23] For more public performances of portions of the epic by Jabaté griots, see Jansen (infra) and Newton (infra).

Kaaba/Kangaba as the historic capital of the Mali empire; and b) some regional states, particularly Kong, subsequently added a connection with "Mande Kaba" to their traditions of origin.

However, in contradiction to the first part of Green's thesis it must be pointed out that the Kandasi Keita of Mininjan had allied themselves firmly with Samory and were thus deposed from power by the colonial regime (Leynaud and Cissé 1978: 41–49; Camara 1990: 286–92). It is true that a fort and eventually (in 1950) a regional administrative center were created at Kangaba (the name preferred by the French). Around 1922 a French colonial officer also recorded the Jabaté version of the epic as "the official legend of Sunjata" (Vidal 1924). However quite lengthy performances of *Sunjata* were recorded well before World War I by Frobenius and Zeltner in other regions of the Mande world (Bulman, infra). Moreover the French administrators of the Bamako Cercle, under whose jurisdiction Kangaba fell, seem to have been entirely ignorant of *Sunjata* and unaware of the Kamabolon ritual even as late as 1954, when it was first described by Dieterlen.[24]

Thus it is impossible to ascribe to the influence of French rule either the prestige of the Kaaba/Kangaba-Kamabolon complex or the primary spread of the *Sunjata* epic. Nonetheless, the observation made by Green about Kong may apply to other local political centers, whose court griots possibly learned of the *Sunjata* epic only after 1900. Such a process is especially intriguing as a possible explanation for connections with *Sunjata* made in contemporary oral traditions of states founded in the eighteenth century by fundamentalist Islamic clerics (Diawara, infra).

Ultimately, however, it does not matter whether domination of the Maninka by the French or by the Bambara, Tukulor, and Samory was the context in which the *Sunjata* epic developed its fullest literary dimensions. What counts most is that after their own empire had unambiguously disappeared, the Maninka created a literary vision of the past that condenses so many aspects of Mande cultural experience: not only the archetypal heroic figures of initiate, hunter, dynastic founder, and universal monarch, but also the link between such male actors and the power of females as well as relationships among clans and between *nyamkalaw* and *horon* (a subject explicitly excluded from the discourse of hunting). It is this contemplation of a socially complex yet, by the time of its telling, largely imaginary "national" identity that endows the epic with its power and, perhaps ironically, gives it meaning to audiences far beyond the Manden or

---

[24] This conclusion is based upon a perusual by myself and Seydou Camara of reports on Kangaba in the Mali National Archives for the years between 1912 and 1954 when the ritual should have taken place. In a 1943 inspection report the Bamako Cercle administration was reprimanded for the absence in its archives of any "coutumier" or "monographie" which would guide officials in dealing with local chiefdom affairs (Archives national du Mali, 2 D 19 Inspection des Affaires Adminstrative, Kouremalé: Rapport de l'Inspecteur Lorine, December 28, 1943, p. 7).

even Africa.

Mande Epic as Written Text

Given the implication of the "classical" *Sunjata* epic in Islamic literacy, regional politics and possibly even the dialectics of colonial rule, we must be somewhat more open-minded in examining further transformations of *Sunjata* into written literary genres. Nonetheless, there remains a marked distinction between the epic as oral performance and written text.

Many written versions of *Sunjata* do consist of direct transcriptions of oral presentations, whether they are the careful work of scholars such as Johnson or the abbreviated and often second- or third-hand accounts recorded by colonial-era administrators or even anthropologists and school teachers (Austen 1990). These efforts are essential for the understanding of African cultural history, but they are not the immediate vehicles by which such history continues.[25]

The criterion used to judge scholarly transcription of an oral work — fidelity to the verbal and other elements of a living performance — are largely inimical to the production of written literature. Not only does the act of reading rather than hearing (and seeing) a narrative of any length require different verbal devices than an oral performance, but the development of a literary culture anywhere in the world involves far more than the technology of writing and reading. Moreover, in the later twentieth century (and especially in Francophone Africa, where until very recently little publication was done in local languages), one cannot expect even written works calling themselves epics to correspond as closely to the poetic or elevated prose models of oral literature as did their European counterparts from classical antiquity to the Renaissance. Thus the *Sunjata* books, which have found wide audiences today, are all prose narratives that critics often place in the same category as novels (Johnson 1986: 233–34; Miller 1990: 89f.).

Certainly if we look for the modern equivalent of jeliw, that is, artists who will continue to compose their own creative works based upon Sunjata's legend, they will have to be novelists as well as practitioners of other modern arts such as the theater, the shorter poem, popular music (Newton, infra), or the cinema. I will consider at least novelists in the last section of this chapter. However, there is also a place in the canon of modern African literature for a "Milton of the Mande," i.e., an author who produces something that we can at once recognize as an epic but also read (and compel our students to read) as an engaging literary text.

The reference here to a single author and the allusion to students are critical. Major literary works like this do not find their audience in Africa or anywhere else through pure market competition. There is always an element of

---

[25] As indicated by virtually all scholars who have recorded *Sunjata* texts, the very presentation of the epic as a single, comprehensive narrative is alien to the experience of Mande audiences (see Bird, Jansen, Newton, infra).

historical accident and institutional constraint. In this case it is a question of which version is first adapted to school and university syllabi and works well enough so that it can hold its position. Thus, for better or worse, the canonical written epic version of *Sunjata* is that of Niane, whose French and English editions have now remained in print for over thirty years.[26]

The canonical status of Niane is clearly not just the result of circumstance and the arbitrary power of educators. Those of us who have taught this text over the past decades do so because it elicits active responses from our students, many of whom have gone on to use the book in their own classrooms at various levels of schooling. We still have to consider, however, what it is that qualifies this version of *Sunjata* to represent the oral work from which it is derived.

Niane, who considers himself more a scholar than an artist, bases such a claim on the fact that his book is essentially the transcription and translation of a performance by a respected and well-trained Kuyaté jeli. This tells us that Niane has directly experienced the epic in its classical form, but it does not indicate to what degree he has altered the written version, because we are not supplied with a literal transcription and/or interlinear translation for comparison. All we can do, therefore, is compare Niane's text with the other *Sunjata* transcriptions (scholarly or unscholarly) available to us.

My own instincts and the more careful comparative analysis by Stephen Bulman (1990) indicate that the narrative content of Niane's version remains within the mainstream of known *Sunjata* oral texts. The ability to communicate this story without changing it to fit the expectations of modern readers (there is even some characteristic narrative backtracking by the griot) is already an important contribution to the "translation" rather than total generic transformation of the epic. Moreover, Niane manages to capture at least some of the diction of the jeli as well as incorporating into his narrative the subgenres of song, praise-poem, proverb, and riddle in a form consistent with Mande epic performance. All of these devices give an archaic flavor to the text that even requires the use of a few footnotes, but for readers and teachers who want this work to provide them with some entree into either a culturally pluralist world or the historic forms of their own culture, such features (within limits) are not only acceptable, but even desirable.

The fact that Niane's text lacks the extensive digressions, the omission or compression of major episodes and other "warts" of normal oral epic performances may be a result of his editing (even fusing multiple performances). It

---

[26] An obvious alternative to Niane is either the prose or poetic *Sunjata* translation produced by Massa Makan Diabaté (1970a, 1975). At the Northwestern University *Sunjata* conference it was suggested that the Diabaté texts, while in some respects more authoritative than that of Niane, are less popular even among Malian audiences precisely because they maintain the allusive and incomplete form of specific, and particularly Jabaté, oral performances; see also Bulman, Conrad, Newton, infra.

may also reflect the "public" character of his Kuyaté griot, who cannot expect his audience to bear with him for the sake of the occasion or fill in the missing narrative from the memory of previous hearings.

The prose form of Niane's text does, nevertheless, deprive its audience of much of the verbal art of the jeli and at the same time omits or represses the disruptive *fadenya* aspect of *Sunjata*, as expressed in such praise-names as "sorcerer-seizing-sorcerer" (Johnson 1986: 135). Indeed, there is a degree of modern nationalism in Niane's work, which presents Sunjata as a model of *badenya* village citizenship, in direct contrast to the understanding of the epic hero in general Mande culture.[27] However, in my own teaching of Niane I have been able to lead students to appreciate the darker aspects of Sunjata through the fidelity of the text to the hunting idiom of the epic and its consequent treatment (or avoidance) of the domains of sexual and agricultural reproduction.[28]

Finally, except for scholarly audiences, there are diminishing returns to reading additional versions of an epic in this form.[29] Thus only one rendition is likely to become canonical, and other authors must find their readers (and also reveal different dimensions of the *Sunjata* story) by more liberal blending of the voice of the past with the media of the present.

The Epic as Novel

It has become almost obligatory for critics of modern African prose fiction to attribute its very considerable power to some generalized roots in "the oral tradition." When examined more closely, the relationship between these two modes of African literature is actually quite problematic, but for this very reason worthy of serious analysis rather than the usual *bien pensant* platitudes.[30] The story of *Sunjata* is an excellent case in point, since Francophone Africa's first

---

[27] See Johnson (infra), but Traoré (infra) argues that *Sunjata* is an exception to this model of antisocial heroism.

[28] Niane/Mamoudou Kouyaté's presentation of the conception of Sunjata as hunting-scene-within-bridal-chamber is (among the printed versions of *Sunjata*) a unique and very striking presentation of the problematic link between heroic violence and domestic reproduction (cf. Conrad, infra, and John William Johnson, private communication, for similar episodes); Niane's account of the seduction of Sumanguru, on the other hand, leaves out one of the key "good parts" (not sexuality but the intervention of Sumanguru's mother).

[29] The recently published paperback edition of Johnson's text (1992) has been selling quite well, but in my own undergraduate classes, at a quite selective university, I find it works only for the most sophisticated students, and even then, only in conjunction with Niane.

[30] For a good critical analysis of claims to orality in modern African literature see Julien 1992: 1–25.

major novelist, Camara Laye, produced his own version of the narrative, while subsequent writers have attempted more complex fusions of the Mande epic with the European novel.

There are very good and instructive reasons why Camara Laye's *Guardian of the Word* has not achieved the same readership or critical attention as his classic *Dark Child*. As with Niane, Camara took his version of *Sunjata* directly from a jeli. His main story thus remains faithful to the narrative line characteristic of oral *Sunjata* performances (Bulman 1990: ch. 1) and is cited by several authors in the present volume as a useful record of yet another variant of the epic.

What makes Camara's book a novel is his rendition of these events through a discourse strongly at odds with the epic and his apparent insertion of details coming entirely from his personal imagination. The incongruities are numerous, including a general use of inner, introspective voices (already noted in Hale 1982) as well as abstract terms such as "development" and "reason of state," and an Islamic prologue locating the Keita ancestor Bilal not only in Mecca but also as a suffering slave in the highly anachronistic site of Yaoundé, Cameroon. Among the apparently inserted details are an extended and literal description of Sunjata's initiation (a conspicuous and significant absence in the oral versions), sentimental references to his love for a Mema princess, and an outrightly pornographic account of Sumanguru's coupling with Sunjata's sister.

As will be seen below, I do not argue that such features in themselves disqualify *Guardian of the Word* from serious literary consideration. What jars instead is the failure of Camara to recognize what he (and perhaps his overly adaptive griot) is doing. He thus insists very literally that we are listening to "living documents," "the wisdom of the Ancients" (Camara Laye 1980: 16) when we know that we are actually hearing a contemporary voice, strongly reminiscent in several passages of *The Dark Child*. These are contradictions that obscure rather than illuminate, because the intended audience has (like Camara) read epics, novels, and books of history and reacts against any text which blends them but does not either respect their mutual boundaries (as do Niane as well as Camara in his first work) or recognize at some level how it is violating them.[31]

The classic theme of the African novel (and especially *Dark Child*) is the painful difficulty of existing with both an African "traditional" identity and the "modern" European-educated consciousness required for the very feat of writing a novel. A nostalgic or even scholarly reflection upon this pain cannot overcome it, since such an act can frame the "traditional" only within a modern discourse even when, as in *Guardian of the Word*, the author seems unaware of his own actions. However the wide repertoire of the novel, especially as developed by various Third World writers, does allow a more conscious use of fantasy, pastiche, heteroglossia, and parody. Through such devices the content and

---

[31] For a discussion of the linguistic and stylistic problems which prevent this book from making the impact which Camara Laye had sought, see Skattum 1990.

generic qualities of the epic can be deployed to reframe the African experience of modernization.

The novel usually cited as the postmodern "anti-epic" of the Mande world is Yambo Ouologuem's *Bound to Violence* (Appiah 1992: 152ff.). However, apart from its many other shortcomings, this work derives its African narrative models far more from the Arabic chronicles of Muslim scribes than from the oral performances of Mande or (in Ouologuem's case) Sonrai griots (Hale 1990). The author whom I would like to propose as a model for using the oral epic as a source of modern narrative creativity is rather Ahmadou Kourouma in his 1990 work *Monnè, outrages et défis.*[32]

Instead of ignoring the barrier between epic and novel (as does Camara) or heartlessly satirizing the past (like Ouologuem), Kourouma has transformed the colonial (and by implication the postcolonial) Mande experience into an epic of *monnew*, a Maninka word that he tells us, in his epigraphic introduction, can be suggested but not summed up by the European terms "outrages, challenges, scorn, insults, humiliations, raging anger" (10).[33] Kourouma's hero is not Sunjata but Djigui,[34] a modern Keita ruler who lives for over one hundred years, enjoys access to preternatural forces, and is patron of the greatest Mande jeliw, but whose identity comes to rest upon an annual ritual of debasement before colonial rule.

In his highly acclaimed first novel, *The Suns of Independence* (1970/81) Kourouma already bent both the form of the novel and the French language in order to depict the more intimate and contemporary humiliation of a Mande dynasty (Miller 1990: 181–245). *Monnè*, however, goes considerably further by presenting a public colonial career in an inverted epic form, within which the narrator's voice is deliberately hidden or shifted and every event is simultaneously an act of heroism and shame. What we experience here is an extremely complex and rich historical encounter in which European domination succeeds in corrupting even the most elevated forms of African cultural expression, but this same transformed discourse becomes a vehicle for African mastery of historical consciousness.

In literary terms, Kourouma's novel returns us full circle to the panegyric; we need to know a good deal about both history and the codes in which it is

---

[32] See also Julien (1992: 51–84) and McGuire (infra) for analysis of other African novels which engage with the Mande epic, in two cases also drawing upon the local trickster genre.

[33] David Conrad (private communication) translates "monnew" as "those things which dig deeply at the ego and the seething anger we feel as a result."

[34] The Kela griots refer to their performance of the epic as "Mansa Djigui" and the name is sometimes identified in Mande folklore with one of Sunjata's successors, Mansa Musa, who is well known in Arabic literature because of his spectacular pilgrimage to Mecca.

expressed to understand what is being evoked. However, rather than the restricted sphere of a royal court, the universe of those potentially able to read the
subtexts of *Monnè* includes all those Africans and Africanists who have been
drawn into the political and cultural turmoil of colonial and postcolonial change.

In conclusion, we can assume that Kourouma's novel does not exhaust
the possibilities for drawing upon the oral epic to represent modern experience.
Likewise, I hope that my own more pedestrian efforts will suggest further ways
of tracing the historical path already traveled by this very dynamic literary creation.

Bibliography

Amselle, Jean-Loup. 1990. *Logiques métisses; anthropologie de l'identité en Afrique et ailleurs.* Paris: Payot.

Appiah, Kwame Anthony. 1990. "The Postcolonial and the Postmodern." In *My Father's House*, 137–57. N.Y.: Oxford U.

Archives national du Mali, 2 D 19 Inspection des Affaires Administrative, Kourmate: Rapport de l'Inspecteur Lorine, Dec. 28, 1943, p. 7.

Barber, Karin. 1991. *I Could Speak until Tomorrow: Oriki, Women and the Past in a Yoruba Town.* Edinburgh: Edinburgh U.

Cope, T., ed. 1968. *Izibongo: Zulu Praise Poems.* Oxford: Clarendon Press.

Cuoq, Joseph M. 1975. *Recueil des sources arabes concernant l'Afrique Occidentale du VIIIe au XVIe siécle (Bilad es Soudan).* Paris: CNRS.

Dieterlen, Germaine. 1987. *La Religion Bambara.* Bruxelles, 1987.

Finnegan, Ruth. 1970. *Oral Literature in Africa.* Oxford: Clarendon.

Griaule, Marcel. 1966. *Dieu d'eau: Entretions avec Ogotemmeli.* Paris: Fayard

Hobsbawm, Eric, and Terence Ranger, eds. 1983. *The Invention of Tradition.* Cambridge: Cambridge University Press.

Hunwick, John. 1994. "A Historical Whodunit: The So-Called 'Kano Chronicle' and Its Place in the Historiography of Kano." *History in Africa* 21: 127–46.

Innes, Gordon. 1982. "On the Heroic Age and other Primitive Theses." In Egle V. Zygas and Peter Voorheis, eds., *Folklorica: Festschrift for Felix J. Oinas.* Bloomington, Indiana: Indiana University Press.

Jansen, Jan. 1998. "Hot Issues—The 1997 Kamabolon Ceremony in Kangaba (Mali)." *International Journal of African Historical Studies* 31, 3.

Julien, Eileen. 1992. *African Novels and the Question of Orality.* Bloomington: Indiana University Press.

Kesteloot, Lilyan. 1978. "Le mythe et l'histoire dans la formation de l'empire de Ségou." *Bulletin de l'I.F.A.N.* 40B, 3: 578–611.

Kourouma, Ahmadou. 1970. *Les soleils des independences*. Paris: Seuil. (Trans. Adrian Adams. 1981. *The Suns of Independence*. N.Y.: Africana.)

—. 1990. *Monnè, outrages et défis*. Paris: Seuil. (Trans. Nidra Poller. 1993. *Monnew*. San Francisco: Mercury.)

Laing, Alexander Gordon. 1825. *Travels in the Timanee, Koorankoo and Soolima Countries of Western Africa*. London: John Murray.

Niane, D. T. 1959. "Recherches sur l'Empire du Mali au Moyen Age." *Recherches Africaines* 1–4: 35–46.

Opland, Jeff. 1983. *Xhosa Oral Poetry*. Cambridge: Cambridge University Press.

Person, Yves. 1981. "Nyaani Mansa Mamadu et la fin de l'empire du Mali." In *Le sol, la parole et l'écrit: mélanges en hommage à Raymond Mauny*. Paris: Société Française de l'Histoire d'Outre-Mer.

Skattum, Ingse. 1990. "Problemes de style dans le epopée romancée: le cas du Maître de la parole de Camara Laye." In *Actes du onzième Congres des Romanistes Scandinaves*, 449–60. Trondheim: Institut d'Etudes Romanes, University of Trondheim.

Vail, Leroy, and Landeg White. 1991. *Power and the Praise Poem: Southern African Voices in History*. Virginia: University of Virginia Press.

Webb, C. de B., and J. B. Wright, eds. and trans. 1976. *The James Stuart Archive of Recorded Oral Evidence Relating to the History of the Zulu and Neighboring Peoples*. Pietmaritzburg: University of Natal Press.

Wilks, Ivor. FN/71. June 17, 1966. Africana Library, Northwestern University.

5. *Sinimogo*, "Man for Tomorrow": Sunjata on the Fringes of the Mande World

Stephen Belcher

The fate of heroes rides on the bubble of reputation. Some bubbles, however, are more durable than others, and that of Sunjata is so exceptional as to challenge the underlying assumption of Shakespeare's metaphor, that heroic fame is fragile and ephemeral. Sunjata's story may partake of myth and legend like that of many other African heroes—Mwindo and Ozidi, Samba Gueladio or Lianja— yet its position remains unique. Mwindo, for instance, is the hero of the BaNyanga, whose population Daniel Biebuyck estimated at 25,000–45,000 (Biebuyck and Mateene 1971: 1). But how many millions are covered in the area of the Mande diaspora? Sunjata's fame is of a far greater scale.

Numbers are not, perhaps, the most appropriate measure for heroes. We must recognize that within the last generation, the story of *Sunjata* has acquired a symbolic value outside its homeland; it has become for many the emblematic representative of the potentialities of an African oral historiography, answering the frequently cited Hegelian dismissal of the peoples of Africa as without history.[1] Such a symbolic value necessarily projects a political dimension due to the tensions and irritations within our modern polities, and involves a redefinition of the man who is our concern. In moving outside its homeland, the story is uprooted, and a measure of the dislocation is to be found by comparing the version of *Sunjata* published by D. T. Niane (Niane 1960, which is to be considered the current established literary rendition) with more fastidious

---

[1] My intention in this paper is clearly influenced by the statement of Christopher Miller (1990: 8) that "the challenge now is to practice a kind of knowledge that, while remaining conscious of the lessons of rhetorical theory, recognizes European theory as a *local phenomenon* and attempts dialogue with other localized systems of discourse."

records of the core Manding oral performance tradition such as the versions of
Fadigi and Magan Sisoko (Johnson 1978, 1986) or Kanku Mady Diabaté (Ly-
Tall et al. 1987). Sunjata, the *sinimogo*, the "man for tomorrow," the man who
vowed to rule the jeliw and the *numuw* and the *garankew* and the *finew* and the
three-and-thirty warrior clans—and this enumeration serves to define the peoples
of the Manden—has now achieved somewhat broader recognition, although in
keeping with the traditional pattern of the Mande hero, he still remains a
problematic figure.

This recent fame raises a somewhat contrary question: Might Sunjata be
a recent invention? Might the importance accorded to this ruler of thirteenth-
century Mali reflect our contemporary concerns rather than some more organic
and less anachronistic process? The answer, I believe, is no. The Sunjata
tradition reflects a historical phenomenon quite independent of modern academic
and intellectual interest. The indications of its strength and its independence, I
believe, are to be found on the fringes of the Mande world. Indeed, the last
feature separating Sunjata from the other heroes mentioned above is that of
language. The stories of Ozidi and Mwindo and Lianja possess a certain
underlying similarity, and they are cut from the same cloth. One suspects that
they represent instances of a mobile story-type that tells of the birth and
precocious exploits of a troublesome child, of which vague echoes are to be
discerned in *Sunjata*.[2] But the mobility of the Sunjata tradition is of a different
order. Versions of his story have been collected not only in his mother tongue,
Maninka (or the dialects represented in the area of the Mande diaspora), but in
other languages as well. Versions have been published representing
performances in Wolof, Tukolor (Pulaar), Soninke, Khassonke, and Zarma,[3] and
this claim cannot easily be made for other African heroes. How then, and why,
does or can Sunjata's fame explode beyond the Manden?

A number of mechanisms can be suggested for the wider dissemination
of the Sunjata tradition. The first is simple migration and adaptation, following
the lines of the Mande diaspora. The second would be the natural diffusion of
the story in accordance with the mobility of traditional narratives around the

---

[2] Isidore Okpewho (1980) blends all these heroes in their orality; Christiane Seydou
(1982) has advanced more convincing arguments for distinguishing between West and
Central African epic traditions (such as the *mvet*, the Ozidi Saga, the Mwindo texts) on
performance and stylistic grounds. The question of the difference in narrative patterns is
a broad one, which has not yet been addressed, to the best of my knowledge.

[3] In Wolof, by Ames in Courlander 1975: 71–78; in Tukulor by Gerard Meyer (141–46);
in Arabic and Soninke by Delafosse (1913: 19–30), Arnaud (1912: 166–172), and Adam
(1904: 39–47); in Khassonke by Zeltner (1913: 37–45). None of these versions includes
original language transcriptions. Elements of Sunjata's story appear in Zarma in other
narratives published by Laye (1970: 1–6) and Mounkaila (1989: 145–51).

world, and in this pattern one would assume an absence of historical weight to the tradition and look simply to the travels of the story as a type (as with Mwindo, Ozidi, and others). A third mechanism echoes the second, but restores the historical element: the Sunjata tradition travels as a form of history rather than entertainment. It is appropriated, accommodated, adapted (or even denied) as neighboring peoples construct their own historical traditions. It seems a form of historiography independent of our current academic interest, and thus deserving of exploration in terms different than those of existing work.

The Centrifugal Motion of the Mande Epic

Sunjata is described as the *sinimogo* and the *sini-kini-mogo* ("man for tomorrow," "man for the day after tomorrow") in the performance tradition of the Manden itself, and the process by which, in a curious reversal, the future is projected out of the past of his story to become the present of whichever listener partakes both of the retroactive, chartering function of oral historiography and of the specific energies of this performance tradition. This narrative provides a matrix into which many other legends of origin are affixed, and through which they are thereby validated: social customs, clan origins and names, and national characteristics are all incorporated into the epic tradition.

Such an observation points immediately to a potential tension within that tradition: the competing claims of local interests and the "Pan-Mande" unifying function of the narrative that Gordon Innes and others have observed. While Sunjata is a hero of the Manden, he is not a local or regional hero. The breadth of the performance tradition within sub-Saharan West Africa illustrates his appeal. But although he is not to be pinned to one space he can be called the hero of an anterior time whose story precedes local tradition, and so avoids the pressure toward variation.

This division is perhaps best illustrated in the version of Sunjata from the Gambia performed by Bamba Suso and published by Gordon Innes (Innes 1974: 81):

> This was how Susu Sumanguru's career ended.
> That is where my own knowledge ends.
> Then Sunjata took control of Susu and Manding.
> The mode of life of people at that time
> And our mode of life at the present day are not the same.
> Surnames did not exist.
> All the surnames with which we are familiar
> Were given by Sunjata.

Bamba Suso then continues for another four hundred lines to explain the origins of the various Mandinka clans of the Gambia. This amplification of the story, however, is not purely idiosyncratic. It is to be encountered elsewhere, although the link with the biography of Sunjata proper is seldom so direct. Leo Frobenius (1925: 331–42) adds to his version of Sunjata another thirteen pages of amplifications containing genealogical information and supplements to his story. Diango Cissé and Massa Makan Diabaté (1970) have published *La dispersion des Mandeka*, an account of Mande migrations after the time of Sunjata, based on information from Kele Monson Diabaté. The traditions collected from Wa Kamissoko and published by Youssouf Tata Cissé (1988, 1991) include accounts of migrations, struggles, and further conquests.

Such adaptability to local tradition is only one of the mechanisms at work; it responds to historiographic pressure. The other mechanism, as suggested above, is to be found within the performance tradition itself, and centers on one specific point: the epic of *Sunjata* does not tell of the hero's death. To be sure, there are traditions concerning his death, although they are contradictory and inconsistent. But the moment of his death is not covered in performance; it is left open. Instead, the story-line of a performance moves on to a second generation of victories in Sunjata's name by his generals: Tira Magan takes the Gambia, Fa Koli kills the King of Nyani. Instead of dying with its hero, the story picks up new life and moves further afield—and in fact, the centrifugal motion of the conquests would seem to be a substitute for the death of the hero in ending the story.

The Conquest of the Gambia: From within the Manden

Among the stories of the conquests of Sunjata's generals, that of Tira Magan's expedition against Jolofin Mansa stands out on a number of grounds.[4] It marks the westward movement of the Mandekan into the Gambia, and so possesses some historical weight. By giving such a prominent role to the movement outward from the Mande heartland, it also becomes the metonymic representation of the Mande diaspora within the tradition. Within the Manden this narrative also evokes a potential challenge to Keita rulership by bearers of the Tira Magan's Traore *jamu*.[5] In one version, the story of the conquest of Jolof also involves praise-singing by Sunjata himself in honor of Tira Magan (Cissé

---

[4] The story of Tira Magan's conquest of the Gambia is given by Kele Monson Diabaté and Fadigi Sisoko (Moser 1974; Johnson 1978 or 1986); by Wa Kamissoko (Cissé and Kamissoko 1991: 87ff.); by Bamba Suso, with differences, in Innes 1974; by Frobenius, and by Franz de Zeltner (1913: 33–36).

[5] Earlier in the epic it is two Traore hunters, Dan Mansa Wulanba and Dan Mansa Wulandin, the hunters who vanquish the Buffalo Woman of Du, and thus become potential rivals of Sunjata's father for the propagation of the new hero. In 1968, after the 1968 military coup that deposed Mali's first president, Modiba Keita, in favor of Moussa Traoré, Tira Magan's *faasa* replaced that of Sunjata on the government radio (Cutter 1968).

and Kamissoko 1991: 96); this reversal of roles (kings do not normally act as griots) evokes the much wider issue of how the reputations of particular heroes come to be associated with (or disassociated from) particular praise-songs.[6]

The details of the Tira Magan story are variable more in terms of quantity than of kind; they include an expedition into Senegal (Jolof) to buy horses, the confiscation of the horses by the king of Jolof, and the return of an insulting message linking Sunjata (as an upstart) with dogs, hunting, and walking on foot. Naturally, Sunjata's retainers are reluctant to announce this message to the king, and various *nyamakala* consider the enterprise before a jeli (of course) assumes it and succeeds. Tira Magan wins command of the punitive expedition by digging a grave in which he lies; his subsequent passage through Jolof is swift and irresistible.

The Jolof conquest also deserves attention for the style of the narration in certain of the published versions representing the traditions of Kela/Kangaba. Both Kele Monson Diabaté and Fadigi Sisoko treat this moment with the same technique; they punctuate the account of Tira Magan's conquests with a refrain: "saying they were taking the dogs for a walk" (Kele Monson Diabaté in Moser 1974: 324–28; Fadigi Sisoko in Johnson 1978: 322). The effect is perhaps clearest in the quick-paced version of Fadigi:

> At the Ford of the Cowards
> Tura Magan came to battle.
> He killed the king with the dogs.
> He said he was walking the dogs.
> Tura Magan and war went on.
> He went and killed the king of Nyani.
> He said he was walking the dogs.
> Tura Magan and war went on.
> He killed the king of Sanumu.
> He said he was walking the dogs.
> He killed the king of Badugu.
> He said he was walking the dogs.

(Johnson 1978: 322)

The heavily ironic repetition of the phrase "walking the dogs" serves

---

[6] There is also the tradition that Sunjata first sang the "Janjon" for Fa Koli, as Adame Konaré Ba reports (1983: 100ff.; see also Diabaté 1970b: 43ff.), either for exploits against Sumanguru or for his deed of killing the King of Nyani (parallel to that of Tira Magan in the Gambia). The usual story seems to be that Fa Koli asks for the song and is then given it: cf. the version by Dembo Kanute in Innes 1974: 295ff. See also Bird and Kendall 1980: 20ff. and Conrad 1992.

effectively to erase the original insult, and incidentally to end the performance on a high-spirited note. This point may explain the relative polish of the episode. For the technique of the refrain links this moment of the epic with one other: the extended central passage in which Sunjata rises after a crippled childhood. The latter passage is also marked by a refrain, purportedly spoken by Sunjata's mother Sogolon: "Will you not rise?" she asks at first, and then, "Behold! He has risen!" This refrain structures the several hundred lines devoted to the episode and converts the narrative into an extended paean to the future king.[7] Such a technique does not seem to occur elsewhere in the epic. The various episodes of Sunjata's travels in exile can be punctuated by song interludes. The effect is normally to organize a sequence of encounters rather than to unify the scene and build a crescendo, to structure a sequence rather than to unify the series and quicken the pace, as is the case here. The stylistic feature of the refrain points to a performer-defined significance; the episode must be conceived in advance as a unit and delivered accordingly.

Any reasons I might advance to explain why the conquest of Jolof should be subject to such special handling would be speculation; I have already indicated some of the factors I believe might be in operation, such as external political considerations, or perhaps more credibly the desire to end the performance on a strong upbeat tone. Sunjata does not die, but slips from our attention into a timeless world sustained, in fact, by the actions of his subordinates. The pace of Tira Magan's conquests suggests an insuperable, ineluctable destiny that carries the Mande forward. And here, of course, we find a basis for the forward-looking vision of Sunjata, the "man for tomorrow."

Tira Magan is not the only vehicle for the triumphant energy unleashed by Sunjata. Fa Koli also is attributed a conquest, the King of Nyani, and as David Conrad has recently argued (1992), Fa Koli also leads the epic out of the Manden into the lands of the diaspora. It is an obvious question to ask, then, to what extent this centrifugal motion is represented outside the Manden. How is this episode seen elsewhere, most particularly in the Gambia, the land crossed and subjugated by Tira Magan? Is it central? Is it equally elaborated?

The Conquest of the Gambia: Seen from Outside

The short answer to the preceding questions is "no." Only one of the three Gambian Mandinka versions of Sunjata published by Innes in 1974 deals with this episode. Neither the idiosyncratic rendering of Banna Kanute nor the partial version of Dembo Kanute does so, nor does a published excerpt by Amadu Jebaate (1980). The only published performance version from the Gambia of Tira Magan's feat is therefore that of Bamba Suso, mentioned above,

---

[7] See Belcher 1985: 302–303 for line references to the various reports of this phrase across a number of performances.

and it alters the story somewhat. The Traore hero's suicide-threat is expressed not through a grave, but by a shroud in which he wraps himself before the battle with Sumanguru (Innes 1974: 69, ll. 646–49); he does later proceed to conquer the Gambia, and Bamba Suso provides some detail on the number of his stops and actions and the clan-names that derive from them. Innes's later collection of Gambian historical narratives, *Kaabu and Fuladu*, offers few, if any, references to the time of Sunjata, although Innes notes in the introduction that Kaabu does claim to have been founded by Tira Magan (Innes 1976: 28).

Local historians do consider the connection unquestionable, and the story of Sunjata is associated with the larger history of the Gambia as presented by Hamlyn (1931) and Sonko-Godwin (1988). The history of Kaabu (Gabou) was the subject of a conference in 1980, with some of the papers published in a special issue of *Ethiopiques* (vol. 28, 1981). D. T. Niane has published the *Histoire des mandingues de l'ouest* (1989), filling in the gap left for the Anglophone reader by the more recent focus of Charlotte Quinn's *Mandingo Kingdoms of the Senegambia*.

These works, however, are erudite reconstructions of the past, interpreting their information. Fortunately, we can move somewhat closer to the detail of local traditions for a grassroots perception. Donald Wright (1979, 1980) and the team of Sékéné-Mody Cissoko and Kaoussou Sambou (1974) have each provided a collection of oral historical traditions from the Gambia and Casamance. One might well turn to these works for some indication of both the literary spread of Sunjata's bubble reputation and the role of the Mali emperor in those oral sources that both Quinn and Wright find more useful than the griot performance tradition for reconstructing positive history.

Cissoko and Sambou provide the greater geographic spread, but at some cost in depth; their one-month trip in 1969 took them from Banjul to Tambacounda, and then back along the southern bank of the river. We encounter here a variety of traditions presented in summary form that have, however, the merit of representing many localities along the Gambia River. The informants vary from elders to marabouts and teachers; the circumstances under which the book was produced do not allow complete verbatim transcription of the interviews.

We find few connections with the epic of Sunjata in these traditions, although there is widespread agreement that "ancestors" came from the Manden or that kings brought *mansaya*, kingship, from this region to replace a local tradition of women's rule. Tira Magan is mentioned in the traditions of Kabu. His story is followed by the origin of the *nyancho*, the warlike aristocracy of the last century; it involves a hunter who found a woman living in a porcupine's cave (Cissoko and Sambou 1974: 192ff.). Sora Musa (Fa Koli, the second of Sunjata's generals) is mentioned as the founder of the kingdom of Badibu (46ff.). Surprisingly, the person most frequently mentioned is the sixteenth-century Fulbe leader Koli Tengela, who appears in the traditions of Niumi, of India, of

Kolibantang, and Ndougue Sine, former capital of Nyani. In Niumi he is associated with the Denia dynasty of Futa Toro in Senegal. In Ndougue Sine he is identified as a warrior of Sunjata and named Dembele son of Koli; there it is said that, when the conquests were over, Sunjata told his men to disperse so that they would have lands to rule (152ff.). Wagadu is also mentioned, and this suggests Soninke influence.

   Donald Wright divides his rich collection into two volumes, one dealing with griots and the other with family elders. He worked more exclusively with the kingdom of Niumi, the westernmost of the kingdoms of the Gambia, and his interviews were conducted in 1974–75. Here also, we find that specific connections to Sunjata are scant. Many references to foreign origins are quite general: the ancestors came from *tilebo*, the East, by which is meant the Manden; no king, however, is specified. Darbo elders, whom we might remember because of the way in which Dembo Kanute adjusted his performance of Sunjata to highlight the actions of a Darbo, recall that their ancestors came from the Manding, and one says they came with a cutlass, a golden bracelet, and a Quran,[8] which invites comparison between their tradition and other legends of origin. But they do not claim a connection with Sunjata, and in this they are typical. The Manden is a place, possibly a time, but not often a person.

   One of the few explicit references to be found in Wright's collection of interviews with family elders actually involves Sumanguru. The informant is Lat Grand Ndiaye, a Senegalese from Sine Saloum connected with the royal *guelowar* families of Sine. He reported that:

> The *guelowar* came from Manding in Mali. When Sundiata was living in Mali there also lived a blacksmith there named Sumanguru Kante, who ascended to rule. The *guelowar* gave birth to other *guelowar* and Sumanguru killed every male *guelowar* born in Mali. Sundiata was the one spared because he was feeble in his youth and Sumanguru did not fear him. Of course, you know that when every single male child of a mother is killed, she must panic. A woman called Teneng Kuta Jarbi fled the country with her slave and all of her belongings. (Wright 1980: 170–71)

   An unusual feature of this account is the timing of the departure: the woman's escape is linked to the oppressive slaughter of the innocents by Sumanguru rather than the later triumphant rule of Sunjata; by implication, this form of the tradition is intended to establish a legitimacy prior to the authority of Sunjata. The tradition also appears connected to the question of female rule, for

---

[8] Interviews with Alhaji Sekou Momadou Darbo and Sedia Darbo (Wright 1980: 10, 26); Sedia Darbo is the informant who lists the three objects.

this was an explicit interest of Lat Grand Ndiaye, and in that context the notion of an escape from an illegitimate and socially destructive condition might be considered sufficient justification.

An issue raised by this informant is that of the colonial language barrier and its effects. As a Francophone and a former *fonctionnaire*, Ndiaye would clearly be considered part of the intelligentsia, and his interest in collecting local history reflects the same ideological movement that inspired the historiographic efforts of Niane and later Cissoko and Sambou. Quite possibly Ndiaye's sense of place is somewhat broader than that of Wright's other informants, and for him the neighboring and administratively comparable Mali is a less remote and legendary site. Cissoko and Sambou note in their collection (2–3) that in the Gambia the combination of larger Mandinka villages, and fewer modern schools, permitted better preservation of the traditions than elsewhere.

The question of female rule merits comment (and more research). We find, for instance, an intriguing tradition attached to the king Samake Demba and others (given both by Wright and Cissoko) that women used to rule in the Gambia until men went back to the Manding to obtain mansaya; thereafter, the women yielded power freely and male rule was inaugurated.[9] Birds provide an important thematic element in this sequence, leading men or providing monstrous adversaries.[10] Given the heavily mythical overtones of the stories, I feel it would be rash to construe these traditions as retrievable history, despite possible connections with the matrilineality of the nyanchos and the hypothetical matrilineality of ancient Ghana (Levtzion 1972; Sonko-Godwin 1985: 5).

One griot in Niumi, Unus Jata, does provide us with a specific connection, linking Sora Musa (Fa Koli) and Sunjata (Wright 1979: 30, 47) and thus reflects the tradition given by Bamba Suso and Dembo Kanute (Innes 1974: 66, 302). Unus Jata starts with a reference to Koli Tengela, discusses the Wolof and the Sine-Saloum, follows this with the story of Sora Musa, and then returns to Koli Tengela (his sequence is wildly inconsistent). Sora Musa, Unus Jata says, was a Soninke who went to Mecca, and then returned, stopping in Mali. There, "Sundiata Keita" told him: "My father's blacksmith, Susu Sumanguru, was entrusted this country when my father died. He then refused to surrender the country to the sons of my father. I want you to help us kill him and remove him." This Sora Musa does, and Sunjata then allows him to gain power by washing in the secret waters of the house of Sunjata's fetishes. Sora Musa continues to Bakindiki, in the Gambia, and settles there (Wright 1979: 29–30).

This variant and hybrid tradition deserves dissection. It fuses a number of established legends of origin of power, deriving from groups that are all

---

[9] Interviews with Kemo Kuyate and Sherif Jabarteh (Wright 1979: 73ff., 97ff.).

[10] Interview with Kemo Kuyate (Wright 1979: 73ff.). The story is that of a fight between Jasey and a monstrous bird afflicting the Manding. For other traditions of migrations involving birds see Cissoko and Sambou (1974: 8ff., 26ff.).

represented in the traditions and history of Niumi. We might start first with the question of the Soninke, or Sarakholle. In the Gambian context, the term "Soninke" is ambiguous, for during the nineteenth-century Soninke-Marabout wars it became synonymous with all pagan groups, regardless of ethnic or linguistic affiliation, in much the same way that the *Tarikh es-Sudan* and the *Tarikh el-Fettach* use "Bambara" (Quinn 1972: 53). This confusion should not obscure the genuine Soninke presence in the region and possible influence on local traditions. Quinn (1972: 27) observes that in the 1840s, the king of Niumi, Demba Sonko, recruited a force of 700 Sarakholle (Soninke) mercenaries, and in the interviews conducted by Cissoko and Sambou (1974: 144) we do encounter explicit references to Wagadu and thematic connections of kings and snakes, which recall the Soninke legend of Bida.[11]

The element of Unus Jata's legend that I would identify with the Soninke traditions of Wagadu is the motif of washing in the secret waters, which endows Sora Musa with magical (and creative) power. In the legend of Wagadu, Djabe Cissé takes his brother's inheritance by trickery. He acquires royal power by washing in the waters kept in his father's secret house and then rolling in sand.[12] In his analysis of the figure of Fa Koli/ Sora Musa, David Conrad associates this washing with Fa Koli's "blacksmith/*komo*/sorcerer identity," and suggests that the washing might be a veiled reference to a blood sacrifice (Conrad 1992: 190). Since the interview specifically associates this story several times with the word "Soninke," and the thrust of the episode is to transfer Sunjata's royal authority to Fa Koli (as occurs in the legend of Wagadu), I find it more plausible to see this formulation as an appropriation of Soninke royal traditions, especially given the other borrowings that can be discerned.

Other elements point to Fulbe traditions. Donald Wright (1978) has already presented an analysis of the presence of Koli Tengela, known elsewhere as the founder of the Denia dynasty of Futa Toro. Wright demonstrates that this is a recent accretion to the traditions of Niumi that has now gained widespread credence, displacing an earlier belief (first reported by Golbery in 1786) that the founder was a Mande immigrant named Amari Sonko. In fact, the narrative substance of the two traditions does not seem greatly different, although there is

---

[11] One informant, Mansali Thiam in the village of Palang, makes explicit mention of Wagadu (144). In other testimony, royalty and snakes are linked: the migrants entered the land following a *bida* (testimony of Arfan Mamadou Diane, marabout of Bambine in Badibbu: 124); the king was chosen by a black snake (Lamine Maron, chief of Maron, ibid.: 85); and the king was suckled by a snake (Sori Wali and others in the town of Wouli-Madine, ibid.: 166–67).

[12] Cf. Frobenius 1921: 60–64; Monteil 1953: 376; R. Arnaud 1911: 149–50; Bathily 1977; Soumare and Sylla 1977. These last have been reprinted and updated by Germaine Dieterlen (1992).

a significant change of names. Amari Sonko came and won the country from the kingdom of Saloum, to which it was tributary; Koli Tengela also wins the kingdom from Saloum and ends the tribute that the local population paid.[13] The bridge is perhaps to be found in the complexity of names attributed to the various figures. Sora Musa is also Fa Koli; could the name Fa Koli have been a link to Koli Tengela? Or is the question one of Fulbe influence increased by Islam?

More problematic in Unus Jata's account is the singular description of Susu Sumanguru as the blacksmith of Sunjata's father, which thus presents Sunjata's great rival as a usurper rather than a foreign conqueror or a social upstart. The latter roles are discernible in the Gambian versions of *Sunjata* (Innes 1974: 146ff.), and also in Delafosse's anonymous Arabic manuscript (1913: 20–21), where Sumanguru is king while Sunjata grows up, and thus appears as a reigning monarch who must be overthrown. By contrast, Bamba Suso rather dwells upon the social status of Sumanguru in the context of his seduction by Sunjata's sister (Innes 1974: 73; see also Conrad 1984: 39–41). The relationship of Unus Jata's variant of the story to that of the Kita griots (Kele Monson, Fadigi and Magan Cissoko, Mady Kanku Jabaté) is complex, but essentially involves a simplification of the narrative line: Unus Jata eliminates the succession conflict between Dankaran Touman and Sunjata as well as the dislocating shifts of scene that become necessary when Sunjata goes into exile and the performer must still narrate the conquest of the Mande by Sumanguru.

Another suggestive element of this variant is the semblance of legitimacy it confers upon Sumanguru's initial rule: Sumanguru was "entrusted with power," but later refuses to surrender it, and Sunjata is obliged to go to war, with foreign help, to regain his legitimate throne. This theme brings us into the world of Fulbe traditions of both Macina and the Futa Toro: the same pattern of authority usurped and reclaimed occurs in the story of Samba Gueladio Djegui, a Deniyanke prince of Futa Toro,[14] and in one of the traditions of Hammadi Pate Yella (Hama the Red) of Kounari and Macina (Seydou 1987).[15] It seems clear

---

[13] Koli Sonko comes from the Denia and helps against the king of Saloum, in exchange for a share in the kingship (Cissoko and Sambou 1974: 8ff.); the first king was Koli Bankire, father of Biton Sonko; he twice joined the Wame clan in war against Saloum (ibid.: 26ff.). The variation of names here, and particularly the use of the Bamana title *biton* (associated with the kingdom of Segu) opens up interesting questions of linguistic and cultural influence.

[14] For references to various versions of the epic of Samba Gueladio collected between 1885 and 1989, see Belcher 1994.

[15] Cf. Vieillard 1931: 137–56 and Frobenius 1925: 182ff. and 203ff. for the story of Hambodedio and Besma Sougui. See also Seydou 1987: 5ff. and Meyer 1988: 71ff.

that the specific relations that define, however loosely, the Sunjata tradition are here dissolved into patterns owing more to local folkloric motifs than to historical report.

The general pattern that emerges from this analysis is not surprising: as one moves away from the center, the Sunjata tradition loses its specificity, loses its details, and devolves into generalized legendary material that braids with various other strands of ethnic tradition. The griot performances, as evidenced by Bamba Suso and the others, does seem to preserve much of this specificity, but in reciting more explicitly Gambian traditions, even the master Bamba Suso feels no need to make connections with Sunjata. Outside the formal performances, the historical weight of the Sunjata tradition seems to dissipate. We shall return to the Fulbe and Soninke connections traced above, but let us now briefly consider the possible southward extension of the legend.

Southward Extension

The Gambia lies north and west of those portions of the Manden now in the republic of Guinea. There are also meager reports of the tradition from Sierra Leone, to the southwest of the Manden, which we might examine for comparative purposes.

Michael Jackson, the ethnographer of the Kuranko, provides two fragmentary reports of material from the Sunjata tradition, both of which are of interest (Jackson 1979). The first is presented as a folktale, and recounts the birth and "rising" episodes of *Sunjata* as given in the Kita tradition: a boy (Yata) and his brother are born at the same time; their birth-order is reversed because of delay by the messengers; the second-born/first-announced son is a cripple who eventually uproots a tree and brings it to his mother. When he stands up, his father becomes sick, and so at first he refrains; eventually he rises fully and his father dies. The story mentions griots (*finaba*) and an iron bow on which the boy tries to rise, and there is a song that his mother sings when he rises (Jackson 1979: 97–98):

> Yata tamanda, Yata tamanda, keliya le kake
> Yata tamanda; bi yo, bi yo, bi yo, ma bi nyornye.
> Yata walked, Yata walked; envy made Yata walk;
> today oh, today oh, today oh, there has never been a day like today.

Jackson's informant was his field assistant, Noah Bokari Marah, and the narration was in English. Jackson comments (101):

> At that time, neither Noah nor I was aware of the resemblances and possible connections between the Kuranko narrative (to which Noah gave the aetiological subtitle ["The origin of rivalry between half-brothers"]) and the well-known Mande epic of Sundiata.

Since 1970, when the story was recorded, we have twenty years of documentation to show that the connections are more than possible: we are dealing here with a direct lifting of portions of the performance tradition of the Sunjata epic (the "Rising" scene discussed above is a well-rehearsed episode), and specifically portions that we can recognize as being associated with the Kita/Kangaba tradition exemplified by Kele Monson Diabaté and the other griots of his area. The tradition remains sufficiently coherent for even the song to be recognizable, although that song in particular is one that (perhaps because of its simplicity and the maternal wholesomeness of the sentiment) is unusually widespread and stable within the tradition.[16]

The second version of the story reported by Jackson does, in fact, come from a griot, Yeli Fode Gibate, although it is not presented as a historical epic. Here also, it has become an aetiological legend, this time of the origin of *balafon*-playing, and the substance closely reproduces the rendition of Banna Kanute: after a miraculous and reluctant birth (by means of a mortar) Sunjata acquires the first balafon from a jinn.[17] He then gives this instrument to his griot, Sira Kaarta, in whom it is not difficult to recognize the primeval Mande griot, Surakata (Zemp 1966, Conrad 1985), transposed into the position normally taken by Bala Faseke Kuyate.

These variants leave historical reference behind; they are evidence for the attenuation of the historical value of the Sunjata tradition and for its movement into the floating domain of the folktale. The first instance, in particular, raises the intriguing possibility, outside the scope of this essay, of reading the twin-birth scene of the Sunjata tradition as an originally separate

---

[16] See Belcher 1985: 296–97, for a tabulation (now somewhat out of date) of occurrences of this song in the tradition. The phrase *"keliya le kake"* deserves some attention, for it seems an intrusion intended to buttress the aetiological function of the story: "envy" made Yata walk, and the story accounts for rivalry and envy between halfbrothers. The connections with the *fadenya* rivalry described by Bird and Kendall (1980) are obvious. The phrase does not appear in the versions of the epic I have examined. The word *"kele"* also means warfare, and so one might possibly link this phrase with a line from the performance of Magan Sisoko: "Sun-Jata, i danin kele le kama (Sunjata, you were born for battle) (Johnson trans.)" which is spoken in admiration by Mema Sira, Sunjata's mistress in exile, when Sunjata has told her the secret of the sigi game that she had come to tell him (Johnson 1978: iii 246ff.). This twist on the plot is, among the published versions I have examined, unique to Magan Sisoko.

[17] The same story is told of Sumanguru, and I find it more likely that he is the original protagonist; this is the version given by Bamba Suso, Dembo Kanute, and Wa Kamissoko (Belcher 1985: 253). He is said to have obtained the balafon by giving his sister to a djinn (hence the supernatural origin of his nephew Fa Koli). See Belcher 1991 for a discussion of this theme.

aetiological myth; but the actual references within the story make it clear that the story itself (wittingly or not on the part of the informant) does derive from the performance tradition of the Sunjata epic.

C. M. Fyle (1979: 26–27, 36–37) has provided for Sierra Leone some material analoguous to that of Wright and Cissoko and Sambou for the Gambia. He has collected village traditions, which he presents in summary form with no recognizable references to Sunjata. We do encounter here a Marle Bokari who came from the Manden and may recall Sunjata's brother Manding Bokari, who tore at his sister's skirt (and elsewhere is known as the primordial hunter); but the Marle Bokari of these traditions is explicitly associated with the time of Samori. We also find the ubiquitous Fa Koli Koroma who went to Mecca.

One last association from this region deserves attention. Donald Cosentino, discussing the Mende trickster Musa Wo, has suggested parallels between his story and the Sunjata tradition (Cosentino 1989: 27, 29); given the second variant reported by Jackson above, such a connection may seem to have weight at least within the Sierra Leonean context. But Cosentino's association of the two figures raises, by implication, the much larger question of the relation between *Sunjata* and the enfant terrible story-pattern, widely reported in the areas south of the Manden and apparently stretching into Central Africa and the region of the Mwindo tradition (Görög et al. 1980).[18] The relationship of Sunjata and Sumanguru, which I have viewed as a dialectic opposition between cultural poles in the light of the transference of motifs from one to the other by different griots, loses this dynamic when, and if, we view their story as reflections of the much wider and more evidently mythical pattern of the enfant terrible who overthrows a tyrant king. Here, I believe, we have passed over the limits of the Sunjata tradition and left the Mande world completely.

We have seen above one explicit reference to Samori Ture, the nineteenth-century warlord, which we may view either as historical or (assuming that "Marle Bokari" was once Manding Bokari) as evidence for the telescoping of time and the supplanting of one great king's name with that of another more recent king. Should we continue our survey along the southern borders of the old empire of Mali, I suspect we would find similar patterns: narrative material from the performance tradition of Sunjata metamorphosing into folktale, details perhaps borrowed and incorporated into local traditions. But the historical value of the tradition, outside the Manden, enters into competition with other points of reference. We have seen one such, the mention of Samori in Fyle's material; another, more complex, example is perhaps to be among the chronicles of Gonja (Wilks et al. 1986).

Multiple strands of tradition coexist in these chronicles, which the

---

[18] One serious weakness of these studies by Görög and her colleagues Christiane Seydou, Genevieve Calame-Griaule, and others is the apparently deliberate lack of connection with political traditions and a reluctance to provide wider comparative perspective.

authors attempt to disentangle and identify. An oral tradition speaks of a Malian origin for the ruling "estate," and this belief is echoed by one of the published Arabic texts, the *Amr Ajdadina*, while two others, the *Kitab Ghanja* and the *Ta'rikh Ghanja,* lack such an element.[19] The narrative states that the ruler of the Manden sent messengers to the town of Shighu, rich in gold, to ask for tribute, which was refused. He then sent an army led by two princes and, after conquering Shighu, one of them seized the opportunity to establish his own state (he had been informed by a prophecy that he would never be king in the Manden) and traveled farther on into the land of Gonja.

Without attempting to explore all the aspects of this account, let us pause over a few points, beginning with the names. The *Amr Ajdadina* names the ruler of Mande Kaba "Jighi Jara"; another manuscript mentioned in the commentary gives the form "Jighi Jata." Both forms can, indeed, be connected with specifically Maninka tradition. However, they can also be connected with the Segu of the eighteenth century, when Ngolo Jarra established his short dynasty. Jarra is the dynastic name for Segu from 1750 to 1850 or so, and the name Jighi might well be connected with the frequently used praise-name of the Jarras, *jitigi ni mogowtigi* (master of the waters, master of men) which one encounters in the performance cycle of the epics of Segu.[20] One might further note that the pattern of the legend (a request for tribute that is denied, followed by conquest) is the standard pattern of the epic cycle of Segu (Belcher 1985: 133ff.). The editors argue that the name of the rebellious town, Shighu, should be read as Bighu, a place historically connected with the coastal gold-trade but completely forgotten by the time of the (modern) redaction of the text (Wilks et al. 1986: 8, 38). However, the assumption of a time of conflict between "Mande Kaba" and "Shighu" would take us back to the period in which Bighu was flourishing. The conservative connection with the local site (Bighu) appears to obscure a borrowing of legends of origin. The question involves, in part, the gold: Segu produced no gold, while Bighu was a gold-trading center, and the story speaks explicitly of gold.

---

[19] The *Ta'rikh* (158) says that a notable came from Mali, but it is given simply as a place rather than a kingdom.

[20] The phrase is frequently encountered in the collection translated by Lilyan Kesteloot (1972), *Da Monzon de Segou.* For other occurrences with the original language, see Dumestre 1979: 66–67: "a ko ji tigi Jara / fanga tigi Jara / mugu tigi Jara / kolon tigi Jara / mogow tigi Jara [He said, 'Diarra, master of water, / Diarra, master of power, / Diarra master of gunpowder, / Diarra master of cowries / Diarra, master of men']." I realize that it may seem inconsistent to read the name of the aggressor (the king of Mali) in the praise-names of the victim (Shighu), but my presumption is that the traditions have, in fact, been somewhat confused. Kathryn Green (1991: 131ff.) presents evidence that references to "Mande Kaba" in traditions of origin is probably a recent accretion, and specifically discusses the case of Gonja.

The gold, however, is magical. It "grows from the ground by the power of Allah," and is kept in two houses without doors (ibid.: 44). Here we have perhaps a legendary report, which fuses traditions from the North without much regard for their origin. Could we see the gold as a reflection of the Soninke traditions associated with Wagadu and Dinga's house of secrets? Is gold that "grows from the ground" to be compared with gold showered from heaven by a benevolent bida-serpent? The question seems open and deserving of wider investigation.

Let us present two final details from the Gonja chronicles as evidence for possible Mande influence. I do not believe the question can be fully answered here, but it does look to the dissemination (as identifiable traditions) of Sahelian historical legends outside their homeland.

The first episode concerns the dispatch of an avenging army: "The Sultan of Mandi said, 'Oh, my people, cut down this big tree and lay it across the road so that the horsemen will ride over it.' Accordingly the horsemen went over the tree until the tree was cut in two. It was a *kuka*" (ibid.: 45).

The name of this tree takes us to the praise-songs of the Sunjata tradition: "kukuba ani bantanba, niani niani kambasiga" is a widely reported "song" incorporated into the performance (Belcher 1985: 312–13), although interpretations of the meaning vary considerably. The lines are generally understood as praises for Sumanguru, and a frequent interpretation is that they list the places of his victories over Sunjata. The editors note that "kuka" is not an Arabic word, although it means "baobab" in Hausa; the possibility that it is a borrowing from the Manding performance tradition seems open. The second point about the tree is its function as a counting device for the army, and the editors note reports of a similar practice in Bornu at the end of the eighteenth century. The motif is also found in the traditions of Futa Toro and Bondu, notably with Samba Gueladio, the Deniyanke prince of the eighteenth-century Futa Toro, who is the preeminent Tukolor epic hero. The presence of the motif in Bornu might well owe something to Fulbe connections.

As a final point, we might observe that the *Kitab Ghanja* substitutes an Islamic legitimation for what, from this comparative perspective, should be viewed as an authochthonous composite of borrowed regal traditions. The example of Niumi, discussed above, should serve as a close parallel here: a state that developed recently, just beyond the sphere of hegemony of the older empire, creates its own tradition of origin by fusing a variety of available traditions (Malinke, Bamana, local) into a curious hybrid.

Contrasts of North and South

I hesitate to define a pattern emerging from the evidence reviewed so far. One might argue, on the basis of the Gambian and Kuranko evidence, that the performance tradition of Sunjata is strong enough to retain its identity (or at least to remain recognizable) as it travels. One can also argue that the historical weight of the Sunjata tradition dissipates quite rapidly: the figure of the conqueror of the Manden gives way to those of his generals Tira Magan or Fa Koli (whom David Conrad describes as "the great progenitor," referring to his function as ancestor of so many important clans [1992: 174ff.]). Sunjata may be used for political traditions (see how delegation of authority from the Manden is used as legitimation for male kingship in the Gambia), but not in family and genealogical traditions. He does not serve as a time-marker, but the Manden serves rather as a mythic point of origin. On the southwestern borders of the old Manden, time starts with Mali.

This is not the case to the north. Mamadou Diawara's chapter in this volume reviews far clearer patterns of borrowing and appropriation: ones that in fact may serve as the conceptual model by which to measure deviations in the traditions we have examined. For Jara, for Bondu, for the Deniyanke, the role of Sunjata is simple: he provides tokens that subsequently legitimate the authority of the receiver, be it Dama Ngile,[21] Malik Sy, or Koli Tengela. Often, the story of the receipt of these tokens is compounded by other forms of legitimation: Dama Ngile's family supplants a clearly abusive exercise of authority by the Niakhate;[22] Malik Sy also travels to Mecca; Koli Tengela makes war and migrates.

The difference in the clarity with which we see our hero in the northern latitudes (as Niane says, "speak to me in the clear language of the savanna") probably owes little to Islam or to writing, although Soninke marabouts of Nioro have provided early manuscript histories that include Sunjata. Neither the *Ta'rikh es-Sudan* nor the *Ta'rikh el-Fettash* recognizes the hero explicitly, although they follow one sort of pattern in bringing the princely founders of the Songhai state from Mali, pursued by the horsemen of the king. But this legend may also mix traditions, for such a chase on horseback is the characteristic finale to the story of Wagadu's destruction, and its presence may reflect Soninke

---

[21] The pattern, in which Sunjata repeatedly attempts to substitute a less valuable weapon for the true sword brought from Mecca, strongly resembles elements of the Segu tradition in which the young Ngolo Jarra (a destined ruler) is repeatedly tested by Biton Koulibali through deprivation of a token of future kingship (Kesteloot 1972: I 65–83, Conrad 1990: 110ff.). The motif is ancient, and a similar story is told by Herodotus of the child Cyrus.

[22] The Nyakhate prove their unfitness for rule when the king kills a pregnant woman. In the Sunjata tradition, a similar action is attributed to the hero under circumstances which may be interpreted as a sacrifice (Johnson 1986: 147, 209 note to lines 1740–45). Within the Soninke story of Dama Ngile, the figure of Sunjata becomes ambivalent. While he represents a form of authority and a source of legitimacy, he also unjustly attempts to withhold the sword that is Dama Ngile's due. His actions border on those of a jealous tyrant, and one might see the pair Dama Ngile-Sunjata as analoguous to the earlier pair of Sunjata-Sumanguru: the virtuous hunter and the corrupt king.

traditions more than those of Mali.

In Soninke historiography then, Sunjata is incorporated as something other than an anachronistic point of reference. One finds a clear recognition that the Soninke world preceded that of Sunjata and Mande hegemony. A series of manuscripts prepared in Nioro for colonial administrators (see Conrad 1984: 36– 39 and Bulman, infra) take the form of a sequential history of Sahelian kingdoms, in which clear precedence is given to Wagadu. They include the story of Sunjata and the Manden, a mark of its importance, but fit it into a sequence: there were kings before him, and there were kings after him; this is also the message of the "Sunjata" faasa (Diabaté 1970b: 31). The Soninke can and do claim historical priority of place. But at the same time, the Soninke perspective on this relationship seems somewhat world-weary. Their central story, that of the foundation and the fall of Wagadu, ends with destruction and dispersal, and this is a theme carried through other examples from their oral tradition.

To illustrate this last point we should perhaps turn to what is available of the Soninke performance tradition. Meillassoux and Doucoure (1967) have provided one of the few transcriptions of a Soninke griot performance available in print, the *Légende de la dispersion des Kusa* sung by Diaowa Simagha. The legend tells the story of Maren Jaxu and how he avenged his father with the help of his sister. In many ways the plot evokes the pattern of the enfant terrible discussed briefly above; there are also parallels to the Sunjata tradition.[23]

The text ends with a tantalizing, and somewhat irritating footnote: "Le récit se poursuit une demi-heure encore par la légende de Jallo Maxa, puis par celle de Sujatta" (133). One wishes very much to learn the rest of the story, and to see the manner in which the Sunjata epic is performed. But that is not the central point (although one might note that we do have, here, an example of a non-Manding performance version of Sunjata: evidence for the spread of the hero's fame). Let us look to the tone of the traditions, perhaps best summed up by some lines that are repeated three more times after their first utterance:

> This world will come, it will pass
> Other worlds will come after it
> Worlds of turbulence and strife. . . .

It is a somber note; the speaker predicts civil war, dissension, and ultimately the dispersal of the Kusa from their homeland. This epic speaks then of a loss, almost a defeat. The hero's victory is passing, and is even seen as a step

---

[23] The plot outline (avenging a father) is too broad, but elements such as the pairing of brother and sister and the sister's magical abilities are suggestive. Also, the *Dispersion des Kusa* features a *gesere*, a Soninke griot, who takes the form of a gray cat (*jankuma*) to spy out the tyrant's realm. One thus thinks of the griot in the Sunjata epic, Jankuma Doke (Gnankouma Douwa: the spelling may vary), who is renamed Bala Faseke Kuyate.

toward future destruction.

The contrast with the matter and the tone of the epic of Sunjata could hardly be stronger. And it is with this relative and local contrast of ideologies and visions that I think we can, even from afar, grasp something of the significance of the hero and the effect of his epic. Sunjata is not a figure of the past; he is a figure of the present.

Addendum

Since this article was written, I have encountered in E. F. Tamakloe's historical contributions to A. W. Cardinall's *Tales Told in Togoland*, a narrative which seems quite possibly an echo of the *Sunjata* tradition, although it has definitely been transformed. It is the story, given on pp. 239–43, of the hunter-hero Tohajiye (Red Hunter) and his son Kpogonumbo and their dealings with the King of Malle (a note explicitly differentiates this "Malle" from Sunjata's kingdom). Space precludes a full discussion of the transformations, but possible parallels include echoes in names: two brothers named Tindanjiye and Tindanbila (recalling, perhaps, Dan mansa Wulandin and Dan Mansa Wulanba, the Traore hunter brothers) and a maiden named Suhusagba (recalling the various witch-oriented compound names of the Sunjata praise tradition, such as *subaa-mine-subaa*, "sorcerer-seizing-sorcerer"), the motif of finding a hero by the use of plants/foodstuffs, the selection of a deformed and lame maiden as a bride, and the transformation of the hero from hunter to king. It is in this case the combination of these different motifs that suggests the connection with the epic of *Sunjata*.

Bibliography

Arnaud, Robert. 1911. "La singulière légende des soninké." In *L'Islam et la politique musulmane...*, 149–50. Paris: Comité de l'Afrique française.

Bathily, Abdoulaye, ed. 1977. *Documents du Colloque de Niamey*. Paris: Fondation SCOA.

Belcher, Stephen. 1991. "Sunjata, Sumanguru, and Mothers." Paper presented at the African Studies Association Conference.

—. 1994. "Constructing a Hero: Samba Gueladio Diegui." *Research in African Literatures* 25, 1: 75–92.

Bérenger-Féraud, L. 1885. *Recueil de contes populaires de la Sénégambie*. Paris: Leroux. Reprint 1970.

Biebuyck, Daniel, and Kahombo C. Mateene. 1971. *The Mwindo Epic*. Berkeley: University of California Press.

Cardinall, A. C. 1931. *Tales Told in Togoland*. Westport, Connecticut: Negro University Press.

Cissoko, Sekeny-Mody, and Kaoussou Sambou, eds. 1974. *Recueil de traditions orales des mandingues de Gambie et de Casamance*. Niamey: Centre régional de documentation pour la tradition orale.

Cosentino, Donald J. 1989. "Midnight Charters: Musa Wo and Mende Myths of Chaos." In W. Arens and I. Karp, eds., *Creativity of Power: Cosmology and Action in African Societies,* 21–37. Washington and London: Smithsonian Institution Press.

Delafosse, Maurice. 1913. "Histoire de la lutte entre les empires de Sosso et du Mande." In *Traditions historiques et légendaires du Soudan Occidental*. Paris. Reprinted in *Notes africaines* 83 (July, 1959): 76–80.

Dieterlen, Germaine. 1992. *L'Empire de Ghana: le Wagadou et les traditions de Yéréré*. Paris: Editions Karthala: Association ARSAN.

Dumestre, Gerard, ed. and trans. 1979. *La geste de Segou*. Paris: Armand Colin, Classiques Africains.

Frobenius, Leo. 1921. "Die Wiederentdeckung Wagadu." In *Atlantis VI:*

Spielmanns-geschichten der Sahel, 60–64. Iena: Eugen Diederichs. Martin Sändig reprint 1978.

—. 1925. "Die Sunjattalegende des Malinke" and "Ergänzungen." In *Atlantis V: Dichten und Denken im Sudan,* 303–43. Iena: Eugen Diederick.

Fyle, C. Magbaily. 1979. *Oral Traditions of Sierra Leone.* Niamey: Centre for Linguistic and Historical Studies by Oral Tradition.

Görög, Veronika, Diana Rey-Hulman, et al. 1980. *Histoires d'enfants terribles.* Paris: G.P. Maisonneuve et Larose.

Hamlyn, W. T. 1931. *A Short History of the Gambia.* Bathurst [Banjul]: Department of Education.

Innes, Gordon. 1976. *Kaabu and Fuladu: Historical Narratives of the Gambian Mandinka.* London: School of Oriental and African Studies.

Jabaté, Kanku Madi. 1987. *L'Histoire du Mande.* Collected, translated, and annotated by Madina Ly-Tall, Seydou Camara, and Bouna Diouara. Paris: Association SCOA.

Jebaate, Amadu.1980. "La jeunesse de Soundiata." Ed. and trans. D. Creissels and S. Jatta, *Recueil de Littérature Mandingue,* 108–25. Paris.

Kamissoko, Wa. 1991. *Soundjata, la gloire du Mali.* Paris: Karthala/Arsan.

Laya, Dioulde, ed. 1970. *Traditions historiques des ethnies de la région de Dooso (Dosso).* Niamey: CELHTO. Second edition.

Levtzion, Nehemia. 1972. "Was Royal Succession in Ancient Ghana Matrilineal?" *International Journal of African Historical Studies* 5: 91–94.

Meyer, Gerard. 1988. *Paroles du Soir: Contes toucouleurs.* Paris: L'Harmattan.

—., ed. and trans. 1991. *Récits épiques toucouleurs.* Paris: Karthala.

Quinn, Charlotte. 1972. *Mandingo Kingdoms of the Senegambia.* Evanston: Northwestern University Press.

Sawse, Ali, and David Ames. 1975. "The Lion of Manding." In Harold Courlander, ed., *A Treasure of African Folklore.* New York: Crown.

Seydou, Christiane. 1987. *Des preux, des belles, et des larrons*. Paris: Nubia.

Sonko-Godwin, Patience. 1986. *Social and Political Structures in the Precolonial Periods (Ethnic Groups of the Senegambia Region)*. Banjul: Sunrise Publishers.

—. 1988. *Ethnic Groups of the Senegambia: A Brief History*. Banjul: Sunrise Publishers. Second edition.

Soumare, Mamadou, and Diarra Sylla. 1977. In Abdoulaye Bathily, ed., *Documents du Colloque de Niamey*. Paris: Fondation SCOA.

Vieillard, Gilbert. 1931. "Récits peuls du Macina et du Kounari." In *Bulletin du Comité d'études historique et scientifique de l'Afrique occidentale française* 14: 137–56.

—. N.d. *Récits peuls du Macina, du Kounari, du Djilgodji et du Torodi*. Ed. Eldridge Mohamadou. Niamey: n.p.

Wilks, Ivor, Nehemia Levtzion, and Bruce Haight. 1986. *Chronicles from Gonja*. Cambridge University Press. Fontes Historiae Africanae Series Arabica IX.

Wright, Donald. 1979. *Oral Traditions from the Gambia. Volume 1: Mandinka Griots*. Athens, Ohio: Ohio University Center for International Studies, Africa Program.

—. 1980. *Oral Traditions from the Gambia. Volume 2: Family Elders*. Athens, Ohio: Ohio University Center for International Studies, Africa Program.

—. 1987. "The Epic of Kelefa Saane as a guide to the Nature of Precolonial Senegambian Society—and Vice Versa." *History in Africa* 14: 287–309.

Wright, Donald. 1991. "Requiem for the Use of Oral Tradition to Reconstruct the Precolonial History of the Lower Gambia." *History in Africa*. 18: 399–408.

6. Searching for the Historical Ancestor: The Paradigm of Sunjata in Oral Traditions of the Sahel (13th–19th Centuries)[1]

Mamadou Diawara

The name of Sunjata irresistibly recalls that of Mali, the political formation he founded toward the start of the thirteenth century. At its apogee in the fourteenth century, under Kanku Musa, the area of influence of imperial Mali extended well beyond its Manden core: from west to east it covered a belt stretching from present-day Senegal to the Aïr in Niger. From the north to the south it reached from the Sahara to the southern marches of the Sudanic zone.[2]

Mali thus included in some sense the three states covered in this article: the Zarmataray, the kingdom of Jaara, and Bundu. The Zarmataray, or land of the Zarma, located in the present Republic of Niger, is said to have been organized into a state between the eleventh and the fifteenth centuries. According to Fatoumata Mounkaila (1988: 25, 225, 235) the Zarmataray included the Dallol Bosso, the plateau lying on either side of the Dallol, the region of the Niger River, as well as the Zarmaganda (also Hale 1990: 132, 142,

[1] This chapter was composed in 1993, during my stay at the University of Bayreuth as a guest professor with the SFB 214 and the Institut für Afrika Studien. I would like to express my profound gratitude to both those institutions. I also thank Odile Goerg, Denise Paulme, Adam Jones, and Karim Traoré for their willingness to read, correct, and discuss preliminary versions.

[2] Researchers have produced little precise information on the relations between Mali and its dependent political units. Therefore, I prefer to talk of areas of influence, which seem to me more credible than the notion of territorial borders inherited from European historiography.

291). Within this larger territory a distinction can be drawn between the northern Zarmaganda, "cradle of the Zarma people," and the Zarmataray to the south (Olivier de Sardan 1984: 18, 21–23). The major population groups of the state were the Zarma (or Djerma), the Sonrai, the Dendi, and the Twareg.

As for the kingdom of Jaara, it rose from the ashes of the empire of Wagadu (the Ghana of Arab travelers? Cf. Conrad and Fisher 1982). The city of that name, nowadays reduced to a modest village of a few hundred souls, lies some thirty kilometers east-northeast of the Nioro in Mali. This polity, whose area of influence covered the triangle between the borders of modern Mali, Mauritania, and Senegal, was ruled by two dynasties from the fifteenth to the mid-nineteenth centuries: the house of Nyaxate (fifteenth century) and that of the Jawara (sixteenth to nineteenth centuries). Its main inhabitants were Soninke, Fulbe, Moors, and Bamana.

The foundations of Bundu were set by Malik Si around 1690 (Curtin 1971: 471; 1975: 189). This state lay in present-day Senegal, at the confluence of the Senegal and Faleme rivers, and its very diverse population consisted of Fulbe, Soninke, Moors, and other groups.

The history of Mali and its founding hero had a profound impact throughout the Mande cultural world. This chapter will address the following questions: What was the influence of Sunjata and his story on a dynasty with a history older than that of Mali (the Zarmataray)? What is that influence on the marches of Mali among both the Zarma and Jaara, who link themselves to a primordial past, that of Wagadu (eighth to eleventh centuries)? And finally, what is the value of the epic of *Sunjata* among peoples lying even farther from the center of the Mali empire, for instance in Bundu?

John William Johnson (1986: 3) has defined Sunjata as "a culture hero. The epic which celebrates his memory constitutes a political charter of Mande culture." Should we thus approach the phenomenon of *Sunjata* as a model of heroic traits and literary composition imposed on other peoples and cultures? Or should we adopt a more interactive perspective, in which local chroniclers, through continuous productive efforts in contact with other historical and literary sources and in exchanges which are both conscious and unconscious, direct and indirect, negotiate the broadly common elements of a heritage belonging to the entire Mande world?

The Narratives
Presentation

I shall not here recount the story *Sunjata*; other chapters within this volume present it in detail (cf. also Bulman 1989: 171–72). The following paragraphs summarize traditions of the birth, in the case of the Zarmataray and Bundu, or the evolution, for Jaara, of three political entities, stressing those sequences in which Sunjata appears linked with their respective founding fathers (see table 6.1). It is notable, however, that no Maninka chronicler of Sunjata

TABLE 6.1: FOUR HEROIC TRADITIONS

Hero and State	Location and Dates	Eastern Origin	Local Ethnicity	Pilgrimage to Mecca	Sunjata Linkage
Zabarkane (Mali Bero) ZARMAT-ARY	Niger 11th–15th centuries	Zabarkane of Yemeni ancestry	Zarma	Zabarkane encounters Muhammad	Zarma in Malian exile; S. forces them to return home on a flying granary
Daaman Gille JAARA	Mali/Mau-ritania/ Senegal 15th–19th centuries	descended from Julxar-nayini	Popula-tion: So-ninke, Wagadu Daama: Maninka (Xanyaag a)	Pilgrims obtain magic knife from Mecca in return for Daama's aid	Daama retrieves knife from S.; conquers local foes, marries d/o S., urged to depart
Malik Si BUNDU	Senegal 17th–19th centuries	no claim of origin	halpulaar	Malik, a de-vout and learned cleric, undertakes his own hajj	S. encoun-tered at Kaaba, prepares Malik for rulership
Sunjata MALI	Mali–Upper Guinea 13th–14th centuries	descended from Bilal (all ver-sions) and Julu Kar-nyini (some)	Maninka	The jinn Tan-imunari takes S. to Mecca as a child	no men-tion of other 3 heroes in any Mande Sunjata texts

mentions any of the three heroes whose stories follow.

Zarmataray

The legend of Zabarkane (or Mali Bero), founder of this dynasty, come to us through seven accounts recorded by Mounkaila, includes some essential elements that send us back to the Sunjata/Mali narrative. Four of them retain the primordial Middle Eastern origin of the Zarma. According to Saley Sandi and all the other chroniclers, the Zarma stopped for a time in Mallé, west of their present homeland, the Zarmataray, in Niger. According to Mounkaila (1988: 179), "Mallé" is a land of exile, the final stage of the westward migrations of the Zarma, the starting point of their peregrination toward the east. Mali Bero, the ancestor-hero, is said to have been driven out of Mallé by Sunjata (Magan Soundjata) himself (ibid. 1988: 23, 189). The flight of the Zarma, led by Mali Bero, alias Zarmakoye Sombo (ibid. 1988: 91), "the best known leader of the Zarma migrations out of Mallé" (Mounkaila 1988: 168)—ends in the Zarmataray, using the vehicle of a flying granary.

Jaara

Daama is considered to be the common ancestor of the Jawara dynasty (Boyer 1953; Diawara 1990). Originally from the East, he apparently became a wandering hunter in the game-filled lands of Wanta (Manden), south of the present city of Bamako. By chance, Daama also met pilgrims leaving for Mecca, and performed valuable service for them, receiving as a reward the gift of an enchanted knife from the holy places. The weapon was entrusted to Sunjata and delivered only after Daama, in exchange, had defeated irreducible enemies of the Mali emperor stationed in two sites. Worried by the power of this dangerous warrior, Sunjata granted him the hand of his eldest daughter, requesting that he leave the Manden. Thus began the lengthy peregrinations of the hero searching for his land.

Bundu

The story of Malik Si, a hero from Bundu (now in Senegal), and his foundation of the kingdom of Bundu is "one of the best remembered and the most frequently retold of all Senegambian oral traditions" (Curtin 1975: 189). We will use here the version by Saki Olal N'Diaye, as translated and edited by A. Neil Skinner and Philip D. Curtin (1971).

Malik Si, a cleric from Suyuuma (near Podor in the Fuuta Tooro), first came to the region known as Bundu to study the Quran. His learning and holy life won him the titles of *tierno* (cleric) and *waliyu* (saint), but "The sons of his father conceived jealousy and hatred for him [. . .]" (473). Malik then traveled to different places within his own region and, finally, set off for Mecca. There at the Kaaba he found Sunjata who "was not a tierno, he was not a waliyu, but he was a wise man" (473–75).

At Malik Si's departure Sunjata "brought him three men. . . . [and]

bestowed on him a basket called Dantuma [a charm]" (475). Malik then went back to Bundu and, while crossing an important river along the way, prophesied, "Bismillahi, Almamy from Malik to Malik [. . .] Bismillahi, waliyu from Malik to Malik, sainthood from God arose with Malik and will pass away with Malik" (475). Malik took control of Bundu by asserting his religious power over the autochthonous Fadube, a troglodyte people with tails who could not complete their great project of digging a well because the wood of all the local trees were protected by jinn (477).

The Places of History
<u>The Social Context of the Production of the Stories</u>
        I do not propose to undertake here a critical analysis of each available version of the stories of Zarmataray, Jaara, or Bundu. However, it does seem useful, before studying the relation of these chronicles with that of *Sunjata*, to describe their circumstances of production and collection.
Zarmataray
        The seven texts presented by Mounkaila divide up as follows: three testimonies by *jassere* of the same family (texts I, II, III; cf. Mounkaila 1988: 222), the fourth a composition on the occasion of National Youth Day in Niger, based on a text from an elderly woman of Zarmataray; the fifth a text in Arabic from a cleric; the sixth from a community leader; and the seventh from an old Zarma servant. The jassere are the heralds of Zarma aristocracy. They are of Soninke origin, and their name recalls that of the *geseru* (sing. *gesere*) of the area around Nioro in Mali, whom they claim as ancestors.[3]
        The texts may be classified in the following manner:

> a. Three oral accounts from dependents of the Zarma aristocracy (I, II, III)
> b. One oral family narrative (VII) that echoes the first three in glorifying the Zarma aristocracy, benefactors of the jassere and, in the past, patrons of the former servant who is the narrator
> c. Two accounts from local savants (V, VI), of which the first is literate in Arabic
> d. Finally (IV), a popular version specially arranged and broadcast over the national radio airwaves

While we do not intend a historical analysis of the Zarma narratives, one should note that we only have more or less official versions, although those of the weaver (VII) and the radio (IV) do not dwell on the role of Islam in the hero's story (Mounkaila 1988: 13).[4]

---

[3] Moraes Farias 1991, 1992 (see especially the bibliography of 1992: 5); also Hale 1990: 175–76; Mounkaila 1988: 43–48; Olivier de Sardan 1982: 224–30, 310, 330–32, 354.

[4] The weaver's narrative may be considered as emanating from a jassere, considering the

Jaara

Agents of the French colonial regime recorded at least eight accounts dealing with the Jaara kingdom; some administrators, such as Gaston Boyer, even collected several snatches of narrative at the same time. The oral traditions dealing with Daaman Gille, for which data on the informants is precise, include ten testimonies from aristocratic dependents, against four aristocratic accounts and three from royal servants. A host of oral narratives from the common people, from Arabic-writing men of letters, and servants complete this list, including the remarkable text of the *garanke* (leatherworker) Dogo Jawara, recorded by A. Bathily and C. Meillassoux (Bathily 1975). This last is one of the counterpoints to the official versions derived from noble families and their retainers.

Bundu

Of the twenty-five versions of this history analyzed by Curtin (1975: 201–202), twelve are oral texts transcribed and translated by European agents of the colonial administration, by explorers (eight), or by native researchers, Fulbe-speakers and others (four). No indication is given about the original authors of the collected texts. As for the other thirteen oral versions presented, Curtin distinguishes six testimonies from the Sisibe, members of the Si family and their allies: two from the Fadube, defeated by the Sisibe, and three from the Soninke who, like the Jakhanke (one text), represent the "other ethnic groups in Bundu."

To bring the social context into clearer relief, let me present the sampling thus: two oral traditions from the Sisibe aristocracy, four narratives from bards, and one from a blacksmith (all dependents of the triumphant family). The Fadube, the group displaced by the Si, provide two testimonies. Local savants of various social and political categories also contribute: two local leaders, a leatherworker, and a former servant. Analysis of the narratives collected by the French, looking to the social and political origins of the informants, proves impossible for lack of data. Neither can one speak definitively about the content of the other thirteen accounts, of which seven are directly or indirectly distilled from members or followers of the family of the hero being celebrated.

Placement in Time and Space

All testimony on Zabarkane of Zarma comes from the present Republic of Niger. As for the accounts dealing with Daaman Gille, they come from spots as different as the villages around Jaara, capital of the kingdom of that name, or Ja, a village in the inland Niger delta, or Kayes, or even Dakar (Bathily 1975).

---

relevant observations by Mounkaila (1988: 51). In the same way, among the Bundu accounts (see below), the narrative by the blacksmith (Bathily 1975), descendant of a family historically linked with that of Malik Si, and with whom the hero entered Bundu, may also be seen as representing the traditions of royal dependents.

Not including Paris, where the latest version of the legend of Daama was narrated by Masuntu, one may claim that the story is found across a broad area, over a thousand kilometers wide, from Dakar to Ja. Of the twenty-five versions of the legend of Malik Si, whose "authors" are quite often unknown (by "author," we mean those who told or sang the story), at least seven were recorded outside of Bundu. One was recorded in Dakar, 600 kilometers to the west; another at a similar distance to the east, in Nioro (Curtin 1975: 189; Skinner and Curtin 1971: 467).

From this we see that the body of the traditions stretches over a territory so vast as to connect the Pointe des Almadi in Senegal to the Aïr in Niger, thousands of kilometers away. Because of migrant African labor in Europe and the subsequent travels of chroniclers who retell the stories in the centers of exile, particularly in France, this area is expanding even more widely in our own time. Exportation outside Africa of music and tales recorded on cassettes, intended for private individuals or the general public, further highlights the mobility of this oral heritage (Diawara 1994). Moreover, the radio-broadcast of the histories of well-known traditionists further extends the field of each story, as well as opening up the possibility of reciprocal influence, which is usually denoted by the denigrating term "feedback" but might also be considered a "fertile echo" (Henige 1973; Chrétien 1985; Amselle 1990: 246; Jones 1990: 85 vs. Rouch 1990 viii).

The first two accounts dealing with Zabarkane were recorded in 1968, the third (a reprise of the first) in 1984, the fourth in 1973; however, the last three are not dated (Mounkaila 1988: 50–51).

The colonial administrator Adam (1904: 232–48) was the first to report in French on Daaman Gille. In 1913, Gaden translated Siré Abbas Soh, and Delafosse (1913) published the translation of an Arabic text. Following these came Arnaud (1913), Blanc (1924), Luciani (1952), Boyer (1953), and Tisserant (1954), all of whom collected traditions that have been translated and either published or deposited in archives. All told, eight texts or collections of information were set down in writing during the colonial period. The most abundant harvest, counting some eighteen versions or fragments, comes between 1975 and 1990, including twelve accounts from my own work (1976, 1978, 1980, 1982, and 1990) and the work of A. Bathily and C. Meillassoux (1975), M. Danthioko (n.d., 1985), M. Baghaga (1977), C. D. Ardouin (1988), and M. Soumaré (1987).

In the accounts of the kingdom of Jaara a single informant, Mamadi Aïssa Diakite, a literate Soninke working in the provincial tribunal of Nioro, appears as the source for at least two documents, those of Adam and Delafosse (Bulman, infra; Conrad 1984). Unfortunately, all of my research in Nioro, Diakite's home town, has yielded no precise indication of his sources; however, there can be little doubt that the "scribe" acted as a conduit for the information of others.

Of the twenty-five Bundu texts studied by Curtin, seven were collected before 1900, five during the colonial period, and the thirteen others, including that of Saki Olal N'Diaye (Skinner and Curtin 1971) date from 1966.

If one examines closely the histories involved, each of the stories we are considering results from a defeat and picks up a challenge; each is in itself a "historical act" (Bazin 1979: 451). After the stinging failure of the Zarma against the coalition of the Fulbe and the Twareg (Mounkaila 1988: 52, 77, 97, 113, 168), and following the flight from Mallé, those who settled in the Zarmataray needed a new set of references. Similarly, when the new military Jawara aristocracy took power in a land where they were suspected to be of servile origin (Meillassoux et al. 1967), they had to demonstrate the contrary. As for Malik Si, the most recent of the Sahelian heroes considered here, he was confronted with a figure of the stature of Koli Tengella, established in the sixteenth century (Curtin 1975: 190; Wright, 1977, 1978; Johnson 1986: 180, 215; Belcher 1992).

The descendants of all these characters may well transcend their ancestral social status through accession to power, but in order to solidify this ascendance, they must achieve recognition through the formal spoken word. As Bazin writes (1979: 457–58), "One may seize power (*le pouvoir*), but powerfulness (*la puissance*) can only *be spoken*" (my italics).

Beside such an original motivation, those regions faced other challenges that each provided a new dynamic to the production of oral histories. One of these was the jihad of al-Hajj Umar, which brought about a defeat of the troops of Jaara and the collapse of the kingdom. The case of Bundu was no different. Thereafter, all the leaders in the land were forced, more than before, to have recourse to the oral histories to maintain the status they had conquered, however artificially. Such imperatives became even greater with the arrival of the colonizer, sworn enemy of al-Hajj Umar, before whom it was imperative to demonstrate one's superiority over the Muslim invader. The work sometimes moved at a very brisk pace as the colonizers, eager to establish the *pax gallica* with partners of their choice, had their own motives for collecting oral traditions (Amselle 1990: 240–41).

This context for the production of historical narratives covers all the areas included in this article, even though the Zarma narratives are the fruits of more recent collecting efforts. At present, it is impossible to demonstrate such distortions as Kathryn Green found in reference to "Mande-Kaba" (1991). One may of course dispute the analyses of the authors (Austen and Jansen 1996), but it is not impossible to observe a similar reflex on the local level.

The resurgence of traditions appears again following independence, as is seen by the massive volume of recordings after 1960, the date at which postcolonial states appeared in the region. The patriotic call for nation-building was articulated through music and local histories. Opportunities were also seized to provide a historical foundation for the rule of the presidents of the new states, along with their allies. Was it not said that Modibo Keita of Mali descended from Sunjata, that Hamani Diori of Niger was the heir of Zabarkane (Johnson

1986: 123, v. 824ff. n. 824, p. 203; Jones 1990: 90, and cf. especially bibliographic n. 47; Manthia Diawara 1992: 157)? And were not the officers of Diori's army, in overwhelming majority Zarma, also gratified by the same praise-songs?

The new states, equipped with national radio stations, along with secondary and postsecondary schools, went to work at producing a national history, often reinforced by the researchers of the former colonial power (e.g., the French scholars assigned to the different regional centers of the IFAN) along with other expatriates. Collection campaigns multiplied, the cultural heritage became fashionable, UNESCO and the Agence de Cooperation Culturelle et Technique participated. Politicians glorified the state, magnifying the history of their glorious ancestors, even at the risk of getting lost in their past and avoiding the burning responsibilities of the hour (Bagayoko 1987). The collecting programs also owed their energy to the technology that allowed recording on audio, and then videotape, and subsequent broadcast of the material.

Text, Context, and History

Of the fifty-eight presently extant accounts of Mali Bero, Daaman Gille, and Malik Si, we know the social context of production of thirty-eight, of which seven deal with Mali Bero, thirteen with Malik Si, and eighteen with Daaman Gille. Of that total, nineteen, that is the half, are derived from the official spokesmen of the aristocracies in power, from groups termed "jassere" in the Zarmataray, "*geseru/jaaru*" in Jaara, and "*gawlo*" in Bundu. In fact, one can increase that number beyond nineteen, for the private family oral traditions are influenced by those spread abroad by griots, and vice versa.

The Zarma jassere of Niger are of Soninke gesere origin, although according to Mounkaila (180) the Zarma do not claim any Soninke origin. Given this fact, it is hardly surprising that the geseru of the west, once they had emigrated to the Zarmataray, incorporate the Manden and Sunjata in their accounts. Moreover, the Zarma are not unknown to the Soninke, who call them the Janbaramanu (sing. Janbarama). Ivor Wilks deals with this question in passing in the course of his conversations with al-Hajj Siddiz b. Said (Fanta Sidiki, born in 1897), a savant of the gold-producing town of Obuase in Ghana. Al-Hajj Siddiz had preserved a book that he called a *silsila* and whose content he described to the researcher (1989: 59–60). A year later, in 1964, in the course of a follow-up interview, the savant gave this account of the origins of the Tarawiri Limamyiri, the family that filled the position of Imam of Wa (ibid.: 61):

> The name of our forefather (*jadd*) who sired seven sons was Jata. 1. The eldest of the sons was Musa who was called Jiki. . . . 4. Mali Biri. 5. Mali Kinana. . . . The descendants of Mali Biri and Mali Kinani, their descendants are in *Jabirima* (the *Zabarima* country). (My italics)

The terms "Jabirama," "Jabarima,"and "Mali Biri" are quite similar to "Janbarama" and "Mali Bero" (cf. also Streicker 1980: 104, cited in Hale 1990: 132).

In Jaara, the geseru and the *jaaru* (sing. *jaare*) *sodoga* are the official proprietors of the legend of Daama. The sodoga, who are lower than the geseru on the social scale, are intimately connected with the jeliw of the Manden, their ancestors, whose name they borrow. Indeed, the ancestor of the sodoga was formally linked with the jeliw of the Manden by marriage. Since that time their descendants maintain regular, reciprocal matrimonial ties. Thus one finds a pronounced Mande cultural influence on the output of the sodoga, which, as can be noticed, differs more and more from that of the geseru, their teachers in the art of narration. At some point in the past, the jaaru sodoga become full-fledged members of the court at Jaara. Until the end of the 1970s, the best specialist in the kingdom's history was a sodoga woman, descended through the maternal line from the famous Jabaté/Jabaxate family of Manden (Cissé 1988: 65, 67, 87). She passed this skill on to her son.

In Bundu, the professional bards are called *awlube* (sing. *gawlo*; see esp. N'Diaye 1971: 467; Curtin 1975: 202). The families with the patronymic of Curtin and Skinner's main source, N'Diaye, and the Si are "cousins," because they share the lion as a collective taboo (Curtin et al. 1971: 470). Moreover, we know that N'Diaye, Konde (name of Sunjata's mother), and Jara are equivalent patronymic, and those who bear them are also "cousins." We have every reason to suspect heavy influence in Bundu from Mande narratives such as the epic of Tira Makan Traoré and his conquest of the Jolof (Johnson 1988: 180, 215; Wright 1977, 1978; Belcher 1992) through the medium of the locally established Maninka and their allies. Similarly, the traditions about Bundu recorded around Nioro in Mali did not escape local influence, which might explain in part the relations between Malik Si and Daaman Gille that are underlined in certain versions.

Sunjata as Model
Sunjata: The General and His Challengers
       The traditionists of the Zarmataray and of Jaara all provide accounts in which Sunjata is identified both as a preeminent military leader and a person who must be challenged.

Let us begin with the documents about Jaara, since they deal with this relationship most explicitly (see table 6.1). According to the narratives, Daama, offspring of a jinn-father, was a hunter. Having given help (without exchange) to pilgrims, Daama is rewarded with an enchanted knife from Mecca by his guests. According to the oral traditions of the clients of the local aristocracy, when Daama was absent, the blade intended for him was given to Maxan Sonjata (Sunjata), the sovereign. As soon as he learned of the travelers' return, Daama left Sankaran for the Manden to claim his knife. According to some versions, the hero was also a geomancer and learned that the pilgrims had come back from divination. The sovereign ordered a slave to fetch a sword and two knives for Daama from the storeroom. The slave obeyed, and brought *haxala*, the blade on which the name of Daama was written. The sovereign sent the slave back to another weapons store, hoping to give Daama a different blade. Three times the slave tried different storerooms, but each time he brought the same blade.

Boyer's informant (1953: 24) even details the king's desperate attempts to retain the marvelous weapon. Convinced he could not keep the enchanted knife and desiring to keep his throne, the sovereign acknowledged that he possessed the weapon. But having heard of the qualities of the hunter Daama, he intended to make use of his services before handing the knife over. Employing Jugu, the leatherworker who had introduced Daama to the court, as an intermediary, the sovereign proposed to the hunter that he should attack the rebellious villages of Toxo and Haanu, who had defeated the elite troops of the Mande armies, composed of the renowned *Manden jon tan ni wòrò* or "the sixteen Mande clans" (Cissé et al. 1988: 226–29). Should he win, the sovereign promised Daama the knife and the hand of his own daughter, Soxona Suuxo. Daama accepted the proposal, overcame the villages in succession, and handed the booty over to Sunjata. Then the sovereign proposed to the leatherworker, "Either leave the country with your foreigner and his weapon, or give it to him and drive him off." In fact, the emperor gave Daama his daughter Soxona in marriage, and she bore three sons, of whom two were twins. But the sovereign, anxious about his guest's power, begged him to leave the Manden. Daama left, and never boasted of having shaken the throne of the most powerful sovereign of the period.

However explicitly Daama may have defied Sunjata, he also challenged him implicitly by serving as his "chief huntsman," supplying the court without immediate reward, and refusing any offers of payment. In the Soninke view of social status, such a relationship of receiving without giving anything in return places the emperor in a position of inferiority. This imbalance was corrected when Sunjata offered Daama his daughter in marriage.

Throughout the Zarma narratives one also finds the founding hero compelled to compete with the prestigious figure of Sunjata. The informant of text IV "specifically accuses Sunjata of having threatened the Zarma and of driving them out of Mallé" (Mounkaila 1988: 189). The speaker narrates the following to Dioulde Laya, cited by Mounkaila:

So he sent to Sombo partridge feathers, pottery shards, and charcoal. "What is this madman sending me?" asked Zarmakoye Sombo [Sombo-Mali-Bero]. "You know that one only finds partridge feathers on ancient sites, and that pottery shards and charcoal are the sign of former villages! Sunjata informs you that *if you don't emigrate, he will burn down your town, and partridges will scratch about in the ashes.*"(italics mine)

The similarity with a classic episode of the *Sunjata* narrative is obvious. The chronicler here repeats almost word for word the message from Sunjata to Prince Birama of Mema, who was going to refuse him ground in which to bury his mother (Johnson 1986: 166, 167, esp. ll. 2512–32; Cissé 1988: 1145–49). We have no irrefutable proof that the motif was borrowed from the Mande story. However, it is hardly risky to suggest that the narrator is evoking the atmosphere of the Manden before referring to its most glorious son. As Mounkaila suggests, "Having been banished from Mali, they [the Zarma] preferred to hold Sunjata responsible, rather than some coalition of unknown kinglets."

Whether in victory or in defeat, it is better to have met the best of adversaries; the masters of Malian and Nigerian tradition know this and make use of Sunjata, the man who founded one of the most celebrated of sub-Saharan African states.

Sunjata and Mali: The Political and Social Model

The accession of Malik Si to power in Bundu is prepared by the prophecies and dialogues of his encounter with the ruler of the Manden in Mecca. The text of Saki Olal N'Diaye is specific on this point: "He [Sunjata] made him [Malik] stay there for a long time, *and they did that which had to be done, and spoke the words that had to be spoken, and they took the steps which had to be taken*" (N'Diaye 1971: 474–75; my italics).

Sunjata is first concerned with the magical preparation of Malik, a neophyte in the management of men and power. That this preparation takes place in Mecca, seen as a center for Islamic and animist practices, only makes it more perfect. Thereafter, Sunjata enriches his protege with a supreme political gift: "Soundiata brought him *three men.* One of the men was called Tamba *Kante*, and he was a *blacksmith (bailo).* The second man was called Keri *Kafo*, and he was a *captive (maccudo).* The third man was called Layal, and he was a minstrel *(jareejo).* He was surnamed *Kouyate. . .*"(my italics).

Kante is the name of the blacksmiths descended from Sumanguru of Sosso, the unfortunate adversary of Sunjata; Kouyate is the patronymic of the first griot of the Manden, the very one who under the name Bala Faseke Kuyate, captivated Sumanguru with the tones of the magical *balafon* belonging to his admirer (Johnson 1986: 149–51; Cisse 1988: 165; Moraes Farias 1992). Although the Bundu narration takes place in a Fulbe world, in which the official clients of the aristocracy are the awlube (see above), Malik is given a bard of the jeliw Kuyate family, exactly as in Mali and against all expectations. Kafo, the slave's name, curiously echoes the names of the postimperial political units (*kafuw*) in the Manden. So it is hardly by accident that Sunjata offers his apprentice a *kafo*, symbol of Bundu, the polity founded and ruled by Malik Si. Further, the king of Mali endows Malik with the essential attributes of power: a blacksmith, the source of equipment for the warriors who found states and provide slaves, whether named Kafo or not. Those slaves constitute the economic foundation for the ruling class, while at the same time playing eminent and innumerable political roles throughout the region (Meillassoux 1986). Malik receives a further essential attribute, the griot: state archivist, irritant of the powerful, but above all else the person who provides the patron with the ideological foundation of authority, and thus an essential part of power (Sory Camara 1976; Bazin 1979; Meillassoux 1986; Mamadou Diawara 1990).

In the land of the Zarma, the claim on the Manden is less explicit but just as strong. The ancestor Zabarkane (or Mali Bero) comes from Mali on a flying granary (Mounkaila 1988: 29). No matter where one places this country, "Mallé" and the flying granary recur in four of the seven stories treated by Mounkaila (1988: 168). In text I, the speaker names the *Mallinke lemmey* (Malian fruit-offshoot), a term also used in Soninke territory to refer to the children of Mali (people of Malian origin). "Mali" represents a pivotal period that the author describes as follows: "Mallé constitutes the final stage in all the westward migrations of the Zarma, and the starting point for those heading eastward to the Zarmataray." One possibly important detail is that the son of Zabarkane, the Arab, who is named Zarmakoye Sombo and from whom the princes unanimously claim descent, also has a surname, Mali Bero, which explicitly recalls the state created by Sunjata (ibid: 91).

Later, Mounkaila writes (1988: 180), "In the conditions created by the texts, one might imagine Mallé fully in Soninke lands. . . . But nowhere do the Zarma claim to be Soninke in origin." Is this surprising, when we have already seen a similar phenomenon in Jaara and the topos is widespread not only within the Mande cultural sphere, but throughout the entire Niger bend (Terray 1988: 6; Amselle 1990: 126)? Daaman Gille, ancestor of the princes in a kingdom in the heart of a land populated by a majority of Soninke, is considered a "Mallinke," someone from the Manden. As proof, the speakers narrate his legend, which sends him wandering over thousands of kilometers, at the expense of any realism. The geseru name him "*Mallinko hanan hanan, Haayan gunbo nyogome Daama* " (People of Mali / first / first / of Haaya / male / camel / Daama = Daama, first of the Mallinko [princes], bull-camel of the forest of Haaya).

Like the Zarma aristocracy, the princes of Jaara consider themselves foreigners, people of the Manden called to rule over commoners (Soninke, Fulbe, and others). Their ancestry ensures them superiority over their subjects. Through some logic, "Mallinke" becomes a synonym for prince, emptied of its ethnic-cultural connotation (Diawara 1985: 264ff.; 1990: 83). It could well be that as a state situated within the area of influence of Mali, the rulers of Jaara enjoyed confusing themselves with their sovereign. Whatever the case, no ethnic claim coming from the princes of Jaara or from Zarmataray can serve as foundation for their predestination to power. The Zarma also may well have had Soninke or other origins, and still, like the people in Jaara, claim some attachment to Mali. A Malian origin enjoys the same value as an Arabian one; the essential point is that the proclaimed identity corresponds with the political landscape of the period. It is better for a prince of the Sahel to come from the

Manden at a time when the empire of Sunjata is at the height of its power, and to come from Mecca after Islam begins to exercise influence. Thus does one keep one's place among the powerful.

Sunjata: The Blesser, Master of Cults

Mali Bero, sometimes called Zarmakoye Sombo, eldest son of Zabarkane (Mounkaila 1988: 91), is also named Sombo-Mali-Bero (ibid.: 219). In the case of texts that constantly evoke Mali, it does not seem out of place to connect "Sombo" with "Simbon/Sinbon." This Maninka term serves as an honorific title for great hunters and has become one of Sunjata's praise-names.[5] The king of Mali was thus able to link himself with the masters of the bush: father and food-supplier, healer, geomancer, knower. His name becomes a synonym for that expertise. The term "simbon" also leads us through many versions to Bilal, companion of the Prophet, who sent his three sons (or grandsons, depending on the version), among them the first "Simbon," who is also the founder of Manden. Observing the Zarma tendency to attach themselves to the Middle East and to the Manden, it therefore seems quite likely that "Sombo" is a form of "Simbon."

This connection appears all the more believable since Sombo-Mali-Bero, "the most famous of the leaders of Zarma migrations out of Mallé" (Mounkaila 1988: 168), was a formidable specialist in occult lore, which he used to transport his people and their belongings from Mallé to the Zarmataray on a "flying granary." Only the Arabic-reading cleric, author of text V, attributes the mysterious take-off of this magical device to the intervention of a marabout.

Daaman Gille is also a great hunter. His skill and his valor get the better of the king of Mali, who tests him against hitherto unconquerable enemies. Like any master of the bush, he hunts the great game animals: buffalos, elephants, and hippotragues (a kind of antelope). Daama even manages, without any aid, to carry his kill to the local villagers thus becoming, in the course of his travels, a food-bringing father for a wide region, including the inhabitants of the site inhabited by Sunjata himself. Having pursued animals through lands as different as the Manden, Wanta, Segu, Faya, and especially Sankaran, land of the Buffalo of Do and the mother of Sunjata, Daama reveals himself to be a hunter without peer. Is he not named, in his Maninka-language praise-song, "*donsolu benba*" (the father of hunters)? Like the master hunters of those lands, Daama is also a redoubtable healer. Early in his relations with the court of Jaara, he manages the cure of a prince or a princess (depending on versions). He is also a geomancer, since it is thanks to this knowledge that he becomes aware of Sunjata's attempt to cheat him of his Meccan knife (Diawara 1985: 277;

---

[5] John Johnson (1986: 185, n. 32) translates "Sinbon" literally as "lion-born-of-the-cat"; see also Cissé 1988: 2, 43, 77, 101, 386, 402; 1990; Niane 1965: 86, n. 5, cited in Johnson 1986; Innes 1974: 154, n. 106.

Daraame, BB 1979: CII 3m. 6, 12, 54).[6]

In his peaceful confrontation with Sunjata, Daama manages to escape through the use of occult knowledge, as is always the case in encounters between hunters. However, this complete mastery of secrets and forces of the bush does not exclude a certain ascendancy of Sunjata over the heros of Zarmataray and Jaara, to say nothing of Bundu, where no such claim is even made.

Saki Olal N'Diaye, the informant for Skinner and Curtin, tells us that Malik Si, the hero of Bundu, encounters Sunjata at the Kaaba in Mecca as a combined sage and visionary. Sunjata recognizes Malik Si's exceptional qualities despite the fact that the latter ruled from 1690–1707, i.e., more than three centuries after Sunjata's death (N'Diaye 1971: 471, n.b.; Curtin 1975: 189, 200; 1974: annex 8, in 1975: 200, n. 12).

The sovereign of Mali bestowed upon the pilgrim a basket named Dantuma, which contained a marvelous object, the *Sige Jinne Jolof* (literally, the feather of the jinn of the Jolof), a small box made of wood previously used in a funeral bier. This charm allowed Malik Si, once back in his own land, to break the flow of a river and enable his companions to cross without getting wet (Curtin 1975: 197, 198). The charm was also decisive in the conquest of Bundu. Some (eleven versions, cf. Curtin 1975: 191) state that Malik gained victory without striking a blow, after helping his adversaries finish digging a well that they had not been able to complete (N'Diaye 1971: 191). For this purpose, he used a small copper tablet that Allah had given him; he dropped the tablet into the well, which guaranteed him the power to reach the water source at last (Curtin 1975: 195–97). Others claim that his victory followed an armed struggle; indeed, according to one account of the words uttered by Malik Si as he lay headless before his final set of adversaries, "power is born from a drop of blood" (Curtin 1975: 191).

None of the heroes really succeeds without the blessing of Sunjata. Even Daaman Gille, who actually challenges Sunjata, is no less a beneficiary of the Mande sovereign's magical power. By marrying Sunjata's daughter, Daama implicitly but automatically obtains the former's blessing. One cannot offer one's daughter to a man and curse him at the same time. Moreover, by going off to fight for the great mansa, Daama likewise appears to enjoy his psychological and magical support. The accounts, as though establishing the warrior's destiny, are quite clear on this point: Sunjata must have observed in Daama the qualities of statesman, and this is why he sends him out of the land.

To these accounts, which rely upon direct examples and in which we discern a mixture of pre-Islamic beliefs with some elements of Islam, we may add others that link their native Sahelian zone with the Middle East, reflecting contacts that go back for more than a millennium.

---

[6] CII indicates the number of the field-recorded cassette; 3 is the number of the research mission (m.); the other numbers refer to the page of the transcript.

The Connection to the Middle East
A Common Cult of the Model Ancestor
       The variously spun ties to Sunjata are rarely direct. The only exception
is a Zarmataray text (number VI, from an unidentified informant) that makes
Sunjata a close relative of Mali Bero.
       In other accounts the link is more sophisticated, and the hero becomes a
de facto ally of Sunjata through a common relationship with a third party. The
most frequent case is a figure called Tanimunari by Fa-Digi Sisòko, the source
of Johnson's *Son-Jara* (1986: 132). According to Fa-Digi it is Tanimunari,
Sunjata's "Muslim jinn" who takes the young hero (still crippled at this time) to
Mecca. It is Tanimunari who also claims that God has revealed to him:

> When the month of Domba is ten days old,
> Son-jara will rise and walk. (135)

       This jinn is oddly similar to another among the Zarma named Tamimun
Dâri, mentioned by the author of text V, dealing with Zabarkane, the Zarma
ancestor. The marabout-informant for this account begins:

> We the Zarma are of Arab origin.
> . . . yes , the Yemenites gave birth to the Tamimun.
> And so Tamimun Dâri came from our group.
> Tamimun was a companion, a companion of the Prophet.
> Tamimun begot Zarah
> Zarah begot Zabarkane
> Zabarkane begot Zeinabou, who was the cause of his departure from
> Medina. . . . (Mounkaila 1988: 139)

       According to this source the patronymic of Tamimun Dâri is the root
for the Zarma term "Tamima," which refers to the "good servants of Allah."
Mounkaila (1988: 205) quite rightly, wonders whether one should not identify
this character with his homonym from the popularizing texts of Islam, a figure
known for his piety despite "the adventures he gets into because of the pagan
jinn Ifrutu."[7]
       Three narratives dealing with Daaman Gille provide a similar name. A
collation of the various traditions shows a Tamimu Daari at the center of the
genealogy of the Zarma, of the Jaara royal princes, and in the career of the
young Sunjata. While no speaker dares to establish a direct kinship relation on
the basis of this character, it is clear that Tamimu Daari provides a formal link
between the three men. Sunjata's guardian spirit, who is claimed by everyone,

---

[7] See also a reference in a Nigerian text to the same figure (Labarin Tamimuddâri, in
Mounkaila 1988: 205, n. 89), which suggests a wider range for the story.

becomes the father, the grandfather, or preferably an ancestor.

We also find, in examining the family trees of Sunjata and Daama, another common forefather: Julxarnayini. According to the account edited by Johnson (1986: 188, n. 164) this figure, who is none other than Alexander the Great, was an ancestor of Sunjata. The oral sources emphasize both the military prowess and the wealth of Alexander, "The Man with Two Horns" (Dhu al-Qarnayn in Arabic).

Boyer (1953: 22) collected the same type of oral text for Jaara. This genealogical reference, like a bravura piece, can be found in several versions of the legend of Sunjata (Niane 1960: 21; Diabaté 1970: 34; Cissé ed. 1976). One might object here that Middle Eastern origins can be established by traditionists independently of Sunjata, which is true. The point is not this evidence, but that the link with the Middle East is not exclusive of the link with the Malian ruler.

Son of the Primordial Man

Fa-Digi Sisòkò's version of the legend of *Sunjata* brings Adam and God on stage, and God asks what he may offer Adam in life. God had already granted beauty and moral integrity to Jinns and Angels, respectively. So Adam says, "I will accept what you give me." God grants him dignity. Thereafter, God removed Adam from Paradise and placed him in Hindi (India), "The land where the sun rises; the land where the moon rises" (Johnson 1986: 103). Johnson suggests that India might simply mean the East (1986: 187, n. 130). In the same narrative, Bilal, companion of the Prophet, fathers a son named Mamadu Kanu, who in turn fathers three others: Kanu Simbon, Kanu Nyògòn Simbon, and Lawali Simbon. The two first sons settle in Wagadu, which they then leave for Jara (Jaara), and then move on to found a hamlet named Kiri-Kòròni, the first village of the Manden.

All accounts of Sunjata mention this Middle Eastern Arab, or even Meccan, origin. We find the same thing with traditions about Daaman Gille, Zabarkane, and Mali-Bero. As for Malik Si, while he was born in Suyuuma, near Podor in the Fuuta Tooro (Curtin 1975: 190), the traditionists devote more effort to narrating his life in Mecca with Sunjata than to anything before this period. We also find an insistence upon a Middle Eastern or Arabic or Meccan phase in the narratives dealing with:

a. The clients of the descendants of the heroes in question, be they called "gesere," "jeli/ jaare," "gawlo," "jassere," "griots," "men of the mouth," (Diawara 1990) or people of the word (Camara 1976); Fa-Digi Sisòkò of Mali and Badié Bagna of Niger, informants for generations of Africanists, are quite representative in this regard.

b. Family savants relating the past of their own group or that of others.

c. Men of letters (in Arabic or French), or people who speak at least one of those languages, distilling a variety of information ranging from the life of the Prophet, from colonial administration, and from local history; Samany Sy of Bakel (in Senegal), a war-veteran (Curtin 1975) informant of many researchers, may well represent this type; these are intellectuals, authentic ideologues, or the theoreticians of power (Amselle 1990: 125, 1127; Moraes Farias 1992a) in the communities for which they serve as spokesmen.

Following Fa-Digi Sisòkò's narrative (Johnson 1986: 103), mankind comes from the East; this idea pervades many of our texts, including those dealing with Daaman Gille, Zabarkane, and Mali-Bero, as well as the legend of Wagadu (Monteil 1953; Dieterlen and Sylla1992).

The Predestined Heroes

Malik Si is a vivid example of the predestined hero holding his power from two sources: Allah and Sunjata. After he completes his pilgrimage to Mecca, "*God gave* him the kingship. But he also *showed him* that the country he was to rule over was the country called Bundu" (N'Diaye 1971: 473; my italics). Only later, according to Saki Olal N'Diaye, when Malik sets off for the Kaaba does he meet a man named Sunjata. The chronicler does not explain how one may accomplish the Muslim pilgrimage before even reaching the Kaaba.[8] But we must take it for granted that the hero's wishes and those of the narrator are fulfilled, once Malik is endowed with the sign of royalty by Allah, and that is the essential point of the story. His predestination is reinforced by Sunjata's recognition in him of the signs of power (cf. above).

The fourteenth of the texts studied by Curtin, produced in the court of Sada A. Sy, *chef de canton* of Bundu from 1918 to 1954 (1971: 202), states that the hero received a copper tablet from Allah, which he used as a support for writing, unlike the other ordinary marabouts, who were content with a piece of wood. The savants using this form of instrument constituted a minority of fearsome ability,[9] which is underlined here by the point that the gift comes directly from Allah.

Here our hero is destined to reign, and more; he is equipped to perform miracles worthy of his stature. Curtin sees the pilgrimage episode as a late addition, especially since it is not found in the versions collected before 1950, and justifiably supposes that the composition of this sequence is probably due to the pilgrimage of the hero's famous namesake, a leader of the Tijaniya sect of eastern Senegal and descendant of another branch of the Si family from the central Fuuta Tooro (Skinner and Curtin 1971: 471 n.b.). Nor should one omit to

---

[8] Trans. note: There may be some confusion here with the Malian town of Kangaba, which in some pronunciations becomes Kaaba.

[9] This belief is widespread in the Sahel. Among the Soninke, the tablet is called *kiri walaha*, in opposition to the wooden version termed *walaha*, used by students as well as humble marabouts.

mention the intensified Islamization of Senegal during this period. But such factors emphasize, rather than reduce, the influence of Mecca and the Middle East.

Malik Si may well be predestined, but so also is his entire dynasty. On his return from Mecca, while crossing the Senegal river, he prophesied: "Bismillahi Almamy from Malik to Malik," meaning that his descendants, the Sisibe, would rule as Almamy of the Bundu from Malik Dauda to Malik Hammady Sy (who died in 1905; cf. Skinner and Curtin 1971: 475, note c). Predestination is also a dominant theme in the legend of Daama Gille, punctuated by the following observation: "If Allah Has Intended You for Something, You Cannot Avoid It."

The magical character of Daama's knife or sword is noted even in several portions of the Malik Si narrative collected in the Fuuta Tooro, which note that whoever saw it was destined to reign (Curtin 1975: 198). We may recall the surprising scene from the Jaara tradition in which the knife repeatedly puts itself into the hands of the servants Sunjata sends to fetch a substitute weapon. Moreover, according to a version collected by Delafosse (1913: 302), Daama asked the pilgrims to request a hunting knife from the Sharif of Mecca. The version recorded by G. Boyer (1953: 24) specifies that the pilgrims, forgetting to transmit the message, were reminded by the Sharif himself, who then gave them the weapon that would become the scepter for the dynasty founded by Daama.

The hero, some say, accepted the weapon only after a marabout had read the inscription etched on the blade: "Wo lawolina Daama, wo laxirina Daama / the first owner [of the weapon will be named] Daama, the last owner [will be named] Daama" (Diawara 1985: I 273, n. 1). So the knife, which serves as a symbol of power, comes from the grand Sharif of Mecca, and again, as with the story of Malik Si, the narrators wait until the end of the dynasty to observe the coincidence of the surnames of the first and last sovereign and thus to seal the destiny of the weapon or the writing tablet.

As Curtin notes (1971: 475, note c), this phenomenon is widespread not only within Sudanese oral tradition, but also in the Bible. The narrators know the Quran, or have heard parts from marabouts. Thus, after a thousand years of coexistence with Islam and religious observance (however loose), the similarities are hardly surprising (cf. Amselle 1990). Indeed, we find the same things told by the storytellers and poets who celebrate the Prophet Muhammad, such as Dirini, the thirteenth-century Egyptian mystic who wrote:

> Mohammed said: "The first light created by Allah is my light. It is said that when Allah created his divine throne, he *wrote upon it with letters of light*: there is no God but God and Mohammed is the Messenger of God." (Rodinson 1961: 343; my italics)

One crucial aspect in the exceptional destiny of Daama is a similarity with the parentage of Sunjata, who was born of the relations between a human, the king of the Manden Fatama Magan the Handsome and a buffalo-woman, Sugulun Konde (Johnson 1986: 129, 115; Cissé 1988: 57ff.). Sunjata is thus an exemplary *over-conceived* character (Smith 1979: 338). In Jaara, we are dealing with a mortal woman, Siga-Xeero, and a father who is a jinn, which allows Daama control both in this world and in the invisible one. Such a birth is believed to guarantee the origin of political power, which rests not only on physical prowess but particularly upon a control of strange and occult forces (Amselle 1979, 1990: 154; Johnson 1986: 42; Bagayoko 1987).

Thus we see Sunjata, gifted through the spirits of Do, his mother's land, those of the Manden, his father's land, and last but not least by a Muslim jinn, Tanimunari, who leads him to Mecca and imparts to him the date on which he will at last walk. Such a "mixed ancestry" (Terray 1988: 5–6) allows him not to be a foreigner. At the same time, it allows the hero to keep a certain distance from his subjects and to rule by right of his very nature. Terray, speaking of the heroes of the Niger bend, emphasizes that they are descended from parents of different nations. Again, there is a strong temptation to make comparisons with the life of the Prophet. In the words of another thirteenth-century Egyptian source, the pious Berber poet Bushiri:

> Mohammed is the Lord of the *two worlds,* the *two races* [men and jinns]
> Of the *two nations*, the *Arabs* and the *foreigners*. . . . (Rodinson 1961: 342; my italics)

It is possible, without necessarily implying a Middle Eastern or particularly Arabic origin for the West African narratives, to establish such parallels, especially since the cultures involved have been in contact with the Middle East for over a thousand years.

The Pilgrimage and the Pilgrims
    A pilgrimage to Mecca is a constant element in the tales about these heroes (see table 6.1). Zabarkane, the father of the Zarma leader Mali-Bero, is said to have lived at the time of the Prophet (Mounkaila 1988: text II, 91ff.); he emigrated from Medina, says the teller of text V (ibid: 141), which makes him a contemporary of the Prophet. In the course of text III, the informant recounts an animated discussion between Zabarkane, the Prophet (to whom he had come to make his submission), and others of the faithful (ibid: 107). This places Mecca, Medina—Arabia, in short—at the heart of the story.

As for Malik Si, he trod the soil of the holy places of Islam, and it is there that he met Sunjata. The latter, according to Fa-Digi Sisòkò, came to Mecca as a child in the company of Tanimunari, his Muslim jinn (Johnson 1986: 132).

However, Daama did not travel to Mecca, as the Bundu version claims for Sunjata (cf. above, "The Predestined Heroes"). But his fate is bound up with pilgrims who, departing for Mecca, were welcomed by the hero in his hunting-camp. The travelers unfortunately forgot their supply of gold in the camp. According to some informants, the hunter immediately caught up with them to return their property; according to others, the travelers sent one of their number to claim the property. The guests, touched by the honesty and the generosity of the hero, asked him what he wanted as a gift from the holy city; he was content, it is said, to ask for a hunting knife.

The identity of Damaan's pilgrims varies considerably depending on its source in the oral traditions of the clients of the aristocracy of Jaara, represented by M. Daraame and B. B. Daraame, or in the aristocratic traditions culled from B. Jawara or N'Ba Moodi Jawara. The names given are, respectively, as follow: Kankan Musa, Alafayi Jigi Musa, Alafayi Hasiliman Banna, and Alimaami Maaliki Si; Alafayi Musa, Jigi Musa, and Kankan Musa; Sunjata; and finally Sora Musa, also called Alafayi Musa Jigi. We shall not go into detail on this issue here (cf. Diawara 1985). However, some names are quite revealing. Kankan Musa is of course Kanku (or Mansa) Musa, the famous sovereign who made the costly trip in the fourteenth century. It is hardly surprising that intellectuals, informed of writings on the subject, should make use of the name of this pilgrim. N'Ba Moodi settles the question of the many given names of Alafayi Jigi Musa, called Alafayi Musa Jigi, Sora Musa, Alafayi Musa, or Jigi Musa. According to N'Ba, these names all refer to the same person. Alafayi is a variant on the title "al-Hajj," given to pilgrims on their return home from Mecca; it can mean "foreigner" with reference to their status during their stay in Arabia. The stimulating article of Moraes Farias (1989) casts light on Musa, a multifaceted character. M. Daraame includes Malik Si among the travelers. This is hardly surprising, since numerous miracles are attributed to his personage, including some performed in Jaara (Curtin 1975: 192, 198). There is no need to introduce Sunjata, except to say that he was, like the other characters, an intermediary between Daama and the Meccan authorities (in this case, the great Sharif) for the acquisition of power. In all cases, the pilgrimage or direct contact with the travelers to the Holy Places is a necessary step for the heroes on their path to the throne.

The Network of Statesmen

Slowly but surely, these different narratives weave together a network of statesmen who come together, plausibly or not, whether this is stated directly by the tellers or left to be understood.

Sunjata and the Others

Thus Sunjata, whom historians place in the thirteenth century, becomes the contemporary of Malik Si, the seventeenth-century ruler of Bundu (1690–1707). Daama, who lived toward the end of the fifteenth or the beginning of the sixteenth century (Diawara 1990), also meets Sunjata. Mali-Bero, expelled de facto from the Manden by Sunjata, at least belongs to the thirteenth century.

However, the chronology that Mounkaila establishes to argue the contemporaneity of the two heroes, perhaps to support the content of the oral traditions (that she elsewhere criticizes), is highly doubtful. According to one of the proposed time-schemes, we would date Sombo and the migration from the Manden to 1280 (Mounkaila 1988: 221). More interesting is the establishment of a network of leaders who all claim a mutual link, against any considerations of chronology.

Daama, His Successors, and Malik Si

Six texts from Curtin's sample, as well as traditions collected in the central province of the kingdom of Jaara, the Kingi (see especially Boyer 1953), claim that Malik spent time in Jaara. The marabout was called on to treat the sterile wife of the ruler of Jaara. According to the texts of Bundu, the marvelous scepter of Jaara conferred royalty on any person who saw it. Having healed his patient, who bore a boy, Malik was shown the flash of the blade by the delighted ruler. But the king, aware of the seriousness of the action, lost no time in driving away the now-dangerous guest to rule elsewhere (Curtin 1975: 198). The people of Bundu thus locate the origin of their power in Jaara. As Curtin observes, this fragment of the legend of Malik looks like a borrowing from the Jaara tradition (ibid.: 199); but the important point is that it exists and that it legitimates the power of Malik and his family through Jaara (cf. above, "A Common Cult of the Model Ancestor").

In a strange, echoing effect of the two traditions, the Bundu narrators ascribe Malik's power to his having seen the blade of the enchanted scepter of the Jaara dynasty, while the chroniclers of Jaara (see above) place Malik among the holymen who originally brought the weapon from Mecca.

Tamimu Daari, Sunjata, Daama, and Mali-Bero

No informant derives the relations of his hero with Sunjata from the common relation all three have with Tamimu Daari. Each includes the Arab for quite practical reasons: the direct legitimization of power. The characters develop in isolation from one another; the only virtual, but unrecognized link, is Tamimu Daari, which seems quite odd in a region in which the slenderest thread of kinship is carefully cultivated. Through Sunjata, we find the assembly of heroes: himself, Daama, Mali-Bero, and Malik Si; Tamimu, however, links the first three. And so Sunjata remains the great Connector, despite the Middle Eastern claims of the others.

Sunjata and Tamimu Daari therefore belong to the pantheon of "political ancestors" invoked principally for establishing a charter of rule. At issue is more the intent to establish a claim to power, "born of a drop of blood," than to compose a chronicle of the past (Amselle 1990: 126, 127). This is how certain stories, like bravura pieces without obvious links, should be seen; their function is to remove impurities from the blood and to replace them with more acceptable bases of authority.

"To Be Means to Come From, and Most Particularly to Be Descended From"

The strong tendency among Fulbe, Maninka, Soninke, or Zarma historians to invent such prestigious origins grows out of a belief founded upon their very conception of power: to be, one must already have been (Braudel 1985). To achieve this, one must break with ordinary mortals, and this occurs principally through one's ancestry. Therefore, as the Zarma proverb says, "To be means to come from, and most particularly to be descended from" (Mounkaila 1988: 203). When one reaches the sovereign, or the personality most visible to local theoreticians of power, one stays with him. Thus, the people of Bundu, of Jaara, of Mali, and of Zarmataray settle on the best source: Sunjata Keita.

What is there upstream from there? Who, beyond Sunjata, can be evoked as a source of legitimacy by these people of the word, these ideologues of power? If we lay out the products of the clients of the aristocracy (jaaru/ jeliw, awlube, geseru, jassere, commonly termed "griots"), we see the Middle Eastern origin emphasized.

My hypothesis is as follows: oral traditions, which may sometimes be transcribed in Arabic,[10] and in which magic and myth dispute the field with history, all derive from local religious beliefs. When the power upheld by such narrative encounters another religion, when the people who create the narratives come into contact with Islamic traditions, then a greater challenge appears that becomes ever more pressing as people convert to the new religion. Foreign Muslims, then local converts, and finally even indigenous marabouts appear on the scene. Those in power must find a way to dominate these Muslim groups. Sufficient material is available for the purpose in the texts spread among the neophytes; sometimes the latter are prepared to abandon their pre-Islamic beliefs. The newcomers, armed with Islamic (and thus Middle Eastern) texts, sometimes themselves of pre-Islamic inspiration, provide the aristocrats and their agents who specialize in the production of history/ideology with the means for updating their past. Ingenuity helps to integrate the new elements, as has always happened in the case of contact with foreign cultures—in this case, Islam, which has been present for over ten centuries in certain regions of the Sahel.

Thereafter, one finds subjects who have become marabouts or even Sharifs (descendants of the Prophet, named the Hayidara) who, because they know the Quran, are believed blessed and able to bless. They specialize in various propitiatory rites and in the healing of ills (see the holy marabout Malik Si). This used to be the domain of a variety of healers, miracle-workers, hunters, geomancers—specialists, who had a place in the current social system and thus came more or less under the chief's control. Sometimes, the political ruler was in the same social category as the experts, and his family maintained a relationship

---

[10] See the case of Mamadi Aïssé Diakité of Nioro (above and Bulman, infra); see also the studies on the *ajami*, works in local languages written in Arabic letters.

with theirs. Once outside sources of powers begin to compete with established authority, however, the latter seeks to domesticate them by assuming an effective ancestry. At the same time, the specialists of old update themselves and take from the new knowledge what they need. A typical case is that of the folkloric pilgrim, Makan Ta Jigi, or Alafayi Jigi Musa, although some will deny any contact between the two belief systems even here.

The more the Muslim savants negotiate the transition by hybridizing their practices, the more the hereditary power holders get to work to avoid being left behind and losing control of the new converts. Thus one can explain how and why the aristocracies—Soninke in Wagadu, Maninka in Mali, Halpulaar in Bundu, Zarma in the Zarmataray—discover their Middle Eastern ancestors. There is a constant coming and going between Islam and its symbols and the indigenous religion, as a reflection of a real bridge between the two. Very few people pass from their ancestral religion to Islam without holding onto a private stock of belief.[11] Only thus can one understand that people such as Daaman Gille are considered by the chroniclers to be apostates and not perfect animists (Moraes Farias 1989; Amselle 1990: 181ff.).

Far from being borrowings in which a traditionist in awestruck admiration assimilates foreign ancestors, these are deliberate and reflected actions, the source of new power for the dominant class and others in power, for the chiefs are not the only ones in the lists.[12] Marabouts also have a place in the arena. While they are busy drawing up new genealogies reflecting their status of apostate to their pre-Islamic faith and neophytes in Islam, they also join the service of the court and the military aristocracy, for whom they are perfectly ready to compose texts via an intermediate griot (Diawara 1990). A sort of competition arises between the traditionists who specialize in oral narratives and the marabouts who control written accounts. It would appear that the first, fearing dispossession from their function and their raison d'être, seize on elements produced by the latter; thus, Islamic and Middle Eastern narratives slip into the indigenous oral heritage. This happens all the faster because everyone, Muslims and others, turn to the oral transmission of knowledge, and one often finds borrowings that show a surprising knowledge of Quranic literature.

The Necessity for Mutual Recognition
        The practice of trade by foreign agents as well as by apostate marabout traders creates new relations within the society and also between the sovereigns and the traders. Reinforcement of these new relations requires mutual

---

[11] Note that Malik Si, the holyman, is considered by his family to have been initiated by Sunjata; on hybridizing (*métissant* in the original) see the stimulating work of Jean-Loup Amselle, *Logiques métisses* (1990).

[12] This is why Mounkaila's analysis of the presence of Muslim elements in the Zarma texts seems to me insufficient.

recognition by the parties involved. Hence the need for local marabouts to proclaim themselves members of the *umma* and for the locals, in particular those associated with the court, to prove themselves worthy partners. For these, the royal way is to claim an origin that links them with their new partners. Thanks to the two social categories that develop the same type of arguments, the locals seem to be saying to the foreigners, "Behold! Our history/origin is not as strange as all that." This seems all the truer because Mecca itself, according to the Quran, was once a non-Muslim sanctuary, and even in Arabia the Prophet coexists with the jinn—and therefore why not the hunter, be he named Sunjata or Makan Ta Jigi (Moraes Farias 1989)?

Strengthened by this implicit argument, the spokesmen of the Sahel endow themselves with the most redoubtable ancestors; Sunjata becomes the living symbol for a number of states and traditions created by their agents. All that is left is to integrate them with local legends and history to provide permanent self-justification!

These stories, derived from very evident Sahelian sources, are grafted on to other narratives that have the apparent aim of further exalting the power of their heroes. This is true for Wagadu, for Mali, and for Jaara. One can find the same tendency in the old store of legends drawn upon by the early Muslim men of letters in Arabia, whom Maxime Rodinson (1961) describes as follows:

> It [this heritage] comes from the legendary treasure-trove of the Christian Middle East, through the medium of Syriac literature. . . . Thus the legend of Moses . . . in which one finds echoes of the old Sumero-Akkadian epic of Gilgamesh, poured again into the Hellenistic Romance of Alexander. Then again, the story of this same Alexander, under the name Dhu al-Qarnayn, the two-horned (since his "father," Jupiter Ammon, had two horns), who built a wall at the far ends of the world to prevent over-running by the fabulous folk of Gog and Magog.
> . . .

From Dhu al-Qarnayn, which the Soninke pronounce Julxaranayini and the Malinke render in the form Julu Kara Nayini (Johnson 1988: 188, n. 164; Moraes Farias 1989: 158), the peoples of the Sahel have retained an image of power, wealth, and Arab identity. None of these groups openly claim a Judeo-Christian origin, although given such borrowings elsewhere on the continent, this might have occurred if the appropriate traditions had been better known in the Sahel.[13] The same holds true for the allusions to the Middle East in the widest sense of the term. It will be interesting to see the fruits of future

---

[13] I am not disregarding the Biblical echoes in the legend of Wagadu (Monteil 1953), but they are hardly as explicit as in other cultural zones. See the work on this topic by Chrétien 1981, 1986, 1993; Henige 1982. Adam Jones (1990: 85) speaks of the borrowing of "foreign historical models" (*die fremden Geschichtsmodelle*).

collecting, for it is quite possible that new elements are already being added to these essentially mutable compositions.

The intrusion of Alexander the Great into the legends of *Sunjata* and Daama seems equal to that of Malik Si in the chronicle of Daama. The irruption of the Prophet Muhammad into the story of Zabarkane is the structural equivalent of Sunjata's appearance in the accounts dealing with Zabarkane, Daama, and Malik. One can hardly analyze the problem purely in terms of the borrowings by a more recent civilization from an older one. We cannot see this as a question of simple diffusion from thirteeth-century Mali, from eighth- to eleventh-century Wagadu, or from whatever Middle East it may be; otherwise, how can we understand the statement recorded in 1898 by Charles Monteil on the subject of the empire of Ghana or Wagadu: "They say that the Sise of Mali go back to Dyabe in a curious way: Dyabe [who lived prior to the eighth century, according to historians] apparently sent the king of Mali, Sun Dyata, as a sign of neighborliness, a woman he had made pregnant. . . ."

Bibliography

Ardouin, Claude Daniel. 1988. "Une formation politique précoloniale du Sahel occidental malien: le Baakhunu à l'époque des Kaagoro." *Cahiers d'Etudes Africaines* XXVIII: 3–4, 111–112: 443–61.

Bagayoko, Shaka. 1987. "L'Etat au Mali: représentation, autonomie et mode de fonctionnement." In *L'Etat contemporain en Afrique*, ed. Terray Emmanuel, 91–122. Paris.

Baghaga, Moussa. 1977. *La légende de Daaman Guille*. Bamako: Mémoire ENSup.

Bathily and Meillassoux. 1975. *Lexique soninké (sarakolé) -français*. Dakar: Centre de linguistique appliquée de Dakar.

el-Bekri, Abou Obied. 1965. *Description de l'Afrique septentrionale*. MacGuckin de Slane, trans. Paris.

Belcher, Steven. 1992. "Sinimogo—The Man for Tomorrow." In *"Sunjata* Epic Conference," November 13–15, Institute for the Advanced Study and Research in the African Humanities, Northwestern University. Transcript at Northwestern University Library.

Blanc, E. 1924a. "Contribution a l'étude des populations et de l'histoire du Sahel Soudanais." *Bulletin du Comité d'Etudes Historique et Scientifiqus de l'Afrique Occidentale Française (BCEHSAOF)*: 259–316.

—. 1924b. "Notes sur les Diawara." *Bulletin du Comité d'Etudes Historiques et Scientifiques de l'Afrique Occidentale Française (BCEHSAOF)*: 86–99.

Boyer, Gaston. 1973. *Un peuple de l'ouest soudanais: les Diawara*. Dakar: IFAN.

Braudel, Fernand, ed. 1985. *La Méditerrannée: l'espace et l'histoire.* Paris: Flammarion.

Bulman, Stephen P. D. 1992. "An Examination of the Role of the Literary Mediator in the Dessemination of the Sunjata Epic." In *"Sunjata* Epic Conference," November 13–15, Institute for the Advanced Study and Research in the African Humanities, Northwestern University. Transcript at Northwestern University Library.

Chrétien, Jean–Pierre. 1981. "Du hirsute au Hamite: les variations du cycle de N'Tare Ruhatsi, fondateur du royaume du Burundi." *History in Africa* 8: 3–41.

—. 1985. "L'empire des Bacwesi: la construction d'un imaginaire géopolitique." *Annales* 41: 1335–377.

—. 1986. "Confronting the Unequal Exchange of the Oral and the Written." In *African Historiographies: What History for Which Africa?*, eds. Bogumil Jewsiewicki and David Newbury. New York: Sage.

—. 1993. *Burundi. L'histoire retrouvée. 25 ans de métier d'historien.* Paris: Karthala.

Conrad, David C., and Humphrey Fisher. 1982.

Curtin, Philip, D. 1971. "Jihad in West Africa: Early Phases and Inter-Relations in Mauritania and Senegal." *Journal of African History* XII, I: 11–24.

—. 1975. "The Use of Oral tradition in Senegambia: Malik Sii and the Foundation of Bundu." *Cahiers d'Etudes Africaines* 58, XV–2: 189–202.

Danthioko, Oudiary Makan. N.d. *La légende des Nyaxate recueillie et transcrite par Oudiary Makan Dantioko.* Manuscript.

—. 1985. *Soninkara Tarixu. Récits Soninké.* Niamey.

Daraame. 1979. Cassette no. II, 3m.

Diawara. 1976. Cassette.

Diawara. 1978. Cassette.

Diawara. 1980. Cassette.

Diawara. 1982. Cassette.

Diawara, Mamadou. 1985. *La dimension sociale et politique des traditions orales du royaume de Jaara (Mali) du XVe au milieu du XVIe siècle.* Two vols. Thèse de doctorat de 3e cycle, EHESS. Paris.

Dieterlen, Germaine, and Diarra Sylla. 1992. "L'Empire de Ghana. Le Wagadu et les traditions de Yéréré." Paris.

Henige, David H. 1975. "The Problem of Feedback in Oral Tradition: Four Examples from the Fante Coastlands." *Journal of African History* XIV: 223–235.

—. 1982. "Truths yet unborn? Oral Traditions as a Casualty of Culture Contact." *Journal of African History* XXIII: 395–412.

Jones, Adam. 1990. "Kolonialherrschaft und Geschichtsbewußtsein. Zur Rekonstruktion der Vergangenheit in Schwarzafrika 1865–1965." *Historische Zeitschrift* 250: 73–92.

Luciani, J. 1952. "Etude sur le canton Kaarta Soninké." Nioro n, serie 1D7, Archives Nationale du Mali, Bamako.

Meillassoux, Claude. 1986. *Anthropologie de l'esclavage. Le ventre de fer et d'argent.* Paris: Presses universitaires de France.

Moraes Farias, Paulo Fernando de. 1991. "Praise as a Foreign Language: The Gɛsɛrɛ of Borgu" In *Conference on Power, Marginality and Literature in Africa*, London, SOAS, January 17–19.

—. 1992. "Praise as Intrusion and as Foreign Language: A Sunjata Paradigm Seen from the Gesere Diaspora in Béninois Borgu." In *"Sunjata* Epic Conference," November 13–15, Institute for the Advanced Study and Research in the African Humanities, Northwestern University. Transcript at Northwestern University Library.

N'Diaye, Saki Olal. 1971. "The Story of Malik Sy." A. Neil Skinner and Philip D. Curtin, eds. and trans., with the assistance of Hammady Amadou Sy. *Cahiers d'Etudes africaines* 43, XI: 467–87.

Niane, Djibril Tamsir. "Mythes, légendes et sources orales." *Recherches Africaines* 1, 4: 36–42.

Olivier de Sardan, Jean-Pierre. 1984. *Les sociétés songhay-zarma (Niger-Mali).* Paris: Karthala.

Piault, Marc Henry. 1982. "Le héros et son destin. Essai d'interprétation des traditions relatant la genèse d'un Etat du Soudan Central, le Kabi, au XVIe siècle." *Cahiers d'Etudes Africaines* 87–88, XXII, 3–4: 403–40.

Rodinson, Maxime. 1961. *Mahomet.* Paris: Editions du Seuil.

Rouch, Jean. 1988. "Quand les griots entrent à la Sorbonne." In *La grande geste du Mali*, eds. Y. T. Cissé and W. Kamissoko, 5–11. Paris: Fondation SCOA.

Samaké, Maximin. 1984. *Pouvoir traditionnel et conscience politique paysanne: les kafo de la région de Bougouni, Mali*. Thèse de doctorat de 3e cycle, EHESS, Paris.

Sclee, Günther. 1988. "Die Islamisierung der Vergangenheit: Von der Rückwirkung der Konversion somalischer und somaloider Gruppen zum Islam auf deren oral tradiertes Geschichtsbild." In W. J. G. Möhlig, H. Jungraithmayr and J. F. Thiel, eds., *Die Oralliteratur in Afrika als Quelle zur Erforschung der traditionellen Kulturen*, 269–99. Berlin.

Siddiz. 1989.

Smith, Pierre. 1979. "Naissances et destins: les enfants de fer et les enfants de beurre." *Cahiers d'Etudes africaines* 73–76, XIX–I–4: 329–52.

Soh, Siré-Abbâs. 1913. *Chroniques du Foûta Sénégalais*. Paris.

Soumaré, Mamadou. 1987. *Wagadu-Biida und Kaagoro. Text, Übersetzung und Analyse oraler Literatur der Soninke (Mali)*. Inaugurale Dissertation, Philipps-Universität Marburg.

Streicker, Allen Joseph. 1980. *On Being Zarma: Scarcity and Stress in the Nigerian Sahel*. Ann Arbor, Michigan: University Microfilms International.

Terray, Emmanuel. 1988. "Tradition, légende, identité dans les États pré-coloniaux de la Boucle du Niger." *Cahiers d'Études Africaines* XXVIII (1), 109: 5–11.

Tisserant. 1954. *Etude sur le canton des Diawaras*. Nioro n., Archives Nationales du Mali, Bamako, serie 1D9.

Wilks, Ivor. 1989. *Wa and the Wala. Islam and Polity in Northern Ghana*. Cambridge: Cambridge University Press.

7. The *GƐSƐRƐ* of Borgu: A Neglected Type of Manding Diaspora

Paulo Fernando de Moraes Farias

One of the recurrent motifs in the oral literature of the Maninka—the inhabitants of classical Mande or Manden, the motherland of the Sunjata stories and songs—is a tale of two brothers who are traveling together. When food proves unavailable, one of the brothers feeds the other from his own flesh/blood. Hence they evolve into the prototypes of two highly distinct cultural roles and social strata. The one who gave from his own substance becomes the praisee and patron, while the other becomes the praise-chanter and client. In the Manden this motif, in slightly modified form, is incorporated into versions of the Sunjata epic (Bulman 1990: 334). But it is also often narrated without connection to the epic, to figure out the origin of the relationship between those two social categories (Zemp 1966: 632–33; Smith 1973: 477; Camara 1976: 100–101, 147–48).

The same motif reemerges, very far from the Manden, in Borgu—a region straddling the international border between the north of the Republic of Bénin and northwestern Nigeria. This is not merely an instance of the well-known phenomenon of a story being borrowed across language barriers and over vast geographical distances. Rather, it reflects a connection that is more immediate than the simple adoption of a loan-motif, but which involves a double historical articulation: first, the presence in Borgu of the Gɛsɛrɛ (plur. *gɛsɛrɛbà*) category of praise-chanters/traditionists, historically derived from praise-chanters/traditionists in the far-away Soninke heartlands; and, second, the fact that the Soninke-heartland praise-chanters have shared over the centuries some of the motifs of Mandenka lore. In fact, the Mandenka tale of the two brothers also occurs among the Soninke in stories about the origin of oral specialists (Diawara 1990: 73–74).[1]

---

[1] On the currency of this tale among the Mandenka and the Soninke, and its occurrence in other linguistic communities in contact with the Mandenka and the Soninke, see Zemp (1966: 632-33), Smith (1973: 477), and Camara (1976: 100-01, 147-48).

The role played by ɢᴇsᴇʀᴇ praise-chanters/traditionists in Borgu is striking evidence for one mode of long-distance communication (and metamorphosis) of cultural forms in West Africa, namely the migration and resettlement of oral specialists. This particular mode has been much less studied by historians and social scientists than others involving military conquest, trade diasporas, and traveling Islamic teachers.[2]

As we will see, ɢᴇsᴇʀᴇ migrations have sometimes been linked with armed invasions and with the "hyper-mobility" of people fostered by the entrepreneurial dynamics of precolonial African merchant capital (cf. Collins and Richards 1982: I, 131). However, it is also clear that those migrations did not primarily depend on conquest and commerce.

To a large extent, the ɢᴇsᴇʀᴇ progress across West Africa can be understood in terms of labor migration and the supply of know-how—provided we remember that we are not dealing with a waged proletariat, but with a clientage (educated into the high degree of specialization assigned to them by the hereditary division of labor in their society of origin) in search of new patrons with matching requirements. In other words, members of a social category trained in certain professional skills made their services available abroad. Over the generations, they found gainful employment where there was not only demand for their services, but also the capacity to reward them.

In our own late twentieth century, in Mali and elsewhere, the decline of the power and wealth of the traditional patron strata has induced praise-chanters/traditionists to gravitate within their own societies toward new (and hence "illegitimate") patrons—nouveau riche traders, politicians, and bureaucrats—rather than old royalty and "aristocracy." Alternatively, they endeavor (often successfully) to explore the international entertainment market opened by the global electronic media (Diawara 1997).

In centuries past, changes in the balance of West African imperial power (notably the decline of old Mali and the rise of the Soŋoy or Songhay empire in the late fifteenth century and later the collapse of Soŋoy after 1591) played a part in spurring migrations of Soninke-speaking praise-chanters toward new patronage sites located to the east and southeast of the Soninke heartlands. But variations in client/patron demographic ratios are also likely to have contributed to the process. Members of client groups competed for a finite number of patrons within each society. In situations in which the critical demographic mass of praise-chanters was exceeded, and in which the praise-singing categories consequently became too numerous for the carrying capacity (itself dependent on the vagaries of harvests, trade-derived income, booty capture, etc.) of the local patrons, the incentives to migrate must have loomed large in many ɢᴇsᴇʀᴇ minds.

---

[2] On warriors on horseback, trade networks, and Islam, with particular attention to speakers of Mande idioms, see for instance Brooks (1993).

Over the generations, migrating praise-chanters/traditionists were successively "hired" by different royal and chiefly courts, ever farther removed from their original point of departure. But prior to embarking on the study of the GESERE oral specialists of Béninois and Nigerian Borgu in their present location, we must examine the professional and linguistic genealogy, and the route on the map, which attach them to the Soninke heartlands and to the Manden, that is to areas situated in Mali, Mauritania, Senegal, and Guinea-Conakry, at considerable geographical distance from Nigeria and the Republic of Bénin.

Classical Mande or Manden has for geographical axis a stretch of the upper valley of the Niger. Manden traditionists are fond of saying that the northeast limits of that axis are the outskirts of Bamako, the capital of Mali, and that its southwest extreme is the town of Korosa or Kurusa, in Guinea–Conakry (Moraes Farias 1993: 14). Maninka, the vernacular of the Manden, and closely related idioms like Juula (Dyuula) and Banmana (Bambara), together constitute what is usually referred to as Manding (Vydrine 1995/96). Linguists place Manding within a wider language family that includes Soninke, and which we will refer to as Mande.

The Soninke-speaking heartlands are in northwestern Mali, eastern Senegal, and southern Mauritania. Soninke-speaking societies in these regions share with the Manden not only certain narrative motifs, but also some other cultural traits. These include religious rituals brought to the Manden by Soninke migrants (Dieterlen 1975), as well as the presence among the Soninke of a category of oral specialists called *Jaaru* (sing. *Jaare*). Their name and role are derived from those of the jeliw (sing. jeli) "griots" of Mandenka and Banmana societies. The majority of the Jaare groups are regarded as being of non-Soninke origin (Diawara 1990: 40–43).

In the dialects of the Soninke language spoken in the Soninke heartland, the counterparts of the GESERE traditionists/praise-chanters of Borgu are called Geseru, sing. Gesere. It is said that the Geseru have roots in the medieval Soninke state of Wagadu, called "Ghāna" by external Arabic sources (Monteil 1953: 363–66; Meillassoux, Doucouré, and Simagha 1967: 8,11). However, their presence is not recorded by the extant medieval Arabic evidence on "Ghāna"(Tamari 1991: 232).

In common with other Sahelian societies, both the Manden and the Soninke possess "casted" categories of specialists who are set apart by their artisanal skills (including word craft), perceived capacity to manipulate supernatural forces, and constraints on the selection of marriage partners. These categories are subsumed under an endogamous social stratum which is called ŋamakalaw (sing. ŋamakala) in Maninka, and ŋaχamalo (sing. ŋaχamala) in Soninke.

Together with other griot categories (including the Jaaru), blacksmiths, and leatherworkers, the Soninke-heartland Geseru belong to the ŋaχamala hereditary client groups or castes of traditional society. The Geseru are historically attached to the Wago (sing. Wage)—the Soninke patronymic-name groups who trace themselves back to Wagadu aristocracy. But Gesere groups also came to be strongly attached to the Jawara dynasty, which ruled the Soninke state of Jaara in the Kingi region (mostly within Mali but also extending into Mauritania), from the sixteenth century until the overthrow of this state by the conqueror al-hājj ʿUmar Taal in 1862 (Diawara 1989: 131; 1990: 35–36, 42, 186). Yet other Gesere groups attached themselves to the Sempera—Bacili dynasty that ruled the Gajaaga or Galam area (in the Senegal valley) up until the colonial conquest at the end of the nineteenth century (Bathily 1989: 11, 217–18).

    While Gesere presence has remained strong in the Soninke heartlands through the present, the sixteenth-century Geseru were to be found much farther to the east, attached to the court of Askya Muhammad I of Soŋoy, who reigned from 1493 to 1528, and who was himself of Soninke paternal descent (Monteil 1965: 510; Cissoko 1975: 75; Hunwick 1985: 24, 109–10). That attachment continued during the reigns of Askya Muhammad's successors, through the Moroccan conquest in 1591.

    Oral traditionists bearing the title (in Arabic transcription) *Gissiri Dunka*, *Gisari Dunka*, or *Gasiri Dunka*—cf. *Tunka* (king, chief) in Soninke—are attested from the sixteenth-century Soŋoy empire centered on the city of Gao (Gaawo in Soŋoy, Gǎwgǎw in Tǎmašǎq). Information provided by informants holding that title is incorporated in a Timbuktu chronicle that was completed in the second half of the seventeenth century but which draws on earlier information (Ta'rīkh al-fattāsh 1964: text 11, 94, 155; transl. 14, 177, 276; Hunwick 1970–1971: 69).

    The Soŋoy-speaking regions remain host country for the diaspora of oral specialists who use Soninke (or Soninke-based idioms) as a performance language. But the diasporic territory extends much farther to the southeast. It forms a geographical arc that now begins in the border areas of Mali and Niger, and stretches across Niger toward Gaya and the meeting point of the borders of Bénin, Nigeria, and Niger. Then, falling away from the Niger valley, the end of the arc extends into the north of the Republic of Bénin, to reach the Bwɛ or Bwɛɛ (Bouay on maps, also known as Gamia) and Nìkì (Nikki on maps) districts of Béninois Borgu. Gesere oral specialists may also be found across the international border, in southern areas of Nigerian Borgu (southwest of Kǎǎma or Kaiama Emirate) that are part of the Baruten Local Government Area of Kwara State.[3] My Bénéinois colleague, O. B. Bagodo, and I interviewed one of

---

[3] "Baruten" is a bureaucratic misspelling of the expression Bàrù–tẽm, which means "Bàrù Country" in the Bàatɔ̀núm language of Borgu.

them in this area, at Gbere Bɛrɛ, in April 1993.[4] But as a rule these specialists
are absent from other parts of Nigerian Borgu, though some Borgu stories tell of
an early GESƐRƐ presence at Busa or Buss (Lombard 1965: 207, 208 fn.1).

Geseru are no longer established in the Gao area of the Soŋoy-
speaking region, but they are still found farther downstream along the Niger
(Hale 1990: 64; Mounkaila 1989: 10–11).

In the Kaado dialect of Soŋoy spoken in the Teera and Tilabeeri areas
of the Republic of Niger, close to the border with Mali, those who continue the
work of the Geseru are known as *Gyèsérè* or *Jèsérè* (Prost 1956: 384; Ducroz
and Charles 1978: 135). Ìrokò (1974: 273f.) reproduces, in French translation,
traditional narratives from those areas collected in the late 1940s and early 1950s
by French colonial officers (Larue, Captain Buck, and Colonel René Dutel).
These narratives quote a few Soninke words and often refer to Jèsérè
traditionists, and to the title Jèsérè Dunku or Jèsérè Donkoy borne by "the royal
'griot'" in the imperial past.[5] This title is clearly the same one that was used at
the Askya court, but its rendition in Kaado is influenced by the Soŋoy word *koy*
(chief, master, owner).

At the other (southeastern) end of the section of the Niger valley
included in the Republic of Niger, the oral specialists performing in Soninke-
derived idioms are called *Jásárè* or *Jásárà* (plur. *Jásárài*) in the Dèndí variety of
the Soŋoy language (Tersis 1968: 74). In between the regions inhabited by
Kaado-speakers and Dèndí-speakers, similar denominations are applied to oral
specialists by populations speaking the Zarma variety of Soŋoy.

Interestingly, among Zarma-speakers the name *Jèsérè* or *Jàsárè* (plur.
Jèsérèy) is extended to all types of griots, whereas the denomination *Jèsérè
Dunka*—cf. again the title reported from the Askya court— is reserved for the
category of master oral specialists who can perform in the Soninke-derived
idiom locally known as Sillance, or Sillince, which is then translated into Zarma.
These specialists are also referred to as *Nyamkaaley*, sing. *Nyamkaale* or
Nyamkaala (cf. the Maninka term amakala, and the related Soninke term
ŋaxamala), *Timmey* (sing. *Timme*), and *Sillince* or *Silence*.[6] This last
denomination is formed with the Soninke patronymic-group name *Silla* (plur.
Sillanu) and the Zarma suffix *ce* (which signifies "originating from" or "people
of"). It is virtually identical with the designation *Sillankī* given, in Arabic
transcription, to both Askya Muhammad I of Soŋoy (who was Soninke on the
paternal side) and his father in Timbuktu literature (as-Saᶜ dī 1964: text 71, 134;
transl. 117, 212). The patronymic-group name "Silla" continues to be borne by
certain Gesere lineages in the Soninke heartlands.

---

[4] Interview jointly conducted with my Béninois colleague O. B. Bagodo.
[5] See Ìrokò (1974: 273, 278, 289-90, 293, 342-43, 352, 355).
[6] See Olivier de Sardan (1982: 82, 224-30, 310, 330-32, 354) and Mounkaila (1989:62).

In Zarma country the Jèsérè Dunka or Sillince oral specialists are regarded as an aristocracy of traditionists several notches above other griots. In oral tradition, their eponymous ancestor Jèsérè Dunka is associated with the Askya dynasty of Soŋoy. But his putative ancestry is then traced back to a paternal ancestor identified as Sii Baaru (the name of the last ruler of the pre-Askya Soŋoy dynasty of the Sonyii or Sii) and a Soninke woman called Faata (Olivier de Sardan 1982: 225–27).

The Zarma term "Jèsérè Dunka" reemerges in Béninois Borgu. Under the form "*GESƐRƐ Dunga*," it is the title given to the chief GESƐRƐ (and head of all griots) of the Bagana or Bãgana (traditional ruler) of Kpande or Kouandé (Akognon 1980:89, 91). "Dunga" also appears in the name of Mamadu (or Maamu) Dunga, an ancestral figure referred to in some of the stories of origin of the GESƐRƐbà of Borgu, and reappears in the title *Bàà Dunga*, said to have been used in the past by the head of the GESƐRƐbà of the royal city of Nìkì.[7]

Mounkaïla (1989: 62–127) has performed the very valuable task of collecting a number of texts in the Sillance idiom, accompanied by their parallel Zarma versions, and translating these Zarma versions into French. But the Sillance originals she recorded will require special study in order to establish in detail their kinship with, and deviations from, the vocabulary and grammar now used in the Soninke heartlands. It will also be necessary to identify the borrowings from languages other than Soninke. However, even a cursory examination of verses 1 through 40 of the first Sillance originals yields words that have identical, or virtually identical, counterparts in heartland dialects of Soninke, like *faana* (first), *fo* (thing), *lammu* or *lemmu* (sons, offspring), *liɲo* (sweet, pleasant), *safe* (to speak), *saara* (to father, to engender), *tunku* (king). Other comparisons reveal sound shifts such as X ↔ k, as in the case of the word *konne* ("enemy" in Sillance), which corresponds to the modern Soninke word *χonne*. Yet other Sillance words are influenced in their form by Zarma grammar, like *maamey* (ancestors), which corresponds to the Soninke *maame*, but which mimics the Zarma plural in *ey*.

Hale (1990: 184–279) and collaborators have also helpfully transcribed and translated a long Zarma text that includes Sillance word sequences. Some of these sequences proved impossible to translate at the time (Hale 1990: 181). One of them was the expression "Tuuri Siino" (verses 352–53, 367–68). Actually, it corresponds to the modern Soninke Tuuru Sinna or Tuuru ʃiɲa ("Mount Tuuru," or Jabal ath-Thawr in Arabic). It is a reference to one of the places visited by pilgrims near Mecca.[8] Other Sillance expressions, translated in Hale's

---

[7] Interviews: B. Adam, April 1988 and January 1990.

[8] It is believed that the Prophet Muhammad found refuge in a cave on this mountain while escaping from Mecca to Medina.

work, closely parallel modern usage in the Soninke heartlands. Among them is
"*a falle na a dagante*" (verses 490, 495, "he departed after him").[9] In other
cases, words may have been distorted by the particular diction of Nuhu Malio,
the reciter of the text (see Hale 1990: 180–1). Thus, for instance, *a gamjimini*
("he didn't drink water") and *hille* ("millet") in verse 531, and *Gommo cillany*
("on the road to Gombo") in verse 543.[10] Words like *ndaba* ("village," verse
749–59) and *saara* ("to father," verses 496, 773) have obvious counterparts in
modern Soninke (respectively, *debe* and *saara*).

The GƐSƐRƐbà of Borgu

The GƐSƐRƐbà (sing. GƐSƐRƐ) represent the outer limits of the diaspora
of oral specialists who use performance idioms derived from Soninke. They are
Muslim praise-chanters and specialists of the past. Traditionally, they were
clients only of kings, princes, and chiefs. In Borgu they coexist with other griot
categories, but are usually ranked above these.

In Borgu the GƐSƐRƐbà have historically operated within traditional
political structures of considerable complexity, located in a region that was one
of the great commercial crossroads of precolonial Africa (Lovejoy 1978). It is
also a region of considerable linguistic diversity. In Béninois Borgu and in the
southern parts of Nigerian Borgu, the majority language is Bàatɔnúm (a Gur or
Voltaic language).[11] Another major Borgu idiom is the Manding language, which
will be called Bo'o-Busa or Boko-Busa in this chapter.[12] This language
comprises several dialects distributed over Béninois and Nigerian Borgu. Boko-
Bàrù, a variant of Boko-Busa strongly influenced by Bàatɔnúm, is spoken in the
Kã̀̀ma or Kaiama area of Nigerian Borgu. Other widespread languages in the
Borgu region are Fulfulde and Dèndí—a variety of Soŋoy established in the
country by precolonial networks of long-distance traders (Heine 1970:161). In
addition, Mokɔle (said to be a dialect of the Yorùbá language) is spoken around
Kã̀̀ni (Kandi) in Béninois Borgu. Other Gur languages besides Bàatɔnúm are
spoken in Béninois Borgu, for example, Gulmacema and Ditamari.

---

[9] In modern Soninke: *a* ("he," "him"); *falle* or *halle* ("after," "behind"); and the verbal
form *dagante*—from *nan daga* ("to depart, to leave"). I thank my colleague Mamadou
Diawara for his comments on the texts collected by Mounkaïla and Hale.
[10] In modern Soninke (verse 531): *a ma* ("he did not"), *ji* ("water"), *nan mini* ("to
drink"), and *yille* ("millet") instead of *hille*; and (verse 543) *killen di* ("on the road to"),
with the name Gommo following this expression rather than preceding it.
[11] Bàatɔnúm-speakers call themselves Bàatɔmbù (sing. Bàatɔnù).
[12] However, other authors reserve the name Boko-Busa for one of the dialects (spoken in
the Busa and Wawa areas of Nigerian Borgu) of this Manding language (see Stewart
1993: 46).

The GƐSƐRƐbà are found in areas in which Bààtɔnúm is the predominant language, in Nìkì, BwƐƐ or Gamia (Bouay), Kpande (Kouandé), Kãni or Kandi (in Béninois Borgu), and in the Baruten Local Government Area of Kwara State (Nigeria).

GƐSƐRƐ formal praise performances are in a language that is unintelligible to local society and therefore requires translation. This special performance language is called WakpaarƐm by some, but not all, of the GƐSƐRƐbà. For reasons that will be discussed later, WakpaarƐm has been consistently mistaken for a form of Soŋoy by anthropologists and historians, including scholars from Borgu. But we will demonstrate, in the light of recently collected language material, that WakpaarƐm is basically derived from Soninke.

Unlike the griots of the Manding-speaking heartlands, the GƐSƐRƐɓ are not part of an endogamous social stratum. Borgu is outside the West African areas in which griots and other categories of craftspersons, occur as hereditary professional and status groups bounded by endogamy and often described as castes (Tamari 1988: 205; 1991: 223; and map 1). By origin the GƐSƐRƐɓ are one of such castes. But the Borgu society into which they have migrated has no system of endogamous specialist groups (Lombard 1965:145). The GƐSƐRƐ mode of insertion into this society combines highly diversified marriage alliances with a high degree of professional and linguistic specialization.

Historical and ethnographic evidence supports the identification of WakpaarƐm with Soninke. GƐSƐRƐ linguistic behavior in Borgu follows a pattern that can also be observed elsewhere, within the far-flung diaspora of oral specialists who all use Soninke-derived performance languages requiring translation into local, quotidian languages. WakpaarƐm is one of these performance idioms, comparable to the Sillance used by the Jèsérè Dunka of the Zarma-speaking areas in the Republic of Niger. Its Soninke vocabulary and grammar were not lost during the GƐSƐRƐɓ 's passage to Borgu.

It is pertinent to ask how the linguistic and professional distinctiveness of the GƐSƐRƐbà has been preserved over the centuries, in a country where they could have easily fused with the rest of the population as other caste people supposedly sought to do elsewhere through migration (Tamari 1988: 534). We will examine this question first from the point of view of the GƐSƐRƐbà themselves, i.e., from their position as an immigrant group achieving implantation in a new host society. Then we will introduce the point of view of their patrons into the discussion, and the various advantages these patrons found in their association with a clearly distinct, WakpaarƐm-speaking, griot group.

Intermarriage and Gender-Bound Transmission of the WakpaarƐm Performance Idiom

By contrast with the Soninke heartlands, in which Gesere praise-chanters and their patrons share the same language but do not intermarry, in Borgu the GƐSƐRƐbà chant formal praise in a language not understood by those being praised, but marriage exchanges take place between these GƐSƐRƐ specialists and their patrons.

Similarly to the Jèsérè Dunka of Zarma country, GƐSƐRƐ traditionists seem to work by contraries. By definition, a medium for the public broadcast of praise would be expected to ensure relatively easy communication with the praise addressees and the wider audience. Moreover, GƐSƐRƐ performances have long been part of the local culture, most likely since the sixteenth century. There has been plenty of time for the GƐSƐRƐbà to adopt a local language for all their praise performances. Nevertheless, when performed for traditional patrons in a traditional setting, GƐSƐRƐ praise is still not chanted in Bààtɔ̀núm (a language well known to the GƐSƐRƐbà) or any of the other main languages of Borgu. The Wakpaarɛm praise language deployed by the GƐSƐRƐbà is therefore unintelligible to all other sectors of the local population. A translation into Bààtɔ̀núm has to be intercalated by auxiliary GƐSƐRƐ performers, or by other performers schooled in the role of interpreters.[13]

Performances in Wakpaarɛm are a familiar feature of the culture of Borgu, yet their linguistic medium defamiliarizes them. Wakpaarɛm opens up a distance between the performer and audience which is incomparably greater than that which can be created by the skillful deployment of genre conventions and language registers when both sides share the same language. The patrons of the Gesere and the general public are thus unable to assess the literary skills of the performers.

It is not through mutually energizing interaction (between GƐSƐRƐ performers and a linguistically competent and critical public outside the GƐSƐRƐ social category) that the survival of Wakpaarɛm can be explained. Rather, it has survived as a badge of identity owned by the GƐSƐRƐ group. At this level, the task of maintaining Wakpaarɛm falls entirely on the GƐSƐRƐbà themselves.

In the case of the Zarma-speaking areas in the Republic of Niger, it has been suggested that the Sillance idiom is used by the Jèsérè Dunka oral specialists "to communicate secretly" with their patrons (Hale 1990: 64), although this suggestion has been contested (Olivier de Sardan 1990: 208). In the Borgu case, it is clear that Wakpaarɛm is not a medium for secret communication between the GƐSƐRƐ oral specialists and other social categories,

---

[13] Interview: B. Adam, April 1988.

not least because esoteric knowledge in Soninke-derived language is not disseminated throughout society, by contrast with what has been said to apply in Zarma-speaking areas (Mounkaïla 1989: 48, 181; Hale 1990: 179, 181).

As a most conspicuous, unmistakable, emblem of uniqueness in a country where, save exceptions controlled by the GESEREbà, it is not available to others, Wakpaarɛm continues to mark out the GESERE métier in spite of the absence of endogamy barriers. Wakpaarɛm clearly separates the GESEREbà from other local categories of oral specialists and musicians, who do not have a special performance language. It decisively helps the GESEREbà to keep their distinction while exploring the advantages of marriage alliances outside their own group. These alliances have reinforced GESERE implantation in Béninois Borgu by allowing extended kinship networking with other groups at various levels of the traditional social hierarchy.

With regard to marriage alliances in the Soŋoy and Zarma countries from which the GESEREbà have moved into Borgu, the situation is intermediate between what obtains in the Soninke heartlands and what applies in Borgu. The Jèsérè Dunka oral specialists and other griot groups (Tamari 1991: 246), and certain other craftsperson categories (Rouch 1954: 34) of these countries have been described as endogamous groups and even as castes, although often in quotation marks (Olivier de Sardan 1982: 155, 225). But it is also stressed that, among the Soŋoy and the Zarma, the caste system has never been as fully developed as in regions farther west, and that marriage prohibitions are rather imprecise in all Soŋoy-speaking societies. However, although no detailed ethnography of the Jèsérè Dunka and other supposed castes is yet available, it is believed that in those societies, unlike in Borgu, women of noble lineage do not marry men of lower groups (Olivier de Sardan 1973: 425).

In the Soninke heartlands, mainstream practice excludes women from the Gesere métier (Dr. Mamadou Diawara, personal communication). In Zarma country, the teaching of the Jèsérè Dunka métier has been described as proceeding "from father to son" (Olivier de Sardan 1982: 331). However Hale (1990: 179) has reported, from the same area, on teaching of the Jèsérè Dunka profession (including teaching of the Sillance performance idiom) "open to both sexes."

In Borgu, the GESEREbà teach their special idiom and other professional expertise exclusively to their sons.[14] But this specialized knowledge is made available to all grandsons, whether born from sons or from daughters (including daughters married to men from outside the GESERE group). Thus male descendants from men who do not speak Wakpaarɛm can become Wakpaarɛm-speaking performers.[15]

---

[14] Interview: B. Adam, April, 1988.
[15] Interview: W. Tokura, January 1990.

These reassimilated grandsons born from non-GƐSƐRƐ fathers keep their non-GƐSƐRƐ patronymic-group names.[16] The process of reassimilation is facilitated by the fact that, in Bààtɔ̀núm-speaking culture, male children are normally educated away from their parents. Their education may be entrusted to either paternal or maternal kin (Lombard 1965: 145,156,165; cf. Tamou Bocko 1983: 37-40).

In the case of GƐSƐRƐ daughters married to men belonging to the Dèndí-speaking "Wangara" communities, the resulting grandsons will bear patronymic-group names that (like those brought into the country by the GƐSƐRƐbà themselves) ultimately are of Manding origin, such as Kurubari or Kuribari, Ture, and Sise, or which were invented as a deliberate allusion to the Manden, as in the case of the patronymic-group name Mannɛ or Mandɛ.[17] GƐSƐRƐ men also marry women from other social categories, including Bààtɔ̀núm-speaking princely and commoner lineages, and the Dèndí-speaking communities.[18]

In addition to the hereditary transmissions of performance skills and the Wakpaarɛm idiom, on occasion male adults from non-GƐSƐRƐ social groups simply adopt the GƐSƐRƐ identity and transmit it to their male descendants.[19] Actually, it is known that even in the Soninke heartland individuals not born within the Gesere status group could sometimes be assimilated to it (Monteil 1953: 364; Bathily 1989: 217).

As a result of intermarriage and assimilation, well-known GƐSƐRƐ patronymic-group names in Béninois Borgu include not only Manding *jàmúw* shared with the Dèndí-speakers (Taruwɛrɛ or Tarawɛrɛ, Fàfana, Mannɛ or Mandɛ), but also other patronymic-group names (Yari, Burɔ, Wɔ̃ko, and Diko) brought into the GƐSƐRƐ group from non-Wangara and non-GƐSƐRƐ sectors of the local population, in other words from different levels of the traditional social hierarchy of Borgu.

It is likely that marriage exchanges between GƐSƐRƐbà and trader communities and the occasional adoption of the GƐSƐRƐ identity by adult men from these communities have historically facilitated the circulation of information and patterns of thought between oral traditions and Arabic literacy, i.e., between Muslim oral specialists and Muslim scholars in the trader communities (cf. Moraes Farias 1992b, 1993).

---

[16] Interview: B. Adam, January 1990.
[17] Interview: B. Damagii, April 1988. See also Lombard 1965: 86 fn. 1, 138-39.

[18] Interview: G. Magasi, January 1990.
[19] Interviews: W. Tokura, April 1988; G. Magasi, January 1990.

Although Wakpaarεm is essential to the Gesεrεbà, their professional competence is not confined to this particular performance language. The education of Gesεre boys includes the mastering of artistic—refinedly metaphoric and euphemistic—Bàatɔ̀núm speech, much appreciated by local audiences (Tamou Bocko 1983: 67–68). The Gesεrεbà use Wàatɔ̀núm for praise delivered in less formal settings, and for narratives about the past, which do not require a formal setting.

In the definition of the Gesεre corporate identity, there is thus an interplay between the use of Wakpaarεm and the use of Bàatɔ̀núm. The Gesεrεbà would probably have survived as professionals of repute even without Wakpaarεm. What, then, is the real advantage of preserving this performance idiom?

Gesεrεbà and Kings

In their historical narratives, which they deliver in Bàatɔ̀núm, the Gesεrεbà consistently state that they came from outside Borgu—from the other side of the River Niger,[20] from ʃɔ̃ɔ̃rai (i.e., Soŋoy or Songhay),[21] from the Gunuma (Gurma) country,[22] or simply from Nisεε, i.e., the Republic of Niger.[23] But their praise performances in Wakpaarεm recall foreign origin with greater immediacy than any story of origin.

By continuing to use their special performance idiom, the Gesεrεbà tirelessly reenact their difference from the patrons they address and the rest of the population. Yet the same performances also reiterate the close association of the Gesεrεbà with traditional political power, i.e., with the Wasangari estate, which includes kings, princes, and most—although not all—chiefly lineages (Lombard 1965: 180–83; Bagodo 1978: 48 fn. 1). The identity of these traditional Wasangari patrons is publicly, and crucially, confirmed by Gesεre praise formulas and genealogical reminders chanted in Wakpaarεm. In principle, such chants may be addressed only to these patrons and serve as a certification of their high status. The survival of the special performance language therefore works to the patrons' benefit. Wakpaarεm becomes their distinctive attribute, as much as it is the Gesεrεbà's. At this level, the patrons collaborate with their praise-chanters to ensure the preservation of a special idiom that they do not understand.

In spite of their "alien" idiom, the Gesεrεbà speak from well within the

---

[20] Interview: W. Tokura, April 1988.

[21] Interview: B. Adam, April 1988.

[22] Interview: Bàà Bwεε, January 1990.

[23] Interview: G. Magasi, January 1990.

ideology of the royal and chiefly institutions of Borgu. They do so not only in their Wakpaarɛm praise performances, but also in the Bààtɔ́núm narrative mode. In line with this ideology, the GƐsɛrɛbà celebrate kings, chiefs, and princely warriors as the force that has shaped local society for centuries. Special story genres proclaim the GƐsɛrɛbà's special relationship with the traditional ruling group. There are exemplary stories about legendary childhood friendships between a chief's son and a GƐsɛrɛ's son (Tamou Bocko 1983: 57). Lombard also reports a parallel genre of GƐsɛrɛ story (1965: 208 fn.1). In this narrative he collected, the patron/client relationship between a king of Busa and his GƐsɛrɛ is reversed, to the extent that—having fallen into poverty—the king becomes the GƐsɛrɛ's slave. Yet the king not only refuses to be ransomed by his own kin, but also fights and kills his relatives when they attack the GƐsɛrɛ and gives him the horses and other booty captured from them.

The closeness between royalty and the GƐsɛrɛbà is also stressed in GƐsɛrɛ accounts by bringing together the putative origin of the two groups, or at least by highlighting homologies between their respective stories of origin. This is best illustrated by a comparison of two accounts, both collected in the commercial center of Kpàràkú ("Parakou") in the Republic of Bénin.

The first narrative is from a non-GƐsɛrɛ informant and office-holder in Kpàràkú's traditional court, who also represents a local line of priestly authority believed to be more ancient than the power of Kpàràkú's chiefly rulers.[24] It states that the GƐsɛrɛbà arrived in Borgu together with the Dèndí-speaking Taruwere, Kuribari, Fãfana, Manne, and Ture, all foreign traders (see also Lombard 1965: 140 fn.1). There is no attempt to link, or compare, GƐsɛrɛ origins with royal origins. GƐsɛrɛ presence is regarded as a by-product of the expansion of commercial networks, and there is an element of truth in this view: trade routes opened the way to GƐsɛrɛ migrations, although the GƐsɛrɛbà attached themselves as clients to royalty and chiefs, not to traders.

By contrast, the second account (which emanates from a GƐsɛrɛ) emphasizes armed invasion. It establishes an analogy between the foreign character of the GƐsɛrɛbà and the equally foreign character not of the long-distance traders, but rather of the Wasangari aristocracy (who are also traditionally described as an immigrant group).[25] However, this account does not depict royalty and GƐsɛrɛ traditionists as having come into Borgu as one group. Rather, the GƐsɛrɛbà are said to have arrived together with invading Sɔ̃ɔ̃rai (Soŋoy) armies and to have found Wasangari rulers already installed at Bwɛɛ and Nikì. After the defeat of the Sɔ̃ɔ̃rai invaders, the GƐsɛrɛbà were left stranded

---

[24] Interview: B. Damagii, April 1988.

[25] Interview: B. Adam, April 1988.

in Borgu. Eventually, they attached themselves to the ruler of BwƐƐ, who was later requested to surrender some of his GESƐRƐ praise-chanters to the king of Nìkì.

Wōrū Tokura, the head of the GESƐRƐbà of Nìkì, went further than this in his own account, postulating the joint arrival of kings and GESƐRƐbà in Borgu.[26] Although he told us that the special GESƐRƐ performance idiom comes from SƐruma (Zarma) country, nevertheless he also stated that the GESƐRƐbà arrived in Borgu from Arabia, "from the land of Mecca," following Kisira—the putative ancestor of the Borgu kings—and his party, who all had refused Islam and had migrated to West Africa.[27]

Another GESƐRƐ informant provided a different version of this supposed joint arrival.[28] His account is in fact a variant of the well-known Manding and Soninke tale of two brothers referred to at the beginning of the present chapter. It also has significant points of contact with a story from the Zarma-speaking country, in which the the Jèsérè Dunka category of oral specialists are classified as bàasèy (joking cross cousins) of the Sii haama (the descendants of the famous Soŋoy ruler Sonni Ali) (Olivier de Sardan 1982: 47, 225–27).

In its Borgu version, the tale makes no reference to Soŋoy, the Zarma country, or Arabia. Rather, the WakpaarƐm idiom and the rest of the GESƐRƐ métier are said to have entered Borgu from the Gunuma or Gurma country, i.e., the right bank of the Niger and its hinterland.[29] The TarawƐrƐ GESƐRƐbà and the Wasangari are described as descended from two brothers who journeyed together into Borgu. As they traveled, the junior brother began to chant a refrain indicating that he was hungry. The senior brother then cut a piece of flesh from his own thigh, roasted it, and fed it to the junior brother. Later the junior brother again felt hungry and chanted, and was fed again in the same way by the senior brother. This establishes the paradigm of the relationship between patron (the Wasangari senior brother, who takes responsibility for feeding the other) and griot (the TarawƐrƐ junior brother who chants for his food, eventually turning into praise-chanter out of gratitude). However, the prohibition of marriage between the descendants of the two brothers, which is classical in the versions of this myth reported from the Soninke and Manding heartlands, is entirely absent in the Borgu version, which has no such rules of griot endogamy.

However, most of the stories of origin associate the GESƐRƐbà with

---

[26] Interview: W. Tokura, April 1988.

[27] On the Kisira or Kisra cycle of stories, see Moraes Farias (1992b, 1993).
[28] Interview: Bàà BwƐƐ, January 1990.
[29] "Gurma" is a name for the right bank of the Niger and its hinterland.

Soŋoy culture. Hence the "foreign" dimension of ɢɛsɛrɛ identity operates as a reminder of the greatest military victories in the history of Borgu, namely, the successful resistance against Soŋoy invasion.[30] These military episodes are recorded both in the Timbuktu chronicles, and in Soŋoy's own oral tradition.[31] In Borgu traditions, ɢɛsɛrɛ presence appears as a valuable prize earned by the local kings and chiefs—once more a living confirmation of their grandeur.

Kingship and Bodily Rites of Islamic Prayer

The ɢɛsɛrɛbà have a long-standing association with Islam.[32] They must have entered Borgu as Muslims following Soŋoy Muslim rulers, in the wake of Muslim traders, or perhaps in an independent search for new patrons after the collapse of the Soŋoy empire. Regardless, ɢɛsɛrɛ praise-chanting and historical narratives circulate the "pagan" symbolic capital of the traditional political culture of Borgu.

In Borgu as elsewhere, there has been a long-standing cultural opposition between kingly status and the prostrations required by Islamic prayer (which is not at all the same as saying that kings were historically hostile to Muslims, nor that kings felt threatened by everything Islamic). This tension pervades the history of Islam in much of West Africa. Prostration of subjects before kings was a widespread feature of court etiquette, while public prostration by kings themselves was unthinkable (Moraes Farias 1990:133).

In practice Muslims have often prostrated before kings (although in principle they should prostrate only before God), and this is true not only in sub-Saharan Africa. Royal and Muslim abhorrence of prostration come together, with an ironical twist, in the episode of the visit to Cairo by the Muslim emperor Mansa Mūsā in 1324. There he showed reluctance, both as a king and as a Muslim, when requested to kiss the ground before the Mamlūk sultan al-Malik an-Nāṣir, as was customary in that Muslim court. He finally complied, but only after pronouncing a formula to the effect that it was actually before Allah that he was prostrating. Yet Mansa Mūsā's own subjects (Muslims included,

---

[30] However, Soŋoy historical records do not yield any clear reference to the areas now included in Béninois Borgu. The only Borgu place name explicitly mentioned in those records is Buṣa (Busa or "Bussa") in Nigerian Borgu (as-Saᶜdī, 1964: text 103, transl. 169).

[31] See as-Saᶜdī (1964: text 64, 76, 103, transl. 105,125,169); Ta'rīkh al-fattāsh (1964: text 39, 69, 71, transl. 67, 133, 137); Rouch (1953: 195-7); Ìrokò (1974: 276-7).

[32] Interview: B. Adam, April 1988. See also Lombard (1965: 140).

presumably) had to prostrate before him, and this court etiquette continued to obtain in Mali under his successors— as noted in 1352–1353 by Ibn Baṭṭuṭā.[33]

But, for strict Muslims, formal prostration (*sujūd*) was reserved for the divinity and could never be performed simply for the sake of honoring kings and other human beings (Fisher 1993:73, 83). Conversely, many rulers felt that prostrating before Allah was repugnant, because it infringed the kingship invested in their own bodies. Hence compromises were often worked out, so that, as in the case of Sonyii Ali of Soŋoy (Hunwick 1985: 70–1), kings prayed without prostrating, and Muslims—in medieval Ghāna (al-Bakrī 1965: text 176, transl. 330) as in the palaces of twentieth-century Yorùbá kings—could greet rulers without either prostrating or kneeling down.[34]

In Borgu the prostration issue is far from forgotten, given that the adoption of Muslim identities by those for whom the GƐSƐRƐbà perform is a comparatively recent phenomenon. In Nìkì (in Béninois Borgu), king Sero Tooru Tunku (1924–1928) was a Muslim before his installation but then ceased to pray, and eventually gave his personal praying beads to the Imām. Kpee Gunu is said to have been the first king to reign in Nìkì as a Muslim (from August 1941 to May 1952). His son, king Séro Taasu (1970–1992), was a Muslim whom we saw more than once with his prayer beads in hands, and who was known to perform the prescribed daily prayers. Of the two kings who reigned between 1952 and 1970, the first—Kpee Laafia or Kpee Daafia—is remembered as a Muslim. But the second, Sero Kpera Wɛ̃ɛ̃ragii, is said to have regarded Islamic praying as unbecoming to a king. One day, when asked why he did not pray, he supposedly answered, "Is there still anybody left above me?! It is for you to prostrate before me."[35]

Yet Muslim and GƐSƐRƐ traditionists with the title *al-ḥājj* attached to their names still glory in this kingly pride. Their professional discourse is royalty-centered, hence it is free to celebrate the distances kings placed between their royal persona and the rituals of Islam. Thus the GƐSƐRƐbà belong firmly in the kings' camp, despite the fact that they are Muslim and associated with Soŋoy's Muslim culture. When talking about their association with kingship, however, GƐSƐRƐ informants systematically play down their association with Islam. One of them explicitly told us that their profession and their religion are

---

[33] See al-ʿUmarī (1963: 54, 58, 61-62; 1927: 68, 72, 76-77) and Ibn Baṭṭūta (1968: IV, 408).

[34] In Nìkì, too, the Imam has been traditionally exempt from the obligation of prostrating before the Sìnà Boko (king). Our personal observations confirm this: during the Gaani festival of October 1990, which we attended, neither the Imam, his deputy, nor any of the other Muslims in their entourage prostrated before the king.

[35] Interview: B. Adam, April 1988.

two separate things.[36] Another stressed that the ɢᴇsᴇrᴇbà who arrived "with Kisira" did not pray, because when one is accompanying an embattled prince, one has no time for praying.[37]

Hence paradoxically, in spite of being Muslim and of foreign origin, the ɢᴇsᴇrᴇbà are now perceived as authentic voices of what is independent of Islam in the culture of Borgu, and especially in the culture of kingship. To grasp this clearly, one has only to compare the difference between local perceptions of the ɢᴇsᴇrᴇ community and local perceptions of Dèndí-speaking communities. In both cases we have long-established Muslim groups equipped with distinctive languages. But the Dèndí are routinely referred to in Bààtɔ̀núm as sɔ̄ɔ̀, plur. sɔbu, (foreigners).[38] By contrast, the ambiguous "foreign-ness" of the ɢᴇsᴇrᴇbà never seems to make them liable to be described as sɔ̄ɔ̀.

The status of the ɢᴇsᴇrᴇbà in Borgu may thus be described as that of an immigrant group that has succeeded in establishing its centrality to local culture and which has done so through the selective cultivation of some of its outsider characteristics and the playing down of others.

The Wakpaarᴇm language

As has happened with the *Arɔ́kin* of ɔ̀yɔ́ (Moraes Farias 1992a), the ɢᴇsᴇrᴇbà have often been used as informants, but there has been insufficient investigation of their own history, social place, and linguistic practice.

In Lombard's otherwise illuminating book (1965: 87, 140 fn. 1, 207–209, 339), he simply states that the ɢᴇsᴇrᴇbà are "of Songhay origin." He does not discuss their Wakpaarᴇm chants, does not examine the linguistic duality of their performances, and assumes that both the ɢᴇsᴇrᴇbà and their special performance idiom are Dèndí—an assumption borrowed by other authors (Levtzion 1968: 176). Yet, although the first ɢᴇsᴇrᴇbà who arrived in Borgu must have been familiar with varieties of the Soŋoy language (into which they had been accustomed to translate their performances), their performance idiom itself was not Dèndí, nor Zarma, nor any other variety of Soŋoy.

Table 7.1: Word List

Wakpaarᴇm	Soninke	Translation*
binnε	binne	black (W, S)

---

[36] Interview: B. Adam, April 1988.

[37] Interview: W. Tokura, April 1988.

[38] On this "eternally foreign" status, see Arifari Bako (1989: 213).

dɛbɛ	debe	settlement (W, S)
dɛbɛ|koore	debe–χoore	town (W, S)
dɛbɛ|tugunne	debe–tugunne	village (W, S)
debunu	lemme, remme,	son, scion (W, S)
	plur. lemmu, lemmunu	
dɛmmɛ	danbe	high birth, noble
		extraction (W, S)
dumɛ, dunnɛ	dunbe	red (W, S)
faabu	faabe, haabe,	father (W, S)
	plur. faabu, haabu	
fangi	faaŋe, haaŋe	river (W, S)
geku**	jaχe, plur. jaχu	sheep (W, S)
gɛsɛrɛ,	gesere,	oral traditionist
plur. gɛsɛrɛbà	plur. geseru	(W, S)
grisaku**	χirisaaχu	W=senior brother;
		S=the status of eldest sibling
kittɛ	kitte	arm (W, S)
kɔmbɛ	konpe	W = house;
		S = hut, room
koore	χoore (or qoore	large (W, S)
	after nasal vowel)	
kulle	χulle (or qulle	white (W, S)
	after nasal vowel)	
maamɛ**	maame	W = grandfather;
		S = ancestors of both sexes
mɛgu	meχe	metal, iron (W, S)
naanu	na, plur. naanu	ox, cow (W, S)

nyommi**	na nyoomi	W = rifle, gun;
		S = to point with the finger***
saage	saaχe	mother (W, S)
saraayẽ	saaraye	birth, ancestry (W, S)
sᴇᴇro	sere, sare,	W = man; S = person, human being
	plur. soro	
siinu	sii, plur. siinu	horse (W, S)
simaarᴇ	kisimare	offspring, grandchild (W, S)
tugunne	tugunne	small, junior (W, S)
tumaane	tunbaare	W = woman; S = slave-woman
tunka	tunka	king, chief (W, S)
yaago, yaagu	yaaχè, plur. yaaχo	eyes (W, S)
yaago, yaagu	yaago, yaagu	shame (W, S)
yᴇmmᴇ, yᴇmbᴇ	yimme	head
yiigo	yigo, yugo,	man, male (W, S)
	plur. yigu	

---

*   W = meaning in Wakpaarᴇm;   S = meaning in Soninke
**   The double asterisk marks lexical items attested here on the authority of
the list of fourteen Wakpaarᴇm words established by Tamou Bocko (1983: 69),
whose transcriptions followed the normal orthography of the French language
but have been retranscribed here.

As yet, neither I nor my colleagues have been able to find Soninke
counterparts for a few of the Wakpaarᴇm words collected by Tamou Bocko, nor
for some of those recorded by ourselves in the field. They may be derived from
languages other than Soninke. They include *sᴇlᴇ* (land), *yandurufa* or *andurufa*
(gold), and *Manta* (God).[39]

---

[39] In Zarma country, "manta" is the name given to a musical tune, and also to the lute
played by the local Jèsérèy (Mounkaïla 1989: 46-7; Olivier de Sardan 1982: 289-90).
This musical instrument belongs to the family of string instruments known as *móólò* in
Dèndí and other varieties of the Soŋoy language (Tersis 1968: 53; Prost 1956: 489).

***   In appropriate contexts, *na nyoomi* may be used in Soninke to mean "to point a target." This may be, through Gɛsɛrɛ poetical metaphor, the origin of the Wakpaarɛm usage *nyommi* (gun).

Table 7.2: Sample of Wakpaarɛm Praise Formulas

1) ʏaago debunu, yaago debunu simaarɛ!
Rendered in B'tɔnfim as: Sekurun bĩ, sekurun debubu (or deubu)! (Son of shame, offspring of shame !). In modern Soninke, the expression *"yaagu lemmu"* (shame children) refers to those who must abide by rules of mutual avoidance (Monteil 1966: 686).

2) Sɛɛro debunu, seero debunu simaarɛ!
Rendered in B'tɔnfim as: Tɔnūn bĩ, tɔnūn deubu! (Son of a man, offspring of a man!). The word order followed in the Wakpaarɛm formula is the same as in, say, the heartland-Soninke expression *Diɲa remme* or "Son of Diɲa" (Sylla 1977: part 2, 21).[40]

3) Wɔllu, wɔllu debunu, wɔllu debunu simaarɛ!
Rendered in B'tɔnfim as: Bɔrɔkĩni, bɔrɔkĩnĩ bĩ, bɔrɔkĩnĩ bĩ debubu! (Man of repute, son of a man of repute, offspring of the son of a man of repute!). The word *wɔllu* appears not to come from the Soninke language.

4) Dɛmmɛ debunu, dɛmmɛ debunu simaarɛ!
Rendered in B'tɔnfim as: Bɛɛrɛn bĩ, bɛɛrɛn deubu! (Son of honor, offspring of honor!).

5) ʏiigo debunu, yiigo debunu simaarɛ!
Rendered in B'tɔnfim as: Tɔn durɔn bĩ, tɔn durɔn bĩ deubu! (Son of a brave man, offspring of the son of a brave man!).

Studies more recent than Lombard's have continued to pay little or no attention to the special performance idiom of the Gɛsɛrɛbà. However, some scholars from Béninois Borgu have called attention to the fact that Gɛsɛrɛ formal performances require translation into Bààtɔnúm (Bio Guéné 1978: 7; Orou

---

This is probably the basis for the name of the *mɔrɔku* or *mɔrɔgu* played by the Gɛsɛrɛbà of Béninois Borgu (though they often chant without musical accompaniment).
[40] Diɲa is the mythical ancestor of the Soninke.

Yorouba 1982: 91). Another of them (himself of Soŋoy–Dèndí descent) has briefly characterized the GƐSƐRƐ griots as being of "Songhay (Soninke) origin" (Arifari Bako 1989: 128). Yet another correctly recorded the name "Wakpaarɛm" as the specific name of the GƐSƐRƐ language, and listed fourteen of its words with their translation into Bàatɔnúm and French (Tamou Bocko 1983:69). But, even then, none of the characteristic praise formulas used in Wakpaarɛm were recorded, nor was the Soninke origin of the idiom demonstrated. Furthermore, most observers have continued to assume that the special GƐSƐRƐ performance language was a form of Soŋoy.

This was an understandable misapprehension. It was largely due to the fact that many GƐSƐRƐ informants call their performance language Sɔɔrai or Sɔɛm (i.e., Soŋoy), and apparently do not remember the name "Wakpaarɛm." Moreover, none of our GƐSƐRƐ informants have displayed any awareness of the connection between Wakpaarɛm and Soninke.

However, while obviously limited in scope, the Wakpaarɛm materials presented in tables 7.1 and 7.2 demonstrate that Wakpaarɛm is basically a variety of Soninke. Both the word list and the sample of praise formulas were collected from the informants listed at the end of this chapter, with the addition of some other individual words recorded by Tamou Bocko (1983:69).

The correspondences between Wakpaarɛm and Soninke were established by us by consulting Soninke vocabularies (Monteil 1966, 1967), and texts recorded from Soninke–heartland traditionists (Bathily 1967, and 1975: 51–94; Meillassoux et al. 1967; Jiri Silla, 1977; Diarra Sylla, 1977). But I have also benefited from the precious help provided by two well-known Soninke historians, Dr. Mamadou Diawara (of the Wissenschaftskolleg zu Berlin) and Professor Abdoulaye Bathily (of the Cheikh Anta Diop University of Dakar).

More crucially than the word list in table 7.1, the Wakpaarɛm praise formulas in table 7.2 display not only a Soninke-derived vocabulary (all listed in Table 7.1), but also a word order that conforms with heartland–Soninke usage.

Tables 7.1 and 7.2 show that the differences between Soninke and Wakpaarɛm include the shifts e ↔ ɛ, o ↔ ɔ, l ↔ d, and X ↔ k, g. As a result of this last shift, which we have also observed in Sillance, the Soninke words for "eyes" and "shame" become homophonous in Wakpaarɛm (yaago/yaagu). The differences also include the use of Soninke plural forms for both singular and plural in Wakpaarɛm (naanu, siinu), and changes in vowel quantity. In addition, the Wakpaarɛm plural form GƐSƐRƐbà follows a B'tɔnfim, rather than Soninke, pattern: in B'tɔnfim, nouns borrowed from other languages take the suffix bà in the plural (Dindi 1984: 97).

Nevertheless, it is clear that Wakpaarɛm's main derivation is from Soninke, not from Soŋoy as has hitherto been maintained. The name

"Wakpaarɛm" itself is a give-away, even though the GESERεbà whom we interviewed did not know its raison d'être. It is a name derived fourteen Wakpaarɛm words established by Tamou Bocko (1983:69), whose transcriptions followed the normal orthography of the French language but have been retranscribed here from a synonym for "Soninke" that occurs, in the Arabic transcriptions Waᶜkuruy, and ᶜHriyyūn (for Waᶜkuriyyūn), in the seventeenth-century Timbuktu chronicles. It also occurs, in forms such as Waakore, Wankore, Waakorey, Wakarey, and Waakaare, in modern Soŋoy dialects.[41]

The sound shifts required for the derivation of the name "Wakpaarɛm" from Waakore can be hypothetically traced with much plausibility, once one takes into account the influence of Bͻnfim (and of the Dèndí variety of Soŋoy) on the Wakpaarɛm language. It is to be assumed that—as happened to some of the words in table 7.1—the vowel *e* in Waakore changed into ɛ. If we also assume a shift o → ͻ as in the words *konpe* (Soninke) and *kͻmbɛ* (Wakpaarɛm) in table 7.1, we arrive at the starred (i.e., hypothetical) form *Waakͻrɛ. In addition, we know that the shifts kͻ ↔kpa, ko ↔ kpa, kw ↔ kpa, and kp ↔ w, are attested in Bͻnfim (and in the Dèndí of Borgu) by alternative toponyms such as Kͻrͻkfi / Kpřkfi (Parakou), and Bānīkͻàrà / Bānīkpàarù / Bͻnīkpàarà (Banikoara), in which *kpàrà* and *kpààrà* correspond to *kòyř* or *kwààř* in the Soŋoy of Gao and in Zarma. From these terms is generated the title of "town chief" (actually the office-holder who mediated between the chief and the Muslims). In Kpřkfi this officer is known as the Bàà-Kpàràkpe, and in Nìkì as the *Bàà-Wàràkpe.*

To complete the tracing of the derivation of the name "Wakpaarɛm," it is also necessary to take into account changes in vowel quantity, as in *saaraye* (Soninke) → *saraayɛ* (Wakpaarɛm, see table 7.1). And, finally, it must be noted that, in Bͻnfim, names of languages are generally formed by adding a final nasal to the name of the relevant ethnic group, as in Faransem—"French"— and Sɛrumam—"Zarma" (Bagodo 1988:3). Likewise, Dèndí is called Dennim in Bààtͻnúm.[42] The name "Wakpaarɛm" follows the same pattern. Hence, we may confidently   postulate   the   series   Waakore   →
*Waakͻrɛ → *Wakpaarɛ → Wakpaarɛm.   ·

Concluding Remarks

---

[41] See as-Saᶜdī (1964: text 9, transl. 18); Ta'rīkh al-fattāsh (1964: text 24-5, transl. 40-1); Prost (1956: 553); Olivier de Sardan (1982: 377-8).

[42] Interview: B. Damagii, April 1988.

The study of the ɢᴇsᴇʀɛbà requires both the examination of their past history and of their present mode of articulation with other sections of Borgu society. In addition, such a study also suggests prospects for the future.

Clearly, the ɢᴇsᴇʀɛ praise-chanters and specialists of the past are not a genetic isolate, biologically descended from nobody else but the ancestors they have in common with their present counterparts in the Soninke heartlands of Mali, Mauritania, and Senegal. Over the centuries, intermarriage of Soninke-speaking traditionists with the populations surrounding them in successive diaspora territories, and other ways of recruiting members of those surrounding populations into the ɢᴇsᴇʀɛ identity, have introduced new blood and new cultural (including linguistic) dimensions into that same identity. Moreover, in their progression from country to country, Jèsérè Dunka, and later ɢᴇsᴇʀɛ, specialists have adapted to (but also explored to their own advantage) the practices of the societies that have successively "hosted" them. These societies have been markedly different from the ɢᴇsᴇʀɛ original communities in the Manding-speaking heartlands. The ɢᴇsᴇʀɛbà do not select marriage partners in the same way as the Mandenka ŋamakalaw and the Soninke ŋaχamalo. Endogamy is no longer a constitutive element of their identity. The mode of clientage has thus changed (not to mention other changes in it, engendered by general transformations in Borgu society since the onset of colonization, with the demotion of old patron strata and the promotion of new, parvenu patrons).

Nevertheless, the fact remains that language and professional specialization, and the preservation of certain shared motifs, have maintained a perfectly recognizable historico-cultural connection between the Geseru of Mali, Mauritania, and Senegal, and the ɢᴇsᴇʀɛbà of Borgu, who live at the farthest end of the diaspora after centuries of progressive displacement over the geographical and social map of West Africa.

The Gesere/ɢᴇsᴇʀɛ communities distributed across the region are living proof of the far-reaching nature of intra-African cultural contacts in the precolonial period. They also bear witness to the multiple roots of African cultures and their capacity to integrate and rework new inputs. This is evidence that runs against any narrowly conceived, hyper-nationalist, present-day vision of cultural identity and authenticity in West Africa.

How does this study suggest new directions for the future of other postcolonial projects? What new understandings can be drawn from this rich past? First, we need to ask whether the performance language of the Gesere/ɢᴇsᴇʀɛ communities is still a fully living language, in the sense of having vocabulary relevant for day-to-day matters that is capable of generating a profusion of statements distinct from the praise formulas inherited from the past. This particular question may be answered only when further research is done into the lives of the communities spread over the diaspora's geographical arc.

However, independent of this, the very persistence of Soninke-derived performance languages in lands so far away from the Soninke homelands is a potential signpost. It points toward a renewed awareness of the intra-African "international" dimension of African cultures. More often than not, the GƐSƐRƐbà themselves are now oblivious of the distant beginnings of their own history and remain unaware of the fact that their performance language is derived from Soninke. Yet as new information becomes available to them and to others in Borgu, it is plausible to expect that a new interest in those (and other) remote connections will awake. One may hope that, ultimately, this will contribute to breaking the mold imprisoning much of the recent writing about West Africa, which has had an almost exclusive concern with what is close at hand, and with narrow definitions of the interpenetrating multiculturalities that characterize so many areas of the region. Then West Africa will fully exist as a historical subject on its own, distinct from a profusion of strictly local monographs.

ORAL SOURCES

This paper draws on oral evidence gathered from the following informants: (a) Sābī Maamaa, also known as Bàbu Adamu, a senior GƐSƐRƐ of the Bàà Maro lineage, interviewed in his compound in the Gàá ward of Kpàràkú (Parakou), Republic of Bénin, once in April 1988 and twice in January 1990; (b) Wōrū Tokura Bukari, the elderly head of the GƐSƐRƐɓ of Nìkì (Nikki), interviewed at the Nìkì–Wɔɔre ward in April 1988 and January 1990; (c) the Bɓ Damagii, a senior traditional office-holder of Kpàràkú, interviewed in his compound in the Sìnà Gūrù ward of that city in April 1988; (d) Iburaima Bàà GƐSƐRƐ, the Bàà Bwɛɛ or head of the GƐSƐRƐɓ of Bwɛɛ (Bouay) in the Republic of Bénin, interviewed in his compound in that town in January 1990; (e) Abudu GƐSƐRƐ Magasi, the head of the GƐSƐRƐɓ of Kãni (Kandi), in the Republic of Bénin, interviewed in his compound in that town in January 1990; (f) the Chief, and several of his courtiers (among them a GƐSƐRƐ), of Gbere Bɛrɛ (Baruten Local Government Area, Kwara State, Nigeria), interviewed in the Chief's compound in April 1993.

All these interviews were jointly conducted by Mr. O. B. Bagodo (a Lecturer at the Université Nationale du Bénin) and myself, in some cases together with Dr. Solomon Oyèéwọlé Babáyẹm (then of the Institute of African Studies, University of Ìbàdàn, now ọba Aknrᵛnọ́lá I, the olúfi of Gbọ̀ngán in Ọ̀ṣun State, Nigeria), who participated in interviews (b) (1988) and (c); and with Mr. O. Banni-Guénné (Secretary General of Bénin's National Commission for the Bo'o Language), who participated in interviews (a) (1990), (b) (1990), (d), and (e).

I also draw in this paper from my video recording of the Gaani festival of Nìkì, made on October 1 and 2, 1990, with the valuable assistance of Mr. O. B. Bagodo.

Bibliography

Akognon, Madeleine. 1980. "L'Organisation du pouvoir politique Wasangari à Kpandé (Kouandé) au XIXème siècle." Unpublished mémoire de maîtrise. Cotonou: Université nationale du Bénin, École Normale supérieure.

Bagodo, Obarè Bouroubin. 1978. "Le Royaume Borgou Wasangari de Nikki." Unpublished mémoire de maîtrise. Cotonou: Université nationale du Bénin, Faculté des lettres, arts et sciences humaines.

—. [1988] 1993. "Jalons et perspectives pour une approche des problèmes de chronologie dans l'histoire du Baruwu (Bargu) précolonial." Communication au Séminaire sur l'histoire nationale, Cotonou: Université nationale du Bénin, Campus d'Abomey–Calavi, 21–26 novembre 1988. *Afrika Zamani*, n.s., 1: 125–48.

Bako Arifari, Nassirou. 1989. "La Question du peuplement Dendi dans la partie septentrionale de la République Populaire du Bénin: le cas du Borgou." Unpublished mémoire de maîtrise. Cotonou: Université nationale du Bénin, Faculté des lettres, arts et sciences humaines, Département d'histoire et d'archéologie.

al-Bakrī, 'Abū ʿUbayd ʿAbdallāh b. ʿAbd al-ʿAzīz [1067–1068] 1965. *Kitāb al-Masālik wa'l mamālik*, joint reprint of the second rev. partial ed. De Slane, *Kitāb al-Mughrib fī dhikr bilād 'Ifrīqiya*, Algiers, 1911, and the French transl. De Slane, Description de l'Afrique septentrionale, second ed., Algiers, 1913. Paris: Adrien-Maisonneuve.

Bathily, Abdoulaye. 1967. "La Légende du Wagadou." Texte soninké de Malamine Tandyan, retranscrit, traduit et annoté par Abdoulaye Bathily. D'après Charles Monteil (1871–1949), *Bulletin de l'Institut fondamental d'Afrique noire* 29, B, 1–2: 134–49.

—. 1989. *Les Portes de l'or*. Paris: L'Harmattan.

Bio Guéné, K. 1978. "La Généalogie des rois de Nikki." Unpublished mémoire de maîtrise. Cotonou: Université nationale du Bénin, Faculté des lettres, arts et sciences humaines.

Bird, Charles S. 1970. "The Development of Mandekan (Manding): A Study of the Role of Extra-linguistic Factors in Linguistic Change." In David Dalby, ed., *Language and History in Africa*, 146–59, London: Cass.

Cissoko, Sèkéné-Mody. 1975. *Tombouctou et l'empire songhay*. Dakar and Abidjan: Les Nouvelles Éditions africaines.

Collins, John, and Paul Richards. 1982. "Popular Music in West Africa: Suggestions for an Interpretative Framework." In David Horn and Philip Tagg, eds., *Popular Music Perspectives*, vol. I, 111–41. Goteborg and Exeter: International Association for the Study of Popular Music.

Diawara, Mamadou. 1997. "Mande Oral Popular Culture Revisited by the Electronic Media." In K. Barber, ed., *Readings in African Popular Culture*, 40–48. Oxford and Bloomington: James Currey and Indiana University Press for the International African Institute.

Dieterlen, Germaine. 1975. "Premier aperçu sur les cultes des Soninké émigrés au Mali." *Systèmes de pensée en Afrique noire* 1: 5–18.

Dindi, J. S. B. 1984. "Le Btɔnfim." Unpublished mémoire de maîtrise. Cotonou: Université nationale du Bénin, Faculté des lettres, arts et sciences humaines.

Ducroz, J.M. and M.C. Charles. 1978. *Lexique Soŋey (Songay)-Français*. Paris: L'Harmattan.

Fisher, Humphrey J. 1993. "Sujūd and Symbolism: A Case Study in the Ambiguity of Symbolic Ritual Action in the Quran and in Western Africa." In O. Hulec and M. Mendel, eds., *Threefold Wisdom: Islam, the Arab World and Africa. Papers in Honour of Ivan Hrbek*, pp. 72–88. Prague: Oriental Institute.

Heine, B. 1970. *Status and Use of African Lingua Francas*. Munich: Weltforum Verlag.

Hunwick, J. O. 1970–1971. "African Language Material in Arabic Sources: The Case of Songay (Sonrai)." *African Language Review* 9: 51–73.

—. 1985. *Sharīca in Songhay*. Oxford and New York: Oxford University Press for the British Academy.

Idris, Musa Baba. 1972. "The Role of the Wangara in the Formation of the Trading Diaspora of Borgu." Paper contributed to the Conference on Manding Studies. London: University of London, School of Oriental and African Studies.

—. 1973. "Political and Economic Relations in the Historical Study of a Plural Society." Ph.D. thesis left incomplete at the author's death. Birmingham: University of Birmingham, Centre of West African Studies.

Ìrokò, Félix [Abọ́ĭ]. 1974. "Gao des origines à 1591." Unpublished Thèse pour le doctorat de troisième cycle. Paris: Université de Paris, Faculté des lettres et sciences humaines.

Levtzion, N. 1968. *Muslims and Chiefs in West Africa*. Oxford: Clarendon Press.

Lombard, J. 1965. *Structures de type 'féodal' en Afrique noire*. Paris and The Hague: Mouton.

Lovejoy, P. 1978. "The Role of the Wangara in the Economic Transformation of the Central Sudan in the Fifteenth and Sixteenth Centuries." *Journal of African History* 19, 2: 173–93.

Monteil, Charles. 1965. "Notes sur le Tarikh es-Soudan." *Bulletin de l'Institut fondamental d'Afrique noire* 27, B, 3–4: 479–530.

—. 1966. "Vocabulaire Soninke." Part I. *Bulletin de l'Institut fondamental d'Afrique noire* 28, B, 3–4: 676–89.

Monteil, Charles. 1967. "Vocabulaire Soninké." Part II. *Bulletin de l'Institut fondamental d'Afrique noire* 29, B, 1–2: 105–33.

Moraes Farias, P. F. de. 1990. "'Yoruba Origins' Revisited by Muslims." In P. F. de Moraes Farias and K. Barber, eds., *Self-Assertion and Brokerage*, 109–47. Birmingham: University of Birmingham, Centre of West African Studies.

—. 1992a. "History and Consolation: Royal Yorùbá Bards Comment on Their Craft." *History in Africa* 19: 241–72.

—. 1992b. "A Letter from Ki-Tooro Mahaman Gaani, King of Busa (Borgu, Northern Nigeria) about the 'Kisra' Stories of Origin (c. 1910)." *Sudanic Africa* 3: 109–32.
—. 1993. "ọ̀ŕnmy̌n's Frustrated War on Mecca: Reflexes of Borgu Ritual in Johnson's Yorùbá Narratives." In T. Fḷọ́ĭ, ed., *Pioneer, Patriot and Patriarch: Samuel Johnson and the Yorùbá People*, 121–32. Madison:

University of Wisconsin, Program of African Studies.

—. 1995. "Praise Splits the Subject of Speech: Constructions of Kingship in the Manden and Borgu." In G. Furniss and E. Gunner, eds., *Power, Marginality and Oral Literature*, 225–43. Cambridge: Cambridge University Press.

Mounkaïla, Fatimata. 1989. *Le Mythe et l'histoire dans la Geste de Zabarkâne*. Niamey: Centre d'études linguistiques et historiques par tradition orale.

Olivier de Sardan, J.-P. 1973. "Personnalité et structures sociales (À propos des Songhays)." In *La Notion de personne en Afrique noire* (Colloques internationaux du Centre national de la recherche scientifique 544), 421–45. Paris: C.N.R.S.

—. 1990. "Un barde, des scribes, et la geste du Songhay. . ." [Review Article]. *Cahiers d'études africaines* 118 (XXX – 2): 205–10.

Orou Yorouba, R. 1982. "La Gani et ses implications socio-économiques." Unpublished Mémoire de maîtrise. Cotonou: Université nationale du Bénin, Faculté des lettres, arts et sciences humaines.

Pacheco Pereira, Duarte [c. 1507]. 1956. "Esmeraldo de situ orbis." R. Mauny, ed. and partial trans., *Esmeraldo de situ orbis: Côte occidentale d'Afrique du Sud Marocain au Gabon*. Bissau: Centro de estudos da Guiné portuguesa.

Prost, A. 1956. *La Langue sonay et ses dialectes*. Mémoires de l'Institut français d'Afrique noire 47. Dakar: IFAN.

—. 1977. "Supplément au dictionnaire soŋay-français." *Bulletin de l'Institut fondamental d'Afrique noire* 39, B, 3: 584–657.

Rouch, J. 1953. "Contribution à l'histoire des Songhay." In *Mémoires de l'Institut français d'Afrique noire* 29: 137–259 and 5 plates, Dakar: IFAN.

—. 1954. *Les Songhay*. Paris: Presses universitaires de France.

Silla, Jiri. 1977. "Légende du Wagadu." Soninke text recited at Yerere (Mali), recorded by Malamine Cissé and translated into French by Abdoulaye Bathily. Niamey: Fondation SCOA.

Smith, P. 1973. "Principes de la personne et categorie sociales." In *La notion de personne en Afrique noire*, 467–90. Paris: Centre National de la Recherche Scientifique.

Stewart, Marjorie H. 1993. *Borgu and Its Kingdoms: A Reconstruction of a Western Sudanese Polity*. Lewiston, N.Y.: The Edwin Mellen Press.

Tamou Bocko, G. 1983. "Intégration sociale et personnalité Baatonu." Unpublished mémoire de maîtrise. Cotonou: Université nationale du Bénin, Faculté des lettres, arts et sciences humaines.

Ta'rīkh al–fattāsh [c. 1665]. 1964. Joint reprint of the 1913–1914 ed. and French transl. O. Houdas and M. Delafosse. Paris: Adrien-Maisonneuve for UNESCO.

Tersis, Nicole. 1968 [reprinted 1972]. "Le Dendi (Niger)." *Bulletin de la Société pour l'étude des langues africaines* 10: 1–88.

al-ᶜUmarī, Ibn Fad'l Allāh [c. 1337]. 1927. *Masālik al-abs`ār fī mamālik al-ams`ār*, partial transl. [Maurice] Gaudefroy-Demombynes, L'Afrique moins l'Égypte. Paris: Librairie orientaliste Paul Geuthner.

—. 1963. Arabic text of the *Masālik's* passages on Mali in s`Alāhu 'd-Dīn al-Munajjid, ed., *L'Empire du Mali vu par les géographes musulmans*, 41–70. Beirut: Dār al-kitāb al-jadīd.

8. Jeli and *Sere*: The Dialectic of the Word in the Manden

Karim Traoré

Introduction

The principal characteristic of Mande studies these days seems to be its dependence on its pioneers, whether colonial Europeans or Africans. This observation does not imply that we should break with our predecessors; far from it. But since these scholars only present a view of a specific period, it would be academically limiting not to dare to go beyond them or to outdo them. The Mande proverb "*i fa de ye i faden folo ye*" (your father is your first rival) deserves special attention, for above all it points to emulation with a view to progress, an indispensable feature of any social body.

But what explains the power of pioneers such as Delafosse, Vidal, and Niane? Apparently, the point is that we do not have especially copious sources. Another reason, linked to the first, is our uncritical attitude toward writing, which Ong (1982) tells us is fundamentally imperialistic. Furthermore, it would appear that we have internalized a perspective common to most of the men and women of the Mande cultural zone with whom we work, that of mythification. We do indeed tend to lack a critical spirit before anything written, or else we echo it to such a degree that we end up distorting the facts. This is true of the way in which scholars have perceived the role of the jeli in Mande society.

This chapter is intended to provide a perspective on certain current axioms of Mande studies concerning the production of knowledge (particularly literature and/or history). I will draw on the polysystematic theory of Even-Zohar (1979) and the "hybrid logic" of Jean-Loup Amselle (1985, 1990). The common point of these two approaches is to apprehend social facts as constructs, to view social boundaries as fluid, while admitting that they do occasionally coincide. Thus they allow a corrective to pure deconstruction, whose ahistorical character seems to me problematic. Although it is true that one cannot avoid *Sunjata* in studies of Mande culture, it does nevertheless seem problematic to assign the source of such knowledge only to the social category termed "jeli." Looking to hunters' literature and to the epic *Sunjata*, I intend to bring out the similarities as well as the differences in the construction of these ideological discourses, which are the most solid support for power systems in the Mande. This initiative is not the first of its sort, since Diawara (1990) had already used it in his book *La graine de la parole*. From the start, one assumption seems fundamental: this is not a historian's analysis, but a purely literary approach, although the genres involved are, in their social context of production, both "true history" (Kesteloot 1989) and fiction. One should see this as preliminary to any other form of literary analysis, for without precise knowledge of the (sociological) context of production, one might be led to confuse genres that are perceived as fundamentally different by all members of the society which produces these discourses.

The People of the Word

The social group which provides those empowered to speak (officially) about *Sunjata* is indisputably that of the jeli, whose essential characteristic is endogamy, as with other *nyamakala* social groups (the *numu, garanke*, etc.). Specialists of hunters' stories are called variously *sere, sora,* or *nkonifo/ngonifo*; they may also be termed *donsojeli*, which is of some importance for my argument. Linguistically, the donsojeli is a particular sort of jeli, since the first element of this compound noun (*donso*, "hunter") determines the second (jeli). Since linguistics is applied not only in the analysis of forms, we should also examine the usage from a sociopragmatic perspective. For we are dealing here with a kind of metaphor, neither fortuitous nor gratuitous: while a donsojeli may not be a jeli, there must nevertheless be some common ground to justify the creation of the metaphor. The donso (hunters and poets) form a society within a society; they are not organized in castes and do not constitute a caste.

The jeli are known as the praise-singers for all other social groups. Thus, they praise Sunjata and through him his "descendants," or, more generally, all the *horon* or even anyone who participates in Mande culture. The nkonifo are dedicated, in a similar fashion, to the hunters whom they will inspire or lambaste, as appropriate, through their stories. So we are dealing with the same principle of loyalty between "patrons and clients" (M. Diawara 1989). Batoma Sanogo expresses it in these terms: "If I see a hunter and I do not praise him, my mouth itches. . . ." (Haidara 1977). Similarly, Tumani Kone uses this leitmotiv in almost all his songs:

> N mana donso ye
> N bere n biran ye.

> When I see a hunter
> I see an in-law.

Baala Jinba baldly terms the hunters' bards (nkonifo) "*donso musoma*" (women hunters). I would not wish to gloss over this potentially antifeminist perspective;[1] I would rather stress the point that hunters and poets are perceived as being in an almost organic complementarity, which translates into a kind of sensuality. The relations of the jeli with his *jatigi* (patron) are not essentially different, and again we can look to a language usage to corroborate such a statement: in some Manden dialects the husband is known as "jatigi."

In these comparisons, the terms are apparently contradictory. While the image of the patron and of the husband (the dominant role) may be somewhat similar in their cultural context, it does seem surprising that Tumani Kone refers to the hunter as an in-law. In the Manden, the in-laws (the wife's family) are people before whom one must be absolutely discreet, for instance by speaking as little as possible. This point runs counter to the bard's almost uncontrollable need to praise. The solution seems to lie in the emphasis in Kone's speech upon gratitude toward the hunter, who gives him everything. A wife, in turn, is considered the most sacred "good" which a family may "offer" to another family or, for that matter, to anyone. So Kone has the same obligations toward hunters as would a young man before his mother- or father-in-law.

All these metaphors lead to a single goal: they mean that, socially, hunters and poets must maintain a symbiotic relationship, even one of total reciprocal trust. This is why, just as any political leader or prince will have his jeli, so also any great hunter has his bard who will know everything about him. This is obviously the minimal condition for any artistic creation intended to last through time. In terms of exchanges, the hunter provides for the material well-being of his poet, and in turn the latter endows his patron with immortality in collective awareness. Seyidu Kamara and Tumani Kone repeatedly say to their patrons:

> I te n son kan na
> N k'i son togo la.
>
> Give me then a tongue
> So I may make your name famous.[2]

---

[1] The problem of women will be treated in more detail in the following pages; see also Traoré 1992.

[2] Here, we note that the hunter is engaged in a perpetual quest for glory, for fame linked to the *togo* (first name)-- which is essentially individual-- while the mission of the jeli is to provide immortality to his jatigi by offering him texts built around his *jamu* (clan name). Further, the text of the quote plays with the polysemy of the word *kan*, which means both "neck" (of game) and "voice" (of a poet). Some poets will use the word *nen* (tongue) instead, which is literally less rich in the Manden; nevertheless, a good

This formulation recalls that which was attributed to Djeli Mamadou Kouyate: "through speech, we [the jeliw] give life to the deeds and feats of kings for the young generations" (Niane 1960: 9). Such a passage suggests another element of similarity between jeli and sere: both will readily dwell upon their skill in speaking and the source of this mastery of speech. In hunters' stories, the formula of choice to express this condition compares the poet to a songbird: Baala Jinba names himself "Badugu kono" (the singing-bird of [his land of origin] Badugu).

So we see that close relations exist between these two groups of "people of the word" (Sory Camara 1976). But the similarity does not stop there. It covers the initiation into speaking-skill as well as the form of literary discourse itself.

Initiation into Knowledge

Within Mande oral literature, *Sunjata* stems from what one might call the serious genre, as does hunters' literature. In opposition to more popular songs and stories, the people empowered to deliver the literary discourse should have undergone several years of professional education. While this training generally begins at home for the jeli, it often operates outside the family circle for those who wish to become hunters' bards, for while no one is born a sere, one must be born a jeli or he cannot be one. In other words, the profession of jeli rests upon a much wider institutional base, since it draws upon the whole of society. The jeli serves the entire society, although he may maintain a special relationship with a given family, while the sere serves only the hunters.

Relationships among Genres

In her article on African epics and identity, Christiane Seydou (1989: 7) brings out three elements shared by all African epics known to her:

> 1. The mode of utterance, which is linked to the formal aspect of speech.
> 2. The narrative logic, which always requires transgression.
> 3. The social function of the text, which consists in the "reactualization of an ideological identity, fundamental to unity in the community."

I intend to employ these typologic criteria to compare the production of hunters' bards with those of the jeli, possessors of the *Sunjata* epic. But before

translation of the quote in a European tongue (!) should substitute "tongue" for "neck" to reproduce the effect of a play with meanings: "Give me a tongue / So I may endow you with fame."

entering into the comparison in this tripartite set of terms, let us pause a minute at what Paul Ricoeur (1984: 60) calls the "narrative class."[3]

Logistic Resources

The two genres of literature that concern us cannot be imagined without a musical accompaniment. While the epic *Sunjata* may involve several instruments,[4] among which one must include the *nkoni*, hunters will provide the rhythmic accompaniment themselves, with a stringed instrument whose name and configuration change according to the region. In the Manden it is called "*sinbi*" and has a myth of origin, which is told much the same way almost everywhere. However, Mamby Sidibé (1982b: 19–43) does report a version that no informant has yet confirmed for me. In the Wasolon and among the Bamana, they call the instrument the "nkoni" or "*ngoni*."

Whether it be the epic Sunjata or hunters' stories, the poet is everywhere supported by a *naamunamine* (*naaumu*-sayer), a respondent, who on occasion may play a second accompanying instrument. In Wasolon, in Kita, and among the Bamana the naamunamine "scratches" the iron, which provides him with another name (*negeshiyen*, "iron-scratcher"). In the Manden, he plays no instrument; however, the poet always performs with a student who plays the second sinbi, and the negeshiyen may be included. Only in exceptional cases will the student fill both roles of musical accompanist and respondent. Most often, the naamunamine is a nyamakala (a numu or a jeli).[5]

As the performance of hunters' stories involves several artistic modes, audience participation is always a possibility; one of these modes is a sort of intermezzo consisting of refrains or popular tunes picked up by a chorus (of women) and/or the audience. Among hunters, those are the moments when dance may occur in the course of the story. Such interruptions are not customary during a classical performance of the epic *Sunjata*.

Terminology

---

[3] Ricoeur (1984: 60) opposes "narrative class" to "written expression" and writes, "We are faced with an almost innumerable variety of narrative expression (oral, written, graphic, gestural) and narrative classes (myths, folklore, fable, novel, epic, tragedy, drama, film, comic strips, not to mention history, painting, and conversation)."

[4] I have only attended sessions in which the musical instrument for the accompaniment was the nkoni. Apparently the *bala* (*balafon*/xylophone) is also used; this would hardly be surprising, especially if the jeli is a Kuyate; is it not reported in the epic that the jeli owe this instrument to Sumaworo, who gave it to Bala Fasseke, ancestor of the Kuyate?

[5] This is what I observed at all the appearances of Baala Jinba Jakite, who uses a numu or a jeli as naamunamine.

The epic *Sunjata* and the hunters' stories belong to the large generic class termed *foli*, which implies that the performance must include musical accompaniment. But beyond that vague designation[6] there are specific terms relating to the genres involved. The most frequent is *maana*, of Arabic origin. The Arabic source-word (*ma^cnaa*) means "meaning"; thus its use by the Mande to refer to a genre is interesting, for it implies that the story cannot be apprehended at the first level, but requires decoding and interpretation. In literature, one might say we are dealing with myth. Please note that I have no intention of drawing up a genealogy for the two genres, nor to explore how the whole of a text (be it epic or *donsomaana*) is/was conceived in its panegyric or narrative elements.[7]

Both sere and jeli view what they produce as maana. Socially, the maana is considered "true history" (Kesteloot 1989), in opposition to another narrative genre, the *(n)siirin* (tale),[8] which is thought be a lie, pure fiction. Indeed, one closing formula for tales stipulates that "*n ye nkalon soro yoro min, n y'a bila yen*" (I take this lie back where I found it). Does this mean that there is no generic difference between the hunters' stories and those told about Sunjata?

---

[6] The word "foli" is vague because it is polysemous. It is composed of *fo* (to say, to play an instrument) and *-li* (a suffix indicating a noun of action); it may have the meaning of "something said," "story," "tale," "tune," "melody," "piece," or "music."

[7] Austen (infra) sees the maana, the epic, as the narrative explication of the *fasa*, the panegyric which becomes obscure through time. This explanation can be supported, but from the perspective of literary sociology and taking into consideration the consumption patterns of literary productions in the region; panegyric and narrative texts may be consumed together or separately. It all depends on the context. As the narrative text is long, it is probable that it is only rarely delivered, or else will only be delivered in fragments. I possess a "daring" version of *Sunjata* spoken by a person whom one could not suspect of incompetence. Nevertheless, this version consists of a fasa sung by a woman and then rapidly commented by the jeli, the prestigious man of knowledge who was supposed to give me the secrets of the epic. Thus *Sunjata* is to be seen rather as a theme whose verbal expression will depend on the situation. My jeli thought he could trick me, thinking he was providing me with flummery; he was wrong, for he showed me much more on the context of production than I would have learned from any number of studies of literary sociology. In short, no extensive version of the epic can have been spoken except in a solemn, and hence artificial, context; I do not see this as a judgment of negative value, because any good literary work avoids spontaneity and presents itself as the fruit of thought-out labor. This also holds for spontaneous poetry in which the element of calculated effect is precisely its spontaneity.

[8] "Siirin" or "nsiirin" is the Bamana word for "tale." In Maninka and other Mandekan dialects this literary genre is called "*talen*" or "*taren*," which moreover may also mean "proverb" in certain cases, as among the Meeka (Marka-Dafing) of Burkina Faso.

No, for the jeli have another term less frequently used but applied only to the epic *Sunjata*: *tariki* or *tariku*. Once again, this term comes from Arabic (*tarikh*), where it means "history" or "chronicle." Here we are closer to reality, to what did happen. For indeed, the fundamental difference of the two genres is that one is of necessity constructed on the basis of history, while the other *may* involve pure imagination, which does not prevent it from being "true." Maana and/or tariki constitute what is generally called *kokoro* (old things), with sacred connotations. That is what makes these two forms of literature prestigious and serious. This is also what gives them an ideological mission, whose first step is to "pour collective and common knowledge . . . which carries the ideological values of the group into a form which will activate that knowledge by reviving in the audience an awareness of their distinctive identity and the desire to fulfill that identity through their participation in exaltation" (Seydou 1989:8). So let us try to discern more closely certain aspects of that activating form which Seydou mentions. It seems one must uncover the aesthetic means used by jeli and sere to recreate the common knowledge.

Aesthetics
        In theory one can imagine a first hypothetical case in which some normative rules of "speaking well" might explicitly prescribe the rules to be observed. Such a situation is comparable to the application of the rules of unity of time, place, and action that held sway over the aesthetics of classical European theater some centuries past. My knowledge of the art of the jeli does not allow me any definitive form of answer to such a question. Nevertheless, it is obvious that some controlling authority does keep watch and maintains a sort of norm in the story *Sunjata*. The control begins with the master from whom the jeli learns his art; it is implicit in the audience reaction when the speaker performs, and it culminates in that highest level of authority constituted by the committee of the *ngaara* (jeli of great talent), who meet every seven years in Kaaba (Kangaba) at the occasion of the reroofing of the Kamabolon, the Mande sanctuary. At that time, the epic *Sunjata* is recited in the presence of the Jabate jeli of Kela, a little village near Kangaba, who are the possessors of the "official version" (see Camara, Jansen, infra). Consequently, the Jabate of Kela judge the performance of other jeli, often their former students who have returned and thus submit to their sanction. In short, the epic *Sunjata* is subject to strict institutional control, and it is expected that initiates shall reveal nothing which might disturb the politico-ideological relationships governing the various actors in society.[9]
        As for the sere, he faces no such rigorous institutional control in the

---

[9] Is it not true that in Mande circles people say that Wa Kamissoko, a jeli of Krina, died because he did not observe these rules and revealed more than he ought? (See Cissé 1988.)

exercise of his art. Hunters expect from him only loyalty to "the children of Saane and Kontoron,"[10] as they name themselves. However, any sere who gives a series of bad performances finds the audience's dissatisfaction translated into a lack of commissions for hunters' gatherings. Moreover, the sere can judge the quality of his presentation from the audience's reactions.

Besides any normative considerations dependent upon an institution, one should also examine the texts for evidence, as they would conform to our literary concerns better than any sociological treatise. Indeed, when one listens to a version of *Sunjata* and to hunters' stories, one is struck by the way both genres delight in extremes and excess.[11] In German I term this literary effect "die Aesthetik des Grauens" (a translation, "aesthetic of horror" seems to me less suggestive). As an example, let us recall the ugliness of the young girl who will be Sunjata's mother. She is hunchbacked and covered with warts. Later, the same aesthetic effect appears when Dan Mansa Wulanba tries to sleep with her. The version published by Johnson (1992) says this:

> Dan Mansa Wulanba rose up,
> To seek pleasure and duty with his wife.
> He laid his hand on the Konde maid.
> Now, all women were taller than Sugulun Konde.
> All of them larger than Sugulun Konde.
> But she stretched out: bililili,
> Putting her feet against the back wall,
> And laying her head at the door,
> And projected two spikes from her breasts.

(Johnson 1992: 47)

---

[10] Variant terms: "Sane and Kondolon," "Sanin and Kontron," etc., but the pair is widely attested.

[11] I was very pleased to hear Karin Barber (1992) use similar terms to characterize a form of Yoruba literature. She described this in a discussion during the Annual Colloquium of the SFB 214 on Gender and Identity in Africa, July 9-11, 1992, University of Bayreuth.

Such an exaggeration may also recall another passage from certain versions of *Sunjata* in which Fakoli, who is known not only for his valorous deeds, but also for his ugliness (*Fakoli kunba ni Fakoli daba*, "Fakoli big-head and Fakoli big mouth"), increases in size. Massa Makan Diabaté reports, in his *Kala Jata*:

> Angered, the son of Kankuba Kante came in and stopped at the doorway of the great hut.
> "Remember," he said, "When I embraced the cause of the Mande, people laughed at my size, although I am already too big."
> Then he stretched himself, and his head knocked the roof from the hut.
>
> (Diabaté 1970a: 70)

The description of the slaughter of enemies is shockingly violent, considering the normal social context. The struggle of the two dogs (Johnson 1992: 63–64) does not appall only the ASPCA. Along the same line, the punitive expedition against the Jolof, and particularly the execution of the Jolofin Mansa by Tira Magan, which has today become almost a proverbial expression, has a violence which the beauty of the lines cannot quite mask. Youssouf Tata Cisse reports that "Malinke griots relate the killing of the king of Jolof in these terms: 'Tira Magan removed the large head from the neck of the Djolofing Mansa, and his buttocks quivered like a common bull sacrificed in the Manden'" (Cissé 1991: 95).

Hunters proceed no differently. One might even say that, for social reasons, their aesthetics of excess are even more pronounced. For while the mission of the jeli is to legitimize a politico-ideological system common to the whole of society, the hunter is less constrained by such considerations. Moreover, the art of the chase is by definition a murderous one; hence, the celebration of *kadogwelenya* and *yirimagwelenya* (ruthlessness and imperturbability) here reaches a paroxysm. The poet calls the hunter *miiribali* (one who does not think), thus signifying that in the course of his activities the hunter can hardly be troubled with domestic concerns. The hunters have an ascetic code of conduct, translated into everyday living by their sober appearance: they pay little attention to clothing; very great hunters bathe only rarely, and further, for several reasons, they do not wash their hunting clothes.[12]

This appearance, sometimes repugnant, is portrayed in the literature not only through profuse descriptions of physical and physiological endurance such

---

[12] The lack of bathing is supposed to hide the hunters' human scent from their animal prey.

as "*minnogolamunyu ni kongolamunyu*" (he who resists hunger and thirst), but also through hair-raising and heart-stopping situations. One of the most repulsive scenes appears in a text by Baala Jinba. Jinba tells how Manbi, seeking hunter's lore, meets a jinn named Nama. Nama is a hideous being, legless and hirsute. His mop of hair squirms with lice, which the person in quest of initiation must kill. After each day of work, Manbi is rewarded with a hunting *boli* (sacred protective object).

As it happens, this text from Baala Jinba well illustrates my remarks about violence. For having been humiliated in this manner during his quest for knowledge, Manbi then kills his initiator and marries his wife. From this union comes a girl named Saane, who will inherit her father's knowledge (his greatest *boli* is Kontoron); Saane and Kontoron are the two greatest hunting deities. We should note that this version by Baala Jinba makes Kontoron a *boli*, while others depict him as a man who may be the son of Saane, or her brother, sometimes even brother and husband, although this last configuration occurs only in the version of Mamby Sidibé (Cissé 1964, 1973; Mamby Sidibé 1982; Traoré 1992, 1994).

An interesting feature of the relationship between Saane and Kontoron (the man) is that Saane is always presented as the possessor of knowledge, from which Kontoron benefits at the price of unconditional allegiance. This contrasts with the numerous hunting stories built around a model of the murder of the (male) being, the father, from whom one gains one's knowledge; such applied knowledge is a secret that cannot be shared.[13]

Hunters and Women

In the course of this summary presentation I pass in silence over many other elements of the aesthetic wealth of the children of Saane and Kontoron. Among these are the innumerable epithets and apparently ordinary phrases (for example, *donso man nyi* [the hunter is terrible], which may be positive or negative in content, but in either case highlights the point that the hunter is extraordinary in the true sense of the word). But we must come to another point

---

[13] The murder of the benefactor could not function in *Sunjata*, which I read as a social charter based upon the principle of *badenya* ("harmony," "accord"; cf. Johnson, McGuire, infra). Obviously, elements of society know quite well that political power goes along with violence ("reasons of state"), but the particularity of *Sunjata* is that it either attributes the scenes of violence to another person (Fakoli, Tira Magan), or it assigns them some other socially acceptable dimension, as in the case of the sacrifice of the unborn fetus and its mother in the version of Fadigi Sisoko (Johnson 1992: 67ff.). Nevertheless, other epic traditions derived from *Sunjata* do operate in the same way as the hunters' traditions, as in the Haalpulaar epic of *Samba Guéladiégui* published by Amadou Ly (1991). The principal characteristic of Samba is his violence, which expresses the *ceddo* ethic.

which is crucial for any comparison of the two genres: the treatment of women.

Jeli and sere both make much of the respect that any child owes its parents, and particularly its mother.[14] Since this stems from social proprieties accepted by all, there would be no reason to dwell on the point in a literary analysis, except that there is an entire discourse based upon, or justifying, this mode of conduct. Indeed, it is supposedly from such respect that the child (mainly male) will derive its later success in life. A proverb says "*musow de be cew bo nyogon na*," which we may translate as "it is women that make men different from one another." According to this adage, all men are born equal, and it is thanks to the virtue of the mother or the wife that one man will surpass another in any enterprise involving a form of competition.

In almost all the versions of *Sunjata* this point is perfectly well illustrated by the contrast between the career of the hero, Sunjata, and that of Dankaran Tuman, his halfbrother and rival. Dankaran Tuman's mother is very nasty, and the effects are felt by her son, who loses in the struggle for succession to the throne. Still within the same epic, Sumanguru, the invader struggling with Sunjata, does not heed his mother and offers her violence when she tries to warn him against a stranger, a one-night woman, to whom he is revealing his secrets. This one-night woman is none other than Sunjata's sister, sent by him on a mission. The mother, the amorous son, and the seductress constitute a typical pattern in hunting stories (Traoré 1992, 1994).

In everyday life, the mother in particular is seen as the founder of her children's future. Among hunters one cannot reduce the mother to a simple source of happiness and success; she provides the very base of the ideological system, as I observed above when discussing the two principal deities, Saane and Kontoron. For while stories about the origin of hunting may diverge on a number of points, all versions insist on the critical and constant presence of a feminine element. This is why we should carry our interpretation of the mother's role beyond that of simple source and condition of success for her progeny; the mother symbolizes the feminine divinity (Saane), who seems the most important spiritual force in the hunters' universe. Is the neophyte hunter not asked to accept the primacy of the hunters' association (expressed as loyalty to Saane and Kontoron) over all other forms of social authority, including that of his mother? There are two presentations of female power in hunting that emphasize both the mother and her opposite.

First, the mother appears as a character in the stories more often than does the father. Even when both parents appear, the mother is assigned the more

---

[14] Here let me refer to the works of Bird (1972) and Bulman (1989). Apparently, Bulman's "Buffalo-Woman Tale" article was slumbering in my unconscious as I began my work on the present theme. I realize that I have picked up a number of his ideas for my own purposes.

active role. One might retort that she is only a helper, but that is exactly the function of a divinity—to help the believer. Moreover, as Sory Camara reports in a story on the origin of power in a tale of the Manden (1980: 126–45), what is involved is not political power in the Western sense but, rather, the whole system of thought that presents power as the skill of joining to oneself superhuman or supernatural forces.

This quest for occult forces, for means of power (*dalilu* and *nya* [secret means and knowledge]), as we have seen, often leads to violence or at least to a very aggressive posture on the part of the quester when faced with the possessor of knowledge. So it is in Sory Camara's tale; with the complicity of an old woman, two young men succeed in stealing the power which was guarded by hyenas in the bush.

Camara provides the interesting comment that men owe their power to their great suspicion of women. This attitude recalls the treatment inflicted by great hunters on the jinns or other supernatural beings who help them in their quest for "power-knowledge." This myth offers another vision of women, hard to reconcile with the idea of the mother since the two brothers show no signs of gratitude toward the old woman. We might recall that the old woman is more to be identified with a mother (grandmother) than with a spouse.[15]

How, then, can we explain the paradoxical existence of two such visions of women? A first explanation might lie within the fact of contact with Islam, which we know projects an image of women that agrees perfectly with the two positions described. One should not reject the idea completely, but it must be placed within a precise social context to be defensible. For we have seen that *Sunjata* and the hunters' stories depend upon specific social levels of authority represented by institutions. Beyond them exists the larger community, in whose name those institutions were established and through which they construct their reality. After all, no institution, no matter how esoteric, can disregard society, as it is for and through the society that institutions live.

Jeli and sere both draw from a popular well in which literary expression (tales, proverbs, songs, etc.) requires no special training. This does not mean that everybody can sing or tell a story very well. The tale published by Sory Camara is indisputably the work of a deeply knowledgeable person, for that tale is certainly the model for the episode of the two brothers and the Buffalo of Do in *Sunjata*. The epic context highlights the badenya (social harmony), later incarnated by the avatar of the Buffalo in the person of Sunjata's mother, whereas Sory Camara's "popular" narrator gives us rather the vision of the community. This point is accepted by researchers, who all agree that epics at all

---

[15] We should observe that a form of generational play makes the grandparents the mates (or rivals) of their grandchildren. But it seems obvious that one cannot interpret the myth through that paradigm.

times have been composite in their motifs, the genres they incorporate, and their functions. To insist upon the portrayal of a world full of harmony on the one hand, and on the Muslim-Oriental origin of Sunjata on the other, well illustrates the quest for integration in the service of legitimation (see Diawara, infra, for the importance of Islam).

Let us return to the problem of women and the second possible explanation for the two visions of them in the epics. Among hunters, it would seem necessary to distinguish clearly between two types of women: first, the woman-goddess, Saane, whose imperfect avatar would be the mother-figure encountered in many tales; next, there is the actual human woman, whose image is ambiguous, to say the least. In other words, hunters experience two realities: that of their ton, which imposes on them a love and respect for Saane, represented in the actual world by the mother, and that of an essentially phallocratic (male-dominated) society. Woman, source of life and knowledge, is unfathomable to the man who can only place the mystery outside the framework of the culture and thus in the bush. This explains why, in some stories, the hunter may make the woman a beast, whom one may not trust and who should be slain. This said, however, it is not the mother—her character is sexually neutral or supposedly pure—who is slain, but a sexed female being, thus comparable to a *faden* (rival).[16] The paradoxical coexistence of positive and negative images is not surprising but logical and, from the literary point of view, fascinating.

Final Remarks

I intended this chapter as a reminder, in very general terms, that our knowledge of African societies, and here specifically a society claiming to belong to Mande culture, is subject to the "people of the word." Speech is so important that it transforms all forms of knowledge in literature, and this makes the classical divisions of literature current in Europe obsolete. For this reason, researchers prefer an interdisciplinary approach to their corpus while still favoring their discipline of origin.

In the construction of knowledge, jeliw seem to hold a monopolistic position, not through their action but, rather, through the ways researchers have concentrated almost exclusively upon them. Moreover, African literary study has developed a metaphor which, from the Mande perspective, cannot apply: one readily compares modern writers to griots.[17]

This is why I have undertaken this presentation of the discursive system

---

[16] See, for instance, the story "Manden Mori" in Cashion 1984: appendix 1.

[17] In contrast, popular parlance uses the term "griot" to refer to hired spokesmen for various dictatorial regimes; "This isn't journalism, it's griot-work" is frequently heard in Bamako, Abidjan, or Ougadougou.

of hunters' bards, to bring out the similarities of jeli and sere. The two literary genres they produce—maana and donsomaana—stem from the same society, and so to place them purely in opposition would be questionable; they do have a relationship of complementarity, each having its own territory.

Thus, the epic of Sunjata fulfills a political purpose. Conceived in an aristocratic milieu on the basis of composite materials deriving from popular tales, myths, and hunters' songs, the epic of Sunjata—and more generally the epic of the Mande—nowadays appears to us a strong figure for identification, both on the national and the pan-African level. This is where one should underline the aesthetic genius of the jeliw who have succeeded in "mythifying" the character so much that they have survived a fair number of their successors, whose names are known only to historians. Institutionally, this mythification is almost a deification, insofar as Sunjata alone fills the epic space both within the "original Manden" and in the whole Mande cultural zone (Diawara, infra).

Dialectically, this apparently enduring omnipresence is hard to imagine without a counterweight elsewhere in the social system. In my opinion, the literary production of the hunters constitutes such a counterweight, although the performers may not necessarily be conscious of this role. Not only do their narratives immortalize Sunjata's generals, almost never mentioning Sunjata himself, but they also develop another ideology. This worldview is admittedly still elitist, but remains significantly more egalitarian and individualistic within a society that normally sets great store by community, and classifies individuals by birth, by sex, and by age.

It is particularly in the context of recent social transformations that the practical effects of the ideology of the hunters' societies as a potential engine for change can be most clearly shown. For although it is recognized and accepted that most jeli nowadays find themselves obliged to change professions, it remains somewhat unacceptable for a horon to earn a living producing modern music. This resistance is not only due to some prejudice against the dissolute life involved but, rather, to the idea that music is part of the domain of the jeli: people still remember the scandal caused by Salif Keita (very evidently a member of a horon lineage) in his family and village during the 1970s. Today this same singer, perhaps the greatest international star of Mande music, is accepted almost everywhere. This normalization is due not only to Salif Keita's success and wealth, but also in large part to his change of artistic inspiration. For now Salif Keita draws most of his repertoire from the hunters' bards, who recognize neither ethnic group nor caste.[18]

---

[18] Salif Keita, like myself, regularly consults the master sere, Baala Jinba Jakite. On the cover of his latest CD, Salif Keita wears hunters' dress, although the volume has an oriental-religious title, "Amen," which is hardly donso (Salif Keita, *Amen*, Island Records Ltd., 1991). On that disk, the song "Lony" (*lonni*, "knowledge") celebrates the greatest source of power in any society, which leads Keita to place Mande sages, such as Suwareba, alongside the modern science that allows planes to fly, the doctor to open up

The example of Salif Keita underlines the general argument which has been made here. By playing on the pivotal role occupied by the hunters' corporations in Mande culture and society it is possible to perceive—and respond to—this world in a new manner.

---

the stomach, etc. Kassé Mady Diabaté, jeli by birth from the prestigious village of Kela, is/was also a student of Baala Jinba Jakite. He has adapted several stories and tunes drawn from the repertoire of the sere, such as "Manden Mori" and "Kulanjan" (Cassette, *Fode*, released in 1988, from which some pieces were reproduced on his CD released in 1990 by Stern's Africa, London and New York).

Bibliography

Barber, Karin. 1991. "Multiple discourses in Yorùbá Oral Literature." *Bulletin of the John Rylands Unversity Library of Manchester* 73, 3 (Autumn): 11–24.

Bazin, Jean. 1985. "A chacun son Bambara." In Amselle, Jean-Loup et al., eds., *Ethnie et espaces: pour une anthropologie topologique.* Paris: Éditions la Découverte.

Camara, Sory. 1980. "Le pagne de la vieille femme ou l'origine de la royauté." In ACCT, ed., *Recueil de littérature manding*, 126–45. Paris: ACCT.

Cissé, Youssouf. 1973. *Un récit initiatique.* Boli-Nyanan: D.E.P.H.E.

Cissé, Youssouf, and Wa Kamissoko. 1991. *Soundjata, la gloire du Mali. La grande geste du Mali* - Tome 2. Paris: Karthala-ARSAN.

Couloubaly, Baba F. 1990. *Une société rurale bambara à travers des chants de femmes.* Dakar: IFAN-Dakar.

Derive, Jean. 1978. "L'utilisation de la parole traditionnelle dans *Les Soleils des Indépendances* d'Ahmadou Kourouma." *L'Afrique littéraire et artistique* 54–55: 103–10.

—. 1990. "L'oralité africaine ou la littérature en kit . Réflexions sur l'apport de l'étude de l'art oral à quelques problèmes théoriques de la littérature générale." In János Riesz and Alain Ricard, eds., *Semper aliquid novi. Littérature comparée et littératures d'Afrique*, 215–25. Mélanges offerts à Albert Gérard. Tübingen: Gunter Narr Verlag.

Derive, Marie-José. 1980. "Bamori et Kɔwulen. Chant de chasseurs de la région d'Odienné chanté par Amara Fofana." Transcribed by Marie-José Derive on 4 March 1975. In *Recueil de Littérature Manding*, 74–107. Paris: ACCT.

Diagne, Bachir Souleymane. N.d. *De l'oralité à l'écriture: transcription et création.* Unpub. ms.

Diarra, Abdramane. 1986. *Politische Sozialisation und Rolle der Frau in Mali.* Aachen: Rader.

DNAFLA. N.d. "Bani ŋenema: un récit de Baatɔɔma Sanɔgɔ." Production,

DNAFLA. Published with the permission of the ACCT, 42 pages; also available as a cassette. Batoman Sanogo presents (Bani Gnanama), Vol. 4., 1989. Producer: Siriman Diallo Immeuble Danzoumana [sic] Fofana, B.P. 346 Bamako (Mali), [SD 004].

Even-Zohar, Itamar. 1979. "Polysystem Theory." In *Poetics Today* I, 1–2 (Autumn): 287–310.

Finnegan, Ruth. 1977. *Oral Literature in Africa*. Oxford: Oxford University Press.

—. 1992. *Oral Traditions and Verbal Arts. A Guide to Research Practices*. London and New York: Routledge.

Haïdara, Gaoussou. 1977. *La légende de Magan*. A recounting of the hunt of Batoma Sanogo, Gaoussou Haidara transcr., trans, and ed. Bamako: Mémoire de fin d'études. ENsup, 103 pages.

Keita, Modibo. 1983. Transcription, traduction et analyse de Nyagalenba [a recounting of the hunt by Baala Guimba Diakité]. Bamako: Mémoire de fin d'Etudes, ENSup.

Kesteloot, L. 1989. "Le pouvoir féodal dans les mythes et épopées du Mandé." Paper at the 15th ALA-Conference in Dakar, 20–23 March. Unpub. ms.

Ly, Amadou, ed. 1991. *L'épopée de Samba Guéladiégui*. The oral version peul de Pahel collected and translated into French by Amadou Ly. Preface by Lilyan Kesteloot. Editions Nouvelles du Sud/IFAN/UNESCO.

Niane, D. T. 1975. *Le Soudan Occidental au temps des grands empires, XIe–XVe siècle*. Paris: Présence Africaine.

Ong, Walter J. 1982. *Orality and literacy. The technologizing of the word*. London: Methuen.

Ricoeur, Paul. 1984. *Temps et récit. Tome II: la configuration dans le récit de fiction*. Paris: Editions du Seuil.

Seydou, Christiane. 1989. "Epopée et identité: exemples africains." *Journal des Africanistes*, 58, Fasc. I: 7–22.

Sidibé, Mamby. 1982a. *Contes populaires du Mali I*. Paris: Présence Africaine.

—. 1982b. *Contes populaires du Mali II.* Paris: Présence Africaine.

Téra, Kalilou. 1980. "Le retour de Jiji-le-Pélerin suivi de quelques chants liturgiques de Seydou Camara." In Kalilou Téra, ed., *Recueil de littérature manding*, 215–37. Paris: ACCT.

Thoyer, Annik, ed. 1986. *Nyakhalen la forgeronne de Seyidou Kamara.* Self-published.

Thoyer-Rozat, Annik, ed. 1978. *Chants de chasseurs du Mali*, vol.3. Self-published.

Thoyer-Rozat, Annik, and Lasana Dukure, eds. 1978. *Kanbili. Chant de Chasseurs du Mali*, vol 2. Self-published.

Traoré, Issa. 1970. *Contes et récits du terroir.* Bamako: Editions Populaires.

Traoré, Karim. 1995. "Bɛɛ y'i ba bolo (Everybody lies in her/his mother's hands): Gender Issues in the Hunters' Songs of the Mande." In Mechtchild Reh and Gudrun Ludwar-Ene, eds., *Gender and Identity in Africa*, 85–97. Munster/Hamburg: Lit Verlag.

Traoré, Karim. 1994. "Les enfants de Saanɛ et de Kɔntɔrɔn: A propos des chasseurs du Mande." In Riesz, János and d'Almeida-Topor, eds., *Echanges franco-allemands sur l'Afrique.*

9. Mooning Armies and Mothering Heroes: Female Power in Mande Epic Tradition

David C. Conrad

"It is hard to give birth to a child who will be famous."
"The father is everybody's, the mother is personal."
D. T. Condé*[1]

Jeli ngaraw, master bards of the Mande heartland who narrate the most substantive variants of their venerable epic tradition, do not usually refer to it by Sunjata's name. To many performers it is Manden *tariku* — the book, chronicle, or story of the Manden. It is to the Arabic derivative tariku (Ar. *tarikh*) and not to the French *épopée* that has, for the Mande people, accrued the mystery and power conveyed by the indigenous phrase *kuma koro* (ancient speech).[2] Kuma koro probably conveys the purest sense of what the "Chronicle of the Manden" means to the jeli ngaraw themselves. In addition to Sunjata, they speak at length of many prominent male and female ancestors, because their discourse represents the Mande people's perceptions of their entire history, not just the story of a single heroic figure. For each clan of the Maninka, Bamana, and other Mande-speaking peoples, the Manden tariku is the true (and in a sense sacred) story of ancestors who remain very much a part of daily life.

Nevertheless, for non-Mande people to refer to the Manden tariku as *"The Epic of Sunjata"* is not inappropriate, because the title *"Sunjata"* evokes homage to the most powerful of mother-son combinations which, for the

---

[2] Chérif Keita told me about the special significance of *kuma*. I use the phrase in this paper as a refreshing synonym for the over-worked "epic" and "oral tradition." In general Bamana and Maninka usage, terms for "epic" include *wasala* and *maana*.

Maninka, represents the defining events of their cultural heritage. The name "Sunjata," in its many manifestations ranging from Soundjata to Son-Jara, derives from the common Maninka practice of linking the offspring's name with that of the mother. The hero of Mande epic is "Sogolon Jara," after his mother Sogolon.[3] Among many of the hero's praise-names "So'olon Jara" is still heard in performances, along with "So'olon Ma'an" (Sogolon's Maghan or "King"). Usually, however, the phrase is contracted to some form of "Son-Jara" which, true to jeli oral artistry, contains multiple praising. "Son-Jara" includes homage to both Sogolon Ba ("Great Sogolon") herself and to Sogolon's Jara ("Sogolon's Lion") or Sogolon's Jala, evoking the bitter bark of the spiritually significant *jala* tree (*Khaya senegalensis*), with which jeliw praise powerful rulers.[4]

The combination of praise for both the thirteenth-century imperial hunter/warrior and for his mother Sogolon that is inherent in the name "Son-Jara" reflects an essential truth of the Mande intellectual system. This is the acknowledgment that men derive their power from their mothers and that human existence and survival depend on the strength of women: "The son's *basi* (medicine/spiritual power) comes from the mother" (Mamady Condé*). In the Bamana/Maninka view according to Sarah Brett-Smith's study of Bamana sculptors, female strength is nothing short of miraculous, owing to women's ability to vanquish death by creating another life. The intrinsic ability of women to produce new human beings is regarded as "the ultimate in human power." The Bamana believe that "men can kill, but they cannot make children. They can guarantee extinction, but they cannot assure survival" (1994: 33).

A scarcity of certain details about major characters and events in the previously available corpus of Mande narrative has dictated that, with the exception of the Do Kamissa buffalo episode (Bulman 1989), discussions of politically significant people of Mande epic have tended to focus on only a few of the most illustrious *kelemansaw* (war kings) of the old Manden's glory, such as Sunjata and Fakoli (Bird and Kendall 1980; Conrad 1992). This chapter introduces material on thirteenth-century *Sunjata* and nineteenth-century *Almami Samori*, selected from Maninka oral tradition of Upper Guinea collected and translated in 1991, 1992, and 1994. These and other recently collected texts have not yet been thoroughly examined and compared with the overall corpus of available sources, so it is too early to assess their possible historical content according to Western ideas of history, which differ from Mande perceptions. The eventual goal of this project would be to explore what the overall corpus of epic oral texts or kuma koro has to say about female power and how that relates to modern cultural studies and confirmed historical evidence. In the shorter

---

[3] For example, a man known as Makula Mamadi is actually "Makula's Mamadi," identified by his mother's feminine name Makula, distinguishing him from other Mamadis in his father's compound or town.

[4] For example, "Sap of the jala tree and *burugu* tree" (Conrad 1990: 111). The tree is known as one of those favored by genies (jinn).

term, the material referred to here draws attention to episodes of Mande discourse indicating that within the kuma koro, women receive a very considerable share of the credit for founding both the Mali empire and its enemy state of Soso that flourished to the north of the Mande heartland.[5] Without entering into lengthy discussion of sorcery and related topics that would be premature at this stage of research, the reader's attention will be drawn to a few recent studies for some indication of how and where the material from oral tradition fits into the Mande cultural context. For example, in considering how jeli discourse reflects attitudes toward women and vice versa, it can be seen that episode after episode of Maninka narrative from Upper Guinea supports Sarah Brett-Smith's (1994) assessment of the Bamana worldview, and her work will be frequently cited here.

By pointing out correspondences between certain rituals and beliefs in today's Manden on the one hand and episodes of oral tradition purporting to recount very early events on the other, I do not mean to suggest that the Mande worldview of today is the same as that which prevailed in thirteenth- and fourteenth-century Mali. We know from the Arab chronicles that there were jeliw in Mansa Sulayman's fourteenth-century court (Levtzion and Hopkins 1981: 293) who fulfilled the same functions that they did in nineteenth-century royal households (Bérenger-Féraud 1882: 267–77; Mage 1868: 307–308; Soleillet 1887: 402–403), and archaeological evidence indicates that in Jenne-Jeno many centuries before the time of Sogolon Condé, blacksmiths (numuw) were probably functioning as spirit mediators just as they do now (Roderick McIntosh 1993). Nevertheless, rituals and institutions of the Mande belief system have doubtless undergone significant change since Sunjata's day, and for the most part we are unable to gauge the nature or timing of that change. Similarly, we cannot pinpoint the insertion of various themes into the epic corpus, or trace the evolution of episodic narrative events. In this discussion I acknowledge some results of recent research into the Mande value system with special reference to Sarah Brett-Smith's work with Bamana sculptors, and I note correspondences between her data and recently translated passages of epic tradition, mostly from Upper Guinea.

If, in the kuma koro or ancient speech, men are the instruments of conquest and destruction, those who can kill but not bring forth new life, women are the sabuw (sources, providers) of all that these men accomplish. Traditional narrative presents the men as instruments (sometimes lethal) that may go astray at any time, requiring guidance by mothers and sisters who provide them with their martial power and lead them to their destined paths, unleashing them upon the world. For every hero such as Sunjata or Fakoli, there is a female sabu. She is usually the mother (or in Fakoli's case his fostermother), but she can also be

---

[5] Master bards of Upper Guinea have no doubt about the location of ancient Soso, which they say was immediately north of present-day Bamako. They also name Soso's four provinces and Sumaworo's spirit centers (or "provincial capitals" in European terms).

the sister, and in some cases these women assume genuine heroic stature. Also prominent in the discourse is another brand of heroine whose credentials are not based on the sabu of motherhood to a hero. These are wives and lovers who risk their lives and are sometimes put to death by the men who benefit most from their deeds.

This chapter will explore how female power — as it appears in Mande epic discourse — is expressed through women's command of metaphysical processes, and also through heroines whose resources are limited to personal courage and traditional areas of female influence. For the sake of this discussion, heroines of kuma koro can be said to occupy those two very rough categories: women who achieve great deeds with sorcery, and those who distinguish themselves without sorcery, through their own innate abilities.[6] Most of the examples presented below were chosen to demonstrate those characteristics with no intention of surveying the entire scope of female representation in Mande narrative. This discussion is therefore biased toward the more dramatic images of powerful women. The epic discourse comprises a vast body of material, and readers are encouraged to consider the overall corpus before arriving at any general conclusions about women as portrayed in Mande oral tradition.

Sabu, Seduction, and Betrayal
In a previous discussion of themes linked to *Sunjata*, I identified a narrative device, for want of a better term, as the "femme fatale" motif (Conrad 1992: 167). At one level of Mande discourse this motif involves the betrayal of some formidable adversary by a "favorite wife" (*bara muso*) or a seductive female stranger as the means by which the hero acquires the information or device necessary for conquest. Beginning in childhood, the hero's path to triumph is arduous and complex, and larger-than-life figures like Sunjata and Fakoli achieve their goals through valences of power originating from a variety of sources. An apparently historical example from the Arabic chronicles will be noted later, suggesting that some heroines of the femme fatale motif are based on recollections, however distorted they may be, of actual ancestresses whose now legendary characteristics and accomplishments reflect values recognizable in today's society. The femme fatale's real cultural foundation is greater than the sum of its anecdotal (or legendary) parts, in that the hard evidence from modern cultural studies provides more insight on ideas of "dangerous" or "threatening" women than can be found in oral tradition (e.g., Jackson 1982: 225–31; Herbert

---

[6] In the overall corpus of Mande oral tradition it is doubtless possible to find a female character who employs both strategies, or who is a sorceress in one text but not in another, e.g., Sogolon herself. Sarah Brett-Smith suggests a correlation between the two groups of women and fertility vs. infertility (pers. comm. June 15, 1995). In some cases, e.g., Do Kamissa, the sorceress does appear to be postmenopausal, but others such as Sogolon and her co-wives are not. On the other hand, the "femme fatale" is almost by definition young, attractive, and presumably fertile.

1993: 85ff.; Brett-Smith 1994: 208–209). It seems justified, therefore, to take this aspect of Mande *kuma koro* as too significant to simply dismiss it as entirely "mythical."

Popular on a superficial level as merely a storytellers' device, the *femme fatale* is a seductive and often treacherous woman who, without the benefit of occult powers, betrays the enemy and provides the hero with the key to victory: Sunjata over Sumaworo, Tiramakan over Jolofin Mansa, Fakoli over Niani Mansa Kara Kamara, Faama Da over Basi of Samanyana (F. Diabaté 1975*; Vidal 1924: 326; Cissé 1975: 105–80; Niane 1965: 64; Kesteloot 1972: vol. 1, 33–58, vol. 2, 34–60). The men whom these women serve and the *jeliw* who tell the story (it is basically all the same one) express their own attitudes toward the *femme fatale* through variations of such sentiments as "never trust any woman" (Jackson 1982: 229), "all heroes who perish, do so as victims of woman's treachery" (Cissé 1975: 163), and "if you see men fighting, it is women who make us fight" (Conrad 1990: 291). Proverbs reflecting female marginalization on the one hand and epic discourse exalting heroines on the other demonstrate the ambiguous position of women in Mande society (Hoffman 1994).

On the negative side of this ambiguity are such institutionalized rituals and processes as the suspicion and apprehension of women by hunters as distracting sexual beings, impeding chances of a successful hunt (Cashion 1984), and the intricate taboos associated with the smelting of iron ore (Herbert 1993). On the positive side are episodes of epic discourse containing implicit acknowledgment that females, however dangerous they may be, lay the foundation of male success.

If the *femme fatale* is an agent of destruction as the betrayer responsible for her male victim's downfall, it is through this process that she becomes the *sabu* (source/provider) of a significant historical person or event. Sijanma the slave girl betrays Basi and brings Samanyana's defeat by the army of Segu, but she is the source of one more success by the ruling Jara dynasty (Conrad 1990: 210–64). In the *Almami Samori* epic of Upper Guinea, Gbankundo Saaji Kamara's favorite wife Kagbé betrays her husband and causes his defeat, but in so doing she becomes a contributing *sabu* of Samori's first empire (Vase Kamala,* Sori Fina Kamara* versions 1 and 2). In these cases men appropriate women's abilities for their own use, but women's power must be contained if it is not to overwhelm the men. In matters crucial to political authority, including the *komo* association, female ability can be accorded recognition and even obedience, but once the presence of a woman becomes threatening, she may be destroyed (Brett-Smith 1994: 254).

Legendary heroines like Sijanma and Kagbé who take grave risks without the benefit of *dalilu* (magic, occult power), thus join Kosiya Kanté (discussed below) as sacrifices on altars of male ambition. Faama Da says to the cunning, seductive slave girl Sijanma, "If you did that to Basi, how do I know you wouldn't do it to me?" And he sends her to the execution ground (Conrad

1990: 263). Samori has a similar view of his late enemy's adventurous wife, and turns her over to his army to be raped to death (Sory Fina Kamara, version 1*). Thus, Faama Da Jara and Almami Samori guarantee themselves that these women will, in death, remain sabuw instead of becoming instruments of their new masters' own future downfall.

In one sense the femme fatale functions as a guide figure providing the key to success, but in the western Sudanic context she can also be earth mother, symbol of fecundity, both destroyer and provider. It is within this purview that we find a link between femme fatale and sorceress. In the context of kuma koro it is possible to regard Mande society's distaff side basically in terms of power: Which women have power to influence armies and affect history? What is the nature of that power, and how do they use it? In oral tradition, the Mande view of miraculous female strength based on women's ability to create new human beings is expressed in terms of sorcery. Mande sorcery is by no means a male-dominated activity, and this is expressed in one local view with the remark that "sorcery is women's work" (Brett-Smith 1982: 28). Through representations of feminine powers of the occult we can identify some factors of historical significance still very much alive in today's Mande society, a point to which we will return later.

Sabu and Sorcery

The legendary Mande woman as sabu is usually the hero or heroine's natural mother, but she can also be a foster mother or sister. Her goals are often, though not always, achieved through *nyagbaya* or *sumusoya* (female sorcery). If she is the mother's co-wife as in the case of the stepmother — sorceress Sansuma Bereté, mother of Sunjata's faden (rival halfbrother) Dankaran Tuman, she can represent the most hazardous of obstacles lying at the outset of the hero's path to glory. In a less familiar episode to be described below in which *fadenya* is absent, Fakoli's foster mother Tènènba Condé assumes the role of maternal sabu for the child's future heroism and all that he will stand for in Mande traditional history (Conrad 1992).

The studies of Patrick McNaughton (1988) and Sarah Brett-Smith (1994) have made it apparent that Mande sorcery is a complex labyrinth of esoteric knowledge, and they have led the way toward illuminating our understanding of how blacksmith practitioners affect the overall social dynamic. Occult practices affect many areas of daily life, and definitions of specialization vary regionally. My sources from Mande regions of Mali, Guinea, and Côte d'Ivoire disagree on specifics because they vary from one region to another, but one definition of *subaya* is that a *suba* (male) or *sumuso* (female) is extremely evil and dangerous, a killer, an eater of human flesh. Subaya has also been described somewhat more benignly as "the practice of secret knowledge, black science at night to harm someone by using magic" (Adama Diabaté*). *Somaya* is said to be the practice of daytime rituals, making offerings to spirit objects (basi or *boliw*), animal or human sacrifices to change or influence the course of an event.

It will be seen below that in texts addressing nineteenth-century events women are sometimes described as at least marginally active on the battlefield. In *Sunjata* however, key roles played by women in the liberation of Mande from Soso are usually represented as sorcery. The sumuso (female practitioner of subaya) is skilled in the field of traditional science, capable of sending her enemies an evil spell or damaging spirit, sometimes styled "bearer of the night venom" (Traoré 1987: 62). She can kill a person or destroy a victim's health, and she is empowered to perform these acts while remaining invisible to ordinary people. The sumuso is mistress of evil forces, but she can do without the use of *korote* (poison). Informants in Upper Guinea describe the *nyagaw* (or *nyagbaw*) as always female, and owners of korote that they can "send" to a victim. Whatever the local term, sorceresses are regarded as extremely dangerous. When Upper Guinea informants declare that a woman possessing korote is stronger and more powerful than a man owning korote (Adama Diabaté,* Magasouba*), they echo Brett-Smith's sources in Mali, from whom she learned that "women's poisons are thought to be even more dangerous than men's because of their smallness, their lack of visibility, and their bizarre effects" (1982: 28). Further evidence for this belief includes the mute testimony of poison contained in komo association flutes (*komo saman*): the poison of the female flute can kill, while that of the male only disables or inflicts illness (Brett-Smith 1994: 213).

Many women of the Sunjata tradition are recalled as sorceresses who had political impact, and some knowledgeable jeliw of Upper Guinea list the names of the most important sorceresses during the course of their narratives. These lists of names are only a small part of the oral literature on the subject, and the material promises eventually to yield some useful information about how this segment of the belief system contributes to the Mande people's own cultural identity. One jeli with family connections in both Siguiri and Niagassola distinguishes between nine *sumusow* (*suba musow*) and nine nyagaw. His list of nine famous sumusow includes Sansuma Bereté, mother of Sunjata's rival half-brother, Dankaran Tuman. The nine nyagaw are said to be female *somaw*, "non-Muslim women who were revered as *basitigiw* (medicine owners)."[7] Among the names of the nyagaw he lists are Fakoli's wife Keleya Konko, Sunjata's mother Sogolon Kedjou, and Sunjata's sister Sogolon's Kolonkan. The other names are not so familiar, but in the discussion to follow, one of these previously unknown sorceresses, Nyana Jukudulaye, will join more famous women as an archetypal manifestation of female power in Mande discourse:[8]

---

[7] The nyagbaw or nyagaw probably get their name from affiliation with nyaguan, the female power association. Brett-Smith reports (1994: 242) that "trying to get women to discuss the nyaguan association . . . is a lost cause."

[8] Excerpts from oral sources presented throughout this paper are reproduced exactly as they are in the transcripts being prepared for publication. Later passages include

There were nine sumusow in the Manden,
There were nine nyagaw:
Sumuso Kounkouba,
Sumuso Songoubètolo,
Sumuso Nyagarigassa,
And Sumuso Siga,
And Solen Sendja of Ton Mountain,
And Nyana Jukudulaye.
Three hundred bells,
Thirty bells,
And three bells,
Encircled her waist at Mande Dakajalan.
When she exposed her buttocks in the direction of any battle,
The warriors would cease fire.

                                              (Aliou Diabaté*)

Regardless of gender, practitioners of the most dangerous sorcery are distinguished by physical anomalies that they either acquire or are born with. Moreover, they are thought never to defecate or dispose of other bodily accumulations by cleaning themselves, lest they weaken their powers.[9] The legendary soma Bagama Banju, as described by the late Laminigbé Bayo, is the most terrifying of sorcerers, a deadly vigilante who sends death to all who offend his sense of justice. The mystery of Banju's personal *nyama* is greatly enhanced by the fact that from birth to death he never cleaned his teeth or bathed: "If a man cleans his mouth every day, people will come close to him when he laughs." As we saw above in the attitude toward women and as seen also in the social dynamics of *nyamakalaya* (Conrad and Frank 1995: 1–16), certain human relationships in Mande are characterized by ambiguity. This includes the mysterious power of sorcery vis-à-vis the rest of society:

---

comments by *naamu*-sayers, i.e., performance participants who encourage the speaker with various comments, especially "naamu" (roughly, "I hear you"), sometimes at the end or in the middle of virtually every utterance. One of D. T. Condé's naamu-sayers, Mamady Kouyaté, is a virtuoso of this practice, with an extensive repertoire of ways to intone naamu. This is why my rendering of this term varies following the lines of D. T. Condé's narrative, though not enough to do justice to the naamu-sayer's oral artistry.

[9] Adama Diabaté, interview at Sebeninkoro, Mali, 2/18/94. Lansana Magasouba, himself a *basitigi* ("owner" of medicine; healer; occult practitioner), confirmed this during the course of our translation of the Bagama Banju story at Macenta, Guinea, during the summer of 1992. It corresponds to Brett-Smith's finding that the medicine-soaked individual becomes a basi in his own right, making it "extremely dangerous to go near them, much less to touch them" (1994: 65).

Oh, genie master approach,
Keep your distance.
When the wind is blowing,
Keep your distance.
Oh, owner of the sorcerer's knife,
The sorcerer's knife can kill you without causing a wound.[10]

Laminigbé Bayo*

Bagama Banju's female counterparts are known to exist among the nyagaw. As another bard expresses it, "Allah created some bad old women" (Fodé Diawara: "Somaya"*). One of the nyagaw receives passing mention by a well-known *fune* of Guinea:

Nyagbamuso who wears no head-tie,
She who has red teeth,
Bird in the air that destroys things on the ground,
If it comes to earth,
The result will be terrible.

(Sory Fina Kamara, Version 1*)

In the Mande epic, female sorcery is articulated through dramatic metaphorical anecdotes that challenge (at least in the case of non-native listeners) the interpretive skills. Nevertheless, the following lines demonstrate that sumusoya (female sorcery) is not perceived as dwelling entirely beyond *musoya* (womanhood) of daily life, or as being apart from questions of male-female relationships:

It is a foolish woman who degrades womanhood.
Even if she were a man,
If she could not do anything with a weaver's spindle,
She could do it with an axe.
It was Maghan Sunjata who first put a woman in government in the
    Manden.
There were eleven women in Sunjata's government,
[From among the] Nine suba women and nine nyagbaw.
*   *   *   *   *
It was these people who first said "*unse*" in the Manden:
"Whatever men can do, we can do."
That is the meaning of unse.

---

[10] These lines exhibit a clear affinity between perceptions of occult power as practiced today and the similarly bloodless removal of wild game parts by Sunjata's sister Kolonkon in an episode discussed below.

It was those women who first said *seedi*:
"Those men who are at war,
The kingship war they are fighting,
The war for territory that they are fighting,
We labored for them.
That was hard work."
The women of the Manden call that seedi,
"That was real work."
It was those women who first said jeeya in the Manden.
Jeeya, Maghan Sunjata made forty-four laws at Kurukanfuwa.
Nobody should make a stranger weep.
The welcoming statement should be,
"Strangers are invited to their lodgings."
                                              (Adama Diabaté*)

The Condé Women

Any discussion of female sorcery in Mande kuma koro should include the Condé women, because the force of their combined impact on events during the time of the establishment of the Mali empire cannot be exaggerated. The most important Condé women in *Sunjata* are Do Kamissa, the "Buffalo Woman"; Sunjata's mother, Sogolon Wulen Condé; and Fakoli's foster mother, Ma Tènènba Condé. These three Condé women were "sisters"[11] of one of the most powerful and influential *mansaw* in the old Manden, Donsamo'o Nyamo'o Diarra, King of Do and Kri, who apparently flourished in the era prior to Sunjata's ascendancy.

Events described in the episode of Do Kamissa establish the basis of practically everything involving the principal hero, because Kamissa is responsible for the fate of her younger sister, Sogolon Wulen Condé, who is destined to be Sunjata's mother. Sogolon's ugliness and physical deformities are both blessing and curse. They signal the secret presence of occult powers qualifying her to become mother of Sunjata. The physical faults also cause her to languish unwed long after her age-mates have gone to their husbands. Her daughter Kolonkan undergoes a similar waiting period in the exile-episode discussed below. These are seasoning periods similar to the ones endured by Sunjata both in the womb and before he can stand and walk, periods during which certain legendary individuals accumulate increasing amounts of nyama with which to confront the ordeals ahead.

A detailed variant of the Mande epic from the Kouroussa region of Guinea explains that Do Kamissa takes the blame for Sogolon's ugliness and

---

[11] Bards of Mali and elsewhere have described the relationship between Do Kamissa and Sogolon in various ways, but the jeliw of Upper Guinea are notably consistent in referring to these Condé women as "sisters," and they provide unusually detailed descriptions of the ruling Condé family at Do and Kri.

physical deformities. In almost all versions of this well-known episode the Buffalo Woman gives herself up to the hunters by providing them with the secret of how she can be killed, but if a narrator gives a reason for Kamissa's self-sacrifice, it is usually not very well integrated with the principal course of action: "I will give myself up to you because you have honored me" (Demba Kouyaté*). The following lines provide some interesting details as Kamissa explains to the hunters why they must not accept as their reward one of the beautiful young Condé women who will be offered to them:

"When they bring out their fine young daughters,   (Naamu)
Do not accept any of them.   (Naamuuu)
Refuse all of them.   (Na-amuuu)
Because my father's last-born [Sogolon] is still in the house.   (Naamu)
Five age-groups of girls have gone to their husbands,   (Naamu)
She has not married.   (Naamu)
If you do not marry her,   (Naamu)
She will never be married. (Naamuuu)
Anyone who marries her,   (Naamu)
Something [Sunjata] will be at her breast.   (Naamu)
You must marry her.   (Na-amu)
You the *Serifu*,[12] (Naamu)
She is very ugly."(Naamu)
Haven't you heard . . . [says the narrator]   (Naamu)
That Sogolon is short?   (Naamuuu)
The Sogolon Kuduma [short Sogolon] that you have heard about,
        (Na-amu)
This is the beginning of it. (Naamu)
Haven't you heard . . .   (Naamu)
That Sogolon is ugly?   (Naamu)
The ugliness of Sogolon that you keep hearing about, (Naamu)
This is the beginning of it. (Na-amu)
Her sister [Do Kamissa] said . . .   (Naamu)
That the youths should marry her.   (Na-amu)
She said, "You Serifu,   (Naamu)
She is very ugly. (Naamuuu)
The duct in her eye is injured and the tears run down, (Naamu)
And I am responsible for that.   (Naamu)
Her head is bald. (Na-amu)
She has a humped back.   (Naamu)
I, Do Kamissa, did that.   (Na-amu)
Her feet are twisted.   (Naamu)

---

[12] "Serifu": The claim in this variant is that the brothers were Moroccan *shurafa* (Ar. sing. *sharif*, of the lineage claiming descent from the prophet Muhammad).

When she walks, (Naamu)
She limps this way and that.   (Naamu)
And I am the cause of that.   (Na-amu)
How was I the cause?   (Naamuuu)
If you see her tear-duct cut,   (Na-amu)
Her head bald,   (Naamu)
A hump on her back,   (Naamu)
I put my far-seeing mask on her face,   (Naamu)
Because of my love for her,   (Na-amu)
Before she was old enough to wear it.   (Naamu)
That's what cut her tear-duct.   (Na-amu)
That's why her hair fell out.   (Naamu)
That's what put a hump on her back.   (Naamu)
I am responsible. (Na-amu)
If she does not get married it will be my curse."   (Naamuuu)
Did you hear it?   (Na-amu)
She said, "If you see her,   (Naamu)
Her feet are twisted.   (Na-amu)
She is knock-kneed.   (Naamu)
I am the cause of that.   (Naamu)
I set her . . .   (Na-amu)
On my sorcerer's horse,   (Naamu)
When she was too young. (Naamu)
That is what caused her veins to be pulled,   (Na-amu)
And her feet to be twisted. (Naamu)
If she does not get married,   (Naamu)
It will be my curse."   (Na-amu)

                                               (D. T. Condé*)

Do Kamissa's concern here identifies her as an archetype of what Brett-Smith (1994: 16) calls "reproductive decision makers." These are women beyond childbearing age, female elders, who protect "the childbearing potential of their juniors." Determined that Sogolon be married and impregnated in spite of her physical problems, Do Kamissa offers herself as a sacrifice that will launch subsequent events leading to the rise of a Mande empire. It will be seen below that the sister of Sumaworo (or Sumanguru) Kanté performs a similar act for Soso.[13]

Narrative from Upper Guinea describing the formidable sorceress Sogolon Wulen Condé bears little resemblance to the sensitive bride found in D. T. Niane's novel-like version of the Mande epic, although there are passages in

---

[13] My renditions of this name are deliberately inconsistent,with "Sumanguru" for texts recorded in Mali, and "Sumaworo" for recordings collected in Upper Guinea (see "Editor's Introduction").

which she appears more vulnerable than she does in the examples to be offered here. Niane describes Sogolon as a fragile ingenue lying on a mat having her hair plaited and weeping softly at the ritual jibes of her future co-wives (1965: 10), but it will be seen below that Sogolon has other uses for plaiting needles. Some published versions designed to preserve the Mande style of discourse at least hint of Sogolon's power, as in scenes where the hunters try to take her to bed and she repels them with a variety of defensive weapons including lion-like claws, porcupine-quill pubic hair, and spikes from her breasts (Zeltner 1913: 6; Camara 1978: 65–66; Jansen 1995: 82; Johnson 1986: 127), but this signals only a fraction of Sogolon's character and powers as they reflect Mande values. Sogolon is as complex and ambiguous a figure as exists in the Mande (or any other) literary world. On the one hand, as she endures the ritual entry into marriage, she cuts a pathetic though undaunted figure with her humped back, bald head, and crooked feet, raising clouds of dust as she is dragged along (Mamady Condé*) and being ridiculed in the bridal songs: "Our heron-head has come this year" (D. T. Conde*). At the same time Sogolon is fierce as a lioness, a potentially deadly, animal-like presence with a distinctly masculine side that is normally associated with elderly women like Do Kamissa. Indeed, Sogolon's masculine side is reasserted in her old age, and when she dies in Nèma she is honored by having her funeral conducted as if she were a man (D. T. Condé*). But that quality is already present to some degree in the prenuptial Sogolon. Far older than most brides, she is already a *musofadi*, a type of woman described by one of my fune informants:

> Ancestor Soumaila had a sister called Maminata.
> She was such a formidable woman,
> Allah did not give that woman any child.
> Maminata was a musofadi.
>   (Sory Fina Kamara, version 2*)

Again demonstrating the ambiguity of matters involving questions of female empowerment in the Manden, my translation assistants emphasize that Maminata is a "real woman," which to them means that she has powerful masculine qualities. Female counterpart to *kefadi* (a formidable male), a musofadi is a woman with a powerful or masculine physique whom my assistants describe as "strong as a man." They claim that in the Voinjama area of northern Liberia (very near the Guinean border a few kilometers from Macenta), a musofadi is allowed to participate in the komo spirit society.[14] Also known as *ngana muso*, the powerful woman is usually postmenopausal. According to

---

[14] Women in komo: Sarah Brett-Smith has evidence that women's attendance at komo meetings is perhaps not as unheard of as we have previously thought, and she suggests that it is certain elderly women who might be allowed to participate in the rituals of some komo branches (pers. com., June 15, 1995).

Brett-Smith (1994: 5), she is "a woman whose sterility, force of character, and ability to master the normally male preserves of ritual knowledge and sorcery endow her with a masculine identity. . . ."

Once Sogolon is married, the sterility of her masculine side will be overshadowed by pregnancy and her struggle against the co-wives' efforts to prevent delivery of the hero she carries in her womb. But as a bride, this formidable creature severely tests Sunjata's future father, Farakoro Manko Faran Konkèn (also Naré Maghan), the ruler (*mansa*) of Farakoro. Sogolon arrives at her husband's house saturated with nyama from her close association with the buffalo wraith and other spiritual forces of Do and Kri. The bride must be subdued and controlled enough for the marriage to be consummated, but without diminishing her power to combat the deadly attacks of her co-wives, each of whom is herself a deadly sorceress.

Sogolon's initial encounter with the future father of Sunjata features supernatural exploits representing the spirit world's necessary involvement in producing the individual who will eventually lead the Mande people to political unification. According to Mande values, heroic birth leading to imperial conquest be achieved only through the kinds of complex ritual preparations, political negotiations, and perilous ordeals already heard in episodes leading up to this meeting that is fraught with danger for both bride and groom. According to one of the Kouroussa variants, when Sunjata's future father learns from Tombonon Manyan Bèrètè that the bride has arrived, he immediately orders them to take her outside the town. Praised in another major variant (Demba Kouyaté*) as "the most powerful sorcerer," the Farakoro ruler already knows what he is up against and requires time to prepare himself: "If you bring her to my house right now," he says, "she will take it away from me" (D. T. Condé*). When the escort does approach with the bride, her head is ritually thrust inside the door three times, and there ensues a sorcerer's contest as deadly and dramatic as any in Mande tradition. From out of her own eye Sogolon shoots a *su bala* or sorcerer's plaiting needle, trying to pierce the groom's eye. She sprays him with scalding breast-milk to blister his skin. With the iron-tipped staff she brought from Do and Kri, she tries to spear him in the chest: "Four hundred thousand *kala*, forty-four kala"; she bombards this man who must prove himself worthy of being Sunjata's father. Sogolon exhausts her *dabali* arsenal and the elder Simbon successfully counters each of her attacks with his own *dalilu*, upon which she enters his house to receive the ten ceremonial *kola* nuts (D. T. Condé*). The Farakoro mansa must establish control over his wife because this will be essential to their child Sunjata's later success. In the following lines, the bard uses the mouth of a hunter to express his version of the Mande philosophy that a woman's character is the overriding determinant of her child's usefulness (Brett-Smith 1994: 86). These lines are part of the complaint of one of the buffalo-killing hunters who acquired Sogolon and was wounded when he tried to bed her:

A man should be able to control his wife.
But here we are with a woman who has more power than men.
The woman should submit,
Even if she has all the power.
A woman should humble herself to her husband.
Anything her husband tells her to do,
She should obey.
That is what will make your children what you want them to be.
If a woman controls her husband,
The child will not flourish,
The child will be no good.
                                          (Mamady Condé*)

    Sunjata's future parents have made the appropriate match and the marriage can be consummated, but Sogolon must yet confront the mansa's sisters and co-wives who realize that she is the designated mother of the future hero: "If you hear about the nine *nyagba musolu* of the Manden . . . " says the jeli, "they came from these fifty women" (D. T. Condé*). These are the sorceresses (nyagba musolu) who place obstacles in the way of Sogolon's giving birth to the one whose coming was foretold. In the jeli *ngara* discourse of Upper Guinea, these women are musofadi, powerful forces that must be reckoned with. Their deadly rivalry reflects the Mande people's own perceptions of the secret and mysterious dangers of daily life. The co-wives' confrontations are concerned with the business of founding the most powerful West African empire of its time, and these women are primed for mortal combat. The only thing that keeps them from killing one another is that neither has dalilu strong enough to entirely overwhelm that of her rival.
    The episode apprising Sogolon's rivals of the extent of her powers comprises one of the great demonstrations of sorcery in Mande tradition. The bride is not allowed out of the groom's house to participate in the wedding dance and fete in the *konye bara* (dance circle), but this is not a problem for Sogolon. With her new husband's permission ("There is no dalilu you can show me that will be worse than what you started with"), she declares that she will remain behind him on the sleeping mat while observing the celebration. She then performs sorcery equal to that of Fakoli, in the famous episode where he increases his size in the council house until he wears its roof like a hat:

>   She put her left hand on her husband.   (Naamu)
>   She was lying behind him on the bed.   (Naaaam')
>   She stretched her right hand,   (Na-amu)
>   She stretched her right hand,   (Naamu)
>   It passed through the straw of the roof.   (Naamu)
>   She stretched her hand,   (Naamu)
>   She stretched her hand to the dance circle,   (Naamu)

She laid her hand on the *dubalen* tree.   (Naamu)

She pointed two fingers down,   (Naamu)
Light was coming out of them.   (Na-amu)
The circle was suddenly full of light, Wa!   (Naamuu)
And she was still lying behind her husband. (Naamu)

Sogolon enjoys the spectacle, commenting on the skills of the different dancers, but suddenly Jonmusoni Manyon notices that the torchless circle is now brightly lit:[15]

She looked up.   (Naamu)
She saw the two fingers hanging down.   (Naamu)
They were shedding light like a pressure lamp.   (Na-amu)
She said . . .   (Naamu)
She said, "Big sister Sansun Tuman Berete, (Na-amu)
Big sister Maramajan Tarawele,   (Naamu)
Raise up your eyes.   (Naamu)
This is the one about whom we said,   (Na-amu)
That we would not be jealous of her.   (Naamu)
That tree that is sprouting,
When it grows to extend its branches,
It will take the Manden from us.   (Na-amu)
Hee! The new bride is lying behind her husband.   (Naamu)
She is watching us with her two fingers, look!   (Naamu)
Do you see the two fingers with eyes?   (Na-amuu)
Mande women, if you are real women . . .   (Naamu)
You had better get ready. (Naamu)
This one must not be successful here."   (Na-amu)
(You heard it?)   (Naaaam')
They suddenly stopped the wedding dance. (Naamuu)
All the women felt cold.   (Na-amu)
They all went home.   (Naamuu)
They all dipped their hands into their dalilu. (Na-amu)
                                    (D. T. Condé*)

Thus begins the battle between sorceresses that will culminate in Sunjata's birth. During the course of ordinary life in the rural Manden, pregnancy "remains an inexplicable process fraught with risk" (Brett-Smith,

---

[15] Beledugu informants reported to Sarah Brett-Smith that "the Daban mask glows with a mysterious light on the night before some major event" such as the death of an important elder (pers. com. June 15, 1995). Sogolon's light-shedding fingers could well owe something to this masking tradition.

1994: 218). In the epic, in addition to the normal hazards involved, the combined power of these rival sumusow is turned against Sogolon, which is why she is said to endure seven years of pregnancy. Sogolon's ordeal reflects the Mande view in which the painful and often life-threatening process of birthing is known as *muso kele* or "women's war" (Brett-Smith 1994: 220–21), as she battles her co-wives to give birth to the hero who is still praised as "Son of the Condé Woman." Through her command of powerful dalilu (or dabali), Sogolon establishes her credentials as a woman capable of bearing the future leader of the Manden.

The third Condé woman, Ma Tènènba, participates in the founding of the Mali empire in ways similar to those of her two "sisters." Ma Tènènba Condé is the wife of Mansa Yèrèlènko of Nègèbòriya. She is also co-wife of Kosiya Kanté, Sumaworo's sister who is Fakoli's natural mother. For reasons to be seen below, Kosiya Kanté abandons the infant Fakoli, leaving him with her co-wife Ma Tènènba Condé. This circumstance leads to Ma Tènènba becoming the sabu of Fakoli's seemingly endless contributions to the Manden (Conrad 1992):

> From then on Ma Tenenba Condé took care of Fakoli.   (Naamu)
> If you see that Fakoli . . .   (Naamu)
> Grew to become a man . . .(Naamu)
> The sabu came from the Condé's place.   (Naamu)
> It was a Condé woman who gave him his dalilu.   (Na-amu)
> (D. T. Condé*)

In another major variant (Demba Kouyaté*) Ma Tènènba is described as "Sorcery Queen," which is consistent with her role in the D. T. Condé text. Here she takes the infant Fakoli on an initiation pilgrimage to all of the great power sources of the Manden to receive instruction, acquire his dalilu, and prepare for his role as "ancestor" of all later sorcerers (Conrad 1992: 174–80). They visit the Kulubali ancestor where the child is bathed in protective medicine that will make him a master hunter. At Sibi, the mansa Tabon Wana Faran Kamara carries the child through the great natural archway of Tabon mountain, introducing him to Jinna Maghan, king of the jinn. At Krina the great ruler Tanan Mansa Konkon rolls Fakoli in the dust of the sacred cave, permeated with the essence of the original creation. They also travel to Nèma and visit Faran Tounkara in his seat at Kountinya, before going on to the ancestral Condé home at Do and Kri. There Fakoli serves his hunting apprenticeship, is schooled in the occult sciences, and acquires the famous sorcerer's bonnet under which he eventually marches back into the Manden. Fakoli's acquisition of an unsurpassed level of dalilu was entirely due to the third great Condé sister Ma Tènènba, remembered here both as the sabu of Fakoli and a major force in establishing the Mali empire.

Sisters as Sabu: Kosiya Kanté and Sogolon's Kolonkan

If the three Condé women are sabu of the Mali empire, Fakoli's natural mother Kosiya Kanté fulfills a similar role for her brother Sumaworo's state of Soso. Some jeliw know far more about Sumaworo than those who recount only the basic outline of *Sunjata*. The bards who claim his father was a jinn are expressing fragmentary impressions of details recounted by jeli ngaraw of Upper Guinea who know the story of how Sumaworo acquired items crucial to his own dalilu including the Soso Bala, the sacred *balafon* that is said to survive today as premier symbol of the old Manden's greatness.

According to the most comprehensive variants, Sumaworo's spirit guide is Jinna Maghan, king of the jinn. Jinna Maghan is sometimes referred to as Sumaworo's "father," and in the version presently referred to, Sumaworo tells the jinn that his real father is dead. In this case the jinn comes to Sumaworo from a secret place in Kodowari (Côte d'Ivoire). Sumaworo returns with the jinn to a cave where for him "the time for sabu had arrived." He is shown several nyama-laden objects including the bala and some magic arrows, the *binye kala* which he secretly covets more than anything else. Sumaworo indicates his desire to possess all these things, but the jinns' price is one human being for each of the four objects, and the people to be traded must be members of his own immediate family.

The idea of offering close family members as a means of obtaining ritual or political power is consistent with the testimony of Salimata Koné, who described this as a process involving both sorcery and a women's initiation society, Nyakuruni. She compared it to komo, saying women brought out their basi at night as the komo society men did and that men had to avoid seeing it. She defined the society by saying "nyakurunnin den caman ye subaga ye de, n'i donna n'i m'i ce folo di, i b'i den folo di, o gundu b'u fe yen" (many of the members of the Nyakurunnin are sorcerers, if you enter, if you don't give your husband, you will give your first child, that is their secret).[16]

In the account where Jinna Maghan demands that a relative be sacrificed, Sumaworo's sister Kosiya Kanté seizes the initiative. Sumaworo first returns to Soso without the coveted power sources because he was unwilling to offer up any of his own people as their price. Kosiya Kanté visits her brother and learns of the jinns' conditions for parting with the four sacred objects. Back at Nègèboriya, Kosiya consults her co-wife, Ma Tènènba Condé who is barren, and determines that if her infant Fakoli were orphaned, he would be well taken care of by Tènènba. Sumaworo returns to the secret cave to renew his efforts to acquire the nyama-laden objects, and Kosiya finds him there negotiating with Jinna Maghan, hoping the king of the jinn will accept an exchange of persons other than his own relatives:

---

[16] Interviewed by Sarah Brett-Smith in the Beledugu region of Mali, September 14-22, 1979.

Kosiya Kanté arrived.   (Na-amu)
Just as he was saying, "The only sister I have,   (Naamu)
I would not give her away, especially since she has been married. . . ."
(Naamu)

Kosiya Kanté appeared at his side . . .   (Naamu)
And said, "Sumaworo?"   (Naamu)
She said, "Whether you send me,   (Naamu)
Or you don't send me,   (Naamu)
I have come myself.   (Naamu)
I prefer your success to my life."   (Naamu)
Then she entered the cave.   (Naamuu)
                                        (D. T. Condé*)

Thanks to his sister's self-sacrifice, Sumaworo is able to acquire the Soso Bala with its mallets, the bell bracelets, the sacred drum Dunu Mutukuru, and the three binye kala, or magic arrows.[17] These are some of the keys to Sumaworo's imperial ambitions, among others mentioned in the tradition. By sacrificing herself to Jinna Maghan, Kosiya Kanté becomes sabu of her brother's successes as leader of Soso. Sumaworo himself is not sabu of the Soso empire. He is the instrument of what has been wrought by his sister Kosiya Kanté, who acquires from the jinn the nyama-laden sources of her brother's power.

Another legendary sister who plays a crucial role in her brother's path to success is Sogolon's daughter, Kolonkan. Kolonkan herself carries abundant credentials as a nyaga, as heard in a variant of the episode of the sorcery contest between her brother, Sunjata, and another Mande ruler, Kamanjan (Faran Kamara):

Kamanjan dashed to the rock face of the nearby mountain.
He cut an opening with his sword and went inside.
At that time Sogolon Kolonkan was looking for her brother behind the town.
She saw them going and she followed them.
When Sunjata tried to enter the mountain she said "Hey brother, Look here!"
Then he looked back.
When he looked back she opened her wrapper.
On the side of her open wrapper appeared a kind of television.

---

[17] In the accounts of the acquisition of the Soso Bala by jeliw from different Mande regions there are many variants of the relationship between genies, Sumaworo's kin, and the nature of the transactions involved. Compare my references to this Upper Guinea version of *Sunjata* with counterpart passages in texts from Kita, Mali (Johnson 1986) and Kela, Mali (Jansen, Duintjer, and Tamboura 1995).

On the screen he saw Sumaworo and his warriors inside the walls of
Soso.
Sumaworo was being fanned by his slaves.
Sunjata was amazed at what he saw.
He said, "Eh!"
He was astonished to see such a thing.
He said, "Your female power is great."
She said, "If my female power impresses you so much,
Stop chasing Kamanjan.
That is not what you were sent for.
You have not yet reached home.
Instead you are doing this kind of thing.
What drives you to do this kind of thing?"
Kamanjan had entered the mountain.
He said "Mother, let him meet me here.
I am waiting for him;
Just come in."
But Sunjata did not go in.
Simbon turned and followed his sister.
They went home.
                                       (Jeli Mori Kouyaté*)

The notion of Kolonkan serving as guide to her brother — keeping him
on the path that must be followed to liberate the Manden from Soso — is
expressed in various ways. Before their mother Sogolon dies she advises Sunjata
to heed "an elder with dalilu stronger than yours." Sunjata's close relationship
with Tabon Wana Faran Kamara (a.k.a. Kamanjan) appears to be the crucial
fulfillment of this prophecy, not only because Kamanjan is one of the most
powerful mansaw of the Manden, but because he is a respected contemporary of
Sunjata's father, relied upon for advice about how to prepare for the inevitable
clash with Sumaworo. His counsel is so important to Sunjata that when
Kamanjan wants to marry Kolonkan, Sunjata at first declines because according
to custom, if they become brothers-in-law Sunjata can no longer confide his
problems to him. In another version of their contest Sunjata matches Kamanjan's
various exploits with a giant baobab tree until Kolonkan issues her warning in
the name of Sogolon:

Before Sunjata could say, "Ah," his sister said, "Big brother,
        (Naaaam')
This is not what my mother told you to do.   (Aaaaa)
Leave it to him.   (Naamu)
Our mother prayed that you be blessed by an elder with dalilu stronger
than yours.   (Aaaaa)
He is trying to demonstrate his dalilu for you.

If you show him your own, he will not give you anything.
        (Naamu)
Leave it to him, and when he is satisfied he will flip the tree back.
        (Aaaaa)
If you get this one's dalilu and add it to what you already have,
        (Naamu)
Maybe you will succeed.   (Aaaa)
You should act like you don't know anything,
So he will give you what [advice] he has,   (Naaaam')
Because he has been fond of you." (Naamuu)

                                                        (D. T. Condé*)

Sabu Scorned
        In Mande oral tradition generally, when someone interferes with a
woman' functioning as sabu and her powers are not allowed to come into play,
serious consequences develop. Texts addressing the earliest of the Mande states
to be recalled in oral discourse, e.g., the Soninke legend of Wagadu, contain the
motif of woman as sacrifice. Initially, in a situation similar to that of Kosiya
Kanté and the enhancement of Sumaworo's power, a bargain is struck with the
local spirits whereby a woman is exchanged for the basic requirements of state
foundation. In the case of Wagadu, annual sacrifice of a virgin to the guardian
serpent Bida is required, with each virgin thereby becoming the sabu of the
ensuing year's prosperity. Eventually, after an indeterminable number of
generations leading up to the late eleventh century, the sacrificial virgin is
rescued from the serpent and destruction of the great Soninke state replaces
prosperity (Adam 1903: 92–93; Monteil 1953: 379; Meillassoux 1964: 188).
        Looking forward some eight hundred years to episodes describing
nineteenth-century events, similar problems result from interference with
woman as sabu, as in the story of *Almami Samori* told by Sory Fina Kamara.*
During the Battle of Sikasso, Samori's brother Kèmè Brèma has an affair with
One-Breasted Denba, sister of Mansa Kéba of Sikasso. She is seen bringing her
lover food, and Samori accuses his brother of fraternizing with the enemy.
Furious at Samori's lack of trust and living up to an earlier oath that he will
never again quarrel with his brother, Kèmè Brèma purposely goes into battle
stripped of his protective amulets and is killed. Samori's dalilu was originally
bestowed upon him by twin female jinns on the condition that he never attack
certain towns including Sikasso.[18] His treatment of Kèmè Brèma and the
brother's resulting death set in motion the genies' retribution for violation of

---

[18] Samori's spirit guides "female genies": According to Sarah Brett-Smith's informants, it
is most common for the genies of men to be female and for those of women to be male
(1994: 54). Biton Kulubali's genie is female (Conrad 1990: 71-74), and a female genie
serves as guide to the brothers who hunt the buffalo woman in a variant of *Sunjata* (D. T.
Condé*).

their taboo. One-Breasted Denba, an agent of peace in the midst of slaughter, might have served as a reminder to Samori of his oath to the jinns. Instead, her angry reaction to Kèmè Brèma's death assures a humiliating defeat for Almami Samori, and she becomes the sabu of Sikasso's victory:

> One-Breasted Denba was told that Kèmè Brèma was killed in the Battle of Sikasso.
>   *****
> First thing in the morning, One-Breasted Denba went to the door of Sikasso Kèba's house.
> She said "Brother, I came to learn if it is true that Kèmè Brèma has been killed."
> Sikasso Kèba said "It is true."
> One-Breasted Denba stripped off her wrapper and threw it at Sikasso Kèba.
> She said, "Give me your trousers."
> Sikasso Kèba said, "Little sister, what are you doing?"
> One-Breasted Denba said, "You will soon know."
> She said, "I invite you to the bank of the old river.
> I invite Almami to go there too."
>   *****
> If you see a woman taking command of a battle,
> Do not wait around for it.
> Before anybody knew it, they started the battle of Woyowayanko.
> Even tomorrow morning there are still some of the muskets at the Woyowayanko.
> It was the woman,
> It was One-Breasted Denba who organized the battle of Woyowayanko.[19]
> The muskets were fired so much,
> They got so they would discharge by themselves.
> Before they knew it Almami's men became few,
> On the banks of the Woyowayanko.
> Almami's army retreated,
> They returned to Bisandu in plain sight of everyone.
>   (Sory Fina Kamara, version 1*)

[19] The first battle of the Woyowayanko (or Wèyawèyanko according to Person), was in April 1883. The Samoriens were commanded by Samori's brother Kèmè Brèma Turé who was very much alive at the time (he died four or five years later at the siege of Sikasso), and the French forces were under the command of Borgnis-Desbordes, in what turned out to be a famous victory for them (Person 1968: I, 407-408). The second battle receives only passing mention from Person (1968: II, 959).

From the Mande perspective, Denba's appropriation of her brother's trousers is especially dramatic because the wearing of trousers can signal a woman's "terrifying ability" to master male skills, including the ability to destroy life (Brett-Smith 1994: 243). As Jeli Mamary Kouyaté* expresses it in his description of another powerful woman:

> To say "I wear a pair of trousers,"
> And "I have something wrapped around my buttocks,"
> These are two different things.

Moreover, it is probably no coincidence that Denba's apparel is mentioned in association with a battle that is represented in a complex Beledugu mud cloth design called "Samori ni tubabu keleyoro Woyowayanko da la" or "the battleground between Samori and the white man at the edge of the Woyowayanko."[20]

In another example of what happens when "woman as sabu" is interfered with, Sunjata's sister Kolonkan finds there is no meat with which to serve the customary "stranger's food" to the delegation that is calling the future Mansa back to Mali. Kolonkan "enters" her dalilu and spirits herself into the bush where her three brothers are hunting. Finding several animals they have killed and left to be collected later, Kolonkan extracts the hearts and livers without cutting into the carcasses and returns to cook for the delegates. When the hunters return, Manden Bori is furious with his sister: "Must she prove her musoya to us?" In the ensuing struggle Kolonkan's wrapper comes loose, and she accuses Manden Bori of shaming her in front of the Mande people just when she was acting in his own interest. Then, defying the convention that sisters are expected to have great influence over the fate of their brothers, Manden Bori further shames Kolonkan by exercising his own subaya, causing fresh blood to flow from the meat she had cooked for the guests. Finally, Kolonkon condemns Manden Bori and his branch of the Keita royal lineage with a curse that is said to explain the troubles of later generations, and whose effects remain evident in today's Manden:

> Ma Kolonkan said, "Are you still trying to shame me?   (Naamu)
> I was protecting your reputation.   (Na-amu)
>
> The Mande people came to you on the question of *mansaya*.
> (Naamu)
> Because you have done this to me, (Naamu)

---

[20] According to Kassim Koné, this *bogolanfini* design was originally called "the battleground between the iguana and the squirrel at the Woyowayanko River" (pers. comm., July 29, 1995). For an illustration of a wrapper with this design see Ahern 1992: 25.

The mansaya will be passed on to you,   (Naamu)
But your descendants will never agree on one mansa until the trumpet
is blown."   (Naamu)

                                                        (D. T. Condé*)

In considering the significance of this scene between Kolonkan and
Manden Bori, the importance of a woman's cloth as well as the general exposure
of her genitalia and buttocks must be taken into account. In Bamana society the
"red" and other kinds of bogolanfini (mud cloth) are central to girls' rites of
passage, including the excision ritual and marriage (Brett-Smith 1982: 25–26).
The reproductive powers of childbearing are also manipulated through ritual
work performed with cloths (Brett-Smith 1994: 16). In Mande oral discourse,
the condition of a woman's cloth can signal various emotions and attitudes, as
where Mamady Condé says of someone: "She tied her wrapper in the way
women do when they are distressed about a child." In a violent scene between
Sumaworo and his mother described by Fa-Digi Sisòkò, she reacts by cutting up
a "menstrual cloth" (Johnson 1986: 172).[21] Bamana women have explained that
the rust-red color of the Basiae and N'Gale cloths worn by women after excision
"will strike fear into the hearts of the initiates' enemies when they see the ritual
cloths, and that such people will die during the succeeding year" (Brett-Smith
1994: 126). Bearing this in mind, it seems clear that when the cloth of a
powerful woman like One-Breasted Denba or Sogolon's Kolonkan is opened or
torn off in an emotional scene with any male character, the event should not be
taken lightly. It is a danger signal, serving notice that men are straying over the
boundary, approaching an area of female nyama.

In the praise-lines quoted earlier, which declare that warriors stopped
fighting when Nyana Jukudulaye exposed her buttocks in the direction of battle,
the point is not that the men stopped to gape at her visible sex. The contrary
would be true because in Mande belief the female genitalia, like ritual objects,
contain dangerous nyama. It is said that when men rest their eyes on a woman's
sex, they will quickly find their way into the grave (Brett-Smith 1994: 209). The
sorceress Nyana Jukudulaye's act of exposure conveys a deadly threat to men in
battle, war being one of the dangerous or secret activities known to the Mande
as "a red thing." According to Brett-Smith's informants, any man engaged in a
"red thing" must not approach a woman or be approached by one, for the power
of female genitalia is stronger than any ritual object (1994: 215). The reason a
woman is not allowed to see the Kòmò is that this would void its power.
Therefore when Nyana Jukudulaye bared her buttocks in the direction of battle,
the warriors could not continue fighting because their protective amulets were

---

[21] In the Mande scheme of secret things, the child was not supposed to know about the
existence of the hidden cloth stained with the mother's first menstrual blood (Brett-Smith
1994: 206), but if this is exactly what Fa-Digi said, it would function as a particularly
terrible curse.

about to be neutralized. Noting that Bamana men — including komo society leaders — swear their most profound oaths by invoking their mother's sex, Brett-Smith observes that "a woman can damn a man forever by removing her wrapper, pointing to her sex, and cursing the offender with its power" (1994: 122).[22]

In *Sunjata* just such an exchange does take place between Kolonkan and her brother, Manden Bori. Brett-Smith's information that "both men and women will forever ostracize a man so cursed, unless he begs forgiveness and persuades the offended woman to revoke her oath" (1994: 123) is supported by the understanding of this distant event in Upper Guinea. Tradition there provides no evidence that Manden Bori ever begs forgiveness, and men of today's Mande heartland continue to discuss the effects of Kolonkan's curse on the Masaré lineage descended from Manden Bori. In lines immediately following Kolonkan's curse, a bard explains that this has caused ongoing problems for the Masaré in regions such as Hamana and Balato:

> You shamed me in front of the people in whose Manden I am to be married?   (Naamu)
> Mba, the mansaya for which they are calling you,   (Naamu)
> Your descendants will never agree on one mansa,   (Naamu)
> Your descendants.   (Naaamu)
> I won't say that you will not get the mansaya,   (Naamu)
> But you will never all agree on one person. (Naamu)
> Anyone you install today, tomorrow you will plot against him. (Naamu)

The performer then repeats the list of Manden Bori's descendants, names the towns involved, and continues:

> Those are the twelve towns of Hamana,   (Naamu)
> And they are the descendants of Manden Bori.   (Naamu)
> If they install a chief there today, tomorrow they will remove him.
>   (Naamu)
>   (D. T. Condé*)

---

[22] Kassim Koné confirms this and notes that of all women, elderly ones and those of slave descent (*wolosow*) command the most powerful nyama through their genitalia. He says that in Bamako during the disturbances of 1991, a grandmother whose grandchildren were killed by soldiers of the Musa Traoré regime went to the cemetery on the morning of their burial (March 26). Stripping herself naked she cursed Musa Traoré, and as it happened, Traoré was overthrown later that day. Koné added that a woman's curses are more dangerous than a man's because she can instantly strip and deliver the curse while standing on the ground, but for the male equivalent to be effective it can only be delivered from a rooftop (personal communication, July 13, 1995).

We know from Ibn Khaldun that the mansaya did pass from the line of
Mari Jata (Sunjata) to that of his brother, known to those sources as Abu Bakr
(Levtzion and Hopkins 1981: 334).[23] When asked about modern jeli involvement
in the matter of Kolonkan's curse, D. T. Condé pointed out that Hamana must
heal the ancient wounds to lift the curse. His explanation demonstrates how
episodes of the epic continue to influence today's rural Mande society:

> I told my brother to tell the people of Balato,(Mmm)
> If they want to install a mansa who will last and not be involved in
> controversy,   (Naamu)
> Let everybody in Hamana offer a cow.   (Naaaam')
> When they kill them,   (Naamu)
> The back part that is the sisters' share . . .   (Naaaam')
> And the internal organs . . .   (Naamu)
> Those must be given to the Mansaré women.(Aaaa)
> After that, each village must offer one wrapper,   (Naamu)
> The wrapper that fell off Ma Kolonkan.   (Naaaam')
> Let them give one wrapper each to their sisters so they can bless them.
>   (Naamu)
> If they do that,   (Naaaam')
> If they agree to that,   (Naamu)
> If the sisters then bless them,   (Aaaa)
> When they put someone in power it will not be disturbed.
> (Naamu)
> But if they do not do that,   (Aaaa)
> Even up to tomorrow,   (The curse will be there!)
> The curse will be there.   (It's true)

Before this last line could be spoken, the attending elders chimed in
together, "The curse will be there!" Rural (and many urban) Maninka of Upper
Guinea retain the traditional worldview, and the curse leveled by Kolonkan on
Manden Bori serves them as a convincing explanation for the lack of continuity
in Mande royal succession from the fourteenth century to the postcolonial
political arena. In conversation resulting from this performance, the learned
elders (*nyarake* or *ngarake*) of Fadama mentioned that results of Kolonkan's
curse are manifest in the cases of weakness among the old Mande mansaw. The
consequences they remember correspond in kind to the disruptions mentioned in
the Arabic sources, including the insanity of Khalifa, various usurpations, and
the tyranny of the later Mari Jata (Ibn Khaldun in Levtzion and Hopkins 1981:
333–35). For modern times, the elders cite the 1968 overthrow of Mali's Modibo
Keita, as well as recent power struggles among candidates and regimes of other

---

[23] Abu Bakr: Possibly Manden Bori (i.e., Bori of Manden), since "Bori" and "Bukari" are
among the Mande renderings of "Bakr" or "Bakari."

countries containing large Mande populations.

Women as Political Actors in Mande Narrative and History

As noted at the beginning, research has not progressed to a point where one can reach definitive conclusions regarding the possible historical content of episodes describing female participation in political events of old Mali. We have seen that Mande oral tradition clearly credits powerful legendary women with a significant share of the glory accruing from the founding of the Soso and Mande states. Female contributions, like those of male heroes, are often described in terms of magic and sorcery with special attention given to the mothering of male heroes. But among the references to female sorcery we find claims like that of Aliou Diabaté cited above: "There were eleven women in Sunjata's government." More specifically and frequently, epic tradition as well as more immediate data from the nineteenth century describe active political roles for women in the formation of alliances through marriage, mediation between major rulers, and the providing of critical food supplies.

When D. T. Condé was asked to elaborate on his earlier reference to a problem in modern-day Hamana that results from Kolonkan's curse, he responded with additional lines indicating that part of the reason she reacted so strongly to Manden Bori's behavior was owing to political circumstances connected with marriage. Mande epic narrative indicates that marriages of the sisters of political leaders formed important political alliances. Kolonkan is not allowed to marry during the long exile in Nema because it would not be of the greatest political advantage. Back in the Manden, she is allowed to marry into the Kamara lineage ruling one of the seven principal Mande chiefdoms. Another important alliance was formed when Sogolon came from the Condé *mansadugu* of Do and Kri to marry the man who would sire Sunjata. The earlier-mentioned marriage between Sumaworo's sister Kosiya Kanté and Mansa Yèrèlenko formed an alliance between Soso and Nègèboriya, which is how Fakoli came to have a father from the Manden and a mother from Soso (Conrad 1992: 168–71). Kolonkan had to wait for marriage until her brother's return from exile, to make the best possible political alliance:

> Ma Kolonkan shouted when she was made ashamed. (Naamu)
> She said, "Big brother Manden Bori,   (Naamu)
> It is my mother who said I will not get married here. (Naamu)
> Otherwise, all my age-mates have already given birth.   (Naamu)
> For a girl to be twenty-seven years old . . .   (Naamu)
> My mother says I will not be married here. (Naamu)
> She says it can only happen in the Manden. (Naamu)
> My big brother Sunjata says I will not be married here,
> (Naamu)
> Only in the Manden."   (Naamu)
>
>   (D. T. Condé*)

In discussing nineteenth-century female Mende chiefs in Sierra Leone, Lynda Day notes how they "made good use of traditional areas of female responsibility to gain political influence." Day says two of the functions that particularly positioned women to exercise influence in the public sphere were "as mediators in intergroup conflicts and as hostesses and providers of food for strangers." All three of the female chiefs described by Day achieved political advantages through effective entertainment of guests and strangers (1994: 488–89). In Mande kuma koro, woman's responsibility for visitors or strangers forms the basis of many female-centered episodes. In the Wagadu tradition, the culprit who destroys the pact with the spirit serpent Bida flees southward to his mother's town. The mother then serves in both of the key roles outlined by Lynda Day, mediating between her son and his vengeful pursuers by offering to feed the population during the famine that has struck Wagadu (Tellier 1898: 208–209, Arnaud 1911: 159, Frobenius 1921: 69, Monteil 1953: 380). This could be merely another trope of female magic, in which the woman produces vast amounts of food from one cooking pot, but it could also indicate the dim recollection of a powerful female leader who controlled extensive food-producing territories.

In a standard episode of the Sunjata tradition, the dalilu of Fakoli's wife Kèlèya Konkon is demonstrated through her single-handed production of an amount of food equal to that prepared by Sumaworo's several hundred wives (e.g., Johnson 1986: 173). Again, it is easy to overlook the public significance of such an overtly domestic action. In this case, detailed versions from Upper Guinea reveal that Kèlèya Konkon is engaged in preparation of a sacrificial feast as a prelude to war. She occupies a difficult position between Fakoli and Sumaworo, from which she must face down Sumaworo's hundreds of co-wives who are threatened by her nyama. The usual result of this scene is that Fakoli returns to the Manden because Sumaworo is so impressed by Kèlèya's excellence that he keeps her (Conrad 1992: 167).

However, a more sinister aspect of female power, as it actually plays out in village life, might lie submerged within this scene. In the Mande scheme of things, especially where perceptions of sorcery are involved, ambiguity is a primary consideration. Although crucial to diplomatic relations, a large volume of food production could also pose a terrible threat, as Brett-Smith describes it (1984: 137):

> Although a cardinal rule of hospitality is that eating out of the same dish links the participants together in perpetuity and no one who has performed this rite may (in theory) act against his fellow communicants, communal meals are favored occasions for administering poison to an unwelcome visitor or rival.

It is interesting to look at oral texts describing events of the second half of the nineteenth century that describe women in situations similar to those found in Mande epics addressing events that allegedly occurred in the thirteenth century. Skeptics could argue that women of recent centuries have influenced images of ancestresses as they are portrayed by the bards who perform *Sunjata*. Defenders of epic portrayals might reply that accounts of historical nineteenth-century women indicate a certain consistency suggesting that narrative conventions and ways of portraying women have survived for very long periods. Whatever century they originated from, the stories of Mande women touch on the crucial issues of gender, descent, and rank, and regardless of how geographically local these episodes may be, they can be linked to the larger picture of the development of social forms throughout Africa (Feierman 1995: 58–59).

The exploits of some nineteenth-century women apparently slipped into the realm of myth and magic so rapidly that little historical residue survived, as in the case of the Sangalan women who participated in the battle of Uyukha-Simbara (N'Daou 1993: 437). Nevertheless, many nineteenth-century episodes describe clearly historical women in various degrees of leadership: usually the wives, sisters, or lovers of *keletigiw* (warlords) involved in a battle or of *dugutigiw* (chiefs) of towns under siege. So far as is known to date, narratives of events in the Mande heartland do not describe actual "female chiefs" like the nineteenth-century Mende women studied by Lynda Day. There does appear to be such a thing for the Manden's eastern periphery, in the person of an unnamed powerful woman (described as "rich") of Bobo Dioulasso, who makes a brief appearance in an episode of the Vase Kamala narrative. She functions as a chief while coping with Samori's invasion in a strategy similar to that of Nwenyekoro of Npebala, who averts disaster by dressing his men as uncircumcised boys (*bilakorow*) and sending them out to meet the army of Faama Da of Segu (Conrad 1990: 256–77 and l. 5762). The woman (chief?) of Bobo Dioulasso sends out the men of her town wearing women's cloth wrappers and carrying pestles, and they prepare "stranger-food" for Samori's army. Samori asks, "Mother- woman, are there no male towns around here?" She admits that there is one, but tries (unsuccessfully) to discourage him from destroying neighboring Nudan by declaring that she loves his warriors too much to see them attack such a powerful place (Vase Kamala*).

If texts from the Mande heartland of southern Mali and northeastern Guinea have not yet revealed any "female chiefs," they have yielded excellent examples of resourceful women seizing leadership opportunities. Aside from questions of official political office, the powerful women of Sunjata's era resemble Day's chiefs in their social positions as "either wife, lover, sister, or daughter of a war leader," and in their ability to convert traditional female roles to political advantage (1994: 488). Indeed, historical nineteenth-century female leaders of both the official and unofficial variety, performed the kinds of exploits that could well have stimulated female characterizations found in *Sunjata*.

The lines quoted earlier, describing the passionate One-Breasted Denba who in her grief flings her wrapper in her brother's face, dons his trousers and leads his men to battle, were stimulated by a known historical event (in this case the failure of Samori's 1887–88 siege of Sikasso). In that case, the alleged drama of female involvement in Kèmè Brèma's death is not confirmed by Person, though it is known that Samori's famous brother fell after imprudently exposing himself to danger during a minor skirmish (1968, II: 770). A different Samori campaign provides a similarly dramatic example of female courage and leadership initiative that can be heard in testimonies from the forest fringe of eastern Guinea, and this one is corroborated by Person. The heroine is Soghoni, wife of Nyénènko, chief of the Toma (southwestern Mande) town of Sélenka in what is now Liberia, near the Guinea frontier. Sélenka came under siege by Samori's army in 1885, but it was not taken until September 1886 when Nyénènko fell victim to an infamous act of treachery. The Maninka besiegers led by Samori's officer Sirifaana Amara had grown discouraged by Sélenka's successful resistance, so Chief Nyénènko was promised safe conduct if he would surrender. Accompanied by his principal officers, Nyénènko left the security of his walls to attend a ceremony where the enemy (Maninka) chiefs prostrated themselves before Sirifaana Amara. When the Toma chief's turn came, instead of giving the customary blessing, Amara shouted a signal in Arabic for him to be killed, and after some confusion Nyénènko was shot and then decapitated (Person 1968, I: 563–64; 583–84, n. 45).

Soghoni's reactions to her husband's death by treachery, as reported by Person, are grist for the mill of Mande oral discourse. Soghoni is quoted as saying, "The sheath has fallen, but the sabre remains" (Person 1968, I: 584, n. 46).[24] Person reports that Soghoni wanted to continue fighting ("voulait encore poursuivre la lutte"), but Toma morale had been broken and most of them fled (1968, I: 564). Soghoni's anger and demand for action are similar to One-Breasted Denba's response to the death of Kèmè Brèma during the siege of Sikasso. If Denba is not mentioned in Person's reference to the death of Kèmè Brèma (1968, II: 770), we can at least consider how Soghoni and her husband Nyénènko appear in testimonies that are only one generation removed from contemporary reminiscences (Vansina 1985: 12–13) and how they are therefore much closer to oral history than most of the traditions cited in this paper.

The first account (Valase Kromah*) was collected from a grandson of the same Bakari Kromah (Person's "Kuruma") who felled Nyénènko as he tried to flee Amara's treachery. This text barely acknowledges the woman's existence, apparently because the informant was more interested in other aspects of the story. Samori sends an ultimatum to Nyénènko, saying "bring his wife here," which is all we hear about Soghoni in this case. The rest of the narrative

[24] Soghoni's characterization of Nyénènko as the sheath and herself as the sword rather than the reverse, is consistent with Brett-Smith's findings on elderly women's assumption of male roles (1994: 16). See also Kassim Koné 1994.

emphasizes the siege and describes Nyénènko's surrender and death in details that correspond to Person's note about ceremonial bowing and clumsy treachery (1968, vol.1: 584, n. 46).[25]

In the second oral version of this event the informant, Kèwulen Kamara, does not seem to consider the wife's name as particularly important (he tells the interviewer, "Since you brought up the subject you should know her name"), but he notes that she "was very fierce," and though he indicates that the town held out for several days after the chief's death, he also says the wife "never went to war" (Kèwulen Kamara*). Kèwulen Kamara provides a detailed account of Nyénènko's surrender and assassination and lays special stress on the wife's famous remark that "you have the sheath, but the knife is still here," which she shouts from a rooftop.

In response to a question about the possible existence of female warriors, the third informant, Kièlè, embellishes what we already know from Yves Person and contradicts the previous assertion that Nyénènko's wife did not go to war:

> She fought a battle for three days after her husband was taken.
> They had captured her husband and killed him.
> That happened in Sèlèga, in Liberia.
> His wife was powerful.
> She fought for three days shooting a gun.
> She had gunpowder and she fought for three days.
> They captured her after they captured her husband.
> They put her husband's head on her [head] and sent her to Sanangolo [Sanankoro] to the *faama*.
> That is the woman I heard about.
>
> (Fata Musa Kièlè*)[26]

The final variant of this event (Tènu Kamâ Kamara*) also fails to name

---

[25] Person says the incident of Nyénènko's death became ludicrous at one point because the Toma-speaking chief did not understand the assassination command in Arabic or subsequent shouting in Maninka so he was slow to react, and when he finally tried to flee in the confusion, the attackers could not make up their minds to fire. Geysbeek's interviews suggest that this contributed to later descriptions of Nyénènko's "gun-proof shirt" that protected him against the first bullet but not the second (Valase Kromah 1984: ll.889-97).

[26] According to Person, Samori was furious about the treacherous killing of Nyénènko, vehemently reproaching Sirifaana Amara and removing him from command. Soghoni had been brought to Kerouane along with the booty and captives, but Samori immediately released the widow and sent her back to Sélenka with salt and grazing animals for her husband's funeral rites (1968 vol.1: 584, n. 46).

Nyénènko's wife, but in this case she is a central figure. She warns her husband against surrender to a Maninka conspiracy, but he ignores her and is killed. Our informant recalls the same famous remark that Person recorded:

> His [Nyénènko's] wife said, "You only have the sword sheath,
> The sword is still here."
> They fought for three days, but they could not get the woman.
> Then they captured the woman later.
> They had cut off Nyénènko's head.
> They made her carry his head on her head to the great faama,
> To the great faama in Kerouane.

Each of these four oral informants was personally acquainted with people who lived at the time of the event described. None of them were bards (jeliw), so their descriptions of Nyénènko's dramatic death and the widow Soghoni's sensational reaction to it probably represent the kinds of ordinary citizens' hearsay accounts that, along with songs exalting hunters' deeds and professional jeli praises of battlefield accomplishments, originally engendered episodes of the Mande epic. Nineteenth-century heroines like Denba and Soghoni seem very close to the historical realities of Samori's campaigns, compared to the sorceresses who orbited the thirteenth-century larger-than-life hero Sunjata. But the fascination with sorcery is still very much alive in today's Mande society, and the fantastic elements of jeli discourse do not entirely submerge the historical personages behind the legendary characters.

Historical evidence adhering to Western conventions that seems to confirm the existence of specific characters in *Sunjata* emerges only rarely. One such instance is Ivor Wilks's description elsewhere in this volume, of the apparent relationship between the fourteenth-century bard Dugha described in the Arabic sources, and the Kouyaté jeli ancestor Nyankuman Dugha of Mande epic. Dugha is of particular interest for the present discussion as well, in that he was the jeli of the Malian emperor Mansa Sulayman who is documented as speaking for this ruler in the judicial proceedings against his "chief wife" Qasa (Ibn Battuta in Levtzion and Hopkins 1981: 294–95). As a wife accused of plotting the overthrow of her unpopular husband, Qasa is an ideal archetype for the femme fatale characters of Mande narrative who conspire against their husbands or lovers by providing enemies with critical secrets. The part played in this account by an accusing slave girl should also not be overlooked when considering the process by which such an event can find its way into the oral tradition of later generations.

Regarding the question of outright female political power in the early Manden, it is curious that nothing in the most hyperbolic praises of Mande song or narrative corresponds to Ibn Battuta's statement that Qasa was Mansa Sulayman's "partner in rule according to the custom of the Sudan" or to Qasa's implied claim (assuming Ibn Battuta got it right) to control of the army: "I and all the army are at your service!" Variants of the Sunjata tradition from Nioro in Mali refer to a woman named Niagalé Missâné who was in charge of Sunjata's armory (Conrad 1995: 107). However, presently available sources do not place a powerful Mande woman at the head of armed troops until we hear of Macarico, who is said to have led an army out of Mande in the sixteenth century (Donelha 1625/1977: 107).

In the seventeenth century at least one powerful Mani woman was still involved in military campaigns, though her gender is said to have barred her from outright rule. In the court of a Mani ruler with the title of Faran, which is the same as that of the Kamara mansas of Sibi in Sunjata's day, the Portuguese priest Bartolomeu Barreira describes the king's aunt, who was obviously a musofadi:

> She would have inherited the kingdom if she had been a man; despite her sex she is so respected and obeyed that nothing of importance takes place in the kingdom without her knowledge. . . . When the inhabitants of this kingdom go to war, this woman always travels in the rear guard with her bow and quiver, and with a club in her hand; and if any man turns back, she makes him carry on forward, by striking him. (Hair 1975: 99–100)

Despite plainly stated references like this to females on military campaigns, we have seen with characters like Nyana Jukudulaye and Sogolon's Kolonkan, that in Mande narrative it is usually a case of powerful women influencing armies and warriors rather than of actually commanding them in the field. I say "appears to be" because we have collected one testimony (Tènu Kamâ Kamara*) claiming that when a woman did go to war, custom dictated that her exploits be credited to her husband.

Mama Siada, the woman in question, is said to have never borne a child. In that and other respects she resembles the earlier-mentioned Maminata ("Allah did not give that woman any child") and conforms to my informants' remarks about Maminata as a musofadi, a formidable woman with masculine characteristics and special privileges. Mama Siada also conforms to Sarah Brett-Smith's description of the type of women known as *ngana musow*, who "develop their tough, achievement-oriented personalities in compensation for their lack of children" (1994: 162). In this case the narrator plainly states that Siada was the war leader and that her husband owed everything to her. The informant accounts for his personal interest in, and knowledge of, the woman because she was responsible for his own grandmother's marriage, which suggests that he could be embellishing her accomplishments to enhance his own image. Note too, that despite his emphasis on Siada's martial abilities and accomplishments, toward the end of the passage Tènu Kamâ Kamara has her back in the traditional role of cook and hostess:

You asked me if there was ever a rich woman,
Who ever gained power in our land.
You said that I should talk about her.
That woman,
Her name was Mama Siada.
That Siada,
She never gave birth.
Her husband,
He was Bòngò Kamã.
It was through Siada,
That our grandmother,
Kagbè Tawulè was married.
Siada became powerful.
She became rich.
It was through Siada that her husband grew up.
          *****
It was that Siada,
Ah, her war slaves,
Were the people of Suludu.
Suludu was a big town.
That was her slave village.
She had many slave villages around Bònkamãnu.
She was a very rich woman.
She was her husband's backbone.
She used to purchase gunpowder and give it to her husband.
They said, "A war can't be named after a woman.
War should be named after a man.
A war can't be named after a woman,
No matter how great she is.
You have to name a war after a man."
Whenever she started a war,
She would name it after her husband.
She used to cook for the war.
She would provide a cow,
And kill it,
And cook it for the warriors.
Siada of Dolè Kamãnu was powerful,
Backwards and forwards.

Have there been historical women warriors and unacknowledged female leaders, childless overachievers whose husbands were credited with their exploits according to Mande convention, and therefore receive only veiled or metaphorical reference in epic narrative? Was the musofadi Kamissa Condé of

Do a great *keletigi* (war chief) whose battle exploits are disguised in *Sunjata* as the murderous rampage of a mythical buffalo? If the sorceress Nyana Djoukoudoulaye "mooned" certain troops, was she really commanding or fighting them?

The search for female leaders in Mande tradition and discussion of their possible historical significance will continue with the exploration of other narratives, especially those focusing on sorcery. Meanwhile, it is becoming increasingly clear that Mande epic is much more than folklore about imaginary heroes from the past. Recitation of descent lists or genealogies is usually done in the present tense, which reflects the Mande view that the earliest ancestors continue to guide their descendants in the maintenance of traditional values.[27] On the occasion of death, the passing of corporeal existence is observed in funeral rites and lamented in the poetic metaphor of *jeliya*, but the spirit remains in the present. The ancestors described in epic narrative form the nexus of spiritual presence in Mande society. This is apparent in the *Mansa su saraka* ("sacrifice for the spirit of the ruler") ritual that must be performed before a blacksmith sculptor will undertake a commission to carve a mask. In Sarah Brett-Smith's experience, the sacrifice for the spirit of the ruler is an offering made to the most famous ancestor of the person commissioning a ritual object (Brett-Smith 1994: 96). In contrast to the skepticism of some foreign scholars regarding the presence of any history in *Sunjata* (e.g., Innes 1974: 26), the view of many sons and daughters of the Manden, including my own informants and assistants, is that the ancestors are simply too important to be forgotten, that they have never been lost to the passage of time because their spirits have never ceased to participate in daily life.

In a society boasting an unsurpassed level of oral art and consciousness, the epic ancestors remain what they have apparently been for many centuries: the means of identification for every stranger entering a town or village, and for every householder receiving the strangers. The ancestors are evoked during any serious greeting, they are regularly praised in songs by the ubiquitous bards, their spirits are present at every council meeting, and sacrificial offerings are made to them before any serious project is undertaken. It is no exaggeration to say that regardless of gender, the ancestors described in kuma koro or "ancient speech" define the identity of each and every member of Mande society. Therefore, if they were to be forgotten, the fundamental essence of the Mande world — as it is perceived by the Mande people themselves — would disappear. For foreign scholars to maintain that it is not possible for Sunjata and his companions to be known after so many centuries and that they and their deeds are entirely mythical (that theirs is "imaginary history" as one

---

[27] When preparing the Bamana Segu epic for publication (1990), I had not yet realized the significance of the present tense. Convinced that it was most important to stress the "pastness" of the people and events described, I erroneously altered tenses in descent lists that should have been left in the present.

colleague has phrased it), is to deny a fact of Mande culture: genuine reverence for the ancestors has kept certain aspects of the past more alive than could have been accomplished by the written word.

Unpublished Oral Sources*

Bayo, Laminigbé. "Bagama Banju." (1,067 lines).

Condé, Djanka Tassey. "Manden Tariku." (16,234 lines).

Condé, Mamady. "Ma Sona Kamara and Almami Samori." (2,521 lines)

—. "Sunjata." (2,450 lines).

Diabaté, Adama. "Ancestors, Sorcery, and Power." (1,489 lines).

—. Interview 2/18/94 at Sebeninkoro, Mali.

Diabaté, Aliou "Ancestors, Sorcery, and Power." (455 lines).

Diabaté, Fanyama. "Sunjata." Bamako, recorded 10/21/75.

Diabaté, Mamady. "Sunjata and Fakoli." (1,333 lines).

Diabaté, Sekou. "Ancestors of the Manden." (1,470 lines).

Diawara, Fodé. "Somaya." (1,106 lines).

Kaba, Jeli. "Almami Samori." (1,368 lines).

Kamala, Vase. "Sunjata, Zo Musa, Foningama, and Samori." (3,147 lines).

Kamara, Sory Fina. "Almami Samori." Version 1. (1,541 lines).

—. "Almami Samori." Version 2. (1,482 lines).

Kamara, Kèwulen. "Foningama." Interview by Tim Geysbeek, Makula Mammadi Kromah, BoakaiYamah, and the speaker's son Jala at Macenta, Guinea 6/28/92.

Kamara, Tènu Kamã. "Foningama." Interview by Tim Geysbeek, Jobba Kamara, and Boakai Yamah at Macenta, Guinea 7/2–4/92.

Kièlè (Kuyaté), Fata Musa. "Foningama and Zo Musa." Interview by Tim Geysbeek and Makula Mohammed Kromah at Douama-Sobala, Guinea 7/12/92.

Koné, Salimata. Interviewed by Sarah Brett-Smith in the Beledugu between

9/14/79 and 9/22/79.

Kouyaté, Demba. "Sunjata." (3,344 lines).

Kouyaté, Jeli Mamary. "Sonsan of Kaarta." Kolokani, Mali, recorded 8/19/75 –
    8/21/75.

Kouyaté, Jeli Mori. "Ancestors, Sorcery, and Power." (1,278 lines).

Kromah, Bakari. Discussions with Tim Geysbeek and Makula Mohammed
    Kromah at Macenta, Guinea, August 1984.

Kromah, Valase. "Almami Samori." Interview by Tim Geysbeek and Makula
    Mohammed Kromah at Macenta, Guinea 8/27/84.

Magasouba, Lansana. Testimony during translation sessions at Macenta, Guinea,
    July 1992, and at Kissidougou, Guinea, June–August 1994.

Sumano, Jamusa. "Sunjata." Maninka tape recording acquired by Kassim Koné
    at Kolokani, Mali in 1983.

*The narratives by Mamady Condé, Mamady Diabaté, Sekou Diabaté, Jeli
Kaba, Demba Kouyaté, Jeli Mori Kouyaté, and Sory Fina Kamara are being
edited for publication by D. Conrad in *Epic Ancestors of the Sunjata Era* and
Almami Samori and Laye Umaru. The texts by Laminigbé Bayo, Aliou Diabaté,
and Fodé Diawara are included in a forthcoming book by Conrad, *Pilgrimage
and Sorcery in West Africa*. The Vase Kamala text and four other lengthy
narratives centering on Musadu but including Sunjata and Samori are being
edited for publication by Tim Geysbeek in *From Sunjata Keita to Bakari
Kromah*. The Djanka Tassey Condé version of *Sunjata* is being edited by
Conrad for publication as *Great Sogolon's House*.

Published Secondary Sources

Ahern, Tavy D. 1992. *Nakunte Diarra: Bògòlanfini Artist of the Beledougou*.
    Bloomington: Indiana University Art Museum.

Bérenger-Féraud, L. J. B. 1882. *Les peuplades de la Sénégambie*. Paris: E.
    Leroux. Reprint, Nendeln: Kraus, 1973.

Brett-Smith, Sarah C. 1982. "Symbolic Blood: Cloths for Excised Women."
    RES: Anthropology and Aesthetics 3:15–31.

—. 1984. "Speech Made Visible: The Irregular as a System of Meaning."

Empirical Studies of the Arts. 2 (2): 127–47.

—. 1994. *The Making of Bamana Sculpture: Creativity and Gender.* Cambridge: Cambridge University Press.

Condé, Mamady. 1989. "Etude d'une école de tradition orale: Fadama (Kouroussa)." Université de Kankan: Memoire de diplome de fin d'études superieures.

Conrad, David C. 1995. "Blind Man Meets Prophet: Oral Tradition, Islam, and *funé* Identity." In *Status and Identity in West Africa: Nyamakalaw of Mande*, ed. D. Conrad and B. Frank. Bloomington and Indianapolis: Indiana University Press.

—. Forthcoming. *Almami Samori and Laye Umaru: Nineteenth-Cnetury Muslim Heroes of Mande Epic Tradition.*

—. Forthcoming. *Epic Ancestors of the Sunjata Era: Oral Tradition from the Maninka of Guinea.*

—. Forthcoming. *Great Sogolon's House: Djanka Tassey Condé's Epic of Manden.*

—. Forthcoming. *Pilgrimage and Sorcery in West Africa.*

Day, Lynda R. 1994. "The Evolution of Female Chiefship during the Late Nineteenth-Century Wars of the Mende." *International Journal of African Historical Studies* 27 (3): 481–503.

De Jorio, Rosa. 1994. "Duguba-Kono-Musow, Aw Ni Baara: Women and Work in Urban Mali." Paper presented at the 37th Annual Meeting of the African Studies Association, Toronto, Canada November 3–6.

Donelha, A. 1625. *An Account of Sierra Leone and the Rivers of Guinea of Cape Verde.* Trans. and ed., A. T. da Mota and P. E. F. Hair in 1977. Lisboa: Junta de Investigações Cientificas do Ultramar.

Feierman, Steven. 1995. "Africa in History: The End of Universal Narratives." In *After Colonialism: Imperial Histories and Postcolonial Placements*, ed. Gyan Prakash. Princeton: Princeton University Press.

Geysbeek, Tim. Forthcoming. *Mande Voices from Southern Guinea: Koniya Traditions of Sunyala, Foningama, and Samori.*

Grosz Ngate, Maria. 1994. "Konowari Jula: Migration and the Construction of Male Identity." Paper presented at the 37th Annual Meeting of the African Studies Association, Toronto, Canada, November 3–6.

Hair, P. E. H. 1975. "Early Sources on Sierra Leone: 5 Barreira Letter of 23.2.1606." *African Research Bulletin* 4: 81–118.

Herbert, Eugenia W. 1993. *Iron, Gender, and Power: Rituals of Transformation in African Societies.* Bloomington and Indianapolis: Indiana University Press.

Hoffman, Barbara. 1994. "Musoya ye divi ye: Woman and Ambiguity in Mande Societies." Paper presented at the 37th Annual Meeting of the African Studies Association, Toronto, Canada, November 3–6.

Ibn Khaldun. 1374–94. *Kitab al-'Ibar wa-diwan al-mubtada'wa'l-khabar fi ayyam al-'arab wa-'l-'barbar.* English tr. by J. F. P. Hopkins in *Corpus of Arabic Sources for West African History*, eds. N. Levtzion and J. F. P. Hopkins. Cambridge: Cambridge University Press, 1981.

Jansen, Jan, Esger Duintjer, and Boubacar Tamboura, eds. and trans. 1995. *L'Épopée de Sunjara, d'après Lansine Diabate de Kela.* Leiden: Research School CNWS.

Koné, Kassim. 1994. "The Female Father and the Male Mother in Mande Cultures." Paper presented at the 37th Annual Meeting of the African Studies Association, Toronto, Canada, November 3-6.

Kourouma, Aboubacar. 1989. "Etude d'une école de tradition orale: Dyéliba Koro (Kankan)." Université de Kankan: Memoire de diplome de fin d'études superieures.

Mage, Eugène. 1868. *Voyage dans le Soudan occidental (Sénégambie-Niger).* Paris: Hachette.

McIntosh, Roderick J. 1993. "Unearthing the Early Mande World of Authority." Paper presented at the 36th Annual Meeting of the African Studies Association, Boston, December 4–7.

—. 1995. "The Power of Place in Mande Social Memory." Paper presented at the Workshop on Global Change in History and Prehistory, Rice University, September 4–6.

Meillassoux, Claude. 1964. "Histoire et institutions du *kafo* de Bamako d'après la tradition des Niaré." *Cahiers d'Études Africaines* 4 (14): 186–227.

N'Daou, Mohamed Saidou. 1993. "History, Memories and Social Differentiation in Sangalan (1850–1958) [Guinea]." Ph.D. dissertation, University of Minnesota. Ann Arbor: University Microfilms International.

Short, Julianne. 1994. "'Now, What Can I Do Besides Eat and Give Advice?': The Social Construction of Senior Womanhood in Bamana Society." Paper presented at the 37th Annual Meeting of the African Studies Association, Toronto, Canada, November 3–6.

Sidibé, Mamby. 1929. "Les sorciers mangeurs d'hommes au Soudan Français." *Outre-Mer* 1:22–31.

Soleillet, Paul. 1887. *Voyage à Ségou 1878–1879*, ed. Gabriel Gravier. Paris: Challamel aîné.

Tellier, G. 1898. *Autour de Kita*. Paris: Henri Charles-Lavauzelle.

10. *Sunjata* as Written Literature: The Role of the Literary Mediator in the Dissemination of the *Sunjata* Epic

Stephen P. D. Bulman

As indicated in the accompanying essays by Ralph Austen and Ivor Wilks, there are great gaps in the written record of both the person of Sunjata as an historical figure and the *Sunjata* epic as a literary work. Between the completion of Ibn Khaldun's *Kitab al-Ibar* at the end of the fourteenth century and the beginning of European imperialist expansion into the Sudan in the late nineteenth century, we have no documents that even mention Sunjata. Such a situation requires us to give very careful attention to the existing colonial and postcolonial texts on Sunjata as a clue to the earlier history of the epic and its historical basis as well as a force in shaping the modern apprehension of this heroic narrative.[1]

Until the early 1960s, when the first tape recordings of actual performances were made,[2] our total knowledge of the shape and content of the *Sunjata* epic depended either upon texts written down by Europeans and Africans attending a performance by a jeli, or inscriptions of non-jeli third-party accounts. Even the early taped versions were published only in the form of conflated and edited prose translations. It is not until 1967 that a recorded performance (by jeli Tiemoko Kone of Mourdiah, Mali) was transcribed and published with a line-by-line French translation (Kone 1970). Beyond this date prose reworkings of the epic—based either upon a single performance, several

---

[1] I am grateful to Ralph Austen, Stephen Belcher, David Conrad, and Paulo de Moraes Farias for helping me in the location of the Sunjata variants and other sources on which this paper is based.

[2] A radio broadcast and recording was made by the bard Kele Monson Jabate for Radio Mali in 1961.

performances, or a number of bards or non-bardic informants—have continued to appear, although line by line direct translation is now the norm.

The work and role of the paraphrasing literary mediators of the *Sunjata* epic is the subject of this chapter—their task of transforming a fluid, oral, and extemporaneous recitation into a fixed piece of literature, first out of necessity, more recently out of choice. The individuals to be discussed here fall into three social/historical groups: literate Muslim notables from Nioro, Mali; early French conquerors and colonial administrators; and European-educated West Africans. My critical goal is to assess the technical skills and shortcomings of these mediators, to determine as far as possible the agendas that motivated their literary efforts, and finally to evaluate the resulting texts. On a more modest level I aim also to provide a checklist of these often pioneering and important written records of the oral poem, and perhaps to stimulate the search for other early versions of the *Sunjata* epic.

The Nioro Chronicle: The Earliest African Literary Variants of Sunjata

From 1904 to 1929 four similar accounts of western Sudanese history emanating from the town of Nioro in the Malian Sahel were published in various French translations. Although mediated by European military and colonial officials, the texts were based on Arabic manuscripts probably produced in Nioro itself, either directly before translation into French, or at an earlier, although undetermined, stage. If the latter possibility is correct, then these manuscripts represent the earliest—and still largely unknown—literate tradition of *Sunjata*.

The story of these accounts involves a chain of transmission beginning with "ancient books" and oral authorities (both unnamed), passing through an Arabic literary composer, on occasion other African writers or speakers, and ending in a series of colonial receptors, whose French translations appeared in a variety of periodicals and books.

The European part of this story begins in 1891 immediately following the French occupation of Nioro by troops under Colonel Archinard. A naval artillery officer named Claude was appointed commander of the *cercle* of Nioro, and either on his authority, or that of his superiors, commissioned a twenty-six-year-old Soninke Muslim resident of Nioro—Mamadou Aïssa Diakité—to write a history of the townspeople.

It is unclear whether the commander's commission was actually the start of the project. The resultant chronicle is long and broad in its coverage, detailing events from the death of Muhammad to the death of al-Hajj 'Umar (1862), switching from the Middle East to the western Sudan via a series of migrations, and including a short section on Sunjata, along with numerous other (mainly Soninke) heroes. Claude may thus have stumbled upon an historiographic effort that was already underway. This hypothesis receives weight when one considers how various later French officials received expanding versions of the chronicle.

Were they simply the fortunate recipients and channels for an undertaking inspired and initiated by Nioro residents themselves?

As for the first known Nioro chronicle variant, Claude passed the completed Arabic manuscript to Archinard, who in turn gave it to the Académie des Sciences Coloniales in Paris. The Académie apparently sat on the document for some three decades, and it was only in 1929 that Henri Labouret finally published a translation (Diakité 1929: 189–225).

In the meantime two—possibly three—further versions of the Nioro chronicle, including a growing section on Sunjata, had appeared in French. In 1904 G. Adam, cercle of Kayes administrator from 1900 to 1903, published a chronicle similar in coverage and style to Labouret's, but longer (Adam 1904). Two facts point to this text being a reworked and expanded version of that commissioned by Claude in 1891 by the same writer.[3] Authorship is attributed to a young Soninke marabout, while Adam apparently received the account as an Arabic manuscript.

Later, around 1910 (according to Conrad's dating), Jean Chartier passed two manuscripts from Nioro to Maurice Delafosse, then in France. One was in Arabic and is credited to Mamadi (sic) Aïssa, *qadi* of Nioro. This is surely Mamadou Aïssa, although admittedly a youngish qadi at forty-six or so. The other was in Bamana and was dictated by two Nioro notables, one of whom (according to Delafosse) was the nephew of the Nioro qadi, making Mamadou Aïssa the likely original source for both. The Arabic manuscript contained additional elements to the Bamana one, though none were relevant to the Sunjata portion of the account. Delafosse later published a French translation of the Arabic manuscript and the familiar pattern of the Nioro history is evident (Delafosse 1913; Conrad 1984). In his book published in the previous year, *Haut-Sénégal-Niger*, Delafosse also employs the work of Mamadou Aïssa (1912: vol. II, ch. 6–7).

Mamadou Aïssa's chronicle had certainly achieved some common currency in Nioro by the 1910s. A further and similar chronicle of western Sudanese history from Nioro was published in French translation in 1912 by Robert Arnaud (1912). Arnaud claims to have received the information orally, although the profession of his informant is unclear. He refers to him as a Soninke of the Bacili family — ruling out Mamadou Aïssa himself — and the source distinguishes himself from the "old griots." Two possibilities can be canvassed: (1) the source was a young jeli who had reoralized the textual chronicle (this could account equally for the broad structural similarities to the earlier Nioro

---

[3] Lieutenant Lanrezac (1907, 1907a) also published similar histori cal information from an "écrivain arabe du poste de Nioro," where he was Deputy Commandant between 1898–1901 (Conrad 1984: 37). Although both articles contain a short incident from the life of Sunjata, this is identified (Lanrezac 1907a: 296) as from Quiquandon's account of the Sunjata epic (see below), and not from the Nioro source.

chronicle variants, the omissions, and the new details that are present); (2) the source was not a jeli, but a colleague of Mamadou Aïssa who preferred to give an oral presentation to Arnaud and included some of his own knowledge in the account.

The specific aims of Mamadou Aïssa and his colleagues in producing textual variants of the *Sunjata* epic remain obscure — did they openly seek Western outlets, or were their primary motives the codification and collation of a "complete" account of western Sudanese history for local consumption? Their overarching goal appears to have been the chronicling of the past within a specifically Islamic frame, a solidifying and categorizing of western Sudanese history, tying in Sudanese heroes with Middle Eastern figures, the savanna with the desert, and spanning the time from the birth of Islam until the time of al-Hajj 'Umar. Certainly the sections on Sunjata Keita were only an incidental episode in this chronicle. At their longest (about 3,500 words) the sections on Sunjata are briefer than the tours de force of Kande Kanote or Kieba Kuyate (see below). And these portions betray a clear Islamic context, conforming in tone to the rest of the chronicle.[4]

On present evidence it is impossible to say if Claude's 1891 commission marks the start of the Arabic literary project or merely the first we hear of it. Certainly the possibility exists that an indigenous literary tradition incorporating the *Sunjata* epic developed side by side with the oral tradition in parts of west Africa before the European conquests. What influence this literary tradition might have exerted over the shape and content of the epic can only be guessed at; but the expansion and alteration of the chronicle's section on Sunjata as well as indications that Arabic textual material was later reoralized to suggest that Nioro was the site of an ongoing oral-literate dialogue.

Early European Literary Versions of *Sunjata*

Nearly all the first European literary versions of the *Sunjata* epic were the result of the imperial activities of European powers—specifically the French seizure and colonization of the western Sudan—and the earliest three come from

---

[4] The desire to make of Sunjata a specifically Islamic hero is of course not confined to these Nioro accounts. Marabouts, for example, are familiar figures in many epic recitations, and in a large majority of published versions Sunjata treats them with respect (Bulman 1990: 304–12). The reference to Bilali as a Keita ancestor is also common (ibid.: 165–70). If the balance between Islam and non-Islamic practices is often uneasy within the epic, it rarely tilts completely to one side or the other. (Exceptions are Bertol 1970, where the hero is the "Sword of Islam" and Sumanguru curses Allah before descending into the underworld, on the one hand, and perhaps Sadji 1936, where Sunjata kills a marabout for the "suspicious" act of praying early in the morning.) Islam is a familiar context for most written versions of the epic, but rarely is the promotion of the Muslim faith a motive for its transcription (or primary oral performance).

military men involved in the conquest under Colonel Louis Archinard.

Lieutenant Hourst of the French navy included a brief summary—just over 1,000 words— of the *Sunjata* narrative in his account of a colonial expedition (Hourst 1898: 50–53). Hourst's mission involved ascending the Senegal River in a boat, crossing overland to the Niger at Timbuktu, and descending the Niger River to the sea. Although he does not name the teller(s) or the location(s) at which he heard the epic, circumstantial details in the account point to Kulikoro, a Niger River village about sixty kilometers northeast of Bamako: the variant ends with the etiological tale of Sumanguru's transformation into the basalt rocks of Kulikoro, and the story appears in the section of the book dealing with that village, which Hourst visited in 1889 and again in 1895.

Captain F. Quiquandon was a member of the army of Colonel Archinard campaigning against Samori in the Sudan. Quiquandon was sent in 1890–91 on a mission to Tieba, ruler of Kenedougou, to make him an ally of the French against Samori and spent some months at the court of Tieba at Sikasso. There he seems to have become familiar with the *Sunjata* epic, although he gives no details as to his specific informant(s). In 1892 he published a version of the epic of about 5,000 words as the start of a survey of Kenedougou history (Quiquandon 1892: 305–18, Méniaud 1931: 529ff.).

Charles Monteil (1871–1949), a French colonial official who went on to teach and write about African languages and cultures, transcribed two brief accounts of the epic in his diary for June 28, 1898, while he was stationed at Médine. One is attributed to the Khassonke marabout Bakary Konte from nearby Komenfara, while the other goes uncredited (Monteil 1966: 166–70). However, according to varying indications from Monteil's accounts of this period, this formally anonymous account of *Sunjata* may be the work of either a Khassonke storyteller (Monteil 1977: 11,) or of the Soninke bard, Tudo Yaresi.[5]

The earliest published version of the epic that attempts to capture jeli performance was produced by another Khassonke, Kande Kanote, and included as a narrative of about 7,000 words ("La Légende de Soundiata") in a collection of folktales (Zeltner 1913: 1–36). The collector of this text, Franz de Zeltner, was sent by the French Ministry of Public Instruction to investigate Sahel archaeology, ethnology, and folklore from 1904 to 1912. In the course of this mission he visited Nioro, where he noted down Kanote's version of the epic, plus a shorter and less coherent rendition by the Nioro jeli Habibou Sissoko (ibid: 37–45).

---

[5] According to his diary, Monteil made notes on a version of the legend of Wagadu by Yaresi at Médine only five days before the unattributed version of the Sunjata story (Monteil 1953: 365). Stories of Wagadu and Sunjata are sometimes combined (e.g., Jali Baba Sisoko "Wagadu and Sunjata," in Conrad 1981: 670–710), and Monteil's anonymous account of Sunjata begins (1966: 166) by naming Simanguru (sic) as a slave of the ruler of Wagadu, Manga Diabé— a key character in Yaresi's legend of Wagadu.

Around the same time as de Zeltner undertook his researches the energetic German anthropologist Leo Frobenius was traveling Africa to acquire cultural artifacts for a Hamburg museum. Among the results of this expedition is a major publication of some 10,000 words, "Die Sunjattalegende der Malinke" (Frobenius 1925: 303–31; 1913: 449–66). The source is jeli Kieba Kuyate, alias Korongo, a griot whom Frobenius encountered (possibly at Kankan) sometime between 1907 and 1912.

Paul Humblot's short summary of *Sunjata*'s story appeared only after World War II, but it is probably the product of efforts undertaken by this French colonial administrator during 1918, when he was based at Baroueli, between Bamako and Segu in the Upper Niger valley. No informant or location is given, and the wide number of alternative details in the account suggest an amalgamation of the information of a number of sources (Humblot 1951: 111–13, ibid. 1918: vols. 3–4, ibid. 1919: vols. 1 and 4). A similarly brief account was published some years later by Robert Pageard, a French colonial official and later judge in Upper Volta during the same period as Humblot's service. This text is based upon the knowledge of an unnamed Segu informant (1961: 53–55).

Humblot's knowledge of the *Sunjata* epic appears to be the by-product of research into the Maninka language: in the same way, another colonial administrator, Jean Vidal, recorded an account of the story in 1922 from unnamed Kela jeliw when he was searching for information on the site of nearby Niani, reputedly the ancient capital of Mali (Vidal 1924).

René Guillot (1900–1969), the French children's author, produced a version of the *Sunjata* story, entitled "La Flèche magique" (Guillot 1950: 54–73). Guillot taught mathematics in Saint-Louis and Dakar from 1923–1948 and developed an interest in African flora, fauna, folklore, and traditional culture, becoming a keen hunter. These facts, plus the paucity of published accounts available by 1948, suggest that Guillot used an original source (Doyle 1968: 126). In the same year that Guillot's book appeared an American Ph.D. student, David Ames, recorded a version of the epic from a Gambian Wolof, Ali Sawse (Courlander 1975: 71–78). Sawse's distant variant of the epic is notable for excluding all reference to Sumanguru.

At least two further variants of the *Sunjata* epic from the pens of French colonial administrators may exist in manuscript form, but have so far not been traced. François-Victor Equilbecq (b. 1872) served in various parts of French West Africa between 1902 and 1932. During this time he collected some 275 folktales, 167 of which were published in three volumes during his lifetime. "Namana Soundiéta," listed among the 275 tales, did not appear in Equilbecq's published volumes, but may exist in manuscript for a projected fourth tome (Equilbecq 1972: 14–15, 26).

Jean François Vuillet (1877–1960) was a colonial agricultural inspector based in present-day Mali from 1898 to 1926 who published work on agronomy and history. Yugoslav poet and painter Rastko Petrovic, who traveled through

West Africa in the late 1920s, writes that Vuillet "discovered the great epic of Sumanguru and wrote it down," noting that it was about 10,000 lines long; but investigations have not thrown up any extant manuscript (Petrovic 1955: 192–203).

Methods

Charles Monteil stressed the importance of mastering local languages to the aspiring French colonial administrator, recommending folktales as learning aids (Grosz-Ngaté 1988: 498). While some administrators—notably Monteil and Delafosse—became competent linguists, most of the literary mediators (including Monteil himself in the 1890s) relied upon interpreters. De Zeltner, for example, admits to employing a translator, and the military officers Hourst, Quiquandon, and Lanrezac would certainly have done the same. French colonial practice, which was to rotate officers from post to post and from one cultural region to another, worked against the development of language skills. Aside from this difficulty, in the age before tape-recording even a linguistically competent scribe would have found it impossible to keep up with the performance of a jeli, and it must be surmised that several sittings were employed for the accomplished versions that Frobenius and de Zeltner present.

Attitudes of the European writers to the epic varied considerably from contempt to enchantment. Quiquandon and Vidal openly admit to editing elements of the tradition: Quiquandon writes how "j'ai essayé de débarasser le plus possible ces récits légendaires de miraculeux dans lequel ils sont noyés" but concludes that if he did this completely there would be nothing left (1892: 306). Likewise Vidal admits discarding details of the story that he considered "far too puerile and childish" or episodes "too long and tedious." It is almost certain that he censored the episodes dealing with Sunjata's exile; with regard to this portion of the narrative Vidal writes of "prouesses sans nombre dont le détail serait fastidieux." Vidal also inserts a modern judgment of the hero, stating that he achieved success only by gathering mercenaries eager for booty from across Africa (1924: 318, 322, 326).

Monteil's attitude to his informants could also be high-handed. Grosz-Ngaté writes of how he summoned two praise-singers to hear their traditions for his book *Les Bambara* (1924). Running short of time for the interview, "he solves the problem by cutting short their disquisitions, qualified as 'tirades,' and points out confidently that he believes nothing essential has escaped him" (Grosz-Ngaté 1988: 500).

On the other hand Frobenius was clearly impressed by his informant, Kieba Kuyate, whom he praises thus:

> And Korongo—how he delivered this! The voice modulated; the facial features mimed in numerous nuances individual words and gestures; and the delivery was delayed or sped up, subsided and increased.

Verily, a mighty heroism, a living epic, and a born artist—this Korongo. (Jahn 1974: 9)

Frobenius paid his sources well, believing this produced the best results (Jahn 1974: 8). De Zeltner appears not quite so enchanted with the jeli Kande Kanote, whom he calls "assez réputé," but that did not stop him from spending two months in an effort to secure a "version complète," after repeated requests, and an apparent abridgment of the tale (Zeltner 1913: ii, 37). Perhaps he was not so well financed as the German? De Zeltner also tells us how he tried to recapture in French the style of the bard's performance, with "ses courtes phrases, ses tournures un peu gauches, ses répétitions, ses images, ses longeurs . . ." (ibid: ii).

Motives
Lanrezac ends his article on Sudanese legends with the statement:

J'espère seulement avoir démontré . . . que nous n'avons pas affaire à de véritables sauvages, mais à des êtres humains ayant véritablement une âme vibrant sous les mêmes joies, sous les mêmes douleurs que celles qui émeuvent notre coeur. (1907: 619)

Equilbecq justified his efforts on the grounds that "it is necessary to know those whom one wishes to dominate." But he also argued that "these traditions are the supreme vestiges of the primitive beliefs of the black race and, on this basis, deserve to be saved from oblivion" (Equilbecq 1971: 22).

Leo Frobenius's motives are neatly summarized by Austen (1990: 35–36): "a simple instinct to collect (inspired by the museum sponsors of his several expeditions), a German romantic vision of Africa's anti-rational civilization, and commitment to a radical theory of cultural diffusionism." Hourst's travelogue was part of a vogue for African adventure stories, particularly prevalent in fin-de-siècle France, in the aftermath of French imperial successes.

Disparate aims — but all of the early literary accounts of the *Sunjata* epic were produced under colonial conditions and most served specific needs of colonial rule. We have already noted that Captain Quiquandon became familiar with the *Sunjata* epic while negotiating an alliance with the ruler of Kenedougou during the period of territorial conquest. By the turn of the century increased knowledge of African society, history, and culture was seen as a prerequisite for successful continuation of French colonialism. David Conrad (1984: 37), citing the evidence of the French Soudan archives, notes that "it was a matter of colonial policy for officials at regional offices to inquire into the historical background of local cultures." Even efforts by French administrators to demonstrate that Africa had attained something that could be regarded as "civilization" may be seen as responses to the generally low esteem in which colonial service was held by the public at home.

Charles Monteil was thus charged with producing a questionnaire concerning the legal customs of Africans for a colonial handbook when he included two brief accounts of the epic in his diary. The specific ethnographic, linguistic, and historical projects of colonial officials de Zeltner, Humblot, and Vidal have already been noted.

The most impressive result of French imperial desire to study, catalogue, and lay bare African achievements can be found in Maurice Delafosse's three-volume *Haut-Sénégal-Niger* (1912), which included an early attempt to integrate medieval Arabic information on Mali with oral sources such as *Sunjata*. Delafosse's undertaking was the brainchild of Governor Clozel of Haut-Sénégal-Niger who, upon arriving in Bamako in 1908, initiated the project by requiring all cercle administrators to fill out lengthy questionnaires on their regions. The resulting book reshaped the administrators' raw data, along with material culled from other sources, into chapters that deal in turn with the land, peoples, languages, history, and cultures of the regions under French control.

Delafosse's courses at the Ecole Coloniale in Paris from about 1910 are described by William Cohen as "the highlight of every cadet's education." Cohen cites the well-published administrator, Robert Delavignette:

> [While] Seignobos at the Sorbonne was declaring that the blacks were mere children and had never formed nations . . . Delafosse . . . was teaching his students that they were men and in pre-colonial times had even founded empires. (Cohen 1971: 49)

Delafosse was an advocate of the "associationist" approach to colonial governance, meaning that France should encourage its African subjects to develop within their own social and political structures rather than assimilate to the metropolitan political model (Grosz-Ngate 1988: 498, Cohen 1971: 49). Clearly, the dissemination of medieval African history via figures such as Sunjata gave added weight to such objectives by stressing the long-standing political accomplishments of West Africans.

Early African Literary Variants in French—Franco-African Culture and L'Ecole Normale William Ponty

From the mid-1930s written versions of the *Sunjata* epic produced by Western-educated West Africans began to appear, first in learned journals, then also in book form. Those Africans who first published French language accounts of *Sunjata* were all products of the elite school for French West Africa, L'Ecole Normale William Ponty. As authors and often teachers they sought to disseminate and celebrate African culture and history through the new medium of French, employing *Sunjata* as a didactic tool and, in some senses, adopting the role of literate jeliw. Their written versions of *Sunjata* were both spontaneous reactions to the cultural hybridization resulting from French colonial presence and products of a Franco-African culture consciously fostered by French educationalists during this period.

One of the earliest *Sunjata* variants in French produced by Africans is a short three-act play, originally performed by Ponty students at their annual fête in 1937 and entitled "La ruse de Diégué." Its script survives, and was published anonymously in *Présence Africaine* in 1949.[6] The play begins with Sumanguru resisting all Sunjata's attempts to defeat him, goes on to describe how the hero's sister (Diégué) discovers Sumanguru's secret source of strength, and ends with the triumph of the hero. Dialogue is in French but the numerous songs (to be accompanied by dances) are in Maninka (anon. 1949, Traore 1972: 45–46; Diawara 1981: 34–35).

Shortly before World War II the Senegalese writer Abdoulaye Sadji (1911–61), then a school teacher at Saint-Louis, published a version of *Sunjata* of about 6,000 words in a colonial educationalist journal (Sadji 1936: 119–72). All of Sadji's work manifests an effort to marry African and European practices and values. He went on to publish three novels (Sadji 1958, 1965, 1965a); one of these, *Tounka* (actually written in 1946), is placed among "the earliest known treatments of a legendary African theme in the form of a novel in French" (Blair 1976: 71). Sadji, who went on to become an inspector of primary education in Senegal, also wrote a book (1964) on educational theory, which seeks to draw lessons for Africa from ancient Greek and Roman practices.

Sadji's informant, jeli Bakary Diabaté, originated from Khasso province, Mali, and was the grandson of one of Samori Turé's jeliw, Mariniang Diabaté (or Kinya-Mori Dyubaté). The undated encounter that produced the epic variant, as recounted by Sadji, recalls the experience of Franz de Zeltner with Kande Kanote. Diabaté too was reluctant to give up his knowledge, and the school teacher had to wait for days before the griot felt in the right mood to perform (Sadji 1985: 11–12). Bakary Diabaté's recitation is an unorthodox treatment in many respects: Sumanguru is Sunjata's brother, and their contest occupies only a few brief lines. Characterization revels in extremes: Sunjata is portrayed as an excessive figure. Undeniably superhuman—prodigious in development, appetite, and strength—he is also malicious, killing a marabout on a slim pretext. The piece feels disjointed and episodic but is also racy, sharp, and funny.

In the same number of *L'Education Africaine* the Soninke Ibrahima Bathily, also a school teacher, reports traditions which include elements of the

---

[6] Bakary Traoré (1972: 45–46) identifies "La ruse" as the work of two unnamed Malian students. The published version of this play also contains one of the earliest references to the connection between the Sunjata epic and the septennial Kangaba reroofing ritual, at which the epic is regularly performed (anonymous 1949: 296; cf. Austen, Camara, Jansen, infra).

Sunjata story (Bathily 1936). Bathily's unnamed informants from the upper Niger and Sahel tell the story of a Diawando ancestor, Mokhondji, who is given a leading role in Sunjata's defeat of Sumanguru. In this account it is Mokhondji who suggests to the Keita ruler that he send his beautiful sister to Sumanguru in order to discover the latter's *tana*, or secret power. The successful mission leads to a fruitful alliance between the pastoral and trading Diawandos and the sedentary Malians.

Mamby Sidibé's approximately 6,000-word version of *Sunjata* was written in 1937 in Bamako but remained unpublished for twenty-two years (Sidibé 1959). We do not know but can guess that Sidibé (yet another school master) employed his treatment in the classroom long before its publication. Perhaps because he was Fulani rather than Mande, Sidibé reduced the epic to a rather dry and scholarly narrative, segmented into short, headed sections, interspersed with commentary and comparison, amplified with photographs and accompanied by footnotes that betray a wide knowledge of variant details.[7] Like Sadji, Sidibé appears keen to link Africa and Europe, and he compares the epic to non-African traditions: for example, Sumanguru's seduction is related to the stories of Samson and Delilah and of Hercules and Diana. While at one level a research achievement in its own right, the account is also a potential class-text with didactic elements — Sidibé labels his account of Sumanguru's seduction (in which Sunjata's sister achieves her goal by plying Sumanguru with drink) "In Vino Veritas."

The life of Sunjata Keita as told by Mande griots was also a theme for some early Négritude authors. Maximilien Quénum, from Cotonou, Dahomey, was in the first wave of this school; his French-language literary versions of traditional tales have been compared to those of Birago Diop and Bernard Dadie (Blair 1976: 34). Shortly after World War II he produced a volume containing a variant of *Sunjata*, along with two other non-Mande traditional stories (Quénum 1946).

Quénum's book was addressed to the French public "with the hope that you may get to know and love beautiful Africa." His *Sunjata* epic is lyrical and imbued with a sense of mystery and awe. Quénum clearly relished the characters of Sunjata and Sumanguru, treating them as opposites. The hero is a model of balance and modesty, while Sumanguru is portrayed as enormously fat and is brought low by his appetites. But Sumanguru is not judged; the tale ends enigmatically with his death and transformation into a stone in the rocky landscape of Kulikoro, where his spirit remains. By way of an epilogue, Quénum

---

[7] Bolin Jigi, father of the great Kita griot, Kele Monson Jabate, is said to have been Sidibé's informant (Diabate n.d.: 684). Sidibé (d. 1977) produced scholarly articles on Maninka culture and history and also became a well-known storyteller (*Veillé avec le vieux Mamby Sidibé*, Bamako, ca. 1977–78). It can be noted that both Sidibé and Sadji taught at Saint-Louis. Did Sidibé introduce Sadji to Sunjata?

contrasts the materialistic/mechanistic Western conception of the universe with that of traditional African holism, where "the universe is alive." The lavishly produced and illustrated volume evidently appealed to the French, and Quénum received a prize for it from the Académie Français (Blair 1976: 34).

Quénum used various sources for his version. These included a specific reference to the Ponty theatrical performance discussed above and memories of the jeliw from Quénum's childhood: [8]

> Souvent, et toutes les fois avec le même plaisir intéressé, je retrouve ces heures inoubliables pendant lesquelles quelques anciens, érudits et loquaces, nous faisaient le récit des belles épopées de notre race. (Quénum 1946: 45)

Among all the literary accounts of *Sunjata*, Djabril Tamsir Niane's prose narrative (1960, 1965) has had by far the greatest impact, both in Africa and the rest of the world. The year of original publication was perhaps a fortuitous one, with the eyes of the world on the many states in Africa transforming from colonial to independent entities. The impact of Niane's text was also due in no small way to its scale. At over 30,000 words it was about three times as long as any previous variant. With this length it was better able to convey the tradition's depth and complexity to a literary audience. It was also unusually palatable to Western audiences curious about African art.

Soundjata marks a stylistic break with most earlier literary accounts of the epic: although Niane did not reject the magical elements of the tradition, he grounded his narrative in a recognizable and believable historical context. In contrast to the texts of Quénum or Sadji, *Soundjata* does not emphasize the excesses of the characters or revel in the "chaotic" nature of some themes; neither does Niane openly philosophize about the African soul and African culture or eulogize the African past. Instead, the author assumes a direct and (perhaps disingenuously) simple style, leaving all generalizations to the griot whose words he is recording.

Niane was born into a Tukolor family that settled in the northern area of Guinea where he was to hear his version of the epic. In 1958 Niane was a history teacher and headmaster in Conakry when an old school friend introduced him to Mamoudou Kouyate, jeli (and later *belen_tigi*, or "master bard") at Djeliba Koro in Upper Guinea. Niane found Kouyate eager and open and describes him as possessing "la verve." Elements of the epic were heard at many sessions over a period of several weeks; Niane then conflated these performances into a single,

---

[8] A dramatized variant of Sunjata by the Malian Sory Konake (b. 1922) may have been influenced by the same source, since Konake had himself been a William Ponty pupil (Konake 1973).

seamless narrative (Miller 1990: 75; Niane, personal communication, 1988).

    Soundjata was composed more as an historical and educational project than a literary work, and quickly became established as *the Sunjata* text. At the same time that the book was published, Niane's impressive thesis from Bordeaux was appearing as a series of articles detailing the economy, politics, and society of medieval Mali from Arabic and oral sources (Niane 1959, 1961). *Soundjata* is dotted with circumstantial and historical detail much of which derives from these studies. Footnotes explaining obscure points and noting variant traditions— plus something of Niane's attempt to codify Maninka oral art into traditional "schools"—all add to the impression of scholarly weight and balance.

Literary Variants since 1960

    Five years after Niane's effort, fellow Guinean Camara Laye followed a similar path in the village of Fadama, near to Djeliba Koro. Camara Laye approached Belen Tigi Babou Conde bearing gifts and dressed traditionally to avoid being mistaken for a government official. The preliminary visit secured permission to tape-record Conde's recitations of the epic over a month in early 1963 (Camara Laye 1980: 27–30).

    While Niane maintained Mamby Sidibé's sober approach, *Le Maître de la parole* of Camara Laye is in the same tradition of celebration as Sadji and Quénum, although much further developed. It is an attempt to explore, interpret, and disseminate African themes and concepts clustering around Sunjata through the Western literary mode of the novel.

    Camara Laye's interest in African oral tradition was manifest immediately upon his return from France in 1956. After the immense success of his two early novels, he began to travel through West Africa collecting oral tales. In the next twenty-three years he covered twelve states, excluding his native Guinea (King n.d.: 94–96). The *Sunjata* epic is the only product of this effort that made it, at least in extended form, into a full-length publication—and only just. The tapes of Babou Conde's recitations were not fully transformed into book form until two years before Camara Laye's death in 1980.

    The resulting work is clearly multifaceted but, on one level at least, it constitutes an homage to the writer's Maninka heritage, a brave attempt to realize the epic's range, depth, and complexity in a single, lengthy narrative. *Le Maître de la parole* clearly shows the limitations of such a European-African synthesis, uneasily combining the conventions of a limited narrator and psychological insights with the epic's traditional characters, plot, and themes.

    Camara Laye brings elements of his own Maninka childhood to the story of *Sunjata*, such as the circumcision ritual. But we should be careful not to overdraw the role of the modern African literary mediator by attributing to him themes in *Le Maître* that are actually stock elements in the *Sunjata* epic. For example Adele King (n.d: 93–94, 124) implausibly argues that the prominence of women in the book, the description of the hero's arduous initiation into manhood, and exile are Camara Laye's additions to Conde's recitation. Likewise, Eric Sellin (1980: 393–94) attributes the book's concentration on the hero's early years to Camara Laye when this is clearly a feature of most oral variants of the story.

Camara Laye is not afraid to employ the epic's story to highlight contemporary dilemmas. In the introduction (1980: 32) he attacks modern African rulers who "turn politics into a bloody massacre." Implicitly, he may be comparing Sumanguru to Sekou Touré. The narrative ends (ibid: 220) with the exhortation, "May the example of Sundiata and his family illuminate us in our progress along the difficult road of African evolution." Some literary critics have compared this theme in *Le Maître* to an earlier and more explicitly political novel, *Dramouss*, implying it derives entirely from Camara Laye's own preoccupations. Yet Camara Laye is only employing oral tradition for an accepted purpose among the Maninka. Ibn Battuta thus describes fourteenth-century Maninka bards exhorting the mansa to good deeds by recalling the actions of previous occupants of his position (Levtzion and Hopkins 1981: 393).

By the time *Le Maître de la parole* appeared (1978) most published variants of the epic were direct translations of single performances, or sets of performances, by specified jeliw. A few important literary reworkings were, however, still produced (Bertol 1970, Konake 1973, Gbagbo 1979, Konaré Ba 1983, Sidibe 1980). Two versions of *Sunjata* particularly indicate the continued role of the epic in the modern West African school curriculum.

Bakari Sidibe's English synthesis of four recitations, mainly of Gambian bards, follows the same path and pattern of Niane's *Soundjata* and is directly designed for educational use (Sidibe 1980). The narrative is clear and concise, lucidly extrapolating from the often abstruse language of the original performances, three of which were published earlier in linear form and direct English translations by the Scottish researcher Gordon Innes in collaboration with Bakari Sidibe (Innes 1974). Sidibe, a Banjul school teacher and researcher, arranged some of the recitations, and one of the performances (by Bamba Suso) was given in a school hall, before an audience that included senior school pupils.

Sidibe's book is introduced by Winifred Galloway, who provides explanations for various elements in the narrative. The epic is presented here not simply as cultural history (although that is given importance too) but as a socially progressive force for today's children. Sunjata is held up as a "paragon of leadership," while Fakoli is castigated for his torture of a freeman (Sidibe 1980: xv, xvii).

Adam Konaré Ba's lengthy synthesis also has a wide educational rationale. The author (now wife of the president of Mali, then a lecturer at the Ecole Normale Supérieure, Bamako) states as her aim to make known to as large a public as possible "Maninka society, its philosophical concepts, ways and customs" (Konaré Ba 1983: 11). As in both Niane and Camara Laye's accounts of the epic, considerable attention is given to Sunjata's role in the formation, ordering, and stratification of Mande society.

The versions of Niane, Camara Laye, and Konaré Ba each present an episode in which Sunjata, having defeated Sumanguru, sets about endowing the world with a new structure, rewarding his supporters and establishing relations between clans and hereditary professionals. Elements of this episode are also present in many other accounts of the epic, and Sunjata is often referred to as the ultimate authority for Mande social norms—the originator of the frame in which social actions occur. Nonetheless, in most narratives such elements appear piecemeal—an episode may incidentally explain the origin of a relationship of *senankuya*, for example. But among the versions of the epic known to me, only in these three literary renditions do such elements combine to form a separate section of the story. Here literary mediators appear not as inventors of tradition but as its narrative codifiers: reconstituting, ordering, and tidying up the scattered accounts of social etiology into a neat and easily comprehensible statement.

As Camara Laye employed the epic to contrast the rulership of Sunjata Keita and Sekou Touré, Konaré Ba appears to use the epic as a vehicle for her own agenda. For example, she places particular emphasis on the role of women. Sunjata's sister (here Nana Triban) is portrayed as agonizing over whether to prostitute herself on behalf of the hero and the future of the Maninka state; the fundamental debt Sunjata (and Maninka society in general) owes his sister is then explicitly stated, with Sunjata offering Nana Triban part of his kingdom as an expression of his gratitude (Konaré Ba 1983: 63–89). Most traditional accounts do not spell out so explicitly Sunjata's dependence on his sister, although many Maninka oral narratives and proverbs recognize the powerful role of women in both the domestic sphere and the allegedly pure masculine realm of hunting (Bulman 1989).

Conclusion

This chapter underlines the importance of the *Sunjata* epic to elites in Africa. Of course the significance of the story to traditional African rulers and ruling families throughout the Maninka world is well known; and the use that some modern political leaders in West Africa have made of the epic has also been documented (e.g., Cutter 1968). In the present account, however, emphasis is placed upon the employment of the epic by three less likely sets of elites: literate Muslim notables in turn-of-the-century Nioro; early French conquerors and colonial administrators; and Western-educated West Africans from the 1930s onward. Each group has used *Sunjata* to promote specific, although different, projects.

Viewed from the 1990s, the phase of these rewritten accounts of *Sunjata* is linked in part with imperialism and with African responses to European conquest. Directed to learn about and comprehend Africa, French colonial officials were the first to produce literary versions of *Sunjata* for Western consumption. For them, *Sunjata* demonstrated the history and culture of West Africans. By recording and publishing versions of the story they might have hoped to raise their own prestige as conquerors and colonizers from its generally low level, and to aid in their task as governors through their increased knowledge of their subjects' culture. By disseminating the history of their new dominions they may have sought to win continued French backing for the colonial project in general, or for particular versions of that project (e.g., Delafosse and "associationalist" policy).

For the jeliw who acted as their informants, the white newcomers could on occasion prove a receptive and prestigious audience, replacing or supplementing traditional African elites as a source of patronage.[9] Claude and the other European officials who produced variants of *Sunjata* from the Nioro Muslims also acted as channels for a newer African elite—literate Muslims. Either responding to European approaches, or on their own initiative, this group employed the knowledge of jeliw to create a local Islamic history, a chronicle that linked their own region and the heroic deeds of Sunjata within the wider history of a universal religion. Both the Muslims of Nioro and the European colonials thus employed the jeli's knowledge of *Sunjata* to help situate their own power within local tradition. Control of the jeli and his words was apparently as important to these elites as it had been to the earlier African patrons of bards.

Modern African literary mediators like Mamby Sidibé, Quénum, Sadji, Niane, and others employed writing to solidify and disseminate the epic. *Sunjata*'s story was one element of traditional African art to be celebrated and documented in the form of printed texts and dramatic performances. None of these authors were jeliw by descent or training, but as African educators, historians, and novelists writing in French, they may be considered the twentieth-century equivalents of griots. More recently, especially through the examples of Camara Laye, Konaré Ba, and the playwrights Konake and Gbagbo, modern interpreters have used the epic for social and political commentary, thus replaying in their own day the role of jeliw in the medieval Mande empire over which Sunjata himself once ruled.

---

[9] However Grosz-Ngaté (1988) suggests French administrators used the status of their office to exact information.

Bibliography

ARSAN   Association pour la Promotion de la Recherche Scientifique en Afrique Noire, Paris. Formerly Fondation SCOA.

C.E.A.   *Cahiers d'Etudes Africaines.* Paris: Ecole des hautes études en sciences sociales.

C.E.H.S.A.O.F.   Comité d'Etudes Historiques et Scientifiques d'Afrique Occidentale Française. Paris.

C.N.R.S.   Centre National de la Recherche Scientifique, Paris.

HiA   *History in Africa: A Journal of Method.* Los Angeles: African Studies Association.

I.F.A.N.   Institut Fondamental d'Afrique Noir. Dakar: Université de Dakar. (Formerly: Institut Français d'Afrique Noir.)

J.A.H.   *Journal of African History.* Cambridge: Cambridge University Press.

J.S.A.   *Journal de la Société des Africanistes. Paris: Musée de l'Homme.* (Now: *Journal des Africanistes.*)

N.A.   *Notes Africaines.* Dakar: Université de Dakar, I.F.A.N.

P.A.   *Présence Africaine: Revue culturelle du Monde Noir.* Paris.

R.A.L.   Research in African Literatures. Austin: African and Afro-American Studies and Research Center, University of Texas.

SCOA   Société Commerciale de l'Ouest Africain.

S.O.A.S.   School of Oriental and African Studies, London University

Anonymous. 1949. "La Ruse de Diégué." *Présence Africaine* 5: 796–809.

Bathily, Ibrahima. 1936. "Les Diawandos ou Diogorames: Traditions orales recueillies à Djenné, Crientzé, Ségou et Nioro." *L'Education Africaine* 94, April–June:173–93.

Bertol, Roland. 1970. *Sundiata: The Epic of the Lion King.* New York: Thomas Y. Crowell.

Blair, Dorothy S. 1976. *African literature in French: A History of creative writing in French from West and Equatorial Africa.* Cambridge: Cambridge University Press.

Cohen, William B. 1971. "The French Colonial Service in French West Africa." In C. T. Hodge, ed., *Papers on the Manding*, 183–204. Bloomington, Indiana: Indiana University Press.

Conrad, David C. 1981. "The Role of Oral Artists in the History of Mali." Two vols., Ph.D. dissertation, S.O.A.S., London University.

Courlander, Harold, ed. 1975. *A Treasury of African Folklóre: The Oral Literature, Traditions, Myths, Legends, Epics, Tales, Recollections, Wisdom, Sayings and Humor of Africa.* New York: Crown Publishers.

Delafosse, Maurice. 1972. *Haut-Sénégal-Niger.* First published 1912, three vols. Paris: G. P. Maisonneuve et Larose.

Diabaté, Massa Makan. N.d. "Essai critique sur l'épopée Mandingue." Docorat de troisième cycle, Centre de Recherches Africaines, Universite de Paris I, Sorbonne.

Diakité, Mamadou Aïssa Kaba. 1929. "Livre renfermant la généalogie des diverses Tribus noires du Soudan et l'Histoire des Rois après Mahomet, suivant les renseignements fournis par certaines personnes et ceux recueillis dans les anciens livres." Henri Labouret trans. *Annales de l'Acadèmie des Sciences Coloniales* 3: 189–225.

Diawara, Gaoussou. 1981. *Panorama critique de théatre malien dans son évolution.* Sankore, Dakar, Senegal: Sankore.

Doyle, Brian. 1968. *The Who's Who of Children's Literature.* London: Evelyn.

Equilbecq, F.-V. 1972. *Contes Populaires D'Afrique Occidentale.* Originally published as *Contes indigènes de l'ouest-africain français*, Paris, 1913, and further volumes in 1915 and 1916. Paris: Maisonneuve et Larose.

Frobenius, Leo. 1912–3. *Und Afrika Sprach.* Berlin and Charlottenburg: Deutsches Verlaghaus.

Gbagbo Laurent, Koudou. 1979. *Soudjata, le lion du Manding*. Abidjan: Editions Ceda.

Grosz-Ngaté, Maria. 1988. "Power and Knowledge: The Representation of the Mande World in the Works of Park, Caillié, Monteil and Delafosse." *Cahiers d'Etudes Africaines* 28: 498.

Guillot, René. 1950. *La Brousse et la bête*. Paris: Librairie Delagrave.

Hargreaves, John D., ed. 1969. *France and West Africa*. London: Macmillan.

Hourst, Lieutenant de Vaissau. 1898. *Sur le Niger et au Pays des Tuaregs: La Mission par le Lieutenant de Vaisseau Hourst*. Paris: Librairie Plon.

Humblot, Paul. 1918–19. "Du Nom Propre des Appellations chez les Malinké des Vallées du Niandan et du Milo (Guinée Française)." *Bulletin du C.E.H.S.A.O.F.* 1, 3–4: 519–40; 1, 2, and 4: 7–23, 393–426.

——. 1951. "Episodes de la légende de Soundiata." *N.A.* 52: 111–13.

Jahn, Janheinz. 1974. *Leo Frobenius: The Demonic Child*. R. Sander, trans. Austin: Afro-American Studies and Research Center, University of Texas.

King, Adele. N.d. *The Writings of Camara Laye*. London: Heinemann.

Konake, Sory. 1973. *Le Grand Destin de Soundjata*. Paris: DRTF-DAEC.

Kone, Tiemoko. 1970. *Soundiata*. Trans. Mme. Marta & Lassana Doucouré. Bamako and Niamey: Institut des Sciences Humaines du Mali and Centre Régionale de Documentation orale.

Lanrezac, H.C. 1907. "Légendes Soudanaises." *Bulletin du société de Geographique Commerciale de Paris* 29: 607–19.

——. 1907a. "Au Soudan: la légende historique." *La Revue Indigène* 16: 292–297.

Méniaud, Jacques. 1931. *Les Pionniers du Soudan, avant, avec et après Archinard, 1879–94*. Paris.

Monteil, Charles. 1924. *Les Bambara*. Paris: Larose.

—. 1966. "Fin de Siècle à Médine (1898–99)." *Bulletin de l'I.F.A.N.* 28, B, 1–2: 82–172.

Monteil, Charles. 1977. *Contes soudanais*. First edition, Paris: Ernest Leroux, 1905. Nendeln, Liechtenstein: Krauss Reprint.

Niane, D. T. 1959, 1960, 1961. "Recherches sur l'Empire du Mali au Moyen Age." *Recherches Africaines: Etudes Guinéenes*. Conakry, Guinea: Institut National de Recherches et de Documentation.

Pageard, Robert. 1961. "Soundiata Keita et la Tradition Orale. A propos du livre de Djibril Tamsir Niane: Soundjata ou l'Epopée Mandingue." *P.A.* 36: 51–70.

Petrovic, Rastko. 1955. *Afrika*. First edition 1930. Belgrade: Prosveta.

Quénum, Maximilien. 1946. *Légendes Africaines: Côte d'Ivoire—Soudan—Dahomey*. Rochefort-sur-Mer: Imprimerie A. Thoyen-Thèze.

Quiquandon, F. 1892. "Histoire de la puissance mandingue." *Bulletin de la Société de Géographie de Bordeaux* 2, 15: 305–18, 369–87, 400–429.

Sadji, Abdouyale. 1936. "Ce que dit la musique africaine." *L'Education Africaine* 94, April–June: 119–72.

—. 1958. *Maïmoiuna*. First published 1953. Paris: Présence africaine.

—. 1964. *Education Africaine et Civilisation*. Dakar: S.AF.E.P.

—. 1965. *Nini, mulâtresse du Sénégal*. First published 1934. Paris: Présence africaine.

—. 1965a. *Tounka*. First published 1952. Paris: Présence africaine.

—. 1985. *Ce que dit la musique africaine*. Paris: Présence africaine.

Sellin, Eric. 1980. "Trial by Exile." *World Literature Today* 54.

Sidibe, Bakari K., ed. and trans. 1980. *Sunjata: The Story of Sunjata Keita, Founder of the Mali Empire*. Banjul: Oral History and Antiquities Division.

Sidibé, Mamby. 1977–78. *Veillé avec le vieux Mamby Sidibé*. Bamako: Ministère de la jeunésse, des sports, des arts et de la culture, Direction nationale des arts et de la culture, division arts et lettres.

Traoré, Bakary. 1972. *The Black African Theater and Its Social Functions*. Dapo Adelugba, trans. First published in 1958. Ibadan: Ibadan University Press.

11. Butchering Heroism?: *Sunjata* and the Negotiation of Postcolonial Mande Identity in Diabaté's *Le Boucher de Kouta*[1]

James R. McGuire

"We can negotiate."
–Solo in *Le Boucher de Kouta*, 1982

The purpose of this chapter is to investigate the way in which Mande novelists can redeploy the narrative codes of the *Sunjata* epic as a means of negotiating shifting concepts of national identity in postcolonial West Africa. By examining one such example, Massa Makan Diabaté's 1982 *Le Boucher de Kouta* (*The Butcher of Kouta*), we can see how this Malian francophone writer freely isolates and selects narrative techniques, tropes, and culturally embedded concepts of social action and conflict resolution from the epic as a way of updating and keeping alive a Mande literary culture. Diabaté recasts and rehabilitates traditional epic modes, using them to confer on the modern Malian state a history and legitimacy beyond the material reality of its formal borders, suggesting that the recognition of a national identity does not necessarily exclude a will to ethnic or regional identity.

For Diabaté, there is no contradiction between writing in French while employing culturally and regionally specific narrative practices; there is no contradiction in writing an imaginative modern novel that insists on harking back to the complexities and strictures of the form, content, and context of a jeli's versified epic recitation. He constantly juggles these seemingly irreconcilable ambivalences posed by the postcolonial era precisely in order to set forth a

---

[1] Much of the material for this essay is taken from a previously published article (McGuire 1993) as well as from a chapter of my dissertation (McGuire 1994).

decidedly hybridized way of seeing the modern Mande world. His goal is both to preserve this world and to reimagine the identity of those within it.

The first part of this chapter undertakes to locate Diabaté's project as a francophone African writer within the framework of recent questions regarding the relationship between cultural identity and literary practice. I also attempt to show how certain Mande concepts governing social action, conflict resolution, and heroism, as posited inter alia by the *Sunjata* epic, must inform the way one goes about reading a Mande text. The rest of this chapter is focused upon *Le Boucher de Kouta*.

Toward Reading Epic Identity in the Mande Novel

I will refer to Diabaté as a "Malian" writer writing about the "Mande" since he has reflected publicly and at great length upon his cultural and national identity (see bibliography). Diabaté's discussion of postcolonial identity informs the use of the *Sunjata* epic in his novels. In his essays Diabaté fully recognizes the oscillating duality of the term "Malian." He writes as a man who traces his own origins, without question and without irony, back to the medieval Mali empire. At the same time he presents himself as a citizen of the modern nation-state of Mali who has proclaimed his commitment to the building not only of a nation but of a national literature.

The Manden is thus a region that, paradoxically and in spite of the arbitrary yet utilitarian borders drawn up with the emergence of the African nation-state, serves for Diabaté as the cultural bedrock for the formation of a national literature.[2] This apparent incongruity does not pose the same quandary for Malian literary practitioners that it seems to for some Western and African literary scholars. Christopher Miller (1990: 118) notes that:

> the question of national literatures is a topic of current debate, divided between critics such as Mohamadou Kane of Senegal, who advocates broad cultural and traditional categories he calls "*aires culturelles*" [cultural areas] . . . and critics like Adrien Huannou, for whom national literatures are already a fact.

In such a debate, Diabaté might claim the best of both worlds. His treatment of the Manden as the cultural sphere informing his work is inseparable from his devotion to the definition of a Malian national literature. In 1986, for example, he contributed three articles to *Littérature malienne*, one of a series of special issues of the journal *Notre Librairie* devoted to national literatures from francophone African countries and the Diaspora (Diabaté 1986a).

---

[2]The figure of ethnicity crossing enforced political borders is memorably dramatized in, among other novels, *Les soleils des independences* by Ahmadou Kourouma.

In another central document regarding the development of a Malian national literature, Titia Singare (1977: 16) argues that nationalization does not necessarily exclude a will to cultural identity based on precolonial history, myth, and tradition. Singare here cites a key phrase from the Malian novelist Seydou Badian Kouyaté, who recommends that conflicts between "modernist" and "traditionalist" generations reach "a mutual understanding based on the double necessity of taking root and opening out."

This apparently contradictory figure of gesturing simultaneously toward interior and exterior, of "taking root and opening out," is crucial to the point I want to make regarding Diabaté. Both his essays on, and his practice of literature reveal a commitment to the dialogical and open-ended relationship between Old Mali (and the Manden as a contemporary cultural area) and the modern state of Mali. It is under these circumstances that I propose considering Diabaté's novel *Le Boucher de Kouta*, and his novels in general, as dialogical in the very broadest sense of the term. Singare justly noted (1977: 17) that Malian literature of the 1960s and 1970s manifests the pessimistic revolt of a new generation of modernist writers in which "dialogue with the past has not yet really been established." Diabaté's 1982 novel, however, is a positive response to Badian's appeal for the "taking root and opening out" of Malian letters.[3]

As the principal, if imaginary, founding text of the Mali empire and the Mande, *Sunjata* is clearly the richest source of Mande narrative elements, to repeat Manthia Diawara's 1992 formulation. I focus here on certain aspects of *Sunjata* that have had a marked impact on Mande identity processes, as they are intrinsically related to the manner in which Mande novelists narrate their historicity. As Diawara puts it, Mande novels can either "recreate or challenge the ideas of kinship and taboos that the 13th-century epic posited" (1992: 6).

An article by Amadou Sy Savane, which also appeared in the 1986 *Littérature malienne*, is a very useful benchmark for identifying what he calls the centripetal and centrifugal currents of the Mande novelistic tradition as it has manifested itself in Mali. Savane states (1986: 123) that:

> Until recently Malian literature has been dominated by what one might call the traditionalist current whose representatives would be Ahmadou Hampaté Bâ, [and] Massa Makan Diabaté. . . . The evocation and restitution of an intact and sympathetic past has been seen by these writers as their duty.

---

[3]Chérif Keïta (1988: 65) has already pointed out how, in his novels, "Diabaté uses traditional institutions such as the *fadenya* . . . [and] the fraternité de case. . . . He shows his characters struggling with modern governments and their designs, that in most cases conflict with the imprint the Mali Empire and its glorious past have left on the mind of the Mandenka."

However, Savane goes on to recognize Ouologuem's *Le devoir de violence*, along with Diabaté's later novels, as the first works to "abandon the traditionalist current." Diabaté in particular, through his Kouta trilogy, has presented "a (Malian?) society in all of its contradictions, that is to say its present destiny."

The dimensions of Mande society that are challenged or reaffirmed in the numerous texts Savane lists all find their initial thematization in the *Sunjata* narrative. To be more specific, one finds moderate to acrimonious critiques of traditional kinship and taboos such as: gerontocratic, patriarchal, and "class" power structures and discourses (i.e., *horon, nyamakala,* and *jon*); polygamy; excision; arranged marriages and women as objects of exchange; initiation rites; sorcery and the supernatural, etc.

Massa Makan Diabaté legitimizes his use of the *Sunjata* epic by referring to his personal lineage. He is a descendant of a long line of royal Kitanke bards. With the fall of the Mande ruler Samory Toure in 1886, French colonialism began the long and complex process of manipulative intervention into Mande social and political structures that has continued into the postcolonial era. One of the groups most affected by such state action is the jeliw. As occupants of an important public platform they are often forced to sing the political praises of whoever holds political or economic power.

This recent history is important for Diabaté, because in order to authenticate his use of tradition, he has to establish an integrity and authenticity in direct contrast to the modern social understanding of "griot." In Diabaté's case, legitimation has been conferred by other scholars. For example, Chérif Keïta (1988: 57) gives great attention to how attempts by the French to dissolve the elaborately structured Mandé society have forced Malians to reassess the status of "traditions" and their relationship to modern nation-building. He examines in particular the jeliw, many of whom are unable to resist the temptation of easy money through indiscriminate praise-singing and "selling out" to the stardom of the pop music industry. But within this caste "two of its most distinguished members in the Republic of Mali, the late Banzoumana Sissoko and the late Massa Makan Diabaté," have somehow managed to retain the integrity expected of jeliw by "tradition," while at the same time endorsing the cultivation of the modern republic.[4] Thus, even though he writes in French, Diabaté is considered to be Mali's "griot of modern times" (Zell et al. 1973: 373).

Having outlined Diabaté's complex relationship to the traditional world as well as his discussions that center around modern nationalism, it is possible to

---

[4] See also the seminal article by Bird and Kendall (1980); see also Keïta 1995 for a biography of Massa Makan Diabaté.

explore the techniques he borrows from the *Sunjata* epic. In this chapter, I focus principally on the use of two fundamental Mande concepts, *fadenya* ("fatherness") and *badenya* ("motherness"), which motivate the action of *Le Boucher de Kouta*. Since these concepts are discussed at length elsewhere in this book (Johnson, *infra*) I will not explain them here. It is the force of these concepts and the dynamic tension between them that drive the plot of this novel forward and distinguish it from Western works of fiction.

The paradoxical relationship between *fadenya* and *badenya* in the Mande narrative can be expressed metaphorically as a negotiation between chaos and order, exile and return, or isolation and connectedness. The introduction of tropes here is not an effort to overly familiarize these concepts, but rather a way of proposing what I will cautiously term a paradigm for action in Mande narratives–the epic of *Sunjata*.

For anyone who writes fiction about the Mande, *Sunjata* is an inescapable intertext. For Diabaté especially, who published several versions of the epic before embarking on his novelistic career, the fictional representation of the Mande world seems to depend on having to deal first with the tropes of *Sunjata*. Diabaté's mission to "rescue" Mande oral tradition manifests itself conspicuously in his repetitive reproduction of the *Sunjata* epic.[5] One might even suggest that he is obsessed with the Mande notion of heroism and the way it plays itself out in postcolonial literary practice.

My discussion of *Le Boucher de Kouta* proposes that Diabaté's preoccupation with the Mande paradigm of heroism in *Sunjata* is a preliminary effort to hybridize in his fiction the epic and modern conceptualizations of heroism. In the foreword of his first published work, *Si le feu s'éteignait* (the first story of which is "La Légende de Soundiata"), Diabaté announces, quoting Brecht: "[The author] has sung of the Hero, the ordinary man, who in an ordinary situation makes an extraordinary gesture: 'Pity the country that has no heroes. . . . Pity the country in need of heroes.' Yet today in Africa the true heroes, the true princes, are those who take up arms courageously against poverty" (Diabaté 1967: 7).

This characterization of today's true African heroes prefigures by thirteen years the parodic version of the princely hero in *Le Boucher de Kouta* who, in his own devious fashion, will "take up arms courageously against poverty." Moreover, this initial involvement with the figure of the timeless, epic hero Sunjata provides half of the frame that surrounds Diabaté's entire work. For in 1985, after a hiatus of nine years during which he wrote his four novels, Diabaté returned to *Sunjata* by reworking his 1970 *Kala Jata* as *Le Lion à l'arc*. Thus, Diabaté's departure in 1976 from the task of transcription and translation

---

[5] Diabaté holds degrees in both sociology and political science. He has produced numerous versions (transcription/translations and novelizations) of the *Sunjata* epic (see bibliography).

and his consequent venture into fiction writing is not an abandonment of his initial mission to preserve and update Malian tradition. As Diabaté stated at the outset of his literary career (1967: 7): "[The author] has sung of the past, fixed upon the beautiful faces of children, and of the future." One hears most clearly in Diabaté's novels this melody of the future, the invigorating parody of the past.

Suspicious Meat and the Novelty of Namori: Negotiating a Postcolonial Mande Hero
        Diabaté's representation of Namori, the titular protagonist of *Le Boucher de Kouta* is clearly a dialogue with the epic paradigm for heroism, which produces by means of the novelistic medium a paradoxically idiosyncratic, flexible, and living version of Mande tradition. Without suggesting that this novel is in any way a retelling of the *Sunjata* epic, I propose that the modes of behavior that advance the story's narration and the conflicts they produce and resolve follow the general patterns mapped out above.[6] What I will discuss here is the way the butcher will plot to regain his heroic status, and how this action amounts to a distorted mirroring, or parody, of Mande epic heroism.[7]
        The present reading of *Le Boucher* focuses on the concluding scene of the novel, a public debate over where the Kouta butcher ought to be buried after he falls ill and dies. An imbroglio between Muslims, Christians, the town poor, and the local imam over Namori Coulibaly's funeral occurs when the legitimacy of the butcher's heroism is put to the test. During a devastating drought, Namori had earned a reputation as the town's savior by miraculously providing fresh meat daily, even during the most punishing periods of the crisis. However,

---

[6] Manthia Diawara's project complements mine in that he examines novels that "redeploy the narrative elements of *The Epic of Soundiata* . . . [to] see the ways in which they appropriate European languages as instruments through which themes and motifs anchored in pre-colonial traditions are repeated and transformed" (1992: 156).
[7] Although my goal here is to elucidate the connections between the Mande novel and epic, the ironic distortions of heroism identifiable in Diabaté's novel can also be seen as deriving from another Mande artistic genre, the traditional Bambara theater *kotèbà*. Indeed, in his foreword to Diabaté's *L'Assemblée des djinns*, Demba Diallo observes: "Satire agrees with Massa, like a Koteba performance" (12). For more on this often satirical genre see Maiga and Joulia in *Littérature malienne* (1986: 135–36, 137–39), G. Diawara (1981: 18–30), and Schipper 1982. Namori's trickery can also be associated with another independent genre, the trickster tale. In Diabaté's novel, a group of village women even refer to stock trickster tale characters in describing Namori's improbable marriage to Doussouba, a train station food vendor: "'The hyena and the dog are bad travel companions'" (*Le Boucher*, 121). Furthermore, the sense of Namori's travels abroad as a confusion or loss of identity rather than (in the case of initiation rituals or Sunjata's exile) the acquisition of new powers, knowledge, and dimensions of identity is very much aligned with the trickster tale genre. For more on the trickster figure as heroic parody see Austen 1986.

unbeknownst to anyone but his initiate brothers, his ex-wife Doussouba, and the imam, the butcher produces this miracle by covertly slaughtering donkeys belonging to one of these initiate brothers and selling the meat to the starving population. Namori did indeed save the starving population; yet, he also became very rich in the process. But most importantly and scandalously, he secretly caused the collective breaking of Muslim taboo by inveigling the masses to consume the flesh of an "unclean" animal. After Namori falls ill and dies, his funeral cortege sets out for the cemetery but is met by the town's poor, who insist that the butcher receive a hero's burial in the local mosque. Having summarized the events leading up to the novel's climax, I shall return to this crucial moment below, after tracing Namori's very idiosyncratic passage along the Mande heroic trajectory.

Namori is a horon (freeman), and therefore possesses by birthright a quantity of *nya* (occult power), which is commensurate with the reputation of his Coulibaly *jamu*. In an analeptic passage describing Namori's legendary refractoriness toward the colonial authorities, one detects the expectations the jamu imposes. Compelling a man to act in accordance with the status of his jamu can be a strong means of persuasion: "The district officers and policemen assigned to tax collection had the worst troubles with Namori. They implored him, evoked his noble lineage and the memory of his father. Namori remained deaf to their ruses" (46–47). The police attempt cleverly to show that Namori's intractability is a refusal to measure up to the social expectations of his patronym.

In fact, it is shameful cooperation and submission to authority, the signs of badenya, that Namori is resisting. His behavior toward the colonial authorities is motivated by selfishness, self-aggrandizement, and rebellion against authority. He becomes a hero in the eyes of the Koutanke for the very reason that "he has the capacity to act when social conventions paralyze others" (Bird and Kendall 1980: 16). Yet, although he behaves "as if impervious to the primary instrumentality of the *baden* group, which is *malo*, 'shame'" (15–16), he is eventually broken by the French commandant, Bertin. This instrumentality of the baden group is most effectively expropriated and exploited by Bertin, who ruins Namori's reputation as an *ngana* (hero). Namori's initial fall from heroism, the tarnishing of his jamu, is but one motivating precedent for his desire to regain heroic status by plotting against his rivals in the story's present.

Namori's fadenya strivings are played out at the most intimate level in the company of his initiate brothers (*frères de case*). Keïta (1988: 65) describes the traditional Mande institution of the initiation brotherhood as "the bond that ties together a group of men who have been circumcised at the same time."[8] The

---

[8] Diabaté's *Comme une piqûre de guêpe* (1980b) is one representation of the *frère de case* relationship ("*case*" here refers to the hut within which a group of initiates is confined).

initiation brotherhood provides an arena for the rivalry with one's peers necessary for living up to or surpassing one's jamu. The relationship between the initiate brothers in *Le Boucher* is summed up quite succinctly by the narrator: "All four loved one another, helped one another, yet never displayed mutual regard or respect. At times, seeing them quarrel noisily or play extraordinary tricks on one another, one would have thought them enemies" (38). The rivalry with brothers and peers serves as the proving ground for one's honor and reputation; a man is therefore encouraged to behave in a manner toward them that might seem malicious. Since the master trope of fraternal rivalry is the *Sunjata* narrative, with its potential for the glorification of fadenya, it is not surprising that an individual's worth in society is measured by the quality of the tricks he plays upon his brothers.

Before addressing the topic of Namori's trickery, it is important to see how his character embodies the trope of exile and return, so central to the epic paradigm. In the Manden, anyone who leaves his town or pursues any behavioral patterns that break with tradition is exhibiting fadenya: "The figures preserved in history are those who broke with traditions of their village, severed the bonds of badenya, traveled to foreign lands searching for special powers and material rewards, but just as important, they are also the ones who returned to the villages and elevated them to higher stations" (Bird and Kendall 1980: 22).

Diabaté has cast as the title characters of all three novels in his Kouta trilogy persons who have left Kouta for an extended period and returned. As for Namori, the reason for his absence remains a mystery for the Koutanke (though he is suspected of having been a highway bandit). This dark period in Namori's life does not, however, prevent him from receiving the praise and esteem that are the returning son's due in the Manden. It is the imam who, referring to Namori's mysterious absence, recognizes the "good example" of the prodigal whose return benefits the group: "'Those twelve years spent abroad belong to him: a man is what he is, not what he was. Back again among us, I admit that he has disturbed the order somewhat. But he has since made up for that'" (138). Ironically, this passage is from the imam's dialogue with Doussouba, during which she will expose her ex-husband's shameful scheme. Namori's bountiful return to the group thus leads to another spinning out, another disruption of the social order.

The idiosyncrasy of *Le Boucher de Kouta*–it is not a retelling, a version of any other story, but rather the singular unfolding of events in a determined space–suggests the importance of tracing the particularities of Namori's machinations. For it is the singularity of the novelistic form that makes the relationship between Diabaté's fiction and oral tradition so interesting. Namori's scheme to feed donkey meat to drought-stricken Kouta constitutes a deceptive exploitation of the Mande concept of discovering an adversary's vulnerability, or seeking out his occult powers (nya).

The precedent for such action in *Sunjata* is clear. In order to conquer his adversary Sumanguru, Sunjata must discover the secret of his nya. In Niane's version of the epic, Sunjata's half-sister Nana Triban, taken prisoner by Sumanguru, discovers that the only effective weapon against her captor is an arrow with a white cock's spur attached.[9] Similarly, the quest to discover an adversary's nya is aptly illustrated by Namori's ruse to slaughter Soriba's donkeys and feed them to the Koutanke, ironically becoming their hero through the violation of a Muslim taboo.[10]

Initially appalled by Namori's proposed sacrilege, Soriba recalls the warning by the town's diviner, Nogobri, that an anonymous enemy has "slit the throat, while perched in a tree, of a black cock mottled with white, after having buried alive a white and russet dog on the plain west of Kouta" (82). The complexity of Namori's chicanery becomes evident as the reader learns that he had paid Nogobri to create this illusion of sorcery in order to intimidate Soriba. Moreover, Namori reminds his initiate brother: "'You are keenly aware that I lived twelve years in places where the word of God and the ways of his Prophet are ignored, like a woman married to two men at the same time'" (93). Heeding Nogobri's warnings, and terrified of the occult power associated with Namori's "exile" from Kouta, Soriba makes amends by allowing Namori to slaughter his donkeys and sell them as beef in his butcher's stall. For Soriba is convinced that "only a malevolent spirit . . . could have endowed this man, his initiate brother, with such blood, cold as a serpent's, and with such a honed acumen for trickery" (96). Namori's trickery, veiled by an exterior of charitableness, wins him quick fame in Kouta and the Republic of Darako, no longer as "heart-dry-as-a-cock's-gizzard" but as "the-big-hearted-butcher"; and, it is Namori's aspirations to heroism and fortune that compel him to fabricate this illusion of, literally, a change of heart.

Namori's parody of the dynamics of Mande heroism is played out to the fullest. Bird and Kendall (1980: 20) divide the general trajectory of the epic

---

[9] Bird and Kendall note: "The quest for strange or esoteric knowledge, for the secrets underlying an adversary's nya defines the content of Mande heroic literature. . . . As a result of this, the unfolding drama of Mande epics, then, centers more on the acquisition of nya than on any kind of physical heroic action in the Western sense of the word" (1980:18–19).

[10] Johnson (1980: 317) notes this irony: "[although] the hero may bring prestige and even wealth to his people . . . one major method the hero may employ to gain occult power (nyama), which can be used to assist him in fulfilling his destiny, is to violate the tabus of society." In Diabaté's novel Namori's behavior, however, is closer to the model of the Mande trickster figure, for he does not so much heroically defy the taboo as violate it covertly for his own material gain. At the same time the benefit to the community is material and reproductive rather than merely staving off outside violence, as is the case with the epic hero. In this way one can see how the figure of the trickster may be constructed as a parodic foil to the epic hero; the trickster's behavior lacks the grandeur of the hero, but in mimicry it also exposes some of the limitations of orthodox heroism.

narrative into six stages: 1) the hero confronts his adversary with no resolution; 2) the hero consults a magician to determine a course of action; 3) the hero learns that his adversary's power (nya) emanates from an occult source that he must discover and/or obtain; 4) the hero, often with the aid of a woman, discovers the nya and separates it from his adversary; 5) with the knowledge of the nya, the magician develops an antidote, usually in the form of sacrifices and/or *dalilu* (occult power); 6) the latter are used to defeat the adversary.

Although this pattern is recognizable in Namori's actions, he subverts or distorts it at almost every stage. The initial confrontation between Namori and Soriba, the uncharacteristically generous gift of a lean filet that causes the latter to suspect trickery, is carefully created by Namori with precisely this goal in mind. Namori has no need to consult a magician to determine a course of action, for he has already decided upon a very detailed plan of action. Instead, he pays Nogobri to persuade Soriba that his enemy has succeeded in seeking his nya and has performed sacrifices, thus acquiring the requisite dalilu to defeat him. Namori conquers Soriba only by virtue of the elaborately constructed illusion that he has followed the recognizable epic pattern of conflict resolution. His quest to overcome Soriba is clearly a vulgarization, a mockery of Sunjata's quest to discover Sumanguru's nya. If Sunjata is the paradigmatic hero of the Mande epic, then Namori is cast here as the idiosyncratic, mock hero of the Mande novel. His heroism is established in the real unfolding of present events, not in the absolute past valorized by the epic.

The parody of Mande epic heroism in Namori's actions is accentuated by the classic gesture of meat distribution by the fadenya hunter/hero. Most versions of the epic describe the hero's regard for the tradition of generosity surrounding a successful hunt by noting that, despite their otherwise hostile or fadenya-oriented relationship that is normal between siblings of the same father, Sunjata never fails to offer to his half-brother Dankaran Touman meat from the hunt, which is his due as an elder sibling. Contrary to Diabaté's novel, meat distribution in the epic operates in a realm where Islamic strictures do not apply; also, the meat distributed by Sunjata or any Mande hunter would obviously be heroically acquired wild game. In the novel, where the meat is that of the lowly, domestic, taboo donkey, the gesture is multiply debased. Still, the act does result in saving the starving population. The irony is multilayered.[11]

The mock hero proves inadequate in a direct confrontation with public power and is motivated principally by material gain; yet he *is* a savior in terms as serious as the Sunjata model. In the end, the fact that the people do not know

---

[11] Namori's status as a mock epic hero is further supported by the fact that he is not a hunter, actually or metaphorically. Indeed, he is opposed to this role by his vocation as a "butcher," a commercial slaughterer of safe, domestic animals, usually according to Islamic ritual practices. It should also be noted that Namori does not share with the epic hero the kind of relationships with mothers that is, paradoxically but powerfully, at the heart of fadenya (cf. Conrad, infra).

they have been duped is exactly what saved their lives.[12]

Although Namori's path to heroism is more or less a parody of the epic paradigm, his elevation to the role of hero in the eyes of the Koutanke is quite real. The phenomenon of praise-singing in *Le Boucher de Kouta* underscores to what extent Namori's behavior is received by the Koutanke as heroic, as the behavior of fadenya. Bird remarks that the jeli's praise-songs function as "invocations to action, to the creation of disequilibrium through which the entire society can rise to grandeur" (1976: 97). As the donkey meat brings relief to Kouta, Namori's generosity is cited as exemplary by the Imam and his praises are literally sung by the masses, as well as by the jeliw. "His praises are sung like before, when he triumphed over the tortures inflicted by Commandant Bertin. . . . In all the Republic of Darako, the griots sing that in spite of the drought life is sweet in Kouta" (97–98). Although Namori subverts the expected course of heroic action, the illusion he creates of fadenya has the anticipated effect of the solidification of the community.

Diabaté also portrays the voice of badenya in the novel. The plural, synthetic voice of the third person singular and neuter pronoun "*on*" (one) as it is used in the preceding passage is but one sign of the collectivity's voice. The most striking example, however, is the recurrence of passages that are a polyphony of female voices, referred to only as "female gossips" or more simply as "gossip" (41). (One must remember here that fadenya and badenya are gendered concepts.) This synthetic voice of the feminine functions as a social corrective for the actions of individuals. It measures the beneficent or malevolent effects of individual action on the group, thus negotiating public opinion. For example, after the festivities of the marriage of Namori and Doussouba, the female voices splinter into two groups to negotiate the effect of this improbable union: "'He led other men to the gates of paradise,' said the ones. And the others: 'The hyena and the dog are bad travel companions.' And Namori's supporters: 'Change your tune, sisters! The same old song all night long?' [etc.]" (120–21 et passim).

Stylistically, these passages are interesting in that the women's speech is represented as iterative, that is, pronounced as a group ("les unes . . . les autres," or "some" and "others"); yet, the actual words uttered are actually quoted, as from an individual. The voice of badenya never emphasizes thoughts or actions of named individuals, only the synthetic traits of the group. This exchange

---

[12] During a stay with Massa Makan's family in Kita, my host Yssiaka Diabaté and Massa Makan's brother Mulai informed me that the events in the Kouta trilogy are all based on reality. After I met "Soriba," Yssiaka and Mulai confirmed that his donkeys had been slaughtered by "the butcher" during the great drought of the late 1970s and sold in the town market as beef. They claim that the scandal is still not widely known among the Kitanke and that Namori's status as a savior is indeed ambiguous for those who do know about his rather opportunistic business venture. They admit he saved many from starving, and leave it at that.

between negotiating poles of the group's voice underscores the powerful function in the novel (and Mande society) of badenya, the centripetal energy of the collectivity.

Cultural Negotiation through the Novel

It is necessary now to situate my argument on Diabaté's novelistic version of Mande heroism within a broader discussion of the culturally specific relationships between the story and its telling. In the context of reading Diabaté's text, and of the particular way in which it reappropriates the language of the colonizer, I will propose that this text is not what Jonathan Ngate (1988) has termed a "writing back" at the West by renegade African writers, but rather a dialogue between inside and outside, a "writing between." The negotiating nature of the text will provide the groundwork for my reading of the final episode of *Le Boucher*, which might be encapsulated by Solo's words to Namori: "'We can negotiate'" (113).

Regarding his use of French, Diabaté asserts: "I refused to wed this language–which I admire above all others–in order to sire a few little bastards with it" (1985: 9).[13] Diabaté does not view the French language so much as a "miraculous weapon," to use Aimé Césaire's formulation, but rather as a way of mixing blood, of subverting the notion of cultural purity and hegemony. As Bakhtin has so aptly put it, "the word in language is half someone else's" (1981: 293). Diabaté's goals in *Le Boucher de Kouta* enact Badian's call for Malian literature to exhibit the dual tendencies of "taking root and opening out." This "opening out" to the West encourages a reevaluation of the African writer who chooses to write in French not as traitor, but as proponent of cultural pluralism.

As demonstrated in the previous presentation of Mande codes of behavior and their manifestation in one novel, African practice does not accommodate the happy dichotomizations of Western critical discourse, but is more akin to the concept recently proposed by the anthropologist Jean-Loup Amselle (1990) of an "original indistinction" that more aptly describes cultural identity processes in West Africa. Amselle sets out primarily to undercut the long history of European "ethnographic rationality," that has sought to impose arbitrary and essentialist definitions of cultural identity. He proposes instead the more tenable, continuist approach of a "hybrid logic," that is, an emphasis on a certain cultural indistinctness that rejects the rigidity of ethnic classifications.

Without entering into the specifics of Amselle's argument, I simply want to stress the importance of his claims that, instead of striving always to

---

[13] One might recall the disgruntled muttering, "Bastardy of bastardies!" by Fama in *Les soleils des indépendances*, referring to the neocolonial order that had polluted traditional ways. "Bastardization" or the mixing of values finds more positive expression in Diabaté, although the neocolonials are not spared ridicule.

arrive at some comfortable "understanding" of "how one becomes Bambara or Malinke" (79), "it would be preferable to posit an originally multi-ethnic situation" (74). It is through this renunciation of both the traps of cultural relativism and universalism that Amselle sets the stage for his claim that the ethnocentric "anthropology of powers" must ultimately admit that it is "in the relationship between competing terms that identity resides, not in isolated ethnonyms. Identity is defined thus as a displacement or as a difference" (88). Thus, the study of processes rather than typologies guides Amselle's inquiries into ever-shifting West African identities.[14]

One must therefore seek to hear the other's polyvocality in the dynamic relations of power between values the West has recklessly dichotomized. Diabaté and Cissé (1970: 17), in a statement that predates Amselle's book by twenty years, pronounce their mission in transcribing the oral genealogy *La Dispersion des Mandeka* as follows:

> "we must begin by rejecting all the prejudices that weigh upon the oral tradition, by reducing the distance that has separated it from the written source. Even better, by combining the two! To reduce this distance is to consider the oral and written traditions . . . as complementary."

In this statement from the early part of his career, Diabaté sees his role of francophone writer not as one of mediation between opposing constructions, but rather one that fosters a more ambiguous combination by "reducing the distance" between them. The dialogization or hybridization of these categories reveals their fundamental inadequacy in this context, and results in their dismantling.

To understand the concluding episode of *Le Boucher de Kouta* it is necessary to consider how the extreme social complexity and dynamism–the indistinctness–of the fictional Kouta is based on conditions in the real Malian town of Kita. Cissé (1970: 26) describes the ethnic diversity and "blending" (*brassage*) within this community:

> As for the center of this part of Africa one must bear in mind the long succession of the various great Sudanese empires. From these flowed an intense blending which would explain the origin of the ethnic elements that make up Kita's population today.

In other words, Africa is far from being a unitary, monoglot society.

---

[14] We can agree with Miller (1990: 34) that Amselle's effort to deconstruct the notion of "ethnicity" in the essentializing Western myths of tribalism does not necessarily question indigeneous African claims to group identities.

The rather simplistic identification of actual languages spoken in the Manden (Mandekan in its numerous dialects, Arabic, and French) does not even begin to unravel the intensely variform nexus of "voice-zones" present in this society and in Diabaté's novel. Rather than identifying and graphing the stratification of these elements in the text, my aim here is to examine the way they operate together by discussing the scene of Namori's funeral procession, a multifarious interweaving of voices.

Although Namori has become Kouta's hero during the drought, the secret of his deception is on the verge of being revealed. Having found donkey hide in her stew, Doussouba conspires with Namori's initiate brother Solo to blackmail the butcher into sharing his profits. Doussouba, spurned by Namori as a youth, also coerces him to take her as his favorite wife. But this union is ill-fated, and Doussouba reveals Namori's secret to the Imam, hoping to disgrace her new husband. Namori's secret is safe, however, for the Imam realizes he cannot allow such a scandal to become public, and angrily suppresses his discovery.[15]

The imam's inscrutable coldness toward a man who had become "so prestigious and once again highly esteemed in Kouta" (145) bewilders the Koutanke, and when the heroic butcher falls ill, suspicions of sorcery mount (note the collective voice): "There is talk of witchcraft, of spells cast, of verses and suras of the Koran intoned forty times over forty nights of retreat" (151). Namori's condition worsens, and he soon dies. Upon learning of his death, the imam, instead of administering the prayer of the dead himself, sends one of his disciples.

Once again the collective voice functions to influence the action: "The crowd . . . is ready to lynch him [the disciple] and orders him to go find his master. The imam arrives . . . and murmurs more than recites the last words over Namori's body. Half the crowd is indignant" (152–53). As the funeral cortege sets out for the cemetery, it is met by the town's poor whose demand that Namori be buried in the mosque triggers a standoff. The imam, bitter with the knowledge of Namori's treachery, improvises, claiming that Islamic custom prohibits Muslims from being buried in mosques. The poor remind him angrily that it was

---

[15] The revelation of an enemy's secret vulnerability by a woman is a classic epic theme. However, contrary to Nana Triban's discovery and revelation of Sumanguru's nya to Sunjata, the Imam is unable to use the knowledge gained from Doussouba. The tension between the epic hero and the trickster is quite strong here and is intensified by the fact that the secret is not magic, but mundane, just as the accusations of witchcraft are misguided. In this way, the Imam's predicament exposes to the reader Namori's fraudulent reenactment of the heroic relationship between destructive and constructive power, while the general population of Kouta remains ignorant, explaining their high regard for the butcher. It is this tension that must be negotiated in the concluding episode of the novel.

he who had ordered the body of Siriman Keita (another town hero and the subject of the first novel of the Kouta trilogy) to be buried in the mosque.

The imam sends for help from the new African district officer who deploys a small detachment of policemen, stating: "'That was the most I could do. . . . The Republic of Darako is a secular state'" (154). Soon, Père Kadri, a colonial leftover accepted by the Koutanke as director of the Bangassi Catholic mission, offers to mediate between the two groups, but is rejected. The imam explains: "'You are a true Koutanke. . . . But you do not belong to the Muslim community'" (154). Father Kadri becomes recalcitrant: "'Great God Almighty! . . . A man of Namori Coulibaly's goodness belongs to everyone. He fed the poor, whether they be Muslim, Christian, or miscreants. And if you do not reach an agreement, we Christians will seize his body and bury it behind our chapel'" (154).

Tension mounts as the crowd begins to fear the intervention of the Christians, not to mention the effects of the heat on the corpse. As one Koutanke puts it, "'Just a few more hours under this leaden sun and we'll be burying your saint in a state of putrefaction'" (155). At dusk, the negotiations are still stalemated. Père Kadri arrives leading his parishioners, armed with cudgels and iron bars, determined to seize the body. The situation reaches fever pitch when a rock is shot from a sling, landing near the imam. Birima puts it baldly: "'we'll weigh less than a donkey fart against Père Kadri's troops. What's more this quarrel between Muslims has lasted long enough'" (156). The crowd acknowledges Birima's wisdom, and Solo suggests a compromise: that Namori be buried in the courtyard of the mosque.[16] The poor accept joyously, and the Muslims in the procession collectively pressure the imam who finally accepts, albeit "unwillingly" (157).

In this concluding episode of the novel, Namori's body becomes the symbolic locus of discursive difference within Kouta (Kita) and the Republic of Darako (Mali). As a hero in the eyes of everyone except the imam, Namori becomes a symbol not merely of the divisions between competing Mande discourses, but also of the necessity of ongoing conflict resolution that takes the form of a negotiation. This necessity is made all too real by the image of Namori's rotting corpse. Life advances through the compromise between the differing parties. In the face of death and finality, the process of the continual hybridization of values and renewal of identity is the hallmark of this Mande community.

---

[16] Namori's burial in a liminal "betwixt and between" space– almost literally the limen of the mosque– evokes Victor Turner's classic identification of the trickster and "liminality" (Austen 1986: 139). In keeping with the notion of *Le Boucher* as a parody of Mande epic, it should be kept in mind that in Joseph Campbell's adaptation of Arnold Van Gennep's even more classic tripartite progression of rites of passage, liminality is the middle stage between the hero's separation from society and his return as the creator of a new cultural order (Campbell 1949).

Compromise is never final, for it always contains a kernel of instability that threatens to disrupt once again the redefined social order. The imam's observation that Namori's earlier return to Kouta, after having "upset the order a bit," was beneficial for the Koutanke occurs as Doussouba is on the brink of revealing the secret to him; now, as the novel concludes, the compromised site of Namori's burial in the mosque's courtyard and his status as a Koutanke (mock) hero is threatened once again by the revelation of his secret.

The refusal of the district officer to allow state intervention in the conflict over Namori's burial typifies decisions sometimes made by West African governments not to meddle in "traditional" matters. Such a policy indicates the state's recognition of the power and importance of the social values that preceded it. Thus, not only does it encourage the fostering of these values at the local level (as long as they do not threaten the actual power of the state),[17] it often subtly utilizes traditional structures as a means of aggrandizing its own power. Diabaté, as indicated above, was very committed to the formation of a national Malian literature, but was also concerned to avoid entrapment in the propagandistic endorsement of traditional culture by the state.

One thus perceives, in the funeral episode, not the state's intervention in traditional culture but traditional culture's participation in nation-building. For what is at stake in this scene is, ultimately, not merely the salvaging but also the rearticulation and redeployment of traditional values that manifest themselves throughout the novel, in particular those that contribute to the affirmation of a postcolonial Mande identity—fadenya and badenya. The novel's conclusion is a potent dramatization of a dialogue regarding the fate of Mande heroism in a modern West African republic. The verdict is given in the form of a compromise, a willingness to adapt to the sometimes bothersome concerns of the present. Diabaté depicts tradition in Kouta as having the ability to absorb change imposed from without. The town's reputation throughout the trilogy as stubbornly traditional and unwilling to conform to state policies is actually the sign of its desire *not* to be backward, but rather to force the postcolonial nation to build itself around existing structures. Thus, the allegedly "refractory" Koutanke are so only to the extent that they struggle not to be dominated by exterior elements, but rather to incorporate these elements into an enduring sense of who they are and what they will become.

As the incongruities between the Manden and Mali become less problematic in Diabaté, so do those between the paradigmatic epic notion of heroism and the idiosyncratic heroism of the novel. Some of Mikhail Bakhtin's comments may be useful here. Although all of Bakhtin's observations on the

---

[17] In fact, the socialist regime that took power in Mali immediately after Independence attempted to replace chiefdoms and even village authorities with its own political structures.

distinctions to be made between the European epic and novel do not necessarily apply to West African versions of these same genres, his assertions regarding the differing conceptions of temporality of epics and novels, as well as the "parodying-travestying" properties of novelistic writing, shed light on the link between Diabaté's modern fiction and the *Sunjata* epic. According to Bakhtin (1981: 10, 7), the novel always offers a critique of the stilted, unreal, and absolute quality of other genres; it is characterized by flexibility, laughter, and irony: "the novel inserts into these other genres an indeterminacy, a certain semantic open-endedness, a living contact with unfinished, still-evolving contemporary reality (the open-ended present). . . . The novel is the only developing genre and therefore it reflects more deeply, more essentially, more sensitively and rapidly, reality itself in the process of its unfolding."

Although it is not the goal of this chapter to provide a comparative stylistic analysis between oral recitations of Mande epics by jeliw and Diabaté's novelistic writing, there is much evidence for arguing that the latter is a sort of "parodying-travestying," or novelized, reproduction of oral style. In an interview, Diabaté responds to the accusation that to write fiction is to bastardize African orality: "I adopt the same tone, that of a storyteller" (Keita 1988: 65). Diabaté has consciously chosen to break with the medium of transcription and translation that he used to produce his versions of *Sunjata*, in order to project the narrative elements of the epic into the unfolding, idiosyncratic, novelistic language of the present.[18] Namori's travesty of Mande heroism is not, therefore, to be rejected as being unfaithful to the paradigm, but accepted as its most modern reenactment, as an emblem of becoming.

The heroism of Namori in relation to the group, Kouta, is curiously mirrored in Kouta's relation to the Republic of Darako, the nation. If refractoriness is a sign of heroism, then Kouta's obstinacy toward the neocolonial government can be regarded as playing the same role as the individual hero. Moreover, if Kouta (Kita) can be understood here as an individualization of the Mande community, then its heroic relation to the larger group–in this case the modern political state of Darako (Mali)–is one that contributes to the identity formation of the nation by virtue of projecting onto it its own "reputation."

Although Diabaté's writing is always intimate and anecdotal, rather than programmatic, we can still see in *Le Boucher de Kouta* a realization of Badian's call for Malian literature to simultaneously take root and open out, to affirm its

---

[18] The temporal construction of the novel also reflects this goal, as the story is told in the present tense with analepses that fill in gaps of information and inform the unfolding of the story's present. Bird (1971: 284–88) reports a similar narrational tactic used by jeliw, and names "three very noticeable styles or genres" in oral recitations: the proverb-praise mode, the narrative mode, and the song mode, all of which are visible in Diabaté's writing.

identity as different while at the same time participating in a dialogue with the rest of the world as a modern nation.[19] This gesture is affirmed by the fact that Diabaté has chosen to express his ideas in an originally Western medium, and is simultaneously able to address readers both inside and outside the cultural bounds of his writing.

Thus, Diabaté is situated somewhere between the advocates of difference and exclusion, and those of sacrificing difference, of including Africa in the global culture by revealing its "secrets." Diabaté creates a compromise between these two positions regarding the place of African writing and philosophy. For, although he would agree with Singare's observation that "to open out to others, one must first be" (1977: 16), his writing testifies to his commitment toward the unending negotiation between the taking root of Malian/Mande identity and the opening out to the other.

---

[19] Compare James Clifford's compelling discussion of the legal battle of the native American Mashpee, claiming to participate at once in a separate, identifiable ethnic nation and to the American political nation (*The Predicament of Culture*).

Bibliography

Austen, Ralph A. 1986. "Social and Historical Analysis of African Trickster Tales: Some Preliminary Reflections." *Plantation Society in the Americas* 2, 2: 135–48.

Bakhtin, Mikhail. 1981. *The Dialogical Imagination.* Ed. Michael Holquist. Caryl Emerson and Michael Holquist, trans. Austin: University of Texas Press.

Campbell, Joseph. 1949. *The Hero with a Thousand Faces.* N.Y.: Pantheon.

Cissé, Diango. 1970. *Structures des Malinké de Kita: Contribution à une anthropologie sociale et politique du Mali.* Bamako: Editions populaires du Mali.

Clifford, James. 1988. *The Predicament of Culture: Twentieth-Century Ethnography, Literature, and Art.* Cambridge: Harvard University Press.

Club des lecteurs d'expression française. 1986. *Litterature malienne*, special issue of *Notre Librarie* 75–76 (reprinted 1989). Paris: Club des lecteurs d'expression française.

Diabaté, Massa Makan. 1967. *Si le feu s'éteignait.* Bamako: Editions populaires du Mali.

–. 1979. *Le Lieutenant de Kouta.* Paris: Hatier (Collection Monde Noir).

–. 1980a. *Le Coiffeur de Kouta.* Paris: Hatier (Collection Monde Noir).

–. 1980b. *Comme une piqûre de guêpe.* Paris: Présence Africaine.

–. 1982. *Le Boucher de Kouta.* Paris: Hatier (Collection Monde Noir).

–. 1983. Interview. Jeune Afrique, October 12: 90–1.

–. 1985. *L'Assemblée des djinns.* Paris: Présence Africaine.

Diabaté, Massa Makan, and Diango Cissé. 1970. *La Dispersion des Mandeka.* Bamako: Editions populaires du Mali.

Diawara, Gaoussou. 1981. *Panorama critique du théâtre malien dans son évolution.* Dakar: Sankoré.

Diawara, Manthia. 1992. "Canonizing Soundiata in Mande Literature: Toward a Sociology of Narrative Elements." *Social Text* 31–32: 154–68.

Huannou, Adrien. 1989. *La Question des littératures nationales*. Abidjan: CEDA.

Joulia, Dominique. 1986. "Le Kotéba: Regards de l'étranger." *Littérature malienne*, special issue of *Notre Librarie* 75–76 (reprinted 1989), 137–39.

Keïta, Cheick Mahamadou Chérif. 1988. "Jaliya in the Modern World: A Tribute to Banzoumana Sissoko and Massa Makan Diabaté." *Ufahamu: Journal of the African Activist Association* 17, 1: 57–67.

–. 1995. *Massa Makan Diabaté: un Griot mandingue à la rencontre de l'écrtiure*. Paris: L'Harmattan.

Maïga, Moussa. 1986. "Le Kotéba: Le grand escargot bambara." *Littérature malienne*, special issue of *Notre Librarie* 75–76 (reprinted 1989), 135–36.

McGuire, James R. 1993. "Narrating Mande Heroism in the Malian Novel: Negotiating Postcolonial Identity in Diabaté's Le Boucher de Kouta." *Research in African Literatures* 24, 3: 35–57.

–. 1994. "Narrating the Mande: West African Identity Production and the Mande Francophone Novel." Northwestern University Ph.D. Dissertation.

Miller, Christopher. 1993. "Nationalism as Resistance and Resistance to Nationalism in the Literature of Francophone Africa." *Yale French Studies* 82: 62–100.

Mudimbe, V. Y. 1985. "African Literature: Myth or Reality?" In *African Literature Studies: The Present State/L'Etat présent*, Stephen Arnold ed. Washington, D.C.: Three Continents, 7–15.

Ngate, Jonathan. 1988. *Francophone African Literature: Reading a Literary Tradition*. Trenton, N.J.: Africa World Press.

Savane, Amadou Sy. 1986. "Le roman des indépendances." *Littérature malienne*, special issue of *Notre Librarie* 75–76 (reprinted 1989), 123–27.

Schipper, Mineke. 1982. *Theatre and Society in Africa*. Johannesburg: Ravan Press.

Singare, Titia. 1977. "Où en sont les lettres maliennes?" *Etudes Maliennes* 22: 2–23.

Zell, Hans M., et al., eds. 1973. *A New Reader's Guide to African Literature*. 2d ed. New York: Africana Publishing Co.

12. The Production and Reproduction of *Sunjata*

Charles S. Bird

My friends caution me that I should not overuse the present to understand the past. I follow their arguments, but I feel that they can lead to abuse, depriving us of interesting stories to add to the historical puzzle. I believe that the extraordinary diversity in the Mande world is not of recent invention, and I also believe that choices made in the distant past have left their traces in today's practices:

> The past was always disguising itself, disappearing into the needs of the moment. Whatever happened got replaced by the official story or competing fictions. (Stone 1991: 74)

If there is a discernable theme to what I write here, it probably has to do with diversity. How does the diversity of the Mande play itself out it in the epic, a mirror, albeit faceted, of that world? How do we account for the many versions of the *Sunjata* story? Why was *Sunjata* either promoted in the Mande to epic, or demoted to folk story among the Kuranko? The key lies perhaps in its modes of production and reproduction:

> "I was born your servant, you were born my master."
> The warrior aristocracy exercises an actual violence on the dominated social strata, subjected to tributes and razzias. To legitimize this power, it needs to be accepted by all, its ambitions focused then on the public. The princes and their allies in general feel the need to have their traditions proclaimed by their clients. Thanks to them, the patrons can assure themselves of the production of the official version of the country's history. Quickly, this becomes dominant and non-unique, given the means at work to produce and reproduce it— the schools for the transmission of knowledge. (Diawara 1990: 90)

Clan names, like Camara and Keita, spread across many ethnic groups. Camara is found in all the northern and southwestern Mande languages. It shows up in the Kru and West Atlantic languages. The Temne, for example, regard Camara as one of their primordial clan names. This is certainly the case among the Northern Mande. What does this distribution of clan names mean? A plausible inference is that it reflects the long-term movements of families across and through different ethnic groups. In some cases, these clans have preserved the memory of the move. In other cases, the move has been forgotten. This informs my understanding of migration in West Africa as a matter involving, not ethnic groups, but rather individuals and their families.

When a man from Korhogo whose family name I know to be Watara greets the Juula of Korhogo, they address him in return as Traore, a freeman Juula clan name. When a Mande Keita goes north among the Soninke, they may address him as Konate, a name of royal clan. Keita might be thought of as a slave name among those same Soninke. These clan name exchanges are deeply rooted in the social history and practices of the western savanna. It is not difficult to see this exchange as a way of making outsiders insiders. It is a ticket to mobility, a smoothing of the way down the road. If these people were not moving in and out of each other's lives, there would be no need of such practices. Some of that movement was initiated by farming and trade, some by war.

Wherever I went in the Mande world, my hosts would play a language game with me, deciding what my clan name should be. In the Maninka areas, the name proferred would be either Keita or Traore, clan names of freeman (*horon*) history. In Bambara areas, I would be called Jara or Kulibali. I would always cause a big disturbance when I told them I already had a clan name and it was Jabaté. Many people simply would not allow that to be the case. The honored guest could not be a griot.

The play of clan naming games can lead to permanent change, as was the case with my student and friend Ahmadou Toure. His father, of Fula lineage, bore the clan name Bari. He established himself in Sikasso as a practicing marabout, teaching young people to read the Quran. The people among whom he lived called him Toure, probably playfully at first because that was what Muslim clerics were called. Eventually Toure became the only name by which he was known. His children were given the name Toure in conformity to the social will.

Sunjata, too, is a name game.

"If you help us, if you help us, we will write down your words and they will live forever."

"You and your dried words. What are they to me? The meaning of my words is in the moisture of the breath that carries them." (Kele Monson Diabaté and Charles Bird, conversation in Kita, 1968)

I have thought much of the production of *Sunjata*, how the performance sounds, but I have no language to express my thoughts; I can only call upon images that we share and the common feelings they evoke. Most discussions of music as text—notes, rests, keys—lose me quickly. I do not understand music in those terms. As far as I am concerned, music is feeling without graphic representation.

Today, should a student ask me what Kele Monson does with his voice when he sings, I seek that common ground. I might compare it with other musics that we both know, rap, for instance. If you haven't listened to much rap music the comparison might not be helpful. Rap singers have rhythmic and melodic patterns, prosodies, which they use to organize their words. If you are just starting to listen to rap, the recurring patterns may sound repetitious, but after a while you hear hundreds of subtleties in them that skillful singers use to spin their tales. Sometimes it is the accents on the words they use that create the patterns but, most often, the pattern is laid over the speech. Good rappers use many patterns to keep their lines in tension with the background rhythm, but the way the rhythms fall together is of the highest priority. This is likely because rap is almost always danced.

Epic singers like Kele Monson also use hundreds of rhythmic and melodic patterns to organize their language. Some of these patterns are reserved for specific phrases. Other patterns may overlay any line. Some lines have definite melodies. Some lines have no identifiable melody. The sequences of patterns produce a modulated flow of poetic language in every state between speech and song.

The epic singers, however, are more rhythmically relaxed than rappers. They do not use rhyme at all, although they readily exploit alliteration. The meeting points of musical rhythm and metrical language are less determinate. This may be because epics are not danced. They are for listening, usually in the late evening after the dancing is done.

Neither the rapper nor the epic singer can sing without the backing of instruments, guitars, harps, lutes, and *balafons*. The oral epic does not exist without its music. The relation between the two is not simple.

Epic narration is called *maana* in Maninka. The *faasaw* are praise-songs, not narratives. They consist of titles like "Nare Maghan Konate," or "Konate, King of Nare."

There will be praise-names like "Suba Mina Suba," or "Sorcerer-Seizing-Sorcerer."

There will be references to heroic events like "bara kala ta k'i yaala," or "take the bow and walk."

There are homilies, commentaries, and proverbs often dealing with power and destiny like "Jon te Ala lon," or "No slave knows Allah."

These faasaw are sung to inspire the audience, to fire them up. Depending on the setting they are invocations to dance and to reward the singers. Dancing is an important part of the production. Dance requires that the language of the song follow norms expected of the music by those who dance:

> To some of us the Owner of the World has apportioned the gift to tell
> their fellows that the time to get up has finally come. To others he gives
> the eagerness to rise when they hear the call; to rise with racing blood
> and put on their garbs of war and go to the boundary of their town to
> engage the invading enemy boldly in battle. And then there are those
> others whose part is to wait and when the struggle is ended, to take over
> and recount its story. (Achebe 1987: 113)

The *faasa* singers fire us up for the battle. The maana tellers calm the
body and soothe the soul after it is over. Depending on the circumstances, the
narrative maana could go on for hours, but sometimes it could be presented in a
half hour or less. It may begin, as does Kele Monson's Radio Mali version, with
the Old Testament creation of the world and with Adam and Eve in Paradise. It
may end with events that take place on the day you are reading this. Episodes
may telescope up or down, depending on the performer's assessment of the
audience. New episodes can be inserted for any number of reasons. In some
productions, praise-singers will accompany the epic-singer, inserting faasaw at
appropriate moments, as when the entry of Sumanguru prompts the "Janjon."
When I recorded him in Kita in 1968, Kele Monson sang the faasaw himself,
blurring the boundaries between the narrative and the praise:

Sira Mori

> Sinbon!
> It is of Jata, Jata
> For bigger, for taller,
> Baraka didn't leave your likes behind.
> It is of Jata.
> Whatever-the-game Sinbon!

Yamuru

> Masa Kere and Masa Berenu.
> It is Maghan Sunjata's affair.
> It is Sunjata's affair.
> He who fought behind and fought before.
> Jubalifaga.
> Magan Konate!
> Dabalifaga.
> Magan Konate!
> Danfaga, danfara
> It is of that Sinbon.

Sira Mori

> Ayoo, It is of Jata.
> Sinbon, of which Jata is it?
> The Great Neck-breaking Jata.
>
> (Sira Mori Diabaté and Yamuru
> Diabaté, "Sunjata Faasa," Kela,
> 1968)

Seydou Camara,[1] after listening to a hunters' bard sing a story that he had not heard before, asserted that he could sing the same song the next evening. He was not lying. Those of us who have difficulty distinguishing performances from text may have trouble with this. Definitions of sameness turn out, in the end, to be political.

The more I hung out with them, the more I realized that griots were just like us. They often asked themselves why they were doing what they were doing, and they answered these questions in the same way we do, selecting pathways to action that complement their best interests, short term and long. Griots prepare and evaluate their performances in these terms. When I first went to Mali, Modibo Keita was the president. Many griots found it in their interest to link Modibo to Sunjata. Others refused to do so. There is a constant pressure in performance to bring the audience into the story.

Griots are very highly specialized, but they can be roughly classified according to their own categories of performance into those who talk (*kuma*), sing (*donkili da*), and play instruments (*foli*). I have seen the training of griots involving the playing of instruments as described by Eric Charry:

> One cycle of a piece, then, can be repeated over and over again without variation for the purposes of practice. I refer to one cycle of a piece as an exemplar of that piece. These exemplars would usually not be less than one cycle long so that contact with the musical whole is retained. They can be pared down for beginners in terms of the density of hand or finger movement and they can also be elaborated internally, that is the length always remains the same but more movements can be added to increase the density, or new movements added in place of old ones. At any rate, no matter how simplified an exemplar may be made, it is still considered to be the piece, albeit a beginner's version of it. (Charry 1992: 106)

Song is learned in much the same way. Having embodied the rhythms, phrasing, and melodies since infancy, the beginner first learns the unadorned choruses, the exemplars of song, and places them to the master's cues. In this

---

[1] Not to be confused with the author of another essay in this volume.

process, the apprentices hear their master's phrasings and try them out on each other or in private. Eventually, their public opportunities expand if they are good enough. Many bards just learn genealogies and praise-lines of the major Mande families. The learning here is by rote as in Quranic school. As in Quranic school, there is no emphasis on knowing what the words mean.

I have never encountered or heard of anything like the *gesere* schools described by Mamadou Diawara in his brilliant, *La graine de la parole*. Diawara describes what we would all agree to be schools where students come to learn a particular set of facts and skills. This is accomplished by lessons and tutoring. Given their presence among the Soninke, I would expect something like them among the northern Maninka and Bambara, but we have heard nothing. There have been a lot of learned bards who thought deeply about what things in the epic mean. Some of these bards have reputations extending across the Mande world. Bards like Wa Kamissoko could hold forth for hours explaining his interpretations of the things that he sang. Some of the things he would say were also said by others over a large territory; they were common knowledge. Other things that Wa would say were, to me, idiosyncratic. That is, I knew no other bards who said things like that. Did this mean that he was revealing things to outsiders that should be kept secret? I do not know the answer. My feeling is that he was a very original person.

The groundwork for normative interpretation does not get done in school in the Mande. In our culture, normative interpretations of language happen in English classes. In the Kela that I experienced, concentration was on how to perform, more akin to our music and public-speaking classes. For most of the singers whom I knew, faasa was like ritual; its meaning was in the performance, in the doing of it. I think they all believed that there was something lying underneath the words, and that it was something dangerous. They did not have to know it to perform. I do not believe there is anything like a school for *kumala*, the epic narrators (see Camara, Jansen, infra).

I recorded Tahiru Bambira's "Damonson and Samanyana Basi" in Penta Dante's compound in Segou. Her brother, Bakoroba Dante, listened to Tahiru's performance. When it was over, he asked that he be allowed to sing his version. He did not imply that Tahiru's version was wrong or incomplete, but only that his represented different points of view; for instance, there were names that Tahiru did not sing. Tahiru came and listened the next evening. It makes me think that in the dialectic between continuity and change, we are not standing in the same place as the Mande bards:

> The royal couple stopped smiling and focused their attention of listening to the griot. Was it the songs that they listened to? Perhaps. Perhaps they were only thinking of the meaning of the songs and perhaps it was so many praises that intoxicated them and, at the same time, rendered them silent, as if absent. (Camara Laye 1978: 91)

What is the role of the audience in the production of the epic? How does the audience perform as the epic story unfolds? I cannot speak for the states of consciousness of others, so let me try to track mine. What follows is an experiential reconstruction.

I focus first on the language, the words, trying to find out where the bard is in the story. I search in the stream of language for key words—Kiri, Damansa Wulanba, Mande Bukari. If I can't figure out where we are, I have to pay closer attention to the flow of the story. If I recognize where we are, say the Buffalo Woman episode, then my consciousness drifts across the pulses of the performance. It is like being on a familiar path in the woods. You do not have to attend too carefully to where you place your feet. I listen to the sounds of the words, the qualities of the bard's voice, and then my attention drifts to the music, where the hypnotic effects of language and instrument intertwine. My memory takes me to Kita. I see Kele Monson in his robes seated with his *nkoni* before the assembled crowd. Sometimes, the effect is Zen-like. My mind empties and I fill with peace and well-being. Aren't these weavings of associations and shifts in planes of consciousness also part of what the epic means? I feel that I share some of these feelings with my friend, Mamadou Kante, when Kele Monson begins to sing. Some of the feelings are certainly cultural. Both Mamadou and I learned how to have them; but some, I believe, are universal, teased out of "Everyman" by song.

It is impossible to sit before an entourage of singers and musicians performing their age-old art perhaps just for you, and not be affected by it. Praise was invented to energize. It works today as it did many years before. It was invented to go to your head and heart. Centuries have honed its efficacy.

Many bards whom I know operate on the belief that some kind of power, perhaps in the form of a jinn, enters into them while— and only while— they are performing their art. This is not pagan or anti-Islamic; jinns also inhabit the Islamic world. For Baturu Sekou Kouyate, the *kora* virtuoso, such visits came late in the evening while he was playing alone by himself. Inspiration in the form of a muse, a jinn, would take over his hands and he would give himself to its call. These were, he said, his greatest musical moments. For Nantenegwe Kamissoko, it was in public performance. As she rose to sing, you could see her small body fill with energy. She would shine. The memory of her voice filling the Smithsonian's Baird Auditorium sends shivers down my spine:

Nyama be kuma la.

Nyama is in speech

(bard aphorism)

There is an energy in Mande music that flows out of the performers and into me. It pumps me up. It makes me feel bigger than I was before. I think this is nyama. The emotion is deeply spiritual, but at the same time dangerous, narcotic. It makes you feel slightly out of control. The feelings are not generated by the content of the words, as a rationalist social scientist might imagine. Most people affected by this music do not know what the praise-words say or mean. The power is in the performance, in the moisture of the breath. It is certainly not rational:

> Nare Maghan Konate!
> Sorcerer-Seizing-Sorcerer!
> He is the man of the morrow,
> He is the man of the day to follow.
> He will rule the bards,
> And the three and thirty warrior clans,
> And the Mande will be his.
> Biribiriba, Nare Maghan Konate!
> A! Allah!
> A man of power is hard to find.

(Sunjata praise-lines from Fa-Digi Sisoko, Kita, 1968)

The production of text is not easy. If transcription is a journey across the Sea of Despondency, translation is the Wallow of Despair. After recording a bard's performance, I invariably resorted to the "two tape recorder technique." This consisted of leaving one tape recorder running throughout an analysis session. During this time I would play phrases from the master tape on a second machine, then stop it and ask an assistant, often the singer's apprentice, to repeat what he had heard and offer some account as to its meaning. After the apprentice departed, I would listen to the tape recording of our session and decide how to write something down. Let us make one thing very clear. This is not normal behavior in any culture, other than the culture of text producers. Normal people do not sift through language like this. Normal language interactions depend on broad indeterminacies in form and meaning that simply do not need to be resolved. We should not expect our assistants to toil flawlessly for us in an activity that not only strikes them as bizarre, but places inordinate demands on their powers of concentration and focus.

In any case, it turned out that the apprentices, some of whom had been with their masters for many years, did not repeat what the master had sung in one phrase out of ten. I am not being fair here. When I say that they did not repeat what their masters were singing, what I mean is that they did not reproduce the exact words, as we wanted them for our text. We heard something on the tape that the assistant did not say. The apprentices were repeating what they had learned to satisfy the demands of their masters and their audiences. For them, that satisfied conditions for sameness. There was a comfortable indeterminacy in their oral world that was incompatible with our objective and formal concerns. A letter has to be either this or that, either *t* or *d*. Sounds are a lot fuzzier.

Since the master singers would not submit to the kind of interrogation we demanded, we had to patch our transcriptions together as best we could. Thus all of the texts that I have had anything to do with are full of holes at the most fundamental levels. They are certainly not faithful records of performance. But what could be? In some societies it may be the case that oral and literate language are different but equivalent representations of language as formal linguists would have us believe. To traditional Mande griots, they represent different worlds:

> I pledge allegatits to the flag of the United States of America and to the public for riches tanned. . . .

(Lisa Bird, age 6)

> Kuma ka gelen (speech is hard).
> Kumakan ka gelen (the sound of speech is hard).
> Words are hard.
> Giving your word is hard.
>
> (Sira Mori Diabaté, "Sara")

Seydou Camara, in addition to serving as a singer for the hunters, was a dispenser of medicine and medical advice. Incantations constituted a large part of his inventory of devices. He had incantations for almost everything, holding off the curses of your enemies, protecting yourself against random assaults while traveling and assuring success in love. Seydou would regularly supply me with these for my protection, and I of course would diligently write them down. Having written them down, I would examine them and try to determine what they signified, by which I mean, I wanted to see some rational connection between the arrangements of sounds and the meanings appropriate to them. I wanted them to be subject to grammatical analysis. I wanted them to parse. They sounded like pidgin Arabic, but I was never able to find Arabic values for them, as if that mattered. When I asked Seydou what they meant, he looked at me in that funny way of his and said, "Just say them. The jinns will know what you want":

> Nyama, nyama, nyama
> Everything hides under nyama
> And nyama under nothing.

This passage is, they say, a fragment of the song that Bala Fasa Kuyate, the favorite griot of Sunjata, improvised after the battle of Kirina. The hero is here compared to a supernatural force: nyama. This is a dynamic principle, that represents the efficacity of all things. It is a dangerous principle; it is tied to the vital breath that resides in all living things (plants, animals, men). Whoever should fell a tree, kill an animal or a man exposes himself to the evil effects of the nyama that once resided in them. But nyama does not only refer to this supernatural force, its refers also to straw, garbage. The griot plays on this semantic ambiguity (Camara 1976: 217):

> Garbage! Garbage! Garbage!
> Everything hides under garbage
> And garbage under nothing.
> Everything hides under garbage
> But not fire.
>
> (Diabaté 1970a: 25)

Translation is a game where no one is wrong, but no one is right. Where did Massa Maghan Diabaté get "but not fire" from? Kele Monson Diabaté sang something that I transcribed as "nga ne te son o ma nya o nya," or "but I would never agree to that." This is in itself a fairly idiosyncratic line. Massa Maghan heard the line as "gani te son o ma nya o nya," or "fire would never agree to that."

And so the epic reproduces itself in its timeless fashion:

> Tinyesira ye munumunusira ye.
>
> The way to truth is the twisted path.
>
> (Maninka proverb)

There are many stories about the capturing of songs, as part of the hero's booty. According to several sources the Janjon was originally sung for Sumanguru, but Fakoli made the sacrifices leading to Sumanguru's defeat. Fakoli won the song, but it still extolls the power of Sumanguru:

> He entered the Manden in coat of human skin.
> He entered the Mande in pants of human skin.
> He entered the Mande in helm of human skin.
> Ah! Sumanguru, Janjonba!

The epic of Kore Duga Koro tells how Da Monson brought Kore Duga Koro's song, the Duga, to Segu. Once imported into Segu, pieces were pasted onto the song to show that it was Da's property, but old material remained.

Part of the mythology of griots is that they were not made slaves during wars, but rather assumed the bardic condition for new masters. Their repertoires were adapted for new circumstances. Let us think about the possibility that what is now the *Sunjata* epic was captured many times over the last thousand years, and that the singers modified it as they ingratiated themselves to new masters:

> Sosobali Sumanguru
> Mande mansa folo
> Ni Mansa duguren
>
> Sosobali Sumanguru
> First king of the Mande
> And indigenous king.

These are praise-lines from the "Janjon," sung for Sumanguru. Many of those with whom I talked about these lines did not want to take them literally. They would argue that Sumanguru could not have been king, since he was a blacksmith. "He could not have been the first king of the Mande. The first king of the Mande was Sunjata. The lines must mean something else, but we don't know what. We just sing the song." Why weren't the lines edited out or simply shifted in their attribution to Sunjata?

They sing that Sumanguru is the first and traditional king; they say that Sunjata is. This sounds like good evidence for Sunjata's winning the song, and having its accompanying story adapted to fit the new circumstances, but the bards choose to preserve Sumanguru's original claim to the title, and they preserve the role of Fakoli as earning first right to the song. Almost everyone will tell you that the Janjon is Fakoli's song. Why? Why didn't they just attribute everything to the new patron, as they have in so many other circumstances? One way of thinking about it is that the hero's greatness is measured against that of his adversaries. Muhammad Ali is all the greater for the greatness of Joe Frazier. The more that is said of the magical terribleness of Sumanguru, the more terrible had to be the greatness of Sunjata, who defeated him:

> He entered the Mande in pants of human skin.
> He entered the Mande in coat of human skin.
> He entered the Mande in helm of human skin.
> First king of the Mande,
> And indigenous king.

In some versions of the epic Sogolon Konde, Sunjata's mother, drops from the story at the point of Sunjata's exile. He leaves; she stays behind. When he returns she is not picked up again in the narrative. She has no role comparable to Shaka's mother, for example, in the great Zulu narrative. Sogolon's role assures Sunjata's rise to manhood and empowers his pursuit of destiny. It is she who fills him with her magical powers. Her presence in the story ensures us that he is a legitimate son of the country.

This relation between mother and son is formulaic in Mande heroic narratives. Much of the way the bards sing this part of the story seems moveable from one epic to another. I have not heard anything about their relationship that would not be told in other epics dealing with mothers and sons, except for the fact that in some versions she accompanies him on his exile and peregrinations to Mema. This variation is idiosyncratic and interesting. It must be caused by something outside the normal practice of the bard's craft. It might be a response to something that may help us understand why this story was told in this particular way, given the available choices for telling stories.

One possibility is that someone saw it happen who might even have been a bard, and that this story began its life as an eyewitness account of what he or she saw and experienced. It then continued its life as song. It could however be part of a complex explanation that bards insert into moments of the epic's performance. Here, the bard explains why such and so is the state of affairs. These can be simple etymologies like that of the name Keita (which Sunjata did not inherit from his father). In Maninka "*ke*" or "*ce*" means "heritage" and "*ta*" means "take." Thus "he took the heritage." I have heard this etymology inserted into the section where Sunjata's birth was announced first, in spite of the fact that he was the second son. He "took the heritage" of his older brother, Dankaran Tuman. I have also heard it after the account of the victory over Sumanguru, from whom Sunjata seized his rightful heritage.

Seydou Camara told me that Sunjata was a stranger from the north who stole the Mande heritage from the Traores and the Camaras. This is what the name Keita meant to him. The etymologies help to organize the story and sometimes take it over, but we must not forget Vico, who reminded us that etymologies are political.

Some stories involve very complex efforts to explain a certain state of affairs, like when someone comes up to you and says, "Well, if Sunjata's rule is legitimate as you say, how come his mother is buried up there in Mema?" Such things require explanations, and griots are retained to provide them. It is in the griot's interest to make you look good. It is easy for me to believe that the story of how Sunjata's mother came to be buried in Mema satisfied that function. I cannot tell you why they did not just edit it out:

Suba ni mansaya.

Sorcerer and kingship.

Fetishes are the hunter's primary devices—the things that he carries in that sack under his arm, the satchels tied to his biceps and across his calves, the amulets in and on his hat, the bracelets of iron and copper, and the talismans that hang from his neck and adorn his shirts. It is words that he knows to bring help and ward off danger and particularly it is his allies in the spirit world whom he invokes through these devices, and who he wishes us to believe will do his will. The great hunter succeeds not because of his physical prowess, but because his knowledge of the darkness allows him to overcome the forces that lie in wait to bring him down. These skills of the hunter must also be the skills of the political leader:

Mansa bee bora donsoya la.

All kings come out of hunting.

(aphorism sung in *Sunjata* epic)

Both hunters and rulers have adversaries that are trying to bring them down. They must protect themselves against these foes, even disarm and conquer them, and they do so by rendering useless the objects that defend the adversary. The colliding of titans on the Mande fields of battle takes place in the spiritual world. Sunjata kills game by making it surrender to him. His arrows and curses hit their mark not because of his Herculean strength or Apollonian prowess but because he can summon the spirits that make such things happen.

But notice, in the confrontation of titans, that the story turns on a failure of the hero's magic in the face of his enemy. The adversary has defenses that the hero cannot penetrate. There is at best a standoff, and, in some versions of the *Sunjata* epic, Sunjata actually suffers several defeats at Sumanguru's hands. The stalled story of Sunjata's destiny gets its jump start invariably from a woman, the hero's mother or sister. The women have knowledge, gained perhaps in overhearing others, or brought to them by a jinn, that they pass on to the hero, thus enabling him to break down his adversary's defenses. Sunjata appears, not as the agent of his destiny, but as an instrument determined by fate. The women are the determining actors in the story. Their actions make things change. Sunjata benefits only as a consequence. In the Mande world, the mother's nurture endows the child with character. If the mother lacks virtue, for example, the offspring will be flawed and thus unable to achieve the destiny available to him or her.

This relationship of the hero to the women in his life is formulaic in Mande storytelling. The hunter Kambili seems pushed through life first by his mother and then by his wife. The hunter Fakuru is saved from certain death by his wife, after which they exchange clothing, he wearing the woman's skirt and she the hunter's trousers. Da Monson can break Samanyana Basi's power only through the deception of Basi's wife. Sunjata is propelled through the story, first by his mother and then by his sister. The hero achieves his destiny by meeting challenges that demand an ability to summon spiritual support. He meets other challenges demanding intelligence and character, things like generosity, tolerance, and kindness. These properties are not inherited at birth. Some are passed on to the child by the mother; others are commodities that can be accumulated through the hero's alliances. In all cases except that of exile, the relations between Sunjata and his mother are part and parcel of the Mande storyteller's bag of tricks:

Bileman Nguleman Magasugu Dana,
This part was sung for him at Dakajalan.
Bardwoman, that part sung for him at Dakajalan,
Sing it that I may hear,
Me, Jali Mamari, that I may hear it in my ear.

       I yee! Yamaru oo!
Not every child dances the Janjon.
Play does not end the fight.
       Nor does a laugh end it.
Displeasure does not put an end to death.
Janjonba!
       (Mamari and Sira Mori Diabaté, "Janjon," Kela, 1972)

Epilogue

    Much of what follows involves an understanding of West African history that I have derived from reading Patrick Munson, George Brooks, and Susan and Roderick McIntosh. My debt to their work should be obvious to those who are familiar with it:

> A man wanted to know about mind, not in nature, but in his private large computer. He asked it (no doubt in his best Fortran), "Do you compute that you will ever think like a human being?" The machine then set to work to analyze its own computational habits. Finally, the machine printed its answer on a piece of paper, as such machines do. The man ran to get the answer and found, neatly typed, the words: That reminds me of a story.
> (Bateson 1979: 14)

    I believe in stories. I do not believe there is much else to help us understand who we are. I believe in historical narratives, stories that sequence events, offering us explanations of why things are the way they are. We can call these stories history, fact, fiction, legend, or myth. Their names are not important. It is only a matter of their plausibility. I believe that there are bits of language that can be sifted from our *Sunjata* texts and, like pieces of a puzzle, fit with other pieces in series, giving us a vision of the events that may have shaped the epic's language. These bits and pieces and the sequences they constitute are not the same as those used by the bards. We all shape our stories with the contingencies of the present, but we lead very different lives.
The pieces of the puzzle that I have been looking at revolve around the fall of the Ghana empire, the conditions that brought it about and the consequences that

followed from it. For me, there is no way to consider Sunjata and the rise of the Mali empire without this. Ghana dissolved under many pressures not the least of which was long-term drought, a condition that archaeologists confirm and date.

The following climate changes (Brooks 1993: 7) can be delineated from the end of the Atlantic Wet Period (ca. 5500–2500 B.C.):

–a long period of dessication that lasted until ca. 300 B.C.
–a transitional period lasting from ca. 300 B.C. to 300 A.D., during the latter part of which ecological conditions improved sufficiently to permit the development of intra- and trans-Saharan commerce.
–four centuries of moderate rainfall, between ca. 300 and 700 A.D.
–four centuries of abundant rainfall, from ca. 700 to 1100.
–a long dry period extending from ca. 1100 to 1500.

I am interested in knowing what recourses for survival were available to those populations affected by drought. As the McIntoshes tell us, in the period of drought at the beginning of the Christian era, one recourse led to the design of a selective migration for the purposes of surplus agriculture and long-distance hauling back into drought-stricken areas, enabling villages stripped of agricultural resources to survive. Young men went down the road to an area where things were better and served perhaps as tenant farmers, working for new landlords while growing a surplus crop for the people back home. The system still works today where, in a cash economy, young men from these northern villages exchange their work, not for land, but for money with which to buy food for their people. Engaged in such activities, northern Mande peoples developed the practices necessary for cash economies and long-distance trade, activities at which today's Soninke, called Maraka by the Maninka, are held to be masters. The Soninke have, for perhaps one thousand years, been moving through the populations to their south, first the Maninka, but then beyond them into the forest region itself.

The heyday of Ghana was Brooks's fourth period, encompassing four hundred years from 700–1100 a.d. The dry spell that choked it was Brooks's fifth period, another four hundred years from 1100–1500 a.d. The drought required the shifting of political and economic life to the south. This is the climatological context of *Sunjata*.

About 800 a.d., the horse appears in my story, reintroduced into West Africa by the Moors who settled the West Atlantic coast down to the Senegal River delta. The northern Mande, particularly the Soninke, fully incorporated the horse into their culture, where it still plays a central role, both virtual and actual. Today's Soninke represent, to me, the remains of the union of merchants with horse warriors whose descent on the regions to the south is recorded in the political epics of many West African societies. The steppes of the savanna lent themselves perfectly to the technologies of their horsemanship:

During the past two millennia changing rainfall patterns have caused the
"tsetse fly line" to oscillate north and south in a belt approximately 200
kilometers wide extending across western Africa between 13 and 15
degrees north latitude. (Brooks 1993: 9)

That two hundred-kilometer belt from the Niger River to the Atlantic
Ocean is in the geographical stage for the *Sunjata* story. The Mande, as Kele
Monson's epic treatment goes, were not horse people. The Jolof King mocked
Sunjata and his Mande people as barefoot hunters, but they went in search of
horses to protect themselves from and to make war on their neighbors. But who
were these horse warriors? It is easy to picture young men banding together as
warriors and brigands when times get hard. It is part of the narratives of our
American West. It is the story of America's city streets.

From the thirteenth century onward, these and other commercial centers
in the savanna-woodland zone were invaded by Manding-speaking horsemen.
The era of conquests and state-building continued down to the colonial period,
with successive generations of warrior groups raiding along the margins of the
forest zone (Brooks 1985: 14).

The union between the horse warriors and the long-distance traders
resulted in relatively free passage along long-distance trade routes, guaranteed
by every political means including war. The Pax Mande provided the umbrella
for imaginative entrepreneurial capitalism. Sunjata represents this union of
Saharan mercantilism, deeply marked by Islam, with Mande warrior chivalry,
strongly rooted in African spirituality, creating a new society operating in the
mutual interests of these fundamentally different groups:

> If we must trade,
> Then let us trade.
> If we must battle,
> Then let us battle.
> Sunjata is finished.
>   (Kele Monson Diabaté "Sunjata," Kita, 1968)

But what was the old society like? What did it represent? What were
the tensions with the new order? I think the most significant detail represented
in *Sunjata* with regard to these questions is that Sumanguru was a blacksmith.
All of the data reflecting on Mande social practice, particularly with regard to
spiritual matters, point to the blacksmith as the earth priest. The blacksmith
ancestor is responsible for all of Mande civilization. It is he who gave them
agriculture. The blacksmith ancestor came from the sky on a rainbow, carrying
seeds and tools spirited away from heaven. He unites the earth and the sky. He
brings the rains down to the earth:

The smith is three things black:

Black sky. Black iron. Black clay.
The black sky is the rain.
If there is no rain, you will not eat.
The black iron is the hoe,
If there is no hoe, you will not eat.
The black clay is the pot,
If there is no pot, you will not eat.
Those three things are of the smith.
                    (Seydou Camara, conversation, Bamako, 1978)

The blacksmiths maintained strict control over the technology of iron making. They exercised such control by making it dangerous for a non-smith to engage in their craft. Smithing remains the art of the smith because it is held to contain nyama against which the smith is protected (McNaughton 1988).

The technological stranglehold on iron making and the burgeoning importance of iron products placed the smith at the economic and political apex of the Mande world. From this point of view, the epic might be said to symbolize the shifting of power from production, Sumanguru, to marketing, Sunjata.

Blacksmiths are today generally considered *nyamakala*, along with other hereditary craftspeople like bards and leatherworkers. The bards sing that it was Sunjata who organized society into freemen (horon), artisans (nyamakala), and slaves (*jon*). Artisans and slaves are excluded from political power. The story of Sumanguru's fall from power must partially reflect this order of things.

So where does all this take my story? As I argued above, the beginning of the story provided by the bards strikes me as a collage, built up over centuries of telling and shaped by contingency.

My story of *Sunjata* thus begins with Sumanguru:

Sumanguru was a blacksmith.
Sumanguru was King of the Mande.
Mande mansa folo ni mansa duguren.

Sunjata lived in the northern city of Mema (Nema). Sunjata was a member of the court of the Tunkara king. Some say he was his adopted son. The King, Mema Faran Tunkara, a Soninke, gave Sunjata horses. The horsemen were led by the King's son to help Sunjata conquer the Mande. Before leaving Mema, Sunjata's mother dies, and he buries her in that northern soil. Sunjata descends to the south and eventually defeats Sumanguru in battle at Kirina:

The tears went to the Soso.
The laughs to the Mande.

Is it possible to think that Sunjata started out in Mema, and then, having imposed himself militarily on the Mande, proceeded to legitimize his rule using the services of his newly acquired bards? Could it be that Bala Faseke Kuyate was originally the bard of Soso Mountain Sumanguru, for whom he sang the Janjon, and then, after the defeat of Sumanguru, sang the praises of Sunjata? Would this not explain the close relationships between the Kante and the Kuyate who can exchange praises?

> Kukuba ni Bantaba
> Nyaninyani ni Kambasiga

With an even broader brush, can we not think of Sunjata and Sumanguru as allegorical personifications of political and economic forces at play in processes affecting the lives of Mande peoples? As Robert Launay has noted ("*Sunjata* Epic Conference" 1992), if we replaced Sumanguru's label, "blacksmith" with that of "earth priest," we would have in this story one more instance of the clash between the northern horsemen and the earth priest rulers who preceded and opposed them throughout the western savanna. The rulers of Asante, the Mamprusi, the Gurunsi, the Dagomba, the Sonrai, and the Zarma, to mention but a few, trace their history to these horse warriors. In many of these stories, the tellers found it convenient to retain the label of "stranger" for the new conquerors. Strangeness empowers. In other cases, the storytellers convert the stranger into a previously exiled but legitimate son of the country, whose right and destiny it is to rule the land. In my view, this is what happened with Sunjata.

The historical narrative that I have sketched out here is designed in and for literate cultures. It exploits literate methodologies that have no counterparts in nonliterate worlds. Ivor Wilks and David Conrad can hold up five, six, seven versions of the epic and compare them line by line. No illiterate bard, no matter how gifted, can perform any such comparisons. If the evidence is unavailable to him, he cannot arrive at these conclusions. We have available to us in printed form more variants of the epic than any bard has ever been exposed to. In many ways our understanding of the epic is completely inaccessible to the masters who sing it. We should realize that performances of the epic are not common in Mande experience. I know many people who have never seen it performed. Some have heard it only on the radio. Some have heard it but did not choose to listen. Given the relative intensity of our epic experiences, there is no reason then why our stories should correspond in any way to those developed by the bards for their purposes. In fact, the epic of the bards is not an object at all. It is not a text. It is a dynamic activity, more akin to dance or street theater.

In constructing our stories about Sunjata, we too are performers, shuffling through our academic dances. We shape the epic to our individual best interests, whatever they may be. I cannot help but think that, at the same time, Sunjata transforms us with the dances he makes us do:

> For those who would farm,
> Let them farm.

Sunjata is dead.

For those who would trade,
Let them trade.
Massa Maghan has left us.

For those who would battle,
Let them battle.
Sira Mori has left us.

For those who would farm,
Let them farm.
Daman's bird, Kabaya Seydou has left us.

For those who would trade,
Let them trade.
Sunjata is finished.

Bibliography

Achebe, Chinua. 1987. *Anthills of the Savannah*. New York: Doubleday.

Bateson, Gregory. 1979. *Mind and Nature*. New York: Bantam.

Brooks, George. 1985. *Western Africa to c. 1860 A.D.: A Provisional Historical Schema Based on Climate Periods*. Bloomington, Indiana: Indiana University African Studies Program.

Camara, Seydou. 1974. *The Songs of Seydou Camara, Vol. 1: Kambili*. Translated by Charles Bird, Mamadou Koita, and Bourama Soumaoro Bloomington, Indiana: Indiana University African Studies Center.

—. 1975. *Fakuru*. Field recording by Charles Bird, Bamako.

Charry, Eric. 1992. *Musical Thought, History and Practice among the Mande of West Africa*. Princeton University Ph.D.

Diabaté, Kele Monson. 1961. *Sunjata*. Radio Mali recording Bamako (Indiana University Archives of Traditional Music 76-033-F).

—. 1968. *Sunjata*. Field recording by Charles Bird and Massa Maghan Diabaté, Kita.

Diabaté, Mamari, and Sira Mori Diabaté. 1974. *Janjon*. Field recording by John W. Johnson and Charles Bird, Keyla.

Diabaté, Sira Mori. 1966. *Sara*. Radio Mali recording, Bamako.

Diabaté, Sira Mori, and Yamuru Diabaté. 1974. *Sunjata Faasa*. Field recording by John W. Johnson and Charles Bird, Keyla.

Kendall, Martha B. 1983. "Getting to Know You." In David Parkin, ed., *Semantic Anthropology*. New York: Academic Press.

McIntosh, Roderick. 1983. "Current Directions in West African Prehistory." *Annual Review of Anthropology* 12: 225–58.

McIntosh, Susan Keech, and Roderick J. McIntosh. 1981. "West African Prehistory." *American Scientist* 69 (Nov–Dec).

Munson, Patrick. "Archaeology and the Prehistoric Origins of the Ghana

Empire." *Journal of African History* 21, 4: 457–66

Sisoko, Fadigi. 1968. *Sunjata*. Field recording by Charles Bird and Kita Massa
    Maghan Diabaté.

Stone, Robert. 1991. "To Find the Edge." *Harpers* 66–82 (Oct.).

13. An Ethnography of the Epic of *Sunjata* in Kela

Jan Jansen

The town of Kangaba and its neighboring village of Kela (100 kilometers southwest of Bamako, on the banks of the Niger) are often referred to as the best place for learning the entire *Sunjata* narrative tradition. Every seventh year in Kangaba the Kamabolon (a sacred hut) is reroofed, a ceremony during which the whole epic is said to be recited. However, no one has ever been permitted to make any kind of recording during the ceremony, which is why up until now we have only reports by observers of the ceremony.

During the last night of the ceremony the Jabate jeliw of Kela (five kilometers from Kangaba) are responsible for the "definitive" version of the epic. Given the importance that researchers ascribe to this little group of griots in Mande culture, it is remarkable how little information is available about them. In this chapter I want to make a contribution to the study of the Jabate griots by focusing on the ethnographic aspects of their epic performance. After a short discussion of my fieldwork, I will describe what information from the epic is available to whom in Kela. Next, I will elaborate on the transmission of the epic by showing who acquires this information and/or knowledge. Finally, I will address the question of what is recited inside the Kamabolon, the "Secrets of Mande." This article is somewhat preliminary and decidedly untheoretical since it was formulated while I was still in the field.

Research Methods and Fieldwork Setting

Among the approximatley1500 inhabitants of Kela, 15 to 20 percent are Jabate griots or members of their families, living within a section of the village consisting of a public square surrounded by six walled compounds. Within these compounds live five "lineages," or "*bondaw duuru*" (see table 9.1). The only *bonda* that occupies two compounds is number five on the table headed by El Haji Bala (often referred to as Kelabala). El Haji Bala's younger brother El Haji

Table 9.1: The Kela Jabate Lineages

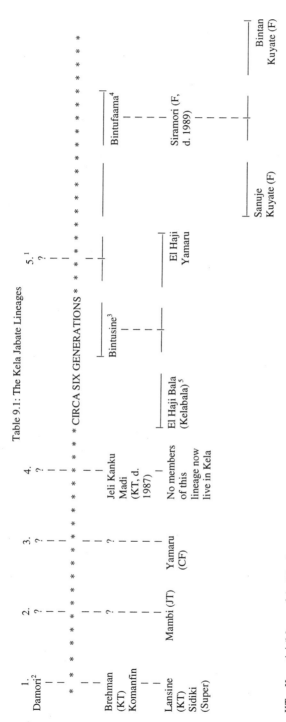

KT = Kumatigi (Master of the Word); see text. JT = Jelikuntigi (Chief of the Griots) = eldest male Jabate in Kela. CF = Classificatory father,
i.e. takes role of Mambi, although slightly younger than he, because Mambi is incapacitated. F = Female.

---

[1] The relationship between well-known members of this lineage is too complex to be indicated on the table. Omitted here is a collateral branch of this lineage
which includes two contemporary singers who have performed and been recorded internationally, Kase Mady and Lanfia.

[2] The Kela Jabate refer to themselves collectively as "Damorila" (descendants of Damori) because Damori was the first Jabate to settle in this place, although
only one of the five patrilineages claims him as a biological ancestor.

[3] Informant of Leynaud and Cissé (1978) in 1960s.

[4] A legendary ngoni player.

[5] Kelabala (c. 1915-1997) was 80 years old at the time of fieldwork and thus the chronological elder of all the Kela Jabate but socially classified as a son of
Mambi (lineage 2) and Yamuru (lineage 3).

Yamuru is the central person in the other compound of the family. The division into two compounds appears to be the result of the large size of this family, which is primarily due to their wealth. Kelebala is a very famous marabout, and El Haji Yamuru was a popular artist in the 1950s and 1960s, when he formed a duo with Bremajan Kamisoko, whose family lives next to the five Jabate families. The Jabate and the Kamisoko (another well-known jeli lineage) consider themselves a unit in Kela.

The other populous lineage (number one on the table), is headed by Lansine Jabate. Lansine is the current *kumatigi*, or "master of the word," responsible for reciting the epic during the Kamabolon ceremonies. I asked him to find me a place to stay in Kela and he brought me to a hut about five meters from his front door; thus we were in close contact during the entire time of my fieldwork. Without Lansine's hospitality and his constant willingness to allow me to accompany him, my research would have been impossible. Altogether, he permitted me to live on his compound from October 1991 to March 1992, from October to Christmas 1992, and, finally, in March 1993.[6]

Most of the research on *Sunjata* focuses on the content of the epic. However, I did not master the Maninke language well enough to enter into profound discussions with the griots. I chose to rely instead upon observations of their practices supported by simple questions about what people do and why they do it. The success of this "low profile" approach was for the most part dependent on my fieldwork setting and the friendliness of the Jabate in Kela.

I know that there is a fine line between observation and voyeurism, especially when one does research within a small group, such as the Kela jeliw. I found that in the community almost all matters were subject to open discussion with the exception of *Sunjata*. I never introduced this topic myself but rather let the griots take the initiative and choose what they thought would be interesting to me when they took me to particular events or invited me for tea. I made a few recordings on my own; most of the performances were recorded without payment, and only after having asked permission. Therefore I can present data about the griots of Kela without fear of embarrassment. My descriptions reflect the unexceptional events of their everyday life.

Available Information about the Epic

There are not very many occasions when the people of Kela can hear the *mansa jigin* ("that which is recited after the death of a king"), as they call the epic of *Sunjata*. Only in the week before the reroofing ceremony, when there are dozens of other griots visiting Kela, do some rehearsals take place (Jansen 1995). It was my observation that in other years a rehearsal can take place after the rainy season. The people themselves say that these rehearsals take place two

---

[6] Funding for this research was provided by WOTRO, The Netherlands Foundation for the Advancement of Tropical Research, Grant W 52-533.

or three times from early September to late November, but I witnessed only one
in 1991 and none in 1992. Everyone gave me the same practical explanation for
this timing: at the end of the rainy season many young Jabate are present in Kela
to work on the fields, thus guaranteeing a large audience.

For the rest of the year information relevant to *Sunjata* can be obtained at
certain formal events and in fireside chats. The last category is, of course, hard
for an observer to understand, but I got the impression that themes from the epic
were not often a subject of discussion. During formal occasions, however, much
information is available, but it is almost always the same: the *fasaw* (praise-
names/genealogies) of the named lineages that live in the Kangaba region. Even
little children already know these oral texts. Sometimes the old men spoke about
the past and referred to the great heroes from the time of the Prophet
Muhammad and Sunjata. Actually, it is remarkable that only three old men told
these stories in public: El Haji Bala, El Haji Yamuru, and Lansine (another Yamuru, the classificatory father of the three other men [see table 9.1], often
seemed to be present to confirm what was said).

Thus it is not easy to catch the griots of Kela in a major performance during which a long part of the epic is recited; during my fieldwork I witnessed
only a few such occasions. These performances, however, give us much insight
into the role of the epic in Mande society, and that is why I have chosen to present fairly extensive ethnographic descriptions of all six.

Performance One:
A Rehearsal of the Kamabolon Ceremony, April 1989

I was not actually at this performance; however, it was partially recorded
by the Belgian photographer Erik Sacré, who sent me the text on a C-90 cassette. On the tape Lansine speaks and Mamaduba Kamisoko, the son of the late
Bremajan, says "*naamu*."[7] The rhythm is that of the "Sunjata" fasa. The performance starts with all the people present singing an a capella refrain. Lansine
is sometimes interrupted by El Haji Bala, and at one moment there is a short
discussion, with many people involved. The stories that are told are about Sumaoro Kante, including his confrontation with the griot, Bala Fasake Kuyate.

Performance Two:
In the Public Square between the Jabate Compounds

"You are lucky that you've arrived today." That is what everyone told me
when I visited Kela for the first time on October 24, 1991. That night after dinner everyone assembled in the public square, which was lighted by a lamp. At
one side of the square is a big wooden platform, upon which Lansine and Ma-

---

[7] See Conrad (infra) for a discussion of this verbal accompaniment to epic recital
("naamu," probably derived from Arabic, means "yes").

maduba took their places with their classificatory father Yamuru next to them. El Haji Bala sat on a chair (because of his hip problems, I assume). In front of Lansine sat two ngoni-players from Bamako. The rest of the platform was occupied by male Jabate and Kamisoko. The audience consisted of women and children and the many visitors from other villages who were at the Jabates' at that time.

All of a sudden, the men started to sing an a capella refrain (Jansen 1995). It was the start of a session that lasted more than three hours and that had the Sunjata fasa as its rhythm. The pattern of the first two hours was as follows: Lansine talked and Mamaduba said "naamu." Sometimes a person gave a gift to El Haji Bala (some coins or a banknote—the total revenue that night was about 4,000 CFA francs, or $16 U.S. in 1993). After a short time El Haji Bala interrupted the performance, said something and gave his blessings, which were answered by the crowd with "*Amina*." A few times someone shouted a benediction to El Haji Bala.

Lansine told the stories of many well-known heroes: Tiramagan, Sunjata, Fakoli, Sumaoro, Bala Fasake, and Sita Fata (the ancestor of the Jawara griots in Kela). Many times I heard him reciting the praise-names for their descendants. Then things seemed slowly to come to an end, which was the moment for which the guests had been waiting. One after another they stood up to praise El Haji Bala and Kela in an almost aggressive way. A few times they were interrupted by Sidiki Jabate, or "Super," Lansine's classificatory younger brother. Sidiki welcomed everyone present and said things that made the audience laugh.

Performance Three: The Inauguration of the President of the Mali Griots

A great ceremony to celebrate this figure took place at Bamako on October 13–15, 1992, and attracted griots from all over Mali and Guinea. The griots from Kela had been invited to legitimize the true successor of Jemusa Sumano.[8] The Kela delegation consisted of a dozen men and one woman, Bintan Kuyate.

On the first night the Kela griots provided a general welcome; different fasaw were played, and families were praised. El Haji Bala's son later stated that "toute l'épopée" was performed, although this did not appear to be literally the case. The second day started with a celebration of the deceased, followed in the afternoon by a celebration of his successors, his "sons." That night, the official inauguration took place. This was a big media event: all the famous griots of Mali sang for the new president and El Haji Bala installed him in his position before the cameras of Radio Télévison du Mali.

But the third night was the most interesting as far as the epic was concerned. That evening after dinner Lansine changed clothes while I happened by

---

[8] President of the Union Nationale des Griots du Mali, a kind of guild or labor union for bards.

coincidence to be in the room. Among the articles donned by Lansine on this occasion was an old leather bracelet placed on the upper arm, which he told me he also wears in the Kamabolon!

The small compound of the late Jemusa Sumano was filled with about 100 people. That evening words were spoken for more than four hours. The first hour Lansine performed to the rhythm of the "Sunjata" fasa and later to that of the "Tiramagan" fasa. Mamaduba said "naamu," and sometimes Super took over for him. Lansine dedicated the greater part of his performance to the exile of Sunjata; he also spoke extensively about Bala Fasake Kuyate. Sometimes Lansine paused to allow Bintan to sing the texts associated with the fasaw melodies ("I bara kala ta" for the "Sunjata" fasa and "Tiramagan muru" for the "Tiramagan" fasa).

After having been in almost complete silence for two and a half hours, the audience relaxed when other people took over the floor, although these also addressed serious topics. One of the new performers was a Fina Camara, who recited what he claimed were 1,000 names for the Prophet Muhammad.

Performance Four: The "Real" Epic

In February 1992 Lansine promised me a recording of "two music-cassettes" on the condition that no one would ever hear them in Mali. Super played the "Sunjata" fasa on the ngoni, together with his son Brehman, and acted as the "naamu"-sayer for Lansine. I had previously asked him to tell the same stories as Jeli Kanku Madi had recited in 1979 (Ly-Tall et al. 1987). Lansine remembered that performance very well because he had participated in it as the naamu-sayer.

To my surprise Lansine more or less replicated Kanku Madi's 1979 recording; he began at the same point, and used the same themes in the same sequence. However, on a more detailed level (character descriptions, for instance) he often deviated, just as his style of performing is completely different from that of Kanku Madi.[9]

Lansine stopped at the moment when Sunjata leaves Nema (Mema in other versions) to return to Mande. At that moment he had talked for almost three hours nonstop, filling two C-90 cassettes. He looked exhausted and complained of a headache. However, within a few minutes he recovered and expressed pride in what he had achieved.

The next morning Lansine said that he had checked the cassettes (as usual I had given him copies) and found that every word was true. Later that day he proposed to record two cassettes again next year. A few days later, laying his hands on his belly he said that there were enough words "inside" to continue for another ten years.

---

[9] For the text of this session see Jansen et al. 1995, lines 1-462.

Performance Five: "Next Year"[10]

In December 1992, during the week before the "Next Year" version was to be recorded, Lansine repeatedly asked me to visit him so that we could discuss what he might recite. Every day I told him to tell "the rest" and pointed out that last year we broke off at Sunjata's return to Mande. Of course, I expected the rest of the copy of the 1979 recording, but I restrained myself from suggesting that he himself had the cassettes of performance (hereafter "P") four.

Two nights before the recording, while I was drinking tea with Lansine's sons and their friends, he told the story of the decapitation of Jolofinmansa (see below). The next morning he asked me if that was what I was looking for, and I said that it would be wonderful to hear that story once again.

During the session Super and Brehman were again the instrumentalists, and again they played "Sunjata" fasa. Lansine started and in one minute he had finished Sunjata's return to Mande and his battle with Sumaoro Kante. Then he gave a long and beautiful version of the decapitation of Jolofinmansa. Having finished this, he then told about Fakoli and some kings after Sunjata. At this time one side of the C-90 was completed, and as I turned the cassette over Lansine asked me what he should talk about now. I suggested that a more extensive description of the battle between Sunjata and Sumaoro would please me greatly. He agreed and proceeded to tell a long story about this event. When two-thirds of the second side was recorded he stopped and said that it was finished. I did not protest, and we went home. Lansine was proud of his stories, which were indeed beautiful, and said that all the words of Africa were "inside."

That evening, I took Lansine aside and told him that I had promised my "chef de bureau" two cassettes, but I had only one. What was I to do? Lansine, friendly as always, told me that this was no problem at all, for we would record a second cassette as soon as possible. I thanked him and said that I would take a C-60 this time.

Performance Six: A "Sudden Death"

The session eventually took place one day before my departure, on December 16, 1992. Lansine started with a long story about Mecca and then seemed to slip automatically into the first passage of the recording of "last year" (P4). I asked him to stop and tell another story instead. Lansine obliged, and after some time he slipped again into a story that I had recorded before.

Then, after forty-five minutes, Yamuru (the classificatory father) entered the room. Lansine immediately switched the subject to well-known praise-lines. We finished after another five minutes, and I never heard a word about what happened or the reason for it (see below for further discussion of this event).

---

[10] This performance is published in Jansen et al. 1995, lines 463-664.

The Epic of *Sunjata*: Text and Comparative Observations

The six performances described above give us insight into the nature of the epic of *Sunjata*. It is clear that Johnson's theses about the African epic are not undermined by the ethnographic data that I collected. In Kela the epic is "open-ended" and "open-starting," as performances four, five, and six demonstrate. Moreover, there is a clear sequence of events for the griot: in P6 we saw that Lansine slipped into another theme known from P4. Thus, the griot is able to pass over some themes without creating a fuzzy version, but he cannot mix themes excessively. However, at the end of the epic the griot seems to have many possibilities. In fact, I was under the impression that P5 contained at least four stories that could be credible conclusions to the P4 recording: the battle; the decapitation; Fakoli's adventures; and the history of Sunjata's successors. But to put these four "endings" together into one story is a more complicated matter.

As far as I know, no one (other than Charles Bird, infra) has previously provided us with a sense of the epic as experienced in "live" performances before local audiences. In the first place, we have seen that a "live" epic is less complete than the best-known written versions. Completeness, however, does not seem important because everyone knows what the story is about; the audience is mainly interested in the way it is recited. It seems to me that the theatrical aspects of the story are just as important as the words themselves.

Completeness is also impossible because there is never enough time. The "live" epic has "extras": interruptions to praise an individual (P2) or song performances by a second griot to give the principal narrator a break (P3). It would take very many hours to give a complete version of the epic because in serious performance the griot elaborates on particular themes, which themselves become real *pièces du théatre*. For example P3, which dealt only with Sunjata's exile, itself lasted several hours.

Therefore, the people of Kela are accustomed to more vivid performances of a less complete epic than we might find in books, a fact that may explain why I never heard a term for "epic" in Kela. People talked about "*kumaw*" (words), "fasaw" (praise-songs), "*gundow*" ("des choses qui restent entre nous," often translated as "secrets"). Lansine usually described what he did as "*kuma*" and sometimes referred to "*gundo*." I did, on few occasions, hear the word "*tariku*," the term for "epic" reported by other researchers, but it was used in Kela only with reference to "a story that belongs to a certain family." Of course, the term "mansa jigin" (see above) is known in Kela, but I seldom heard it, not even when Lansine told me about his activities during the Kamabolon ceremony. Thus Kela people do not categorize epic narratives very strictly; their genre terms are highly context bound.

The Acquisition of the Right to Speak

Up until now I have shown that access to the epic is possible for anyone in Kela. In the following section I will set forth the idea that, although knowledge is widespread, the right to speak is not.

At the end of P6 we saw Lansine switching to another subject when "Father" Yamuru entered the room. I do not think the issue here was whether I was allowed to know the story, but rather Lansine's doubts concerning the appropriateness of the situation for the use of this information. This point is reinforced by another experience.

Everyone in Kela, even the little children, know the praise-lines for the Kuyate, which begin "Kukunba ani Bantanba"; one finds them in any published text of the *Sunjata* epic. As I worked under the name of Sidiki Kuyate in Kela, people often shouted these praise-lines when I entered their compound or when I strolled through the village. However, when Lansine allowed me to write down the praise-lines in my notebook, he said that I was never to show them to anyone. A few months later, the female singer Bintan Kuyate taught me the praise-lines during a chat about everyday events. She warned me, however, to avoid pronouncing these words in public. In addition, she said that I must tell no one that I had received this information from her.

Through this example I want to indicate that a proper use of epic knowledge is more important than the knowledge itself. This connects the epic with education: the epic can be recited only if you have "savoir faire." Thus the epic remains the domain of the old men in Kela. Before I go on to describe the process by which one acquires the right to participate in the epic discourse, I will cite a case in which the old men use the epic to educate their juniors.

One evening I was drinking tea with some young men, along with Lansine and "Father" Yamuru, when all of a sudden Yamuru said something to which Lansine reacted visibly. Lansine then told three stories.

The first story was about Sita Fata Jawara, who had hunted Jolofinmansa with Tiramagan. Tiramagan had already conquered all the cities of Jolofinmansa, but he had not yet captured the king himself. During his flight the king decided to hide in a hole in the ground. Pursuing Jolofinmansa Sita Fata and Tiramagan arrived at the king's hiding place. There the two men saw a foot sticking out of a hole. They proceeded to pull out the foot only to discover that it belonged to Jolofinmansa, the person for whom they had been looking. Jolofinmansa offered them his weight in gold in exchange for his life, but Sita Fata advised Tiramagan instead to kill the king and take the gold, saying "Why take one, if you can have both of them?" And so Tiramagan decapitated Jolofinmansa and took all of his gold.

Lansine continued with a narrative about an "older brother" of Bremajan Kamisoko, the late partner of El Haji Yamuru Jabate. This older brother served in the Guinean army during the colonial era. According to Lansine, in those days the people of Kela suffered from obligatory rubber taxes. Each year, every adult had to bring a certain quantity of rubber to a collection point on the banks of the Niger. If a person did not provide enough rubber he was severely beaten with a whip, thrown into the river, and rolled through the sand. One year, on the day of the rubber-collection, Bremajan's older brother offered to go in his place, to which Bremajan agreed. When it was his turn, the French commander asked, "Where is your rubber?" Bremajan's brother replied, "I don't have any." The French commander ordered him to undress in preparation for a beating. Brema-

jan's brother then said, "I will not undress for anyone ever!" And since that day
the inhabitants of Kela were exempted from taxes.

This account was followed by a story, very popular in Kela, about Komanfin Jabate. In 1968 Modibo Keita, the socialist first President of Mali, delivered a speech in Kangaba during which he denounced the conservatism of the
local population and threatened to destroy the Kamabolon. At this Komanfin
protested, declaring that it would never happen. Modibo was outraged by this
response and threw Komanfin into prison. A few days later the Mali regime was
overthrown by the coup d'etat of Musa Traore, which the people in Kela say was
the result of Modibo's attack upon the Kamabolon.

I cite these three stories as examples of the educational function of griot
narrative. What are they trying to teach? I believe that the stories inspire the
griot to dare to speak in public: "a griot should never be afraid" is a statement
that the researcher will often hear in Kela. The stories and accompanying claims
that the griots from Kela (the Jawara, the Kamisoko, and the Jabate) fear no one
are explained by the belief that the griots know the truth.

As in the case of the epic, all these stories were already known to the
young men who had joined me that night for tea. What made them interesting,
however, was the way in which they were articulated in order to provide a
"deeper" message. It is in this articulation and application of knowledge that the
power of the griot lies. On the one hand, the jeliw liked to tell me everything,
but on the other they were very afraid that I would express the data inaccurately
or, even worse, that I would apply the stories to situations in which they ought
not to be used. That is why I was not allowed to say "Kukunba ani Bantamba."

What then seem to be the general rules about who is allowed to speak, and
when may he do so? First, if one wishes to speak, one has to have the necessary
knowledge. Among the youth of Kela I saw major differences in both interest
and knowledge about Sunjata. Some seemed to know next to nothing, while
others had an almost complete factual knowledge about the deeds of the great
Mande hero and his companions. A similar situation occurs when jeliw try to
master the ngoni, the little lute by which formal recitations are always accompanied in Kela. Some young men play the ngoni, but many quit as early as the age
of ten after having tried for some months. Those who knew the narratives particularly well did not usually master the ngoni.

Thus, at about the age of thirty only the most verbally gifted young people
are competent to participate in the *Sunjata* discourse. However, even they are
not allowed to do so because speaking about *Sunjata* is a tricky business. Since
the epic is related to the organization of society (Jansen 1995), one can easily
insult families by stressing the wrong accents or making dubious statements.
This is the main reason why a thirty-year-old must wait another decade or two to
become a "homo politicus" and discover the true meaning of the epic. In the
meantime he can develop proficiency in the art of speaking during his travels
around the Mande world.

It is from these itinerant individuals that westerners derive their image of
the griot: an aggressive person who wants money all the time. In my own field-

work, however, I got the impression that such men become calmer and more "distinguished" by the age of fifty; they are preparing themselves for the highest stage in their society, that of an elder.

After the age of fifty one is gradually admitted to the top level. If the Jabate from Kela have to send an official delegation to another town or village, they generally choose three old men and two "boys over fifty years old." Sometimes I witnessed a delegation in action, but the "boys" never spoke in public. It seemed that they were responsible for the organizational part of the delegation's visit.

Thus one really has the right to talk at major events only after the age of fifty. Even Lansine participated in training sessions with El Haji Yamuru before the 1989 Kamabolon rehearsals,[11] although he always denied that anyone had taught him anything. He told me once that his knowledge came from a spirit that had entered his body when he was young.

The image that I have given of the epic of *Sunjata* in Kela is that of a performance genre embedded in daily life; it is linked to the status of the aged in Mande society. This contrasts with the picture presented by Seydou Camara (1990: 73ff.; infra) in which he describes a kind of Quranic school with Lansine acting as the master; the pupils learn the epic by heart through listening two times a week to Lansine's words. According to Camara the classes are attended by Jabate and other young griots who come to Kela from the entire Manden.

Camara's descriptions (based on what griots and other informants told him) are not confirmed by my own observations of practices in Kela. Although I lived in the house of Lansine for about one year, only a few times did I witness the performance of the epic (P1-3). Moreover, I believe that Camara exaggerates the role of the pupils from other places. Between 1987 when he became Kumatigi (speaker at the Kamabolon) and 1994 Lansine had five long-term pupils, including myself (other griots came only for short visits). As everyone told me, even Lansine's long-term pupils had come to work in the fields of Kela, and after a few months they left with the benedictions of the older Jabate. On this occasion they are required to recite "all the genealogies that Lansine had taught them," which means that they summarize the praise-names of the families of the Manden. This is not a difficult task for, as we have seen above, even little children have already mastered these lines.

The Status of the Spoken Word in Kela

Up to this point I have shown that performing the epic and using its textual content in political life is a skill that is linked to age. However, this does not explain why the epic is so popular among the Jabate, or why everyone is still so interested in the work. This interest is reflected by the status of the spoken word in Kela.

The Jabate are very proud of what they know, and take special pride in the

---

[11] Personal information from Erik Sacré; see also Camara 1990.

manner by which they retain their knowledge, as illustrated by the following anecdote. All the griots of Kela liked my idea of producing a book about their village, but they were often amused by my dependence on writing in order to achieve my goal. One day Lansine told me some praise-lines, which I then proceeded to write down. When "Father" Yamuru asked me to repeat them, I simply read what I had written. Then Yamuru took the notebook out of my hand and asked me to repeat the lines again; I replied that it was impossible. The two old men laughed, and Yamuru said that his memory was better than mine.

The griots in Kela have an absolute belief in their memories. When I suggested once to my neighbor Mamadi that it would be interesting to write down the epic for future generations he replied, "Why? We are in Kela."

The old Jabate in Kela can all be described as functionally illiterate. When they were young, they were trained for a while in the local Quranic schools, but at the present they are not able to read Arabic quickly. According to everyone, El Haji Bala is the sole exception, because he received a long and intensive Islamic training in his youth. However, when I observed him making amulets he was writing Arabic very slowly, as if it were a sacred art. It reminded me of the practices of the marabouts in Djenne, described so vividly by Mommersteeg (1991). In such contexts of "restricted literacy," the written language is not a medium for general communication, but used only to represent the word of God and His Prophet.

My assessment of the status of the spoken word in Kela once again brings me into dispute with the thesis of Camara, who claims that the *Sunjata* epic also exists there in written form.[12] The first argument against this thesis is the fact that the older Kela men are functionally illiterate. Second, and perhaps even more importantly, the senior griots are so proud of their memories that they would refuse to accept the aid of written sources. Third, I think that Camara is committing an error common among students of the epic: he has forgotten that an oral work of this kind can exist only on the basis of its function in society. As I have shown, the data within the epic is often well known, and it is only through use in special contexts that such data acquire a sacred meaning. According to the impressions from my fieldwork, this relationship of the epic to the sociopolitical arena is a very delicate affair, in which the griots of Kela have proven to be masters. It is only through such mastery that they have acquired their unique present day status.

My final argument against the hypothetical presence of manuscripts in Kela is based on a comparison of sources.[13] At the end of the nineteenth century,

---

[12] Again, Camara's information is mainly based on hearsay: his only cited source is the thesis of Namankoumba Kouyate, a student at the Ecole Normale Supérieure who claims to have seen Arabic manuscripts in Kela in 1967, but who reveals nothing about the content of these documents. Camara does not specify the basis for his further assertions that the *Sunjata* manuscript was completed at the end of the ninteeth century, is written in Maninke using the Arabic alphabet, and is read by Lansine before he teaches his pupils.

[13] I am grateful to Walter Van Beek, University of Utrecht, for suggesting this argument.

marabouts in various parts of the Sudan wrote down local history (Bulman, in-fra). Some of these manuscripts contain versions of the *Sunjata* epic, but these texts are rather short and incomplete. If there was a text in Kela, this is the kind that it would be. Camara suggests that the kumatigi embellishes the written text in order to give his public the impression that he is performing in an oral tradition. However, the length, consistency, and personal variation in the Kela performances, one of which Camara himself helped record (Ly-Tall et al. 1987; Jansen et al. 1995), suggest that they are in no way influenced by any local manuscript which may exist (and I do not believe that one does).

The Final Question: What is Recited in the Kamabolon?

Having now provided some sense of who the Kela Jabate are and how they deal with the Sunjata epic and its ancillary fasaw, we can return to their performances during the septennial Kamabolon ceremony. As already noted, these recitations cannot be recorded electronically nor are outsiders even allowed into the sacred hut to hear them clearly. Instead, observers such as the informants of Germaine Diéterlen and Marcel Griaule in 1954, Claude Meillassoux in 1968, Seydou Camara in 1982, and myself in 1997 have had to spend a long night seated outside and at some distance from the Kamabolon, relying on memory and subsequent writing to gain some idea of what was being recited inside the building. Despite these handicaps, I could hear some parts of the text quite easily (Jansen 1999) and, by comparing them with new information on the 1954 Dieterlen-Griaule project, can claim to have a reasonably good idea of what is actually said.

In order to make sense of what information we have, it is first necessary to consider the critical function of the Kamabolon reroofing ceremony as an ideological statement of the way society should be ordered. At the center of this whole process is the link between the Jabaté and the political leadership of the Keita from Kangaba, another topic, on which more research still must be done. During the rehearsals (see P1) and the ceremony itself, which lasts from circa from 10 p.m. to sunrise, the griots spend most of their time on Sunjata and his companions, preceded by stories about the Mande ancestors in Mecca. The last element was absent in the performances P1-3 that I witnessed and/or recorded, but were important in P4 and P5. One of the reasons that the ceremony lasts so much longer than the performances that have been recorded (by Ly-Tall and myself) is that the griot often pauses, gives the word to another person or adds fasaw to the narration. We see such practices in P1-3, and I observed them in those portions of the 1997 Kamabolon which I could hear clearly.

The most controversial argument made by Camara along with Dieterlen (1955) and Meillassoux (1968), is their insistence that one of the major items recited during the Kamabolon ceremony is the Mande creation myth. Even before I had any direct information on this matter, it seemed impossible to me for Kela Jabate griots to perform such a narrative. I never heard them discuss it, presumably because it is not part of a political discourse like the epic of Sunjata. Ganay's publication (1995: 137–65) of the text actually recorded (however imperfectly) at Kangaba in 1954, as well as my own observations in 1997 confirm this inference. The "creation story" recited in these cases is much like the opening of Kele Monson Diabatés Radio Mali version reported by Bird (infra), i.e., it is based on the Book of Genesis via the Quran and deals with Adam and Eve et al. rather than the ur-Mande ancestors of Dieterlen's account (1955).

The Dieterlen text, with its discourse of reproduction rather than political power and the central role of Faro, the water spirit who is known to many groups in and around Kangaba, might be expected to have another local base, under the sponsorship of the autochthonous Camara lineages. In the classical Mande manner, these latter are given the designation of "dugukolotigiw" ("earth chiefs") in contrast to the politically dominant Keita who are "dugutigiw" ("village chiefs"). However, the preliminary research of Ralph Austen (1996) suggests that this is not the case, implying that Dieterlen's entire construction of a Mande creation myth is based, at best, upon Dogon rather than Kangaba research (van Beek and Jansen 1999).

I also disagree with Camara's further assertion (infra) that the Kamabolon recitations normally conclude with the history of the Manden after the time of Sunjata. Of course this is a subject about which the Jabate enjoy talking, but such information does not have the special status of the Sunjata epic. Kanku Madi did use such material at the end of one of the recorded performances witnessed by Camara (Ly-Tall et al. 1987; see also Austen, infra). I also heard such material in the last rehearsal before the 1997 Kamabolon ceremony, but it was absent from the performance at the actual ceremony. Again, my argument is that these stories do not form part of the same political discourse as the epic.

The arguments in the present section deal mainly with what is *not* recited inside the Kamabolon rather than what is actually stated. However I do believe that the recordings by Ly-Tall et al. (1987) and myself (Jansen et al. 1995 and supra) as well as my 1997 observations (Jansen 1999) also give a good indication of what *is* said. My major point is that any convincing account of Kela Jabate griot performance must be firmly grounded in the kind of direct observation of their social context that I have attempted to provide.

Bibliography

Austen, Ralph. 1996. "The Problem of the Mande Creation Myth." Unpublished paper presented at the African Studies Association, San Francisco.

Camara, Seydou. 1986. "Conservation et transmission des traditions orales au Mande: le centre de Kela et sa place dans la reconstruction de l'histoire ancienne des Mandenka." Thèse approfondie, EHESS, Paris.

Dieterlen, G. 1988. *Essai sur la Réligion Bambara*. Brussels: Université de Bruxelles.

Gaudefroy-Demombynes, Ibn Fa_l Allah al-`Omari. 1927. *Masâlik el abßâr fi mamâlik el amßâr* Vol. I, Paris.

Konaré Ba, Adam. 1983. *Sunjata: le fondateur de l'empire du Mali*. Abidjan: Nouvelles Editions Africaines.

Jansen, Jan. Forthcoming 1999. "The *Sunjata* Epic—The Ultimate Version." *Research in African Literatures* 30.

Mommersteeg, Geert. 1991. "L'éducation coranique au Mali." In *L'enseignement Islamique au Mali*, eds. B. Sanankoua and L. Brenner, 45–62. Bamako: Jamana.

van Beek, Walter E. A., and Jan Jansen. Forthcoming 1999. "La Mission Giaule à Kangaba (Mali)." *Cahiers d'Etudes Africaines*.

14. Out of Print: The Epic Cassette as Intervention, Reinvention, and Commodity

Robert C. Newton

Most students and teachers outside Mali have experienced Mande epics only in printed form. This may involve either a direct transcription or translation by a researcher, or, more likely, an adapted prose narrative, whether D. T. Niane's paraphrase of a performance of *Sunjata* by Djeli Mamoudou Kouyate of Guinea (1960) or Maryse Conde's use of the epics of Segu as a point of departure for her novel of the same name (1984). Although Massa Makan Diabate and Youssouf Cisse have gone to great lengths to fit performances of *Sunjata* by Kele Monson Diabate of Kita and Wa Kamissoko of Krina, respectively, onto the printed page, the vast majority of Malians experience these epics aurally, not as live performances, but as audio cassettes, played on local and national radio stations or on their own cassette players. The experience of reading a transcribed form of the epics in the United States and that of listening to the epics within the context of the admittedly varied cultural competencies that obtain in Mali, are quite separate. In part, this paper is addressed to those who have read but never heard these epics.

It is as a reader that I began my research. Having prepared myself with a review of the pertinent literature and a couple of summers of intensive study of the Bamana language, I left for Mali in October of 1992, under the auspices of a Fulbright grant to study the oral traditions of the Segu region. The title of my research proposal, "Shifts and Variations in the Performances of the Epic Tradition of Bamana Segu," expressed the two-pronged approach I intended to pursue: 1) I would emphasize the performance aspect of the tradition, to counteract the previous transcribed and translated texts that had served as the basis of most studies, and 2) I wanted to compare different versions from different performers, different regions, and different decades in an effort to determine what might constitute variations within a continuity of performance practice versus certain shifts that might mark a rupture within this practice.

In many ways, the essence of my current project followed along this line, but having never been in Mali before writing the proposal and given that almost all my exposure to these epics had been on the printed page, it is not too surprising that my proposal experienced a few shifts and variations of its own. The initial time was spent advancing my rudimentary knowledge of the Bamana language, learning to play the many tunes associated with the Segu epics on the Seguvien instrument of choice, the *ngoni* (a banjo-lute), and becoming a member of the community of Segu. My prior experience as a musician served as a point of entry among the younger musicians of Bamako, the capital city, some 150 miles up the Niger River to the southwest of Segu. Through those musicians who had their roots in Segu, I was given an introduction to their parents and families who served as my sponsors and teachers. It was through this relationship to both the younger musicians and their parents, as a regular presence in their everyday life for over a year and a half, that I came to gain some preliminary insight into the performance of those epics which I had only read. But as I carried out my epic quest for performances in context, what I mostly found were audio cassettes, microphones, and electric guitars. What follows is a brief description of my expectations and how they were met.

Jeliya is the art of words and music practiced by the jeliw, the griots, or masters of the word and music in the Mande-speaking world for the past several centuries. The tasks of the jeliw encompass a wide range of activities employing their verbal and musical skills, including: the role of public speakers and masters of ceremony; negotiators for families and communities; performers and entertainers; reciters of praises, genealogies, and raconteurs of historical events; and advisors and moralists. Many of these tasks are combined in the prestige form of the *maana*, or Mande epic, in which the performer combines praise-singing, genealogies, and proverbs, and dispenses advice and general reflections on life while unfolding a narrative surrounding the exploits of one of the heroes of the great empires in the region.

These epic performances have served to create a rarified space in which past and present merge at a specific moment in the life of the family, the community, or the nation. In their task of simultaneously honoring the past and the immediate, they must maintain a continuity with the history of remembered events and the history of remembered performances— and at the same time fit them to the general cultural conditions and specific social situations of the present. In this sense the performances are both interventions and reinventions.

As an intervention, the jeli inserts himself (the narration aspect of the epics is something performed almost exclusively by men) and his performance within the complex of social interactions as an advocate for his patron (or *jatigi*), but also as a representative of all jeliw as well as his own family and himself. The jeliw are the retainers of the tradition that binds together the community. In this latter role, the function of the jeli is to counsel the community by evoking the actions of past heroes as a model for current leaders and to comment on current events within the context of the epic narratives. The epic narrative form and its themes, main narrative, blocks of lines and formulae are the materials from which he does not so much improvise but, rather, to borrow Albert Lord's term, creates a "composition in performance" (1960:13). His rhetorical task is to preserve and speak the truth in the present, not to memorize. It is to insert the truth of the past into the context of the present as a means of counseling and motivating those present at the performance. It serves to locate and orient both the individual and the community. It is neither a blind imitation of tradition nor an original invention but, rather, a reinvention which breathes the life of shared cultural traditions into the circumstances of the present, and vice versa.

One of the principal means by which this process of location and orientation takes place is through naming. The reciting of family genealogies, the invocation of the praise-songs for a particular last name (or *jamu*), and the recounting of the exploits of notable family members, both past and present, establishes the set of social relations in which the action takes place. The references to the specific towns and villages in which famous events occurred serve not only to evoke the glory of these historical landmarks but also to thicken the meaning conveyed in the course of the narration. Entire sequences of events and relationships are condensed in these names. They are both symbols and concrete markers of the imagination and experience, which prescribe behavior and motivate action among those who have sufficient cultural competence— that is, they have an understanding of certain meanings associated with the names of these people and places.

How does this task play out in the conditions of postcolonial Mali? What has occurred within the performance of these epics to maintain their ability not only to survive but to thrive in the postcolonial era? The epics have always been a means of locating those who identify themselves as members of the collectivity represented by the kingdom or empire from which they emanate and continue to represent. In the era of postcolonial independence, this has been an important point of reference around which to form the new identity as citizens of the nation-state of Mali, distinct from its neighbors who also share the colonial and postcolonial experience. As a landmark and signpost, a source of location and orientation, it takes on added importance in a shifting landscape in which diverse systems and their institutions— Bamana or Maninka (and those of other regional language groups), Islamic, French, Malian state, or those of the international development community— are mixed and matched in the daily struggle to obtain resources and maintain the health and well-being of the extended family and community.

If the epic has retained its privileged status as vehicle of choice for purposes of location and orientation, it has done so through a flexibility that allows the performance itself to be located at the center of events that construct collective identity. One way it does this can be seen in the nature and the practice of epic performance. The epic incorporates the speech styles of several genres, using greetings, conversation, proverbs, ritual and religious language and reference, tales and story-telling, praises and other songs. Prominent members of the audience and their families are singled out in the course of a performance or greeted as they enter to witness the performance. The patrons who sponsor the performance are frequently identified and praised.

The performers have adapted the form and style of presentation to suit the circumstances of the performance and the purposes of the sponsors. Kele Monson Diabate's performance of a detailed and elaborated version of the *Sunjata* epic was recorded by the state-owned and operated radio station as an example of a definitive version by one of the jeliw most renowned for his extensive knowledge of historical details. This same version of the epic has also served as the basis for six different books by Kele Monson's nephew, Massa Makan Diabate, in which he extracts the following from his uncle's performances: songs (*Janjon*, Paris: Presence Africaine, 1970); description of performance (*Kala Jata*, Bamako EDIM, 1970); a description of performance framed with a battery of explanatory notes (*Le Lion à L'arc*, Paris: Hatier, 1986); transcription and translation of performance (*L'aigle et l'épervier*, Paris: P.J. Oswald, 1975); genealogy (with Diango Cissé, *La Dispersion des Mandeka*, Bamako: EDIM, 1970); and, finally, tales (*Si le feu s'éteignant*, Bamako: EDIM, 1967) (see also McGuire, infra).

The version of Banzoumana Sissoko, recorded sometime during his return to Mali during the early days of independence, mostly features songs, condensing long narrative passages into popular soundbites. It was this performance that was played at key times over the government radio station, preparing the populace for impending changes, whether in the form of a coup or conflict with neighboring countries. Once again performing the function of motivating the community on an individual and collective basis to engage in the task at hand, its release in cassette form for mass distribution in the early 1990s is reflective of its adaptability to transformed technological conditions and social relations. Now the citizens of Mali can have a piece of history— contained in both the *Sunjata* epic itself as well as in its performance by the national jeli, Banzoumana Sissoko.[1]

With the many versions of epic performances that are sold on cassette, whether dubs of local performances or concerts, those recorded by the state radio station, or those produced within the studio specifically for purposes of mass distribution, many Malians (more than 80 percent of whom are illiterate) now have home audio libraries of the great works performed by the most prestigious performers.

But what happens to the meaning and communal context of these epics when recording technologies place the act of performance in a time and space entirely removed from personal encounters? How do epic performances now

---

[1]The cassette of Banzoumana Sissoko referred to throughout this paper is labeled "Musique du Mali: Bazoumana (sic) Sissoko, Le Vieux Lion II" Stereo 7372.

enter into the daily lives and discourses of particular communities or within Mali as a whole? In what way does the specific nature of this contact change both the relations between performer and audience and, in so doing, the nature of the performance itself? If jeliya and other services rendered by jeli for their patrons were at one time considered just that, services that would be rewarded by all manner of considerations with both ritualized and pragmatic contributions to their support, what happens when these performances take on the relations of commodities in a national or international market? And if much finger-pointing has always gone on between the jeliw and their patrons concerning lapses in the appropriate conduct and consideration required for the maintenance of these relations in their "traditional" form, how are these dialectics transformed by the communications technology, expanded market, national politics and new definitions of social status in the postcolonial era?

Two examples from the spring of 1994 will serve to illustrate some of the surprises I encountered on my "epic" journey.

I arrived at the village of Djoforongo at the appointed hour for the performance (three hours prior to its actual occurrence). The community was out in force underneath the intense late April sun to greet the delegation of ministers of communication and culture from the national government in Bamako. The anticipated visitors were coming to celebrate this year's National Heritage Day, which was to honor Bakarijan Kone, the greatest general of the Bamana empire of Segu and the most noted ancestor of the town's most prestigious residents, including the mayor. It was to this village that the families of Bakarijan's children and those who served as their jeliw, or masters of the word and music, came after the fall of Segu's Bamana empire to the Islamic Tukulor invaders in 1862. It was and is the role of the jeliw to retain the familial and communal histories that function as the foundation of performances at significant family and public ceremonies. The epic recounting the exploits of Bakarijan in service to Segu is regarded as the pinnacle of such performances. If ever there was a time and place to witness a performance of one of the epic narratives concerning the exploits of Bakarijan, this surely would be it.

Under the post and thatch canopy that sheltered much of the public space between the village's central mosque and the compound of one of Bakarijan's more prominent descendants, several of the villages' elders, including descendants of the generals and their jeliw, were seated in small clusters on the numerous chairs arranged for the speech-making to come. Underneath a large tree dominating the scene from one corner of the seating area, two young men were adding their voices as punctuation to one coming from a cassette, which was narrating an episode in the life of Bakarijan. The voice on the cassette was that of one of the principal singers of the National Instrumental Ensemble of Mali, likely recorded a decade or two prior. The only jeli to speak during the speechifying that was to follow was a voluble and outspoken entrepreneur who was related by birth to families descended from Bakarijan's jeli, Gorodi Kone, but this man had spent most of his adult life in Paris, when not tending to his hotel and bar in Segu, the Bakarijanna.

Shortly after this expedition, I traveled to the Maninka-speaking region of today's Mali, the heartland of the former Mali empire near the southwest border with Guinea. At the secondary school complex of Kangaba, a number of chairs had been rearranged in the back corner of the dining hall. The national school system had been closed down in response to the latest wave of violence in the wake of a long succession of student strikes, often fueled by opponents of the government. The grounds had been temporarily made available to a group of high school-aged students participating in an independently sponsored field trip to research various aspects of the region around Kangaba—history, verbal and musical arts, sociology—and to write about them in Bamanankan, their first spoken and second written language.

A group of jeliw from the nearby village of Kela are known throughout the greater Mande cultural world and beyond as perhaps *the* center of the *Sunjata* epic tradition, emphasized by their connection to some of Sunjata's main legacies, the Keïta families and Kamabulon shrine in Kangaba (cf. Camara, Jansen, infra). For a fee, they had agreed to perform this evening for the research group. The chairs had been moved to circle around a central point, which allowed the overhead lighting to illuminate the faces of the performers for the purpose of collecting a filmed record of the performance. Finally, the entourage arrived from Kela, filling the back of a covered pick-up truck. The village's most renowned jeli, Kela Bala Jabate, had complained of a cold and would stay home for the evening. The narration of the epic was performed by one of his respected brothers, Lansine. The three elder members of the contingent discussed the arrangements for the evening with their hosts, while the band began to set up its equipment under the direction of one of Mali's most noted singers, Lafia Jabate, a former lead singer of Bamako's Super Rail Band and the nephew of the epic narrator. Lafia is an international recording artist like his brother, Kasse Madi Jabate, and other Malian superstars such as Salif Keïta, whose careers began with one of Mali's regional modern orchestras but who have now chosen to live and record in Paris. Lafia, however, continues to reside in his hometown of Kela.

The speakers and microphones were plugged into the amp and a sound check began for the electric guitar, bass, drums, the ngoni with direct amplification lead built-in, and two microphones for the lead singers. The band began the evening's performance with a blend of popular songs and dance music, interwoven with many melodies from the standard repertoire of the Maninka jeliw. Male and female vocalists alternated in singing the lead, one often backing up the other on the chorus. Eventually, these two singers gave way to the superstar who commanded the attention of the crowd with his virtuosity, setting the stage for his revered uncle. The uncle began the epic, the central feature of the performance, focusing on the family praises and a narrative of an episode recounting the exploits of Tiramagan, one of Sunjata's most acclaimed generals. This had been previously arranged with the director of the project, who bears the last name, or jamu, of Traore, the same as that of Tiramagan. "Jamu" is an important component of individual and collective identity in all of Mali and for this reason the director spent much of his own teaching time during this trip delving into the history of his own roots in the nearby town of Balanzan, where the tomb of Tiramagan constitutes a center for most of the Traore of Mali and particularly those of this region.

The jeli's somewhat tentative rendition of the family praises and the narrative itself were overshadowed by the skill and force of the lead singer. The performance concluded with the audience, students and teachers alike, dancing to the more popular dance rhythms and melodies played by modern bands throughout Mali's main cities.

How are we to make sense of these epic "performances" and the contexts in which they are performed? To begin an examination of the once and future nature of the epic in practice, one must be sensitive to the multiple histories of the various aspects at play in any given performance portraying a moving picture of practice viewed from multiple points of reference. Two features in particular I have come to focus on are the influence of audio cassette technology and its appropriation into specific Malian contexts and the incorporation into the jeliya music itself of innovations such as electric instruments and amplification, along with instrumental and singing styles from various parts of Africa, the diaspora, and beyond.

A convenient point of departure from which to examine one such history, which leads to the intersection of these two vectors and their effects on Malian music and the epic today, begins with the period following World War II in Mali. It was at this time that many soldiers returned from Europe and the infrastructures of transportation and communication brought different cultural forms and materials into contact with each other (although radio and telephone were not widely available until 1957 and television arrived only in 1983). Beginning in 1946, the RDA (Rassemblement Democratique Africain) a regional political party, was becoming the dominant force in the push toward independence in then French West Africa. The RDA sought an independence based not so much upon previous empires but related to the boundaries etched during the previous fifty years of French colonial rule. However Mali, even in its previous definition as the French Soudan, is a country where the cultural heritage of precolonial empires has always remained a living presence. Thus the program of establishing and spreading a new national identity has had less to do with reclaiming lost cultural forms and social relations which might be suppressed by the overlay of assimilation policies of the colonial French than with redefining existing structures that had continually resisted such efforts.

In the last decade of colonialism many Malians, like other Africans, had begun to migrate to the cities, whether in search of jobs opened up by new

French development ventures or to flee the rural consequences of such policies, particularly the calamitous Office du Niger irrigated agricultural scheme. These urbanites developed a taste for new musical styles, dances, and instruments, many of which had been imported by the French colonials or brought in as a result of increased contact with the outside world during the war or by the heightened metropolitan investment efforts that followed.

Modern orchestras were formed, with accordions, trumpets, and acoustic guitars soon giving way to saxophones and electric guitars. Drum kits and basses provided a rhythm section, and were soon joined by congas from Cuba and eventually electronic keyboards. Microphones, amps, and speakers were occasionally used to broadcast the sound to large audiences, who flocked to see them in rehearsal halls, street dances, or infrequent public celebrations.

By the early 1960s these bands were a regular feature on the musical landscape and every city featured at least one of these modern orchestras. During this same period, the newly independent Republic of Mali pursued a dual national agenda, on the one hand reclaiming an historical Malian cultural heritage while simultaneously imposing a new socialist model of social relations specifically opposed to the established patronage system. Within this context, two major kinds of musical groups were sponsored by the government to help disseminate this new identity to the citizenry, either in concert or over the airwaves of the state-sponsored radio station, the only non-print medium existing at the time.[2] The National Instrumental Ensemble of Mali was formed at this time and consisted almost entirely of jeliw.

Although the history of the practice of jeliya varied from region to region and its equivalents varied from cultural group to cultural group, this large organization made up of musicians, instruments, and musical traditions from different regions of Mali was a departure from past practice. It constituted a new form and served to represent the newly formed Malian state within its various regions, for the country as a whole, and to the international community. The National Instrumental Ensemble was a symbol of the emerging Malian identity— the possibility of diverse cultures asserting their own specificity while forming a pluralistic blend. It thus demonstrated not only a respect for differences, but also the possibility of maintaining them and using them to create a combined identity based on cultural origins and the current national experience (Taravélé).

The government also opened up another front in its use of cultural forms to frame and reinforce a sense of Malian national identity. By organizing and sponsoring modern regional orchestras not only in Bamako but in the urban centers of the seven designated regions of the country, the government appealed to the aesthetic tastes and the personal and collective identities of the growing number of urban dwellers. This aspect has become even more significant today

---

[2] The station began broadcasting on June 1, 1957 with limited range and hours and was officially inaugurated on September 4, 1957.

given the massive exodus to the cities and Bamako in particular, whose population has continued to expand from around 60,000 in 1960 to over a million today.

Initially, these bands featured some jeliw who had moved away from the confines of jeliya as it was practiced by other members of their families, but for the most part they consisted of young urban men (and eventually a few women) who were excited by the sounds and rhythms of these new forms. The music they played and the instruments upon which they played it were outside the provenance of the jeliw. Above all, these bands played an urban dance music, which, if initially derived from the French, was soon increasingly influenced by the sounds of Cuba and Zaire. The government even sponsored the travel of a dozen of these musicians to Cuba for extensive musical training—reinforcing both the socialist and diaspora link.

In 1962, the USRDA inaugurated the Annual Semaine Nationale de la Jeunesse. After the disruption of the 1968 military coup, this event resurfaced in 1970 as biennial national competitions sponsored by the government. The competition brought together individual and combination troupes playing in various styles: music derived from jeliya or similar traditional regional forms; modern dance orchestras; and dance and theater troupes. In 1970, one regional orchestra, which later became known as the Super Biton National de Segou (a name derived from the title of the founder of the Bamana Segu empire) broke new ground by presenting a modern band interpretation of one of the episodes featuring Da Monzon, the leader most celebrated in epics attached to this precolonial state. To develop this cultural revival performance, musicians within the band consulted the versions of several jeliw from the Segu region.

A tape of this performance was not only aired on national radio but eventually made its way onto numerous albums that were issued at this time with government backing.[3] Several of these albums, by both the ensembles and the modern orchestras, began to feature several of the epics from different cultural traditions throughout Mali. With the advent of cassette technology, not only did these albums become available in a form more accessible to a larger portion of the populace, but many of the performances that had been recorded for government radio also appeared on the market. These were often illegally reproduced in Nigeria and smuggled into Mali. Many musicians would be surprised to walk down the streets and hear their voices unexpectedly coming

---

[3] Although I have found some of the original albums issued by the government under the label "Mali Kunkan," I only found Super Biton's performances of the Bamana epics on homemade cassettes in the marketplace. Their original source was most likely the national radio station, now called ORTM, the "Organisation de Radiodiffusion et Television du Mali," even though they were possibly passed on by a smaller radio station.

from the cassette players that can now be found in almost every home in Mali.[4]

In response to the popularity of these tapes, many jeliw began to record their own versions of these epics and other older songs in one of the growing number of studios either in Bamako, Abidjan, or Paris with the express purpose of mass distribution. Likewise, street-side vendors began to collect versions of these songs and epics from all the possible sources— studio cassettes or albums, recordings from the radio station archives, cuts leaked or reproduced on the side by the cassette producers themselves, or cassettes made at public events or family ceremonies— and would dub them in advance or on the spot for prospective customers.

It was at about the same time in 1983 that Mali's first national television station began broadcasting throughout most of the country. Although initially viewed only in Bamako, live or taped broadcasts from the studio and on location at the site of various ceremonies were seen by a national urban audience and even at the compounds of wealthier villagers who could afford generator-supplied televisions. The video cassette industry entered soon after, and the music videos of the *jelimusow*, the telegenic female stars of this new medium, became a regular part of the Malian-produced programming. As the audio and video cassette markets began to merge, so did the once separate musical forms of modern orchestra and jeliya. Each began to feature the songs, arrangements, instruments, and styles of the other. Zairian guitar riffs and styles were mingled with horn arrangements and dance rhythms of the Afro-Cuban sound in the performance of melodies derived from jeliya. More modern orchestras discovered or rediscovered traditional songs and styles, while the jeliw began exploring new dance rhythms to further excite their growing audiences.

Among the more popular versions sold on the streets are studio-dubbed versions of the *Sunjata* epic as sung by Salif Keita and Mory Kante (Rail Band, Syllart), two former lead singers of Bamako's famed Super Rail Band who have since left the country in the quest of international musical fame. Like the popular version of *Sunjata* performed by Banzoumana Sissoko, those sung by Keita and Kante prominently feature the song aspect of the epic, the portion which is sung by a woman, the jelimuso, and echoed by the women's chorus on the album and cassette of the Ensemble Instrumental National du Mali.[5]   There is the

---

[4] The most common figure I have heard approximating the number of illegally produced cassettes that are sold on the streets of Mali's cities is 90 percent. It is often difficult to determine whether a cassette is legal unless it is bought directly from the producer.

[5] The cassette referred to in this chapter, recorded by *L'Ensemble Instrumental National du Mali* and also bearing its name, has a reference of GP25 and contains performances (or excerpts from these performances) that refer to the historic figures of Sunjata, Ngolo Diarra, Bakarijan Kone, and the song "Janjon."

suggestion, particularly in the work of Lucy Duran (1994) that the big-name singers of electrified orchestras, both those of jeli and non-jeli origins alike, have patterned their vocal styles and arrangements after the singing styles characteristic of the jelimusow. The evidence from the recordings of the Super Rail Band with Keita and Kante supports this contention. In addition, the role of the women's chorus is now taken up by the instruments of the band, forming the chorus of performers who surround the lead singer.

Initially, the epics recuperated by the modern bands for nationally sponsored competitions would highlight the distinctive heritage of each of the different regions of Mali as represented by their designated state-sponsored bands, beginning with the innovative work of the regional band of Segu. Many of these earlier versions dating back to the early 1970s featured long narrative sections. As these epics became a part of the concert repertoire of these orchestras, whether in concert or dance halls, the narrative aspect began to give way to more emphasis on the songs and longer instrumentals. In short, they became more musical and more danceable, highlighting the vocal virtuosity of the lead singer and the dynamic playing of the lead guitarists.

At first, those groups working primarily from the repertoire of jeliya and those playing for modern dance audiences derived their music from different sources, played on different instruments, and used different styles. They complemented each other as the newly independent government attempted to form a new Malian national identity— one derived from the plurality of regional traditions and the emerging urban culture, which was particularly that of Bamako. The challenge of the government in this postcolonial epoch was to utilize the many cultural legacies of the previous empires of these regions, which had simultaneously resisted and been suppressed by the French colonial administrations, in order to elicit a sense of belonging and identity within the local communities of the new Malian state. At the same time, one of the tasks of the socialist government was to undercut the systems of patronage which had always dominated the region's political formations. The contradictory nature of this endeavor is brought out in the epic performance tradition. These epics had been performed specifically for the patron to which the jeli was attached. In fact, what had happened is that the government assumed the position of a grand patron, much as the families of the ruling dynasties and their allies had done during the time of the great empires.

Nowhere is this more evident than on one of the cassettes made of Salif Keita singing the *Sunjata* epic with the Super Rail Band (1988). Near the end of the rather short version of this epic (even when compared to other versions which stress the song mode at the expense of the narrative), he sings the praises of the cadre of military officers who were active supporters of such bands during the regime of Moussa Traore. The patronage system, then, neither began nor ended with the colonial era; rather, it has continued to adapt to the shifting power structure, with different jeliw making different choices from the new assortment of options.

Some have remained faithful to the families which they were attached to under the social contract of *nyamakala-horon*, in which the former provides services in exchange for support by the latter. They have chosen to watch their fortunes rise and fall with that of the families of their patrons. Some, such as Fotigi Diabate, frequently heard over the government radio station in the last decade of the colonial era, have renounced their positions entirely with the death of their patrons, claiming that shifting current social relations have brought about the disappearance of quality patrons who honor their obligations to communities and clients (personal interview, 1993). Other jeliw have taken advantage of the opportunities opened up in commerce with the expansion of the world market economy. But many have chosen new relations with new kinds of patrons.

One such patron, as we have seen, is the government— whether in the form of specific political figures, from local *chefs de canton* during the colonial era, to presidents of the new republic or the more impersonal state-sponsored media or cultural ministries. Almost all musicians in electrified bands were dependent on the instruments and equipment owned by government cultural agencies. Tours were arranged and sponsored both nationally and internationally for the government-sponsored bands and ensembles by these agencies who were also the owners of the principal concert halls.

Many jeliw would make occasional appearances or recordings for the state-run radio or, later, television. Others became regular features. Banzoumana Sissoko was used to promote support for the actions of the government. Jeli Baba Sissoko held his weekly "causeries" every Monday evening on the radio, entertaining the country with his versions of stories, songs, and epic narrations.[6] Modern instrumental versions of *Sunjata* and Da Monzon are often heard before or during Malian-produced news shows and other features on national television broadcasts.[7]

Other new patrons have arrived within the context of postcolonial conditions. From the 1960s onward, researchers, especially those from academic institutions on either side of the North Atlantic, have arrived with access to funds far beyond the reach of most Malians, and they have sought out the best-known performers of the elite form of the epic as the key to historical, social, and cultural understandings of the region. Those jeliw with the appropriate skills have addressed their performances to these audiences and rarely perform except at the most prestigious of events unless an equivalent sum is offered. Other

---

[6] An extensive collection of Jeli Baba Sissoko's "causeries" are preserved at the Bandioteque of ORTM.

[7] Some of the best examples of this music can be found on the cassette "Modibo Diarra et les Frères Tandina (Instrumental Malien) Volume 1," Studio Kemesso, which features electronic synthesizers.

musicians have had their services enlisted by the overwhelming number of development agencies that have sprung up throughout Mali in the last several years, often viewed as well-heeled patrons even as they seek to undermine the patronage system.

But the most significant development affecting the choice of patrons has been the expansion of the world market economy. As a result, wealthy traders and entrepreneurs have emerged and sought out the services of jeliw to sing their praises at major concerts or on nationally distributed cassettes. Many of the titles found on the cassettes of the jelimusow, the women who are the national and international stars of Malian music, bear the names of *commerçants* who have sponsored their recordings and contributed toward their tours, becoming the *de facto* adopted patrons of these artists. In a performance at the French Cultural Center in Bamako, one of Mali's more celebrated jelimusow was alerted that one of the more prominent manufacturers of Bamako was in the audience. During the first song of the evening, she began to sing his praises while trying, with great difficulty, to pick him out of the front row of the audience— a man she had never seen before and of whose family history she has limited knowledge.

In the late 1980s, following the release of several pirated cassettes of epic performances by both revered jeliw and popular modern bands, several jeliw from various regions of Mali began to record studio versions intended for reproduction and mass distribution in Mali. Sponsorship was sought in this money-scarce country among the rising businessmen who would pay for the costs of production. On one cassette from the epic tradition of Bamana Segu (Daouda Dembele, Super Sound Ltd.), the jeli, Daouda Dembele, has filled the breaks in his narration of Segu's most famous general, Bakarijan Kone, with descriptions of the sponsor, his business, Koulibaly Transports, and its services instead of the traditional family praises or social commentary. In effect, a business advertisement has replaced panegyrics and genealogies.

The other opportunity this expanding world market has engendered is the possibility of direct contracts with recording studios. Although most cassettes are made for distribution within Mali (or a greater Mande cultural area), some of the bigger contracts are with studios in Paris, London, the United States, and even Japan. As Malian music has found a broader audience among those listening to varied musical traditions from around the world, many Malian musicians have come to emphasize the musical aspects of their profession to the exclusion of others. As the audience expands, the extent of cultural competency shrinks— and the so-called universal language of music fills the gap.

How has the epic shifted with changes in the patrons and communities for which they are performed? And how has this been affected by the dislocation of the performance, the mutual presence of the audience and the performer that has disappeared with the development of the affordable audiocassette and video? The taped and sold performance has become another among competing commodities in the marketplace. It is no longer under the control of the jeli once it has been reproduced and sold to the owner, who then controls the circumstances under which it is heard. It is fixed, repeatable, and transportable. It does not make the same kind of adjustments to circumstance as might be made by a live performer in front of a live audience. It cannot speak directly to the cultural competence of its listeners. The presumptions regarding the awareness of the audience must be made by the performer at the time of the performance. For this reason, locally recorded performances dubbed on the spot for potential customers exhibit a greater specificity in the use of names of people, places, and things. Those which have been recorded for nationwide broadcast or distribution and are reproduced through studio technology tend to make broader references, use fewer local names, and emphasize more general narrative passages and songs which serve to encapsulate a series of events.

The epic continues as an active intervention into the community and the national life of present-day Mali, reinvented on the cassette to maintain its presence. If few Malians of today have ever seen a performance of the epics of *Sunjata*, Bakarijan, Da Monzon, or the other great heroes of the region's empires, many more have become familiar with them through the playing and replaying of recorded performances. But as these marketplace commodities extend further and further, the meanings embedded in the names, which are available only to the culturally competent of a particular region, begin to diminish. The rich texture that results from the interweaving of narrative, general commentary, personal reference, and pointed advice is replaced with an emphasis on performance virtuosity, which appeals to a wider audience of urbanized consumers. The superfluous praise for scarcely known, publicity-seeking patrons lacks the purposefulness and depth of meaning of the *fasa* that once served to challenge the praised patron to match the actions and strength of character exhibited by his or her illustrious ancestors.

Changes in social relations, economic conditions, and technology have altered patron-performer and audience-performer contracts as well as aesthetics. The resulting shifts in the performances themselves reflect the ongoing negotiations between the performers and the changing world in which they live and perform— and therefore constitutes both a rupture and a continuity of the form and spirit of jeliya.

Bibliography

Durán, Lucy. 1994. "Big Strings and Female Stars: Lyrics, Aesthetics and Gender in the Popular Manding Song Repertoire of Western Mali." Unpublished paper delivered at the annual meeting of the African Studies Association in Toronto, Nov. 4.

Taravélé, Jules. 1965. *L'Essor.*

Discography

Dembele, Daouda. "Histoire de Bakaridjan Vol.1." Super Sound Ltd., SSL 233.

Diarra, Modibo and les Frères Tandina. "Modibo Diarra and les Frères Tandina (Instrumental Malien) Volume I." RM Bamako "Studio Kemesso," Kip 05.

Rail Band. "Rail Band (Salif Keita & Mory Kante)." Mali Stars, Syllart Production, Syl 8357.

Rail Band. 1988. "Rail Band du Mali." Melodias 7137.

Sissoko, Bazoumana. "Musique du Mali: Le Vieux Lion II." 7372.

Super Biton de Segou. "Da Monzon et Bakarijan."

General Bibliography

Adam, G. 1904. "Légendes historiques du pays de Nioro (Sahel)." *Revue Coloniale*, nouvelle série, Juillet 1903–Juin 1904: 81–98, 232–48, 354–72, 485–96, 602–20, 734–44, and Juillet 1904–Décembre 1904: 117–24, 233–48. Published as book in 1904, Paris: Augustin Challamel.

Amselle, Jean-Loup. 1979. "Littérature orale et idéologie. La geste des Jakite Sabashi du Ganan (Wasolon, Mali)." *Cahiers d'Etudes Africaines* 73–76, XIX–I–4, pp. 381–433.

—. 1990. *Logiques métisses; anthropologie de l'identité en Afrique et ailleurs*. Paris: Payot.

Arnaud, Robert. 1911. [1912, 1913] *L'Islam et la politique musulmane française en Afrique occidentale française*. Paris: Comité de l'Afrique Française.

Austen, Ralph. 1990. "Africans Speak, Colonialism Writes: The Transcription and Translation of Oral Literature before World War II." *Cahiers de Littérature orale* 28: 29–53.

Austen, Ralph A., and Jan Jansen. 1996. "History, Oral Tradition and Structure in Ibn Khaldun's Chronology of Mali Rulers," *History in Africa*, 22: 17–28.

Barber, Karin. 1989. "Interpreting Oríkì as History and as Literature." In Karin Barber and P. F. de Moraes Farias, eds., *Discourse and Its Disguises: The Interpretation of African Oral Texts*, 13–23. Birmingham University African Studies Series 1. Birmingham: C.W.A.S., University of Birmingham.

Barber, Karin, and P. F. de Moraes Farias, eds. 1989. *Discourse and Its Disguises: The Interpretation of African Oral Texts*. Birmingham University African Studies Series 1. Birmingham: C.W.A.S., University of Birmingham.

Bathily, Abdoulaye. 1975. "A Discussion of the traditions of Wagadu with some reference to ancient Ghana, including a review of oral accounts, Arabic sources and archaeological evidence." *Bulletin de l'I.F.A.N.* 37 B, 1–94.

Bazin, J. 1979. "La production d'un récit historique." Paris, *Cahiers d'Etudes africaines* 73–76, XIX 1– 4: 435–483.

Belcher, Stephen Patterson IV. 1985. "Stability and Change: Praise-Poetry and

Narrative Traditions in the Epics of Mali." Ph.D. dissertation, Brown University.

Bird, Charles S. 1971. "Oral Art in the Mande." In C. T. Hodge, ed., *Papers on the Manding*, 15–25. Bloomington, Indiana: Indiana University Press.

—. 1972. "Heroic Songs of the Mande Hunters." In R. M. Dorson, ed., *African Folklore*, 275–93. Garden City, New York: Anchor Books, Doubleday & Co.

—. 1974. *The Songs of Seydou Camara*. Trans. C. Bird with Mamadou Koita and Bourama Soumaouro. Bloomington, Indiana: African Studies Center, Indiana University.

—. 1976. "Poetry in the Mande: Its Form and Meaning." *Poetics* 5: 89–100.

Bird, Charles S., and Martha Kendall. 1980. "The Mande Hero: Text and Context." In C. Bird and Ivan Karp, eds., *Explorations in African Systems of Thought*, 13–26. Bloomington, Indiana: Indiana University Press.

Brooks, George. 1993. *Landlords and Strangers: Ecology, Society, and Trade in Western Africa, 1000–1630*. Boulder, Colorado: Westview Press.

Bühnen, Stephen. 1994. "In Quest of Susu." *History in Africa* 21:1–47.

Bulman, Stephen Paul Dusan. 1989. "The Buffalo-Woman Tale: Political Imperatives and Narrative Constraints in the Sunjata Epic." In K. Barber and P. F. de Moraes Farias, eds., *Discourse and Its Disguises: The interpretation of African Oral Texts*, 171–88. Birmingham University African Studies Series 1. Birmingham: C.W.A.S., University of Birmingham.

—. 1990. "Interpreting Sunjata: A Comparative Analysis and Exegesis of the Malinke Epic." Ph.D. Thesis, University of Birmingham.

Camara Laye. 1978. *Le Maître de la Parole: Kouma Lafolo Kouma*. Paris: Libraire Plon.

—. 1980. *The Guardian of the Word: Kouma Lafôlô Kouma*, trans. J. Kirkup. Glasgow: Collins/Fontana.

Camara, Seydou. 1990. *La tradition orale en question (Conservation et transmission des traditions historiques au Manden: Le centre de Kéla et l'histoire du Mininjan)*. Thèse pour le Doctorat de l'EHESS

(Nouveau Régime), Paris, EHESS.

Camara, Sory. 1976. *Gens de la parole*. Paris and The Hague: Mouton.

Campbell, Joseph. 1973. *The Masks of God: Primitive Mythology*. First
     published 1959. London: Souvenir Press.

Cashion, Gerald A. 1984. "Hunters of the Mande: A Behavioral Code and
     Worldview Derived from a Study of Their Folklore." Ph.D.
     dissertation, Indiana University. Two vols. Ann Arbor: University
     Microfilms International.

Cissé, Diango, and Massa Makan Diabaté. 1970. *La dispersion des Mandeka*.
     Bamako: Editions populaires.

Cissé, Youssouf Tata. 1964. "Notes sur les sociétés des Chasseurs Malinké."
     J.S.A. 34: 175–226.

—. 1976. *L'Empire du Mali (suite): L'enfance, l'exile, le testament et les
     funerailles de Magan_Sondyata; les Peuls du Manding: Un récit de Wa
     Kamissoko de Krina*, collected, ed. and trans. by Y. T. Cissé. Fondation
     SCOA pour la recherche scientifique en Afrique Noire: Deuxième
     Colloque Internationale de Bamako, 16 fèvrier–22 fèvrier 1976. Paris:
     Fondation SCOA.

—. 1988. *La grande geste du Mali: Des origines à la fondation de l'Empire
     (Traditions de Krina au colloques de Bamako)*. Paris: Editions
     Karthala/Association ARSAN.

Cissé, Youssouf Tata, and Wa Kamissoko. 1975. [1991] *L'Empire du Mali: Un
     récit de Wa Kamissoko de Krina*, collected, ed. and trans. Y. T. Cisse.
     Fondation SCOA pour la recherche scientifique en Afrique Noire
     (Projet Boucle du Niger): Premier Colloque international de Bamako,
     27 janvier–1er fèvrier 1975. Paris: Fondation SCOA.

Condé, Maryse. 1984. *Ségou*. Paris: Editions Robert Laffont.

Conrad, David C. 1984. "Oral Sources on Links between Great States:
     Sumanguru, Servile Lineage, the Jariso, and Kaniaga." *History in
     Africa* 11: 35–55.

—. 1985. "Islam in the oral traditions of Mali: Bilali and Surakata." *J.A.H.* 26:
     33–49.

—. 1990. *A State of Intrigue: The Epic of Bamana Segu According to Tayiru*

Banbera. Oxford: Oxford University Press.

—. 1992. "Searching for History in the Sunjata Epic: The Case of Fakoli."
    History in Africa 19: 147–200.

Conrad, David C., and Barbara E. Frank. 1995. "Nyamakalaya: Contradiction
    and Ambiguity in Mande Society." In *Status and Identity in West
    Africa: Nyamakalaw of Mande*, eds., D. Conrad and B. Frank.
    Bloomington and Indianapolis: Indiana University Press.

Curtin, Philip D. 1974. *Economic Change in Precolonial Africa: Senegambia in
    the Era of the Slave Trade*. Madison, Wisconsin: University of
    Wisconsin Press.

Cutter, Charles. 1968. "The Politics of Music in Mali." *African Arts* 1, 3: 38–39,
    74–77.

de Ganay, Solange. 1995. *Le sanctuaire Kama blon de Kangaba—Histoire,
    mythes, peintures pariétales et ceremonies septennales*. Paris:
    Nouvelles Editions de Sud.

Delafosse, Maurice, ed. and trans. 1913. *Traditions Historiques et Légendaires
    du Soudan Occidental*. Paris: Comité de l'Afrique Française.

Diabaté, Massa Makan. 1967. *Si le feu s'eteignait*. Bamako: Editions Populaires.

—. 1970. *Janjon et autres chants populaires du Mali*. Paris, Presence Africaine.

—. 1970a. *Kala Jata*. Subsequently as *L'aigle et l'epervier: ou La geste de
    Sunjata*, Paris: P.J. Oswald, 1975 and then as *Le lion à l'arc*, Paris:
    Hatier (Monde Noir Poche), 1986. Bamako: Editions Populaires.

—. 1972. "Le Héros dans la tradition orale du Mandé." Paper presented at the
    Conference on Manding Studies, S.O.A.S., London University.

—. 1973. "Essai critique sur l'épopée Mandingue." Doctorat de troisième cycle,
    Centre de Recherches Africaines, Université de Paris I, Sorbonne.

—, ed. and trans. 1975. *L'aigle et l'épervier: Ou la geste de Sunjata*. Paris:
    Pierre Jean Oswald.

—. 1986. *Le lion à l'arc*. Paris: Hatier.

—. 1986a. "Une voix majestueux s'est tue." *Litterature malienne*, special issue
    of *Notre Librarie* 75–76 (reprinted 1989), 51–54.

Diawara, Mamadou. 1989. "Women, Servitude and History." In K. Barber and
    P. F. de Moraes Farias, eds., *Dis course and Its Disguises,* 109–37.
    Birmingham University African Studies Series 1. Birmingham:
    C.W.A.S, University of Birmingham.

—. 1990. *La graine de la parole.* Stuttgart: Franz Steiner Verlag.

Diawara, Manthia. 1992. "Canonizing Soundiata in Mande Literature: Toward a
    Sociology of Narrative Elements." *Social Text* 31–32: 154–68.

Dieterlen, Germaine. 1955. "Mythe et organisation sociale au Soudan Français."
    J.S.A. 25, 1: 39–76.

Frobenius, Leo. 1921–28. *Atlantis: Volksmärchen und Volksdichtungen Afrikas.*
    Twelve vols. Jena: Diederichs Verlag.

Green, Kathryn L. 1991. "'Mande Kaba,' the Capital of Mali: A Recent
    Invention?" *History in Africa* 18: 127–35.

Greenberg, Joseph M. 1970. *The Languages of Africa.* Bloomington, Indiana:
    Indiana University Press.

Hale, Thomas A. 1982. "From written literature to the oral and back." *The
    French Review* 55, 6: 790–97.

—. 1990. *Scribe, Griot, and Novelist: Native Interpreters of the Songhai
    Empire.* Gainesville: University of Florida Press.

Ibn Battuta. 1355. *Tuhfat al-nuzzar fi ghara'ib al-amsar wa-aja'ib al-asfar.*
    English trans. by J. F. P. Hopkins in *Corpus of Arabic Sources for West
    African History*, eds. N. Levtzion and J. F. P. Hopkins. Cambridge:
    Cambridge University Press, 1981.

Innes, Gordon, ed. and trans. 1974. *Sunjata: Three Mandinka Versions.* London:
    S.O.A.S.

Jackson, Michael. 1979. "Prevented Successions: A Commentary upon a
    Kuranko Narrative." In R. H. Hook, ed., *Fantasy and Symbol: Studies
    in Anthropological Interpretation*, 95–131. London: Academic Press.

—. 1982. *Allegories of the Wilderness: Ethics and Ambiguity in Kuranko
    Narratives.* Bloomington, Indiana: Indiana University Press.

Jansen, Jan. 1995. "De Draaiende Put: een studie naar de relatie tussen het

Sunjata-epos en de samenleving in de Haut Niger [Mali]." Doctoral dissertation, University of Leiden.

—. 1996. "The Reprentation of Status in Mande: Did the Mali Empire Still Exist in the Nineteenth Century?" *History in Africa* 22: 87–109.

—. 1996a. "The Younger Brother and the Stranger: In Search of a Status Discourse for Mande," *Cahiers d'Etudes Africaines*, 36 (4): 659–88.

Jansen, Jan, Esger Duintjer, and Boubacar Tamboura, eds. and trans. 1995. *L'Épopée de Sunjara, d'après Lansine Diabate de Kela.* Leiden: Research School CNWS.

Johnson, John William. 1978. "The Epic of Sun-Jata: An Attempt to Define the Model for African Epic Poetry." Ph.D. dissertation, Indiana University.

—, ed. and trans. 1979. *The Epic of Sun-Jata According to Magan Sisôkô.* Two vols. Bloomington, Indiana: Folklore Publications Group, Indiana University.

—. 1980. "Yes Virginia, There is an epic in Africa." *R.A.L.* 11, 3: 308–26.

—, ed. and trans. 1986. *The Epic of Son-Jara: A West African Tradition.* Bloomington, Indiana: Indiana University Press.

Kanté, Ibrahima. N.d. L'Epopée du Manding. Version de griot: Ibrahima Kanté, Republique Populaire Revolutionnaire de Guinée, Conakry (?), mimeograph, Africana Library, Northwestern University.

Kesteloot, Lilyan. 1972. *Da Monzon de Segou: épopée bambara.* Four vols. Paris: Éditions Fernand Nathan.

Konaré Ba, Adam. 1983. *Sunjata: le fondateur de l'empire du Mali.* Libreville, Gabon: Lion/Nouvelles Editions Africaines.

Kourouma, Ahmadou. 1970. *Les soleils des independences.* Reprinted 1981, *The Suns of Independence*, N.Y.: Africana. Paris: Seuil.

Levtzion, Nehemia. 1980. *Ancient Ghana and Mali.* First published 1973. New York: Africana Publishing Co.

Levtzion, Nehemia and Hopkins, J. P. F., eds. and trans. 1981. *Corpus of early Arabic sources for West African history.* Cambridge: Cambridge University Press.

Leynaud, Emile. 1972. "Clans, Lignages et Cantons." Paper presented at the Conference on Manding Studies, S.O.A.S., London University.

Leynaud, Emile, and Youssouf Tata Cissé. 1978. *Les paysans malinké du haut Niger.* Bamako: Editions Imprimiere Populaire.

Lord, Albert B. 1960. *The Singer of Tales: Epic Singers and Oral Tradition.* Reprinted in 1991. Cambridge: Harvard University Press.

Ly-Tall, Madina. 1977. *Contribution a l'Histoire de l'Empire du Mali (XIIIe–XVIIe siècles): Limits, principales, provinces, institutions politiques.* Dakar and Abidjan: Les Nouvelles Editions Africaines.

Ly-Tall, Madina, Seydou Camara, and Bouna Dioura. 1987. *L'histoire du Mandé d'après Jeli Kanku Madi Jabaté de Kéla.* Paris: SCOA.

McNaughton, Patrick. 1988. *The Mande Blacksmiths: Knowledge, Power and Craft in West Africa.* Bloomington, Indiana: Indiana University Press.

Meillassoux, Claude et. al. 1967. *Légende de la dispersion des Kusa (Epopée Sonike).* Dakar: IFAN.

—. 1968. "Les cérémonies septennales du Kamablon de Kaaba (Mali)." *J.S.A.* 38, 2: 173–82.

Miller, Christopher L. 1990. *Theories of Africans: Francophone Literature and Anthropology in Africa.* Chicago: University of Chicago Press.

Monteil, Charles. 1929. "Les Empires du Mali (Etude d'Histoire et de Sociologie Soudanaises)." *Bulletin du C.E.H.S.A.O.F.* 12: 291– 377.

—. 1953. "La légende du Ouagadou et l'origine des Soninké." *Mélanges Ethnologiques* (Paris): 326–408.

Moraes Farias, Paulo Fernando de. 1989. "Pilgrimages to 'Pagan' Mecca in Mandenka Stories of Origin Reported from Mali and Guinea-Conakry." In K. Barber and P. Farias, eds., *Discourse and Its Disguises: The Interpretation of African Oral Texts,* 152–70. Birmingham University African Studies Series 1. Birmingham: C.W.A.S., University of Birmingham.

—. 1992. "The oral traditionist as critic and intellectual producer: An example from contemporary Mali." In T. Falola, ed., *African Historiography: Essays in Honour of Professor J. F. A. Ajayi.* London: Longman.

Moser, Rex E. 1974. "Foregrounding in the 'Sunjata,' the Mande Epic." Ph.D. dissertation, Indiana University.

Mounkaila, Fatimata. 1989. *Le mythe et l'histoire dans la Geste de Zabarkâne.* Niamey: CELHTO.

Niane, Djibril Tamsir. 1960a. *Soundjata, ou L'Epopée Mandingue.* Paris: Présence Africaine.

—. 1965. *Sundiata: an epic of old Mali*, trans. G. D. Pickett. London: Longman.

—. 1974. "Histoire et tradition historique du Manding." *P.A.* 89: 59–74.

—. 1989. *Histoire des Mandingues de l'Ouest: Le Royaume du Gabou.* Paris: Editions Karthala and Association ARSAN.

Okpewho, Isidore. 1979. [1980] *The Epic in Africa.* New York: Columbia University Press.

Olivier de Sardan, J.-P. 1982. *Concepts et conceptions songhay–zarma: Histoire, culture, société.* Paris: Nubia.

Ouologuem, Yambo. 1971. *Bound to Violence.* London: Heinemann.

Park, Mungo. N.d. *Travels in the Interior Districts of Africa.* First edition 1799. London: Isaac, Turkey, & Co.

Person, Yves. 1962. "Tradition orale et chronologie." *Cahiers d'Études Africaines*, II: 462–76.

—. 1968–75. *Samori: Une Révolution Dyula.* Three vols. Mémoires de l'Institut Fondamental d'Afrique Noire 80 and 89. Dakar: I.F.A.N.

—. 1973. "Oral Tradition and Chronology." In Pierre Alexandre, ed., *French Perspectives in African Studies: A Collection of Translated Essays*, 204–20. London: International African Institute and Oxford University Press.

es-Sadi, Abderrahman. 1900. *Tarikh es-Soudan.* Ed. and trans. by O. Houdas in 1981. Paris: Maissoneuve et Larose.

Seydou, Christiane. 1982. "Comment définir le genre épique? Un exemple: l'épopée africaine." In Veronika Görög-Karady, ed., *Genres, Forms, Meanings: Essays in African Oral Literature*, 84–98. Journal of the Anthropological Society of Oxford Occasional Papers.

Sidibé, Mamby. 1959b. "Soundiata Keita, Héros historique et légendaire, Empereur du Manding." *N.A.* 82: 41–51.

Smith, Pierre. 1981. "Principes de la Person et Categories Sociales." In *La Notion de Personne en Afrique Noire*, 467–90. Paris: Editions de C.N.R.S.

"Sunjata Epic Conference." November 13–15, 1992. Institute for the Advanced Study and Research in the African Humanities, Northwestern University. Transcript at Northwestern University Library.

Sylla, Diarra. 1977. *L'empire du Ghana.* Troisième colloque international de Niamey 30 novembre–6 décembre 1977. Récit de Diara Sylla, transcrit, traduit et annoté par Mamadou Soumaré. Paris.

Tamari, Tal. 1988. "Les castes au Soudan occidental." These de Doctorat d'Etat. Paris: Université de Paris X—Nanterre.

—. 1991. "The Development of Caste Systems in West Africa." *Journal of African History* 32, 2: 221–50.

Vansina, Jan. 1960. *De la tradition orale.* Terveuren: Musée royale de l'Afrique centrale.

—. 1985. *Oral Tradition as History.* Madison: University of Wisconsin Press.

Vidal, Jean. 1924. "La légende officielle de Soundiata fondateur de l'empire manding." *Bulletin du C.E.H.S.A.O.F.* 7: 317–28.

Vydrine, Valentin. 1995/96. "Who Speaks 'Mandekan': A Note on Current Use of Mande Ethnonyms and Linguonyms." *MANSA (Mande Studies Association) Newsletter* 25: 6–9.

Wilks, Ivor. 1968. "The Transmission of Islamic Learning in the Western Sudan." In J. Goody, ed., *Literacy in Traditional Societies.* Cambridge: Cambridge University Press.

Wright, Donald R. 1977. *The Early History of Niumi: Settlement and Foundation of a Mandinka State.* Athens, Ohio: Ohio University Center for International Studies, Africa Series 32.

—. 1978. "Koli Tengela in Sonko Traditions of Origin: An Example of the Process of Change in Mandinka Oral Tradition." *History in Africa* 5: 257–71.

Zeltner, Franz de. 1913. *Contes du Sénégal et du Niger*. Paris: Ernest Leroux.

Zemp, Hugo. 1966. "La Légende des Griots Malinké." *C.E.A.* 6, 24: 611– 42.

Contributors

Ralph Austen is Professor of African History at the University of Chicago. His recent publications include *The Elusive Epic: Performance, Text and History in the Oral Narrative of Jeki la Njambe (Cameroon Coast)* (1997) and (with Jonathan Derrick) *Middlemen of the Cameroons Rivers: The Duala and their Hinterland, c. 1600– c. 1960.*

Stephen Belcher has taught at the University of Nouakchott and at Pennsylvania State University. He is a co-editor of *Oral Epics from Africa* (1997) and the author of *Epic Traditions of Africa* (1999).

Charles Bird was Professor of Linguistics at Indiana University from 1969-1995. His major publications include (with Martha Kendall) "The Mande Hero: Text and Context " in *Explorations in African Systems of Thought* (1980), edited by him and Ivan Karp, and a translation of *The Songs of Seydou Camara* (1974). He currently lives in North Carolina.

Stephen P. Bulman is Head of History at the Newman College of Higher Education in Birmingham, England. His doctoral thesis, completed at the University of Birmingham in 1990, was a comparative survey of variants on the Sunjata epic. He is currently researching oral traditions concerning Sumanguru Kante and Susu.

Seydou Camara (not to be confused with the figure on the cover of the present book) is Head of the Department of History and Archaeology at the Institut des Sciences Humaines du Mali in Bamako. His publications include "La tradition orale en question" (1996). He is also co-editor of *La geste de Nankoman: textes sur la fondation de Naréna (Mali)* (1999).

David C. Conrad is Professor of History at the State University of New York at Oswego and President of MANSA (the Mande Studies Association). He is co-editor (with Barbara Frank) of *Status and Identity in West Africa: Nyamakalaw of Mande* (1995) and editor of *Epic Ancestors of the Sunjata Era: Oral Tradition from the Maninka of Guinea* (1999).

.

Mamadou Diawara is Director of the Center for Research on Local Knowledge in Bamako, Mali. His publications include *La graine de la parole: dimension sociale et politique des traditions orales du royaume de Jaara (Mali) du xvème au milieu du xixème siècle* (1990) and a habilitation thesis, "The Rule of

Speech—The Eloquence of Silence: Studies Toward an Anthropology of Speech among the Lower Classes in the Sahel" (1997).

P. F. de Moraes Farias is Senior Lecturer at University of Birmingham's Center of West African Studies. He has edited (with Karin Barber) *Discourse and Its Disguises: The Interpretation of African Oral Texts* (1989) and written the article "Borgu in the Cultural Map of Muslim Diasporas of West Africa" (1996).

Jan Jansen is a fellow at the Dutch Royal Academy of Arts and Sciences and a member of the anthropology department at the University of Leiden. He has edited (with Clemens Zobel) *The Younger Brother in Mande - Kinship and Politics in West Africa* (1996) and co-edited *La geste de Nankoman: textes sur la foundation de Naréna (Mali)* (1999).

John William Johnson is Professor at the Folklore Institute of Indiana University. He is the editor and translator of *The Epic of Son-Jara* (text by Fa-Digi Sisòkò: 1986, 1992) as well as co-editor of *Oral Epics from Africa* (1997).

James McGuire is currently working as a freelance writer in the Chicago area. His writings include a Ph.D. dissertation, "Narrating the Mande: West African Identity Production and the Mande Francophone Novel" (1994) and the article "Narrating Mande Heroism in the Malian Novel: Negotiating Postcolonial Identity in Diabaté's *Le Boucher de Kouta*" (1993).

Robert C. Newton is the Arts and Media Project Coordinator for the African Studies Program at the University of Wisconsin-Madison. He has completed a doctoral dissertation on "The Epic Cassette: Technology, Tradition and Imagination in Contemporary Bamana Segu" (1997).

Karim Traore is Assistant Professor of Comparative Literature at the University of Georgia. His recent publications include *Le jeu et le sérieux. Essai d'anthropologie littéraire sur la poésie épique des chasseurs du Mande (Afrique de l'Ouest)* (1999) and *Die Verlobte des Marabut. Märchen und Mythen aus Westafrika* (1999).

Ivor Wilks is the Herskovits Professor Emeritus of African Studies, Northwestern University and holds an Honorary Professorship at the University of Wales, Lampeter. His publications include *Wa and the Wala: Islam and Polity in Northwestern Ghana* (1989) and *Forests of Gold: Essays on the Akan and the Kingdom of Asante* (1993). In 1998, he received the Distinguished Africanist Award from the African Studies Association.